RESEARCH STRATEGIES IN THE SOCIAL SCIENCES

A Guide to New Approaches

Edited by

ELINOR SCARBROUGH

and

ERIC TANENBAUM

OXFORD UNIVERSITY PRESS · OXFORD
1998

Oxford University Press, Great Clarendon Street, Oxford OX2 6DP

Oxford New York

Athens Auckland Bangkok Bogota Buenos Aires
Calcutta Cape Town Chennai Dar es Salaam
Delhi Florence Hong Kong Istanbul Karachi
Kuala Lumpur Madras Madrid Melbourne Mexico City
Mumbai Nairobi Paris São Paolo Singapore
Taipei Tokyo Toronto Warsaw

and associated companies in
Berlin Ibadan

Oxford is a trade mark of Oxford University Press

Published in the United States
by Oxford University Press Inc., New York

© the several contributors 1998

First published 1998

British Library Cataloguing in Publication Data
Data available

Library of Congress Cataloging in Publication Data
Research strategies in the social sciences: a guide to new approaches /
edited by Elinor Scarbrough and Eric Tanenbaum
Includes bibliographical references and index.
1. Social sciences—Research—Methodology.   2. Social sciences—Methodology.
3. Social sciences—Research—Data processing.
I. Scarbrough, Elinor.   II. Tanenbaum, Eric.
H62.R4614 1998 300'.7'2—dc21 98–2537
ISBN 0–19–829238–4
ISBN 0–19–829237–6 (Pbk)

1 3 5 7 9 10 8 6 4 2

Typeset by Hope Services (Abingdon) Ltd.
Printed in Great Britain
on acid-free paper by
Biddles Ltd.,
Guildford & King's Lynn

FOREWORD

This volume originates in the teaching programme of the *Essex Summer School in Data Analysis and Collection*, which celebrated its thirtieth year in 1997. The book, with its useful practical aims, didactic and functional, but incorporating broader philosophical and epistemological concerns, is a fitting celebration of the anniversary. The Summer School has always aimed at mediating between social scientists with concrete, substantive objectives and the ever more complicated procedures and techniques which are becoming the tools of their trade.

In the course of offering annual instruction in current techniques of quantitative analysis, the Summer School has, of course, performed many other functions. Beginning in 1968 when social science in Europe was weak and struggling—indeed, barely conscious of itself as a distinctive entity—the Essex Summer School has brought together each generation of social scientists. At first, participants were largely drawn from across Western Europe, but now, increasingly, they come from all parts of Europe and other parts of the world.

The contacts formed at an early age between people of very different backgrounds and nationality have blossomed into networks of teaching and research across the European continent. The Summer School antedated the European Consortium for Political Research, the most active European social science organization, by two years. The success of the Summer School provided a practical demonstration of the feasibility of trans-European cooperation in social science, which induced the Ford Foundation to support the ECPR in the first place. It is no exaggeration, therefore, to say that European social science found its first institutional embodiment in the Summer School. It has remained its mould and matrix ever since.

If the Essex Summer School crucially shaped social science in Europe, it took its form from an American exemplar, the Michigan Summer School of the Inter-University Consortium for Political Research. Michigan provided not only the initial model but also an inspirational instructor, Lutz Erbring, who taught most of the courses in the early years, from 1968 to 1970, of the Essex Summer School. He also operationalized the first suite of analytic programmes for the social sciences on the Essex University computer.

The Essex Summer School continues to operate in tandem with the Summer School at Ann Arbor, but now on a more equal footing. Along with Michigan, Essex has become one of the two leading international schools in quantitative social science, constantly promoting new innovations in order to keep up with ever-changing and expanding specialities in the field. In doing so, it affirms its faith in a quantitative social science dedicated to examining substantively important phenomena in a systematic and rigorous manner. This book forms a practical embodiment of its mission and a strong basis from which to go forward into the third millennium.

June 1997

Ian Budge
Director 1968–73

PREFACE

We owe the genesis of this volume to the, by now, several hundreds of students who have taken part in the *Essex Summer School in Data Analysis and Collection* over the last thirty years. From its tenuous beginnings in 1968 through to the present, the Essex Summer School has sought to respond to the methodological needs and aspirations of social scientists, whatever their specialist discipline. It has been our good fortune that the Summer School has enjoyed the stimulus and excitement of drawing together, each year, an international community of social scientists, young and practised alike.

It has also been our good fortune to enjoy the support of expert social scientists who share our enthusiasm for empirical research. As Instructors on the Summer School programme, their methodological expertise is matched by their teaching skills. Without their commitment to the professionalization of social science, the Essex Summer School could never have grown from a single seminar to the programme of thirty-six courses in 1997. The success of the Summer School owes them a great deal.

Social science methodology is leaping forward at such a pace that a volume about recent advances, and their impact on strategies of research, has to be the work of many hands. All the contributors to this volume are closely associated with the Summer School programme. Some, indeed, in earlier years, were Summer School students. Planning this volume was a collaborative exercise between us, but we, as editors, take responsibility for the final product. Any mistakes are ours alone.

We also take this opportunity to thank others who have done much to ensure the viability of the Summer School. The Economic and Social Research Council has regularly supported the Summer School with student bursaries, for which we are grateful. Similarly, we are grateful for the support we receive from the European Consortium for Political Research. We pay tribute, too, to the foresight of the University of Essex in initiating the Summer School and continuing to nurture it throughout the past thirty years. Without this kind of support, the Essex Summer School could never have become so much a part of the 'map' of European social science.

This volume would not have seen the light of day without the support of Dominic Byatt at Oxford University Press. He encouraged us to pursue our preliminary ideas and showed great patience as our early deadline passed with no product delivered. His insistence that 'getting it right' was the target proved wise. We hope that we have, indeed, 'got it right'.

July 1997   ELINOR SCARBROUGH
                                             ERIC TANENBAUM

CONTENTS

List of Figures   xi

List of Tables   xiii

List of Contributors   xv

1. Introduction   1
   ELINOR SCARBROUGH AND ERIC TANENBAUM

2. Research Strategies in the New Environment   11
   ERIC TANENBAUM AND ELINOR SCARBROUGH

I ANALYSES ACROSS OBSERVATIONS

3. Ordinary Least Squares and Logistic Regression Analysis   29
   DAVID SANDERS AND MALCOLM BRYNIN

4. Linear Structural Equation Models   53
   STEFFEN KÜHNEL

5. Categorical Data Analysis: Log-linear and Latent Class Models   71
   ALLAN McCUTCHEON AND COLIN MILLS

6. Modelling Context and Heterogeneity: Applying Multilevel
   Models   95
   KELVYN JONES AND CRAIG DUNCAN

II ANALYSES ACROSS TIME

7. It's about Time: Modelling Political and Social Dynamics   127
   HAROLD D. CLARKE, HELMUT NORPOTH, AND PAUL WHITELEY

8. Cointegration and Modelling the Long Run   156
   SIMON PRICE

9. Modelling Space and Time: The Event History Approach   191
   NATHANIEL BECK

III NEW PERSPECTIVES

10. The Glass Bead Game: Testing Game-theoretic Models   217
    HUGH WARD

11. Political Analysis in a World without Foundations   249
    BOBBY SAYYID AND LILIAN ZAC

12. Discourse Theory and Political Analysis 268
DAVID HOWARTH

References 294
Index 311

LIST OF FIGURES

3.1   Scatterplot showing the relationship between examination
       grade (Y_i) and income (X_i)   30
3.2   Representation of positive and negative relationships between
       Y_i and X_i 31
3.3   Illustrative representation of strong and weak relationships
       between Y_i and X_i 32
3.4   Alternative sampling distributions of b 33
3.5   Representation of homoscedastic and heteroscedastic residuals   40
4.1   Linear regression   54
4.2   Example of a linear structural equation model   55
4.3   Threshold model   57
4.4   Theoretical model   60
4.5   Modified theoretical model   62
4.6   Extended model   63
4.7   Full extended model   64
4.8   Recall model   65
4.9   Modified recall model   66
5.1   Odds on always buying recycled goods   81
5.2   Local independence   85
5.3   Path model   89
5.4   Estimated class types by gender and education   93
6.1   Multilevel structures   96
6.2   More complex multilevel structures   98
6.3   Cross-classified multilevel structure   99
6.4   Varying relationships between voting and income   101
6.5   Between place heterogeneity   102
6.6   Dot plots of the higher-level distributions underlying Fig. 6.4   102
6.7   Scatterplots of the higher-level distributions underlying Fig. 6.4   102
6.8   Residuals at various levels   106
6.9   Comparing ANCOVA and multilevel estimates: house prices
       in London   112
6.10 Varying relations between Labour voting and mining
       constituencies   117
6.11 Context and composition   118
7.1   Prime ministerial approval and perceptions of the economy,
       June 1979–December 1990   129

7.2 Autocorrelation function (ACF) and partial autocorrelation
     function (PACF), prime ministerial approval   135
7.3 Autocorrelation function (ACF) and partial autocorrelation
     function (PACF), perceptions of the economy   136
7.4 Cross-correlations, prime ministerial approval, and perceptions
     of the economy   141
7.5 Conservative trends, January 1992–November 1995   147
8.1 A stationary series (equation 6)   159
8.2 A non-stationary series with one unit root (equation 7)   160
8.3 The (stationary) first difference of a non-stationary series
     (equation 7)   160
8.4 A non-stationary series with two unit roots   161
8.5 UK GDP (log scale)   162
8.6 Growth in UK GDP (change in log (GDP))   162
8.7 Real UK interest rates (Treasury bill rate less RPI inflation)   163
8.8 Actual and long-run equilibrium values for a non-stationary
     series   169
8.9 Demand and supply for mangoes   172
8.10 Hours worked in UK manufacturing (log scale)   177
8.11 Employment in UK manufacturing (log scale)   178
8.12 Output in UK manufacturing (log scale)   178
8.13 Real wages in UK manufacturing (log scale)   179
9.1 Hazard function for mean cabinet duration   199
10.1 The probability of winning a seat as a function of the
     probability of a randomly chosen voter voting for the opposition 223
10.2 The strategy combination (M_{opp}, M_{gov}) is not likely to be an
     equilibrium   225
10.3 A visualization of the strategies S and T 227
10.4 The distribution of campaigning resources under strategies
     S and T 229
10.5 The form of the variable DX50   236
10.6 The redistribution in lemma 2   241
10.7 The redistribution in lemma 3   242
10.8 The first redistribution in lemma 5   244
10.9 The second redistribution in lemma 5   245

LIST OF TABLES

3.1 Ordinary least squares regression with number of times respondents identified with the Conservative Party as the independent variable   38–9

3.2 Ordinary least squares regression comparing Conservative identifiers and not-Conservative identifiers (1991 wave only)   41

3.3 Logistic regression comparing Conservative identifiers and not-Conservative identifiers (1991 wave only)   46

4.1 Total effects on voting   67

5.1 Percentage distributions for variables used in log-linear and latent class models   72

5.2 Whether respondent always buys versus sometimes/never buys products made of recycled materials by gender   73

5.3 Observed cell frequencies for log-linear models   80

5.4 Fit statistics and conditional tests for log-linear models   80

5.5 Regularly buys environmentally conscious products   83

5.6 Evaluation statistics for latent class model of four environmentally-friendly consumer products   87

5.7 Latent class and conditional probabilities of responding 'regularly purchase' to four environmentally friendly products   88

5.8 Fit statistics for log-linear models with latent environmentally conscious consumerism as the dependent variable   90

5.9 Log-linear (lambda) coefficient estimates for associations with latent environmentally conscious consumerism as the dependent variable   91

7.1 Intervention/transfer function models of prime ministerial approval in Britain, June 1979–December 1990   139

7.2 Unit-root tests for stationarity of Conservative vote intentions, prime ministerial approval, party identification, subjective economic evaluations, and interest rates, January 1992–November 1995   147

7.3 Cointegrating regressions, Conservative vote intentions, prime ministerial approval, Conservative party identification, and personal economic expectations, January 1992–November 1995   148

7.4 Error-correction model of Conservative vote intentions, March 1992–November 1995   150

8.1 Tests for order of integration: ADF(4)   180

8.2	Diagnostics for unrestricted VAR	180
8.3	Tests for number of cointegrating vectors	181
8.4	Normalized β matrix for $r = 2$	181
8.5	β matrix for $r = 2$; identifying restrictions imposed	181
8.6	α matrix for $r = 2$; identifying restrictions imposed	182
8.7	Tests for order of integration: ADF(4)	183
8.8	Tests for number of cointegrating vectors; $p = 2$	184
8.9a	Regression for Δg: Johansen results	184
8.9b	Regression for Δc: Johansen results	184
9.1	Parametric estimation of cabinet durations	195
9.2	Semi-parametric estimation of cabinet durations	202
10.1	Results of three regression models	236

LIST OF CONTRIBUTORS

NATHANIEL BECK, Professor of Political Science, University of California

MALCOLM BRYNIN, Chief Research Officer, ESRC Research Centre on Micro-social Change, University of Essex

HAROLD CLARKE, Professor of Political Science, University of North Texas

CRAIG DUNCAN, Research Fellow, Department of Geography, University of Portsmouth

DAVID HOWARTH, Lecturer in Politics, University of Staffordshire

KELVYN JONES, Professor, Department of Geography, University of Portsmouth

STEFFEN KÜHNEL, Professor of Empirical Research, University of Geissen

ALLAN MCCUTCHEON, Donald O. Clifton Distinguished Professor of Sociology and Director of the Gallup Research Center, University of Nebraska at Lincoln

COLIN MILLS, Lecturer in Sociology, London School of Economics

HELMUT NORPOTH, Professor of Political Science, State University of New York at Stony Brook

SIMON PRICE, Professor of Economics, City University, London

DAVID SANDERS, Professor of Government, University of Essex

BOBBY SAYYID, Lecturer in Sociology, University of Manchester, and Co-director of the Centre for the Study of Globalization, Eurocentrism, and Marginality

ELINOR SCARBROUGH, Senior Lecturer, Department of Government, University of Essex, and Co-director of the Essex Summer School in Data Analysis and Collection

ERIC TANENBAUM, Senior Teaching Fellow, Department of Government, University of Essex, and Director of the Essex Summer School in Data Analysis and Collection

HUGH WARD, Reader, Department of Government, University of Essex

PAUL WHITELEY, Professor of Politics, University of Sheffield

LILIAN ZAC, BBC World Service

1

INTRODUCTION
ELINOR SCARBROUGH AND ERIC TANENBAUM

Social scientists are living in revolutionary times. The experienced and newer entrants to the field, alike, are assailed from all sides by rapid advances in the tools of their trade. On one side, theoretical developments, such as theories of rational choice and discourse analysis, are challenging long-standing traditions of thinking about social science questions. On another side, powerful desktop computers and the arrival of the Internet are transforming our working environment. On yet another side, suites of sophisticated techniques for analysing social science data are demanding feats of methodological agility. Little wonder, then, that social scientists, whatever their speciality, find themselves dazed by this veritable explosion of 'thinking and doing' in the social sciences.

Our purpose in this volume is to introduce some of the more recent developments in social science methodology in a readily accessible manner. Some of these approaches and techniques are set out at great length in specialist texts, but they are usually spread across a number of different texts and often presented in a form of daunting complexity. Such texts are principally aimed at a community of researchers who share a particular specialist expertise. Our aim, by contrast, is to provide guidance on 'other ways of doing things' and on 'other things that can be done' for readers who have already mastered the basic routines for the analysis of social science data and are now ready, and keen, to go further.

Thus, the contributions to this volume are based on two assumptions. First, that our readers are familiar with the fundamentals of statistical analysis, such as normal distributions, means, variances, standard errors, t-tests, and the like. In this sense, the empirical chapters in the volume are primarily targeted towards social scientists with some degree of research experience, whether with large sets of survey data or smaller sets of aggregate statistics. Even so, social scientists who have joined the community of researchers only more recently may find much which opens their eyes to further possibilities. And 'old hands' may profit from reflecting on the substantive implications of the methodological advances discussed here, and, perhaps, pondering the empirical implications of the theoretically oriented chapters.

The second assumption is that our readers are eager to expand their skills, or, at least, to gain a closer understanding of the analytic models employed by their colleagues. As the technology and the techniques available to social scientists have expanded, and continue to expand almost exponentially, it becomes ever more demanding to 'keep up'. Nonetheless, even though we cannot all be experts in every advanced technique now available, we can learn a great deal from those who have expert knowledge, just as the work of those with expert methodological knowledge has often been spurred by colleagues with expertise in substantive fields. There is always the risk, however, as methodological techniques become increasingly more specialist, that methodologists and substantive researchers become increasingly distanced from one another. For this reason, we invited contributions to this volume from social science practitioners known for applying their methodological expertise to substantive questions.

A further objective in this volume is to encourage social researchers to engage in methodological pluralism. As almost every introductory text emphasizes, there are several ways of tackling a set of data, and there are several ways of addressing the questions of interest to social scientists. It is all too tempting, particularly under the imperative to publish, to employ one technique, or a small set of familiar techniques, in which one is adept. By doing so, however, we limit what we can do with data and we limit what we can get our data to tell us. Indeed, the sheer costs of the resources deployed in the social sciences, especially in data gathering, oblige us to maximize the possibilities opened up in the new environment. To do so means knowing what there is and understanding the kinds of questions to which it can be applied. Tukey (1977: p. v) put the point succinctly: 'It is important to understand what you CAN DO before you learn to measure how WELL you seem to have DONE it.' This exhortation, as the following chapters show, applies as much to the advances in technology as to the advances in the methodology of social science research.

In planning this volume we were particularly mindful of the aversion to mathematical complexity among many social scientists, and the dominance of statistical models in empirical social science research. To avoid mathematical complexity, most contributions to this volume focus on outlining a particular technique, which is then illustrated with a worked research example. Mathematical reasoning and notation are kept to a minimum; where even the minimum entails some degree of complexity, the details are presented either in the endnotes or in an appendix. For those who wish to delve further into the mathematical underpinnings of these techniques, we have ensured ample references to the specialist literature. In addition, where specialist software packages are available and represent a considerable advance on general purpose packages, readers are directed to those also—and to Internet addresses for obtaining the most recent updates.

As a response to the dominance of statistical modelling, or hypothesis testing, in empirical research, we have included two chapters setting out the theoretical foundations of discourse analysis. This very different approach to the analysis of social phenomena is only more recently coming to empirical fruition, but already it represents a challenge to many of the conventions in mainstream social science research, especially the emphasis on numerical measures, quantitative analysis, and statistical testing. Here, too, we have ensured that readers who wish to take their understanding further are directed to appropriate source texts.

This volume is not comprehensive in its scope. Nor could it be. If it were, it would be a very fat book with far more in it than social scientists poised for take-off into advanced methods could assimilate. Rather, we have chosen to focus, in the methodological chapters, on developments representing advances on the basic regression model. As the ordinary least squares regression model is probably the most widely used of the earlier generation of multivariate techniques, the 'basics' assumed in this volume will be familiar to readers. The theoretically oriented chapters, by contrast, are designed to give quantitative researchers, on the one hand, cause to reflect on some of their (usually unspoken) assumptions, and, on the other hand, to indicate that the predominance of quantitative methods in empirical research is not unchallenged.

Outline of the Book

In Chapter 2, we, as editors of the volume, consider the several ways in which advances in computer power and information technology can influence the work of social scientists, along with transforming their working environment. In particular, we argue, these advances can free social researchers from the dependence they experienced, in earlier days, on specialists in other fields, such as data management experts, directors of computer services, statisticians, and software experts. Similarly, the arrival of desktop computers frees social researchers to 'play' with their data, or, at least, to spend more time in 'getting to know' their data before embarking on analysis. All this makes methodological pluralism a relatively low-cost exercise. Again, the arrival of the Internet enables social scientists to operate as a genuine community, with daily interactions if they so wish, rather than intermittent encounters at conferences or via the literature. In short, our central argument in the first chapter is that social scientists, old and new, need to reflect on what they are doing; to reconsider the long-standing, conventional techniques used in quantitative social research; and to appreciate the ways in which technological advances release them from earlier constraints. As Keynes declared: 'The difficulty lies not with new ideas but in escaping from old ones.'

The chapters which follow are organized around three themes. The four chapters in Part I focus on methodological advances in analysing observations derived from cross-sectional survey data. The modelling techniques specified and illustrated in these chapters relate to static, or non-dynamic, models, so they concentrate on examining differences across observations; that is, between various subgroups at particular points in time. The principal purpose of these chapters is to demonstrate ways in which conventional techniques can be extended, when applied to time-constrained data, to reveal more about the complex interactions which are typical of social phenomena.

In the first of these chapters, Chapter 3, David Sanders and Malcolm Brynin consider the advantages and limitations of different types of regression models. They take ordinary least squares regression modelling as their starting point, which they then apply to four waves of data, 1991–4, from the British Household Panel Study. This provides a timely review of the basic technique—as much abused as used—upon which the more advanced techniques discussed elsewhere in this volume build. Despite being the workhorse of social research, however, ordinary least squares regression entails a number of restrictive assumptions, which, it has been argued, make it unsuitable for analyses using a nominal or dichotomous dependent variable. Hence, Sanders and Brynin go on to test the ordinary least squares regression model against the logistic regression model, using data from the first wave of the panel survey. Sanders and Brynin conclude, however, that although logistic regression modelling is undoubtedly the statistically correct technique when the dependent variable is not measured on an interval scale, such models can yield results not far different from those obtained from using the linear regression model. Moreover, the results from logistic regression modelling are less readily interpretable than those from ordinary least squares regression modelling. In this sense, logistic regression is not necessarily—as often assumed—the automatic method of choice when dealing with non-linear dependent variables. This conclusion bolsters our plea for methodological pluralism; in particular, that social scientists should maximize the opportunities to experiment with different ways of analysing their data, which is made possible, and easy, by advances in the technology available.

In Chapter 4, Steffen Kühnel sets out the basic concepts of linear structural equation modelling, a technique for testing causal models. Hypotheses about voting turnout are drawn from a brief review of the literature, combined into a single model, and operationalized as a set of linear equations specifying direct and indirect effects. The model is tested using pre-election and post-election survey data on turnout in the 1995 North Rhineland-Westphalia state election. Substantively, Kühnel's models demonstrate that voting turnout can be explained using only a few concepts; also, interestingly, that 'soft utility' concepts can be shown to account for a higher proportion of the variance in turnout than 'hard utility' concepts. Methodologically, Kühnel illustrates not only how linear structural equation modelling can be used to test theoretical models but also how the models can be refined and re-estimated by running a series of experiments. The power of structural linear equation modelling, as this chapter shows, is to yield a more rigorous, and more closely specified, account of behaviour than is possible with conventional multivariate techniques. However, as Kühnel emphasizes, structural equation modelling techniques are appropriate for testing theoretically derived models; they can reveal how good or otherwise a model is, but they cannot supplant the primacy of theory. This message—the primacy of theory when applying modelling techniques—recurs throughout the volume.

Still on the theme of analyses across observations, Allan McCutcheon and Colin Mills, in Chapter 5, focus on recent advances in modelling the kind of categorical data, or nominal data, often found in the social sciences. Log-linear modelling is now a familiar technique for analysing relationships between manifest, or observed, categorical variables. Similarly, the latent class analysis approach is widely used to measure latent, or non-observable, variables. However, whereas these modelling techniques are often presented as independent of one another, more recent developments in the analysis of contingency tables have brought them together, so allowing for the simultaneous formulation of structural models for both manifest and latent categorical variables. Starting with a conventional log-linear representation of data from the 1991 British Social Attitudes Survey on attitudes towards buying 'environmentally friendly' products, McCutcheon and Mills show how the model can be extended to include latent categorical variables. Thus, from data about purchasing dispositions, together with socio-demographic data, they are able to derive three well-specified 'consumer types'. Although the integration of two techniques for dealing with categorical data seems a long way away from regression modelling, McCutcheon and Mills demonstrate that their model is analogous to models usually estimated within the framework of regression analysis.

In the final chapter in Part I, Kelvyn Jones and Craig Duncan demonstrate the opportunities for exploring the context of behaviour opened up by multilevel modelling. Questions about 'contextual effects' have often bedevilled social research using individual-level survey data; for example, attempts to unravel the so-called 'neighbourhood effect' in electoral research. Jones and Duncan demonstrate that such effects can readily be captured using multi-level modelling techniques. First, they specify the simple two-level model, and then go on to show how the underlying concepts can be developed to model heterogeneity in a population of complex structure. Although these techniques are now well established in educational research, such as investigating the effects of different types of schools and/or localities on the attainment of pupils, they have obvious relevance for research in other domains, such as health care and voting behaviour. The great strength of multi-level modelling, as Jones and Duncan show, is that it allows for 'thick' quantitative description, which enables researchers to get closer to the effects for individuals of the environment(s) in which they live and work. Even so, and rather puzzlingly, multilevel modelling is still only rather slowly spreading as a standard methodology throughout social science research.

The three chapters in Part II all deal with advances in the analysis of time-series data. These developments reflect the—albeit, again, slow—percolation of econometric models into other fields in the social sciences. These models not only enable researchers to track change over time but also allow them to test hypotheses about the dynamics underlying such change. The growing use of these models demonstrates the benefits accruing to the social sciences from systematic data gathering and storage by different agencies over what are now long time-periods. Making use of these data requires certain database management skills but, again, developments in technology and software—and archive practices—are making it much easier to access these banks of data. By extending the number of data points in a time-series, researchers can assess the impact of sudden changes in a system, or in the relationships between the elements of a system, thereby capturing some of the essence of a classical experiment.

In Chapter 7, Harold Clarke, Helmut Norpoth, and Paul Whiteley, introduce the basic concepts and methodology of time-series analysis, and outline their applicability to several fields of social science research. They then go on to provide an accessible exposition of transfer function modelling, along with the techniques involved in modelling cointegrated variables and applying error correction models. These methods are illustrated with an analysis of prime ministerial popularity in light of the state of the economy and various critical events—'interventions' in time-series terminology—using British public opinion data over the period 1979–95. As the authors comment, 'time does strange things to data', hence applying the basic linear regression model to time-series data would yield seriously misleading results. This chapter demonstrates how newcomers to econometric techniques can avoid the more obvious pitfalls.

As we have already noted, time-series data are becoming increasingly available in the social sciences but the techniques of econometric analysis are still relatively unfamiliar amongst social researchers. Hence, we have included a second treatment of the topic, in Chapter 8 by Simon Price. The focus of this chapter is the importance of examining information about 'the long run', which entails dealing with the identification of long-run relationships and notions of long-run causality. Although the treatment of econometric modelling is rather more technical here than in Chapter 7, it is nonetheless well within the grasp of readers who are comfortable with matrix algebra. In one example, Price demonstrates the application of econometric modelling to a strictly economic question—the relationship between employment, hours worked, and wages in the manufacturing sector of the British economy—in which all the variables are trended. By subjecting the data to standard econometric modelling, Price can show that it is changes in output and wages which bring the system into equilibrium, rather than employment or hours worked. In his second example, Price analyses the direction of the—well-attested but still controversial—relationship between economic competence and government popularity to demonstrate the application of these techniques in political science research.

The third chapter concerned with change over time deals with the analysis of event histories, using 'count' data and 'duration' data. In Chapter 9, Nathaniel Beck sets out the basic terminology of event history, or duration, analysis, with particular attention to the central concept of a 'hazard rate'. He then goes on to describe the kinds of distributions commonly found in such analyses, and demonstrates the advantages of using a discrete time-framework rather than the more conventional framework of continuous time. Beck also pays particular attention to the estimation and interpretation of duration dependence, and the treatment of 'censored' data. In addition, he shows how event history analysis can provide insights on how to estimate models for binary dependent variable time-series—cross-section data, an aspect of event history analysis which is often neglected in standard treatments. Throughout the chapter, the techniques are illustrated using data on cabinet duration among West European governments. As Beck points out, event history approaches and duration models are especially useful in the analysis of social policy, and their use in international relations is growing. Again, however, as with other techniques described in this volume, this kind of approach is slow to spread more widely among social scientists.

The chapters in Part III are less concerned about methodological advances than with new theoretical approaches. As we noted earlier, the behaviourist assumptions underlying much social science research are being challenged, in particular, by rational choice theory and recent developments in discourse analysis. However, whereas expositions of rational choice theory abound in the literature, straightforward introductions to discourse theory are fairly difficult to come by. Accordingly, the three final chapters in this volume are brought together by a common focus on ways of doing social science research 'differently'.

In the first of these chapters, Chapter 10, Hugh Ward demonstrates how rational choice theory can be operationalized and applied in political science research. As Ward points out, one of the problems about rational choice theory—or game theory—is that its exponents seldom go on to propose testable hypotheses which are then, or can be, confronted with 'real world' data. This is precisely what Ward does. First, he sets out the basic concepts of game theory and shows how they can be used to generate models of individual-level behaviour. He then goes on to illustrate the application of game-theoretic modelling, using the analogy of the 'glass bead game' to indicate the complicated calculations required of the players and their limited room for manœuvre. The model is tested using data on campaign expenditure by the two major parties in British politics. As this example shows, the conventional assumption that parties should, and do, concentrate their resources on the most marginal seats, is not as rational as it appears. Ward's exposition of the mathematical proofs employed in game theory shows the potential rigour of rational choice approaches to analysing behaviour, while his worked example demonstrates how, with ingenuity, some of the problems about operationalizing a game-theoretical model can be overcome.

The last two chapters in the volume set out the theoretical groundwork and empirical implications of discourse analysis. On the one hand, this approach to social phenomena is fast gaining ground in several branches of social science; on the other hand, theoretical discussion of discourse analysis often leaves researchers of quantitative bent rather bemused. In these two chapters, the emphasis is on guiding readers through the epistemological and ontological origins of discourse theory, demystifying its central concepts, and delineating its analytic tools. Both chapters also indicate how the approach can be deployed to unravel the interactive, so often indeterminate, nature of social and political experience. They also offer a response to some of the more vigorous critiques to which discourse theory has given rise.

In Chapter 11, Bobby Sayyid and Lilian Zac start by outlining those developments in several fields of scholarship which have contributed to the emergence of discourse theory. They emphasize, in particular, the significance for social science thinking of anti-foundationalism, which, as they make clear, entails a rejection of essentialism. In short, neither the categories commonly used in the social sciences nor the meaning of social behaviours are given, a priori. Rather, they are fabricated. Moreover, their fabrication, which is encapsulated in the production of meaning, knowledge, and identity, is an essentially political activity, evidenced in the discourses articulated by contenders for power. Sayyid and Zac go on to explain the contribution of theoretical linguistics to the concept of discourse; then they unravel the relationship between the concept of 'discursive formation' and the concept of hegemony; and, most important of all, they spell out the manner in which identities are acquired in the course of discursive engagement. Their reference to Jorge Luis Borges' short story, *Death and the Compass*, provides a simple and elegant illustration of the mistakes that social science 'detectives' can make if they fail to reflect on their working assumptions.

Finally, in Chapter 12, David Howarth delves more extensively into the theoretical antecedents of discourse theory. Although Howarth is primarily concerned with the work of Ernesto Laclau and Chantal Mouffe in developing discourse analysis as an empirical project, he traces the influence of scholars in several disciplines—hermeneutics, structural linguistics, psychoanalysis, literary theory—on the development of a discursive approach to the analysis of ideology and the conduct of politics in ideological terms. As Howarth explains, the essence of the discursive approach is the stress on interpretative methods of enquiry, in contrast to the quantitative methods and statistical orientation of conventional social science. Interestingly, however, at several points Howarth intimates that researchers who apply discourse theory to empirical phenomena are engaged in an enterprise not wholly dissimilar to that which is familiar to quantitative researchers, especially in the primacy of theory and the recognition of what counts as 'social' or 'political'. In addition, Howarth not only addresses some of the more trenchant critiques levelled against discourse theory—referring to a debate which has become particularly vigorous—but also suggests that the empirical application of discourse theory is still hampered by the absence of standard methdological rules of engagement. As Howarth points out, for Laclau and Mouffe's project to succeed, they 'have to provide criteria by which to judge the persuasiveness of accounts derived from applying discourse theory'. At this point, there are still all too few studies in which discourse theory has been applied, empirically, to the analysis of political conflicts.

To repeat the point we made earlier: this volume is not comprehensive in its coverage of new techniques and methodologies for tackling the kinds of problems of interest to social scientists. We have said nothing, for example, about correspondence analysis, the application of network analysis to policy questions, how to use data being made available by geographical information systems, or how advances in ecological modelling can allow for cross-level inference. Nor, indeed, do the contributions to this volume constitute a beginners' guide; rather, all assume that our readers have mastered the 'basics' of quantitative social science research and are in search of guidance when it comes to applying more advanced techniques. The new techniques made possible by advances in technology are no panacea for resolving many of the empirical problems—or the theoretical problems—entailed in social science research. They do, however, extend the reach of social scientists, thus allowing them to present richer, and more accurate, accounts of their subjects and the processes involved in differentiation and social change.

2

RESEARCH STRATEGIES IN THE NEW ENVIRONMENT

ERIC TANENBAUM AND ELINOR SCARBROUGH

The world of social science research has never been so open to new possibilities. Where our predecessors were unable to tread for fear of exceeding the limits of the available data, data access and data transfer, analytic routines, or computing power, today's social scientists can advance with confidence. Where once social scientists of empirical bent struggled with punch cards, chattering computer terminals, and SPSS 'jobs' disappearing into the black hole of remote mainframe processors, often never reappearing, we now enjoy massive arrays of data, powerful personal computers on our desks, on-line access to data, and suites of sophisticated analytic packages. Never before has the social scientist come so well armed.

In this chapter, we review past practices and outline the new techniques and technological developments now available to researchers in the social sciences. We also consider the implications of these developments for research strategies. Our central theme is that advances in technology can free social scientists from the tyranny of simplification which has often hampered attempts to grasp the complexity of the world 'out there'. We begin by noting the major changes in the research environment brought about by technological advances and then go on to point up analytic practices which, we shall argue, are overdue for revision.

Old and New Research Environments

Many of the conventional research strategies familiar to social scientists reflect what was possible given the resources—of data, technology, and techniques—available until around the early 1980s. As technological advances have relaxed these constraints, the challenge now is to recognize that, with the girdle off, researchers can move about more freely, in both designing data gathering and analysing the data gathered. This requires a re-examination of research strategies and a reworking of the decision rules conventionally used to identify successful analyses.

In the first place, increased computer-processing power enables researchers to realize, or come close to realizing, the ideals of statistical analysis. In the early days of applying computer-aided methodologies to social science data, researchers often had to make do with only some rough approximation to those ideals. Moreover, under the weight of convention, these approximations became reified as standard rules of engagement. In the light of current technological capabilities, we suggest that these canons of judgement should, and can, be reassessed.

Secondly, data scarcity complemented underpowered computers. There were simply not enough data available to address many of the interesting, and usually complex, social science questions which deserved close-cutting, sophisticated tools. Moreover, what data there were, other than one's own 'home-grown' variety, were usually difficult to access and wearisome to transfer between research sites. In this sense, it did not really matter very much that researchers lacked high-powered processing capabilities.

These limitations had effects, thirdly, on the skills of researchers. Social scientists themselves often lacked the expertise required to perform complex analyses. Similarly, they often lacked the technical knowledge to master complicated resources. For the most part, research training reflected the common practice of applying prefigured, or 'canned', solutions to familiar datasets. So long as the limited scope of both the data and the technology was accepted within the professional community, standard procedures could be learned with the assurance that they would serve throughout an extended career.

Information technology has changed all this, rapidly and quite dramatically. With processing power doubling in ever-shortening periods of time (Lazowska 1997), it can now be applied to massive data resources. Similarly, the enhanced capacity of information networks allows data resources to be accessed dynamically from a variety of data agencies. Equally, these new information networks provide for easy and rapid data transfer. Training in new approaches and their applications, and, indeed, in techniques specifically fashioned to deal with complex analytic problems, is available at the fingertips of anyone with access to commonly available (although not yet universally available) computer-aided communication facilities. And perhaps most significant of all, the new information technology has fostered a virtual community of researchers, sensitized to analytic problems and readily available to advise on analytic strategies.

In the next section, we focus on ways in which the legacy of practices shaped by the limitations of technology still pervades current research approaches. We then describe how technological innovations can serve to lift the constraints that have traditionally bound social scientists. In the final section, we suggest ways in which new technological capacity offers both a basis for developing flexible research practices and a means of developing new analytical tools.

Traditions of Quantification

Computer-aided statistical tools have been available to social researchers since the early 1960s. In the universities, the first encounters of social scientists with computer-aided analytic tools came from equipment provided for the quantitative analysis of data gathered for the natural sciences. So it is little wonder that the earliest routines used by social researchers reflected the mathematical orientation of natural scientists. They were the main user-base of early computers, and most of the available analytical routines were fashioned around their research interests. In consequence, a strong statistical emphasis biased the development of quantitative empirical social science.

With hindsight, social researchers might, arguably, have benefited more by working in the computing environment created by administrators in their institutions. This might have enabled them, from the earliest days, to adapt the file management facilities developed for administrators, which were functionally similar to the skills needed for data reconstruction and database management. It is just these skills that are necessary for restructuring social science data before they can be analysed. In fact, appreciating these skills, and putting them into operation, is relatively new in the social sciences. This, again, reflects the initiation of social scientists into computer-aided analysis via the mathematical forms of modelling associated with research in the natural sciences.

Marrying data to models

One effect of the mathematical orientation of early modelling techniques was that data were frequently married to existing formal statistical models. Although not designed with social research in mind, they were regarded as providing analogues for the processes being studied. That is, the statistical models provided an expected pattern against which observations from the 'real world' were compared. Close comparisons then led many analysts to describe the world in the language of the formal mathematical model. Poor comparisons, on the other hand, generally led to a rethinking about theory but rarely resulted in challenging or recasting the analogy. Rather, researchers turned to gathering yet more data which, again, were analysed in terms of the existing formal models. In short, early statistical analyses combined inductive pattern matching with deductive theory prescription. The theories, however, were often imported from other disciplines.

John Tukey characterized his approach to exploratory data analysis as 'quantitative detective work'. He argued that researchers should allow the data to speak for themselves before imposing a model for confirmation. In practice, of course, most researchers adopted an exploratory data strategy, but they only allowed the data to speak through the limited vocabulary derived from the mathematical models. Moreover, the models were advanced by statisticians, about whose influence Tukey was decidedly sceptical:

Once upon a time, statisticians only explored. Then they learned to confirm exactly—to confirm a few things exactly, each under very specific circumstances. As they emphasized exact confirmation, their techniques became less flexible. . . . Anything to which a confirmatory procedure was not explicitly attached was decried as 'mere descriptive statistics', no matter how much we learned from it. (Tukey 1977: p. vii)

At the analytical level, confirmation of the appropriateness of an analogue did not distort the data. However, the analyst's interpretative framework was shaped by a Procrustean fit,[1] sometimes knowingly, but often passively. Thus, although analysts did not amputate their data to make them fit predetermined statistical models, they nonetheless shaped what they thought the data were saying to correspond with those models. For sure, applying predefined patterns to data often provided a broad-scale fit, but as though a machete had been used for cutting out the shapes. What these techniques did not allow for was the more refined, close-cut, shapes that might have been achieved using a scalpel.

In particular, the predetermined, 'canned', analytical strategies did not permit the analysis of observations that deviated from the norm. Indeed, deviant cases were usually gathered up in the error term of the model, contributing, at best, to some overall, summary statement of the 'goodness of fit' between the empirical data and the model. Although it has been conventional to describe how well a model fits the world, it was more often the case of transforming the world to fit the model, with the error term mopping up the 'difficult' cases which blurred the fit between model and data.

Of course, there was often good reason for bundling such deviant cases into an undifferentiated error group: the aberrant cases usually fell short of most criteria of sampling adequacy, and many represented unique, or at least infrequent, occurrences. Thus, they did not lend themselves to further analyses that promised to produce replicable findings in other samples taken from the same population. And yet, as we have come to realize, in an increasingly volatile—or, at least, rapidly changing—social world, these aberrant cases may herald changes to come in the broader system. Their characteristics may be advanced signals of impending but unanticipated shifts in the phenomenon under observation.

In short, the limitations of early analytic practices reflected the several limitations facing researchers in the early days of empirical social science: the availability of serviceable theory;[2] our technical abilities to manipulate data; and the scarcity of appropriate data. Shortcomings in each area influenced the development of compensatory analytical strategies, many of which have persisted long after the need for them. As we contend that technological developments have made common analytic simplifications unnecessary, we go on to point up what should be replaced, or, at least, rethought.

Rethinking Analytic Strategies

The impact of early technical, usually technology-based, constraints still pervades a whole range of methodologies in quantitative social science research. Here, we focus on five areas in which the recasting of standard practices is particularly overdue: decision rules, research design, use of data resources, modes of data analysis, and the use of computers.

Simple inferential decision rules

That social scientists felt, in the early days, they needed simple decision rules which could be universally applied to the analysis of data is reflected in the widespread use of significance tests incorporated in typically 'canned' analytic procedures. These were, and often still are, the *sine qua non* that they have 'found' something worth reporting. Certainly, the principle of significance tests testifies to a legitimate concern in the social sciences about the temptation to overemphasize results that may be specific to a particular sample. Even so, the mechanistic way in which such tests continue to be routinely applied suggests that, too often, researchers have stopped thinking about what these tests mean and what claims they can support.

Consider, for example, the widespread adoption of a 5 per cent risk of failing to discard the null hypothesis when it is true. The currency of this test implies that there is something sacrosanct about living with this level of risk (unless, of course, one is designing aeroplanes). There is not. It is almost certainly a throwback to a time when researchers had to look up critical values for their coefficients in printed tables. It was also a convenient tool for researchers who used the *t*-test, or other normal approximations, in which a calculated coefficient of 2 allowed for 95 per cent confidence that the null hypothesis could be rejected. As contemporary computer programs routinely calculate exact probabilities,[3] it would be reasonable to reconsider our dependence on fixed critical values.

We can also question whether describing the statistical significance of a coefficient is the most useful estimate that can be generated from sample data. As a matter of routine, computer packages calculate confidence intervals which are much more informative than the claim that a coefficient of a certain fixed value is unlikely to occur by chance. By the same token, the ease with which computer programs generate inferential statistics compared to hand calculations should alert researchers to the danger of focusing on a few 'statistically significant' coefficients that can emerge from an otherwise 'insignificant' multitude of analyses. That is, given a critical region of $p = 0.05$, we would expect one in twenty of all analyses to produce statistically significant findings in the long run. The problem is that analyses are so easy to generate that the long run can happen quite quickly.

Calculating confidence intervals, in turn, depends on whether the data being analysed meet the criterion that underlies most of the inferential tests reported in standard computer-based packages. All assume that the data are gathered according to the principles of simple random sampling. But a strictly random sample is a very rare species. Even a cursory look at the technical details that now usually accompany data sets reveals that few surveys select respondents using simple random selection. Rather, as is well known but not fully appreciated, quota sampling is widely used; at best, stratified random sampling is the nearest approximation to strictly random sampling. Accordingly, applying inferential tests that require a specific sampling error will be misleading.[4] Complex sample errors, and consequently adjustment for design effects, are not considered by standard computer packages.

Holding on to such conventional practices neglects the fact that the computing power now available makes it possible for researchers routinely to take account of design effects. Moreover, in neglecting these new possibilities, social scientists may be failing to recognize that 'good' research can be achieved using data from a range of different sample designs. Simple random selection is just one of many probability sample designs. Thus, in the light of contemporary computing power, there seems no longer any reason to consider simple random sampling as the only selection strategy for generating sample frames. It would make more sense to use our access to high computing power to incorporate inclusive, comprehensive sample designs. In short, modern computing power can enable social scientists to throw off the tyranny of Tukey's 'inflexible statisticians'.

Increased computing power can also address other remnants of a technologically disadvantaged past. For example, social researchers often use techniques that depend on known sampling distributions. It is not clear that these techniques are appropriate in the majority of research situations. However, computer-intensive routines for generating distributions specifically related to the available data are beginning to appear in many standard analytic packages. Their use as normal practice should be encouraged. Indeed, this recommendation follows directly from the argument that predefined formal models are merely instances of a more comprehensive and inclusive set of models. The formal model may, actually, offer the best fit but it need not be preordained to be so.

The point we are making is highlighted by the way in which factor analysis is often used. Almost as a matter of course, many researchers apply a varimax rotation to their matrices on the implicit assumption that the factors are unrelated. However, they could just as easily apply a more general oblique solution that would allow the uncorrelated factors to emerge—if that is what the data are saying. In other words, we should give precedence to what is in the data rather than requiring our data to fit predetermined models.

Finally, we note the continuing practice of pretending that we have no prior knowledge of the associations among several different kinds of variables. Classical inferential tests assess the independence model but Bayesian estimators that include prior knowledge in the decision rules are much more flexible. This flexibility makes such decision rules preferable. They may require intensive computing but that power is now available. The researcher's task is to learn to harness that power. We return to this point later.

Simple research design

Conventional research designs also still reflect the limitations imposed by earlier resource scarcities. Limited data and processing power enforced an unrealistic attention to the interrelationship of characteristics observed in isolated individual cases. The context in which these observations occurred was invariably ignored, producing overly atomistic analyses. Needless to say, little attention was given to the relationship between (and among) contexts, or the influence of contexts on individuals. Rather, the focus was on the interrelationship between the several characteristics of individuals to the neglect of the environment(s) in which individuals engage in varying types of behaviour.

Contextual information can be social (individuals within families within neighbourhoods) or spatial (households within localities within regions), or, most naturally, a combination of the two. It has long been possible to obtain data about some of these dimensions; for example, British researchers working with survey data have had easy access to geographically referenced census data since the mid-1970s. Even so, the effort to take these data into account would have been largely futile until recently because we lacked the techniques to undertake those kinds of analyses. But appropriate techniques are now available, comprising data-management tools which link disparate data files and statistical tools that support multilevel analyses. At the forefront of these kinds of developments are 'geographical information systems' which even allow researchers to consolidate material observed in units with different spatial organization.[5]

Years ago, Cattell (1966) supported arguments for richer analytical perspectives when he noted that every datum simultaneously describes a characteristic (a 'variable') possessed by an observed unit (a 'case') at a particular time. Although data could be analysed in many different ways to exploit all three dimensions, analysts have usually focused, at best, on only two of them. For example, in two common strategies, analysts conventionally looked at either the change in a small number of variables through time, or they examined interrelationships between many variables at a single point in time. In both approaches, the observed units are usually treated simply as vehicles for the characteristics. Less commonly, the observed units described by the characteristics were analysed to discover how they grouped together. In short, both designs, while informative, yield a restricted description of phenomena.

The phenomena which interest social scientists are usually complex. Capturing that complexity more fully requires the assessment of simultaneous covariation along all three dimensions noted above: the units of observation, their characteristics, and time. That is how behaviour occurs. For example, to obtain a richer, and more accurate, picture of the progress of schoolchildren means measuring changes in their attainment over time together with changes in the school over time. This is simply to recognize that changes in one arena of behaviour are often, indeed usually, contingent on changes in other arenas.

All this was recognized years ago. Even so, progress towards grasping complexity has been slow. But the pace of progress was not due to the reluctance of social scientists, as a community, to grapple with the theoretical problems presented by the multidimensionality of social phenomena. Rather, it was a matter of limited analytical resources. The data required to execute complex designs were, by and large, not available; and even if they were, analysts did not have the tools required to manipulate them. Neither limitation continues to be a constraint in social research.

Simple data resources

Many standard analytic practices took root in a period of data scarcity and still reflect those earlier limitations. The establishment of data archives in the mid-1960s was a major advance in meeting the needs of social researchers. The data archives in the USA and several European countries[6] have developed as centres of specialist expertise in data management and data transfer. They have also been active in recycling quantitative material collected for other purposes, and encouraging researchers to engage in secondary analysis, so maximizing the research potential of disparate data sources. Many of the data deposited in archives have been tied to proprietary analytical systems developed by individual producers. Consequently, they were inaccessible to other researchers unless converted to a more versatile form. The data archives have responded to this need by producing pre-packaged sets of quantitative data to an industry-compatible standard.

Faced with a fairly stubborn technology and data scarcity, researchers tended to work with a particular data file and concentrate on cross-sectional analyses. They only used several data sets simultaneously when they wanted to study change across time. Even then, analyses depended on the availability of similar, or functionally equivalent, cross-sectional studies carried out at different times. This is clearest in the case of electoral behaviour, where it has been possible for researchers to merge repeated cross-sectional surveys containing the same questions. It was also evident in the appearance of several collections of national aggregate-level files generated for cross-national comparative studies, such as the collection published by Taylor and Jodice (1983), for example. What is particularly significant about files of this type is that the data were harmonized by the archives before being released; they featured only structured quantitative indicators; and they were stored as fixed rectangular matrices.

Archives continue to play a critical role in social research but their centralized holdings are now being complemented by data made directly accessible to researchers by the data producers themselves. For example, many data-collecting agencies now make their data available via the Internet.[7] Moreover, these data are not always explicitly quantitative; often, and increasingly, semi-structured textual accounts of events and processes are being released openly into the research domain. Sometimes these data need pre-processing before they can be used, requiring skills that were once, as we noted earlier, the exclusive preserve of data-management specialists. The increasing availability of database management programs, which are accessible to all researchers, mean, furthermore, that we are no longer dependent on the intervention of specialists in data-management skills.

Even so, the sheer volume of data, and data-management technology, becoming available to social scientists has its costs. Now the problem is the potential for excess: the richness of data resources threatens to overload researchers unless they develop the skills to winnow information. Even here, however, techniques are becoming available to identify the various sources of the variables of interest, and to enable researchers to extract, for recombination, items from different datasets.

Moreover, we should not forget that the large information resources now becoming available have one overriding, substantive advantage: they allow researchers to develop and operationalize definitions of social phenomena that correspond more closely to the reality 'out there'. Comprehensive indicators can address multifaceted data resources that provide information on the three dimensions noted above. Extensive data resources, in other words, can help in realizing complex research designs. Even more to the point, these developments can provide the resources required to move away from simple data analyses.

Simple data analysis

We would not want to suggest that large-scale data resources should lead to unplanned research based on serendipity, or simply 'hunting, fishing, and shooting'. Rather, we agree with Leamer (1983) that models should be sufficiently well specified to guard against unexpected, or omitted, measurement error. Even so, the possibility of large databases means that social scientists no longer have the same fear of 'overfitting' their models because they might run out of degrees of freedom as the number of variables in the model approach the number of observations.

Further, both the much larger volume of data and their greater accessibility make it far easier to examine infrequent events or outlying cases. Simply by boosting the number of events or cases available for analysis, it becomes possible to consider whether or not they are an integral part of some phenomenon. To repeat the point made earlier, events or cases that deviate from the mainstream have, traditionally, been thrown into the error term where they were often treated as a nuisance, or 'noise', to be massaged away. With the possibility of examining a much larger number of data sets we can get a clearer picture of what is really deviant and what, much more interestingly, may be early warnings of impending systemic change.

The much easier access to sophisticated analytical resources, both in terms of computer programs and the data to which they can be applied, also argues for a more diverse and pluralistic approach to data analysis. Proponents of methodological triangulation have always pointed to the biased perspective on a phenomenon to which a single perspective gives rise. Given that it is virtually impossible to disentangle the effects of the mode of observation from the characteristics of the observation itself, applying several analytic techniques to the same data can contribute to neutralizing inherent biases; that is, the biasing effects of the mode of observation and the biasing effects of a particular mode of analysis. As the analytic process is now so much faster, and the software programs so much better adapted to the needs of users, there have to be very good reasons for sticking with one routine, or a limited set of routines, throughout a research career.

Simple computer use

Our call for rethinking conventional analytic strategies rests largely on the rapid development of computer power. In contrast to the early days of reliance on distant mainframe computers, processing power is now a personal resource. Compare the current working environment for researchers with that complained of by Allerbeck (1977: 402) only twenty years ago:

Insufficient computing facilities have hindered social research frequently but undesirable local facilities should not suggest the use of analysis techniques that are unable to summarise the relationships in the data adequately if such summary measures are appropriate. In other words, such situations should not lead to complaints about the inadequacy [for example] of the linear model but to *complaints to the director of the computer centre that does not provide decent services for its users.* (our emphasis)

By no longer controlling computing facilities, central computer services no longer control the limits of what researchers can do. Processing cycles, software, and data storage have all migrated to the individual's desk, allowing researchers to design and control their working environment. More than this, social scientists no longer have to compete against researchers in other disciplines, or against each other, to access these resources. The days of overnight working to get around the constraints of computing time and disk space have given way to only the constraints of what research budgets can afford.

This kind of 'free' access to computing power has several implications for the way researchers approach their data. In particular, they are free to experiment. Allerbeck (1977) repeats Stone's recommendation that researchers should take advantage of the accessibility of computing power to encourage 'playfulness' with data. If that was advisable twenty years ago, the current range of data-oriented 'toys' makes the prospect potentially even more rewarding (and enjoyable). For example, data visualization tools enable researchers to investigate suspected 'odd' cases that may yield substantive insights. Again, the application of pattern-recognition techniques developed from work in artificial intelligence, such as neural networks, may point up unsuspected structures.

We are not arguing here that analysts should always 'let the computer do the walking' through their data. Rather, our point is that the occasional computer journey may, serendipitously, discover meaningful tracks. Unlike earlier attempts to automate data analysis,[8] freely available computing resources can wean researchers away from stubborn attachment to findings simply because they were so hard to generate. The possibility of new results which are only as far away as one's desktop demystifies the status of findings, thereby encouraging more flexible and experimental approaches to data analysis. An environment in which different ways of doing things are readily entertained will foster less automatic homage to computer-generated solutions.

The arrival of 'computer freedom' also means that researchers can free themselves from overreliance on a narrow range of investigative techniques. Researchers, whether experienced or newcomers, often tend to apply a single, universal model, modified perhaps by the addition of some qualitative descriptors. As we know, establishing stable taxonomies requires fairly large amounts of data and considerable computing power. Hence, social researchers have, traditionally, treated the world as a single unit which can be described by all the activities that occur within it.[9] Now, however, we have available both the volume of data and the computing power required to establish stable classifications of observations that may reveal different processes. For example, the work currently emerging from multilevel modelling shows how processes may differ within identifiable groups of observations.

A similar flexibility may be forthcoming in the way social scientists treat time. It is odd, but seldom remarked, that according to researchers in the social sciences, social change, if it occurs at all, occurs at only annually, quarterly, or monthly intervals. That is, whereas time is actually continuous, social scientists often treat it as discrete. This, of course, reflects the nature of data-gathering processes and the ability of analysts to process data. However, it certainly does not reflect the actual processes of change. The increased availability of data should allow for a less rigid adherence to such fixed time-points.

We might also note here that the development of 'data warehouses' may have a contribution to make in breaking such rigidities. It is well known that there exist vast amounts of data which might be analysed if incompatibilities between the systems that generated the data can be reconciled. Programmed approaches are being developed, which allow the transformations to be done dynamically as and when required.[10] Although most of these developments are, currently, in the commercial sector, it should not be long before social researchers in other sectors can access these vast stores of data. It is very likely that these data will feature much more accurate time-designations than the familiar broad time-bites.[11]

In reviewing several aspects of data gathering, analysis, and modelling in this section we have highlighted practices which reflect vestigial technical contingencies. In the next section we outline some of the ways in which social researchers can accommodate their practices to the possibilities opened up by the changing technology.

Adapting to the New Environment

Most established social scientists studied social science methodology only as a means of undertaking substantive research. Much the same probably applies to new entrants in the field. Their interest lies in addressing substantive questions, not technique. How, then, can they redress the weaknesses we have highlighted without compromising their substantive work? Fortunately, the new technology offers strategies for keeping abreast of new developments. This can best be demonstrated by describing how social researchers could work if they are prepared to embrace the opportunities offered by the current technology.

Researchers might start by interacting with the 'virtual' community of others with similar interests who communicate regularly via the Internet. Physical isolation no longer limits membership in a working community. Consequently researchers working in a particular substantive area can join the 'centre' where a high proportion of interaction amongst researchers now takes place. Participation in such 'virtual' communities begets several benefits, not least of which is that the stock of experience, and emerging new ideas, can be readily and rapidly shared.

Leading on from participation in 'virtual' communities, collaborative approaches can be developed using tools which are commonly available. Almost all statistical packages allow analysts to create their own statistical algorithms within its broader framework. Consequently, the latest solution proposed for a class of problems can be quickly shared with others and implemented by anyone who cares to do so. As software solutions for analytic puzzles can now be published directly by the author(s), researchers no longer have to wait until a commercially viable market develops before innovative routines are released.[12]

The Internet also fosters data-sharing by removing the technical complexities imposed by incompatible media. Data can now be exchanged just like any other information exchange using the same transfer technology.[13] Moreover, Internet-based facilities for locating multiple data sources are available to help in creating datasets customized to meet particular substantive purposes. Diverse datasets which may feature different logical structures—even if transfers via the Internet make them physically similar—can be merged using non-conventional database management tools.

Awareness of developments such as these mean that applying rigid, 'canned', solutions to substantive problems may no longer be professionally acceptable. Thus, their continued use risks putting practising social scientists at a disadvantage among the community of researchers. Fortuitously, another emerging technology will enable researchers to put into effect many of the new strategies we have highlighted.

One of the most far-reaching changes in computing during the 1990s has occurred in the way in which users interact with computer facilities. The early, character-based interfaces, which assumed that the user was sufficiently aware of what was required of the computer to compose a script of commands, intruded on the relationship between ideas about how information should be manipulated and the process of manipulation itself. Such interfaces are now almost an historical oddity. By contrast, developments in the interface between user and computer have revived symbolic forms of communication, rather reminiscent of (formal) communication in pre-literate societies. Developing such universally meaningful figurative icons depended on the availability of powerful processing capacity, a vivid example of technological developments making life easier for social researchers.

High-level computer power is now also available to the designers of software. Increasingly, researchers have access to facilities allowing them to express their ideas pictorially. These pictures can then be applied, automatically, to the analysis of data. This kind of development extends visualization from the exploratory analyses described earlier to more traditional confirmatory strategies, as well as to the restructuring of complex data series. It is not that we are recommending a return to earlier confirmatory practices but, rather, suggesting that social scientists who wish to take advantage of developments in statistical modelling can benefit from the greater accessibility, and flexibility, of these new visualization techniques. The important point here is that, because visual representations are more readily, and universally, understood than text, new analytic approaches are available to a much wider community of users than was previously the case.

In short, and we conclude on this note, computers have become an integral extension of the mental space of social researchers. Their use no longer requires separate, specialist skills to overcome the intrinsic hostility that marked early developments in information technology. Rather, the operating routines used in contemporary computing regimes encourage, stimulate, and support the imaginative thought processes that traditionally marked creative social science. The barriers that early computers posed to creativity, by forcing researchers to work within artificial constraints, are disappearing. The challenge now is to use them to open up new research strategies and fresh fields of exploration

Notes

1. According to Greek mythology, Procrustes was a hospitable man who was known as 'the stretcher' because he insisted that his overnight guests always had a bed that fitted their frame. As he had only one bed, however, he ensured the fit between the guest and the bed by either stretching those who were too short or chopping the limbs from those who were too tall. Many traditional data-analytic procedures have much the same distorting effects on data.

2. Rational choice theory is one of the few areas in the social sciences where theory has outpaced empirical tests. In too many instances for comfort, however, the theory receives weak empirical confirmation. It remains unclear whether this is due to weaknesses in the theory or the scarcity of appropriate data.

3. Even if most computer programs seem incapable of rounding up very small probabilities. Computer packages usually print these as $p = 0.0000$, suggesting certainty.

4. The effect of false positives created by mis-estimates will increase as computing power is turned to rule-driven 'automatic analyses' that let the computer 'do the walking' through masses of data. Because these systems often invoke decision rules based on statistical significance, the system can be seriously misled if the bases of the inferential statistics are mis-specified.

5. The variety of jurisdictions governed by data-gathering agencies makes life complicated for researchers; e.g., Openshaw (1987: 164) noted that British data are based on a variety of different spatial organizations 'none of which are comparable or, for the most part, nestable'. This problem is magnified by changes to the boundaries of functional and legal entities. The changed boundaries of Germany following reunification is an obvious case; even more complicated is the creation of new sub-national units of local government in several West European countries in the last twenty years or so.

6. Social science data archives exist in over twenty-five countries. They can be located easily on the World Wide Web by accessing URL http://www.nsd.uib.no/cessda/.

7. Data are available directly via the Internet from e.g., the UK's Office for National Statistics located at http://www. ons.gov.uk/; Eurostat, the EU's statistical office, which can be found at http://europa. u.int/en/comm/eurostat/serven/home.htm/; and the UN statistical office at http://www.un.org/Depts/unsd/.

8. One of the earliest of these, the Automatic Interaction Detector (AID), lost popularity as researchers found that the solutions produced often reflected peculiarities in the dataset to which it was applied. AID required more data than were usually available to produce statistically robust findings.

9. The notable exception are researchers interested in marketing strategies, who have developed techniques for market segmentation.

10. Data-mining techniques, not dissimilar to AID in intent, are being developed for

pattern searches through the vast amounts of data collected in these 'data ware-houses'.

11. These developments may be particularly helpful to researchers examining voting behaviour. In particular, it may enable them to address the problems inherent in endeavouring to find consistent behaviour in such a relatively ephemeral, and highly episodic, activity as voting; e.g., it is still unclear whether the instabilities observed in electoral behaviour are due to the unreliability of the measures or to volatility amongst voters.

12. General purpose analytic packages such as *SAS* and *GENSTAT* have always offered a language for programming new algorithms. They have now been joined by packages such as *S-Plus* and *Gauss* that are essentially functional toolkits.

13. According to Lazowska (1997), looking further into the future, the 'real revolution' lies in linking processing power to information sources with intelligent communication paths. See http://www.cs.washington.edu/homes/lazowska/cra/future.htlm.

PART I
ANALYSES ACROSS OBSERVATIONS

3

ORDINARY LEAST SQUARES AND LOGISTIC REGRESSION ANALYSIS

DAVID SANDERS AND MALCOLM BRYNIN

Regression is one of the most commonly used statistical techniques in contemporary social science. This derives from the fact that analysts are frequently interested in applying statistical models to evaluate explanations of social phenomena. For any given *explicandum*, or dependent variable, they wish to know the extent to which a particular theory enables them to identify the minimum, non-tautological set of necessary and sufficient conditions—the *explanans* or independent variables—required for the *explicandum* to occur.[1] Regression provides a statistical counterpart to this notion of explanation. This is because regression models are all based on the idea that prior information about a given set of independent variables, $X_1, X_2 \ldots X_k$, can be used to guess, or predict, the values of a given dependent variable, Y. Regression uses the simple principle that if $X_1, X_2 \ldots X_k$, in some sense, 'explain' the occurrence of Y, then we should be able to use known values of $X_1, X_2 \ldots X_k$ to predict what will happen to Y. To 'predict' in this case means providing either a genuine forecast about the future or a 'postdiction' about events that have already occurred, in which the observed values of Y are compared with the values of Y that would have been predicted if the analyst had only known the values of $X_1, X_2 \ldots X_k$. Predictions, of either type, which turn out to be correct lend credence to the 'explanations' operationalized.

This chapter begins with a review of the basic principles and logic of the ordinary least squares (OLS) model.[2] We then provide an example of an empirical model which satisfies the usual OLS assumptions. In Section 2, we describe the logistic regression model which is now extensively used in social and political research. The logistic approach, however, allows one of the most restrictive assumptions of the ordinary least squares model to be relaxed, so allowing qualitative, or categorical, variables to be employed as either, or both, dependent and independent variables. Section 3 compares the results of using ordinary least squares and logistic estimation to evaluate an individual-level model of partisan support.

The Ordinary Least Squares Model

If we hypothesize that a measured independent variable, X_i, exerts a causal effect on a measured dependent variable, Y_i, then the bivariate relationship between X_i and Y_i can be represented in three complementary ways. The simplest representation is to express the relationship as a symbolic diagram, thus:

$$X_i \xrightarrow[]{\text{(causes)}} Y_i$$

A second, geometric, way of representing the relationship between Y_i and X_i is through the sort of scatterplot outlined in Fig. 3.1. Here we have plotted the scores for seven individuals on two variables, examination performance (Y_i, in percentages) and family income (X_i, in £1,000 units). Note that the figure shows the 'best-fitting line' (its qualities are discussed below) which describes the average relationship between Y_i and X_i. Finally, the relationship shown in Fig. 3.1 can also be expressed as a linear equation of the form:

$$Y_i = a + bX_i + e_i \tag{1}$$

where a and b define the form of the relationship between Y_i and X_i; and e_i represents the error in the relationship; in effect, everything apart from X_i that influences Y_i.

In terms of the geometric pattern shown in Fig. 3.1, a is defined as the constant or intercept, the point where the best-fitting line crosses the Y_i axis. The coefficient b measures the change in Y_i that would be predicted given an

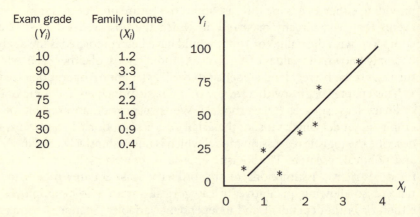

Exam grade (Y_i)	Family income (X_i)
10	1.2
90	3.3
50	2.1
75	2.2
45	1.9
30	0.9
20	0.4

FIG. 3.1 Scatterplot showing the relationship between examination grade (Y_i) and family income (X_i)

increase of one unit in X_i. The two diagrams in Fig. 3.2 indicate the way in which different values of a and b can produce different predictions about the change in Y_i given a unit increase in X_i. Note that b can be either positive, indicating that higher levels of X_i are associated with higher levels of Y_i, and vice versa; or it can be negative, indicating that high levels of X_i are associated with low levels of Y_i, and vice versa. The magnitude of the increase or decrease depends on the steepness of the slope, which is measured by the b term in $Y_i = a + bX_i + e$. For any given Y_i and X_i, the numerical values of a and b can be calculated from established formulae.[3] The a and b thus defined minimize Σe_i^2; that is, the sum of squared vertical deviations (or residuals) from the best-fitting line.

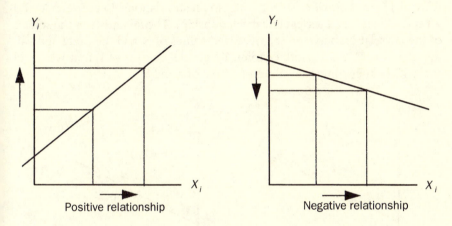

Positive relationship   Negative relationship

Fɪɢ. 3.2 Representation of positive and negative relationships between Y_i and X_i

The underlying principle of ordinary least squares is that we are trying to make a guess at Y (where the guess can be denoted as $Y^\star$) given that we only know (i) the level of X and (ii) the estimated coefficients a and b. For example, if $a = 2$ and $b = 0.5$, and we know that X is 10 for a particular case, then for that case we will guess that:

$$Y^\star = a + b(X)$$
$$Y^\star = 2 + 0.5(10) = 7$$

This guess of Y is the predicted or 'fitted' value of Y that we obtain given X and the relationship between X and Y. The guess may not always be correct (usually it will not be) so there is usually an error, or residual, (e) associated with the guess. The error, e, is the difference between the observed Y and the predicted $Y^\star$. Before going further, readers should convince themselves that, by definition:

$$Y_i = a + bX_i + e_i$$
$$Y_i^\star = a + bX_i$$
$$Y_i = Y_i^\star + e$$

Fig. 3.3 shows how the strength of the relationship between Y_i and X_i can vary independently of the form of the relationship. In Fig. 3.3a, the coordinates (the dots) are all very close to the best-fitting line; the residual for each case is relatively small. In Fig. 3.3b, where the best-fitting line has exactly the same form (that is, the same a and b), the coordinates show much greater dispersal about the line. The closer the coordinates are to the line, the stronger the relationship between X_i and Y_i. This is reflected in the summary statistic R^2, which varies between 0 (denoting no linear relationship between X_i and Y_i) and 1 (denoting a perfect linear relationship). The R^2 statistic is the square of the correlation between the observed values of Y_i and the predicted values of Y_i, or $Y_i^\star$. As we noted earlier, $Y_i^\star$ are the guesses of Y_i that we could make if we knew only the values of X_i and of a and b.

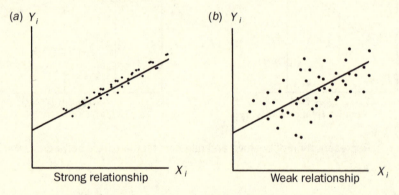

FIG. 3.3 Illustrative representation of strong and weak relationships between Y_i and X_i

Besides being concerned with the form and strength of relationships, regression analysis is also concerned with the problem of statistical significance. This refers to whether or not, on the basis of the observed relationship between the values for X and Y, we can sensibly draw inferences about the underlying relationship between Y and X. In other words, can we generalize from the sample of Y and X values that have been observed to the population of possible X and Y values that could be observed? Significance tests allow us to determine, at specified levels of probability, whether or not we can make such inferences.

The logic of regression-based significance tests is straightforward. Is there enough evidence of a connection between Y and X in our sample to lead us to reject the null hypothesis that there is no relationship between Y and X; in other words, that the 'real' underlying population parameter, B, is zero? The decision rule conventionally applied (which translates roughly into a 95 per cent probability of correctly rejecting the null hypothesis) is that if b—our estimate of B—is more than twice its own estimated standard error, then the null can be rejected.[4] In these circumstances, we can accept the observed b as the best guess of the 'true' population B that can be made. It can also be shown that the least squares estimators, a and b, have a number of highly desirable properties. They are often described as BLUE: the best, linear, unbiased estimators. In this context, 'best' means that the estimators exhibit minimum variance; as Fig. 3.4a shows, the sampling distribution[5] of b clusters closely around the population parameter B. Fig. 3.4b indicates that 'unbiased' means that the sampling distribution of b centres on the population parameter, B.

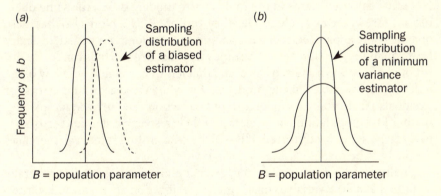

FIG. 3.4 Alternative sampling distributions of b

The attractions of regression analysis, however, go far beyond being able to describe a bivariate relationship in terms of its form, strength, and significance. The model can be generalized from the simple two-dimensional case to the k-dimensional case. In these circumstances, the geometric interpretation of the model is lost. However, symbolic and algebraic interpretations are still available. For example, if it is hypothesized that X_{1i}, X_{2i}, and X_{3i} all influence Y_i, then this can be represented symbolically as:

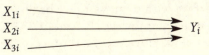

and algebraically as:

$$Y_i = a + b_1 X_{1i} + b_2 X_{2i} + b_3 X_{3i} + e_i$$

where b_1 represents the effect of X_{1i} on Y_i given that the effects of X_{2i} and X_{3i} are being estimated simultaneously or 'controlled for'; b_2 represents the effect of X_{2i} on Y_i controlling for X_{1i} and X_{3i}; and b_3 represents the effect of X_{3i} on Y_i controlling for X_{1i} and X_{2i}. All the other terms have similar meanings to those specified in equation (1) above.[6] The general, linear additive, expression for the multivariate regression model is:

$$Y_i = a + b_1 X_{1i} + b_2 X_{2i} + \ldots b_k X_{ki} + e_i \tag{2}$$

where $b_k X_{ki}$ represents the (controlled) effect of the kth independent or 'exogenous' variable on Y_i. Given that the constant, a, can be regarded as the coefficient on a 'variable' that takes the value of 1 for all cases, equation (2) is sometimes expressed as:

$$Y_i = \Sigma \, b_k X_{ki} + e_i \tag{3}$$

Note that the coefficients in the multivariate model possess the same qualities as those in the bivariate model: they, too, are BLUE. Note also that these qualities only apply if certain basic assumptions hold. In particular, ordinary least squares regression always assumes that the error term is randomly distributed, that it has a mean of zero, and that it is uncorrelated with any of the independent variables in the model. If, for whatever reason, the errors (or 'residuals') from a given model turn out to be non-random, the sample estimates of the population coefficients and their respective standard errors are likely to be seriously distorted. If this is the case, invalid statistical inferences are likely to be made.

Finally, and a point to be stressed, ordinary least squares models generally assume that all the variables in any given specification are measured at interval level. This assumption can be relaxed, however, in relation to 'dummy' independent variables, that is, variables that take the value of unity if a case exhibits a certain characteristic and zero otherwise. The algebraic logic of dummies is simple. Assume that we have a model:

$$Y_i = a + b_1 X_{1i} + b_2 D_i$$

where Y_i and X_i are interval-level variables and D_i is a dummy variable. Suppose that we estimate the model against observed data and obtain:

$$Y_i = 2 + 0.5 X_{1i} + 1.3 D_i + e_i$$

This model says that if we wish to guess Y_i, we begin by adding 0.5 of X_i to 2. If a case scores 1 on the dummy, we then add 1.3 (1.3^*1) to our guess of Y_i—whatever the level of X_i. However, if a case scores zero on the dummy, we add 0 (1.3*0) to the guess; in other words, we keep our guess as it was initially. This means that the dummy effectively measures the extent of the intercept shift that is associated with the cases that score one on the dummy, that is, a shift away from the cases that score zero on the dummy. Given that many concepts in the social sciences can only be measured at the nominal level, the ability of regression models to use dummy variables in this way is important. It means that information about qualitative characteristics can be incorporated into more formal quantitative analysis.

Illustrating the OLS Model

To demonstrate the usefulness of this approach, we model identification with the Conservative Party in Britain over the period 1991–4.[7] Evidence from both aggregate-level and individual-level studies of British voting behaviour shows that support for the major political parties has become increasingly volatile over the last three decades. Panel studies, in particular, have shown a remarkably high level of turnover in respondents' identification with both the Conservative and Labour parties.[8] Between 1991 and 1994, for example, only 20 per cent of the 7,000 or so respondents in the annual British Household Panel Study (BHPS) continuously identified with the ruling Conservative Party, and only 20 per cent continuously identified with the Labour opposition. Here, we seek to establish what affected voters' propensities to identify with the Conservatives. Our dependent variable is the number of times that each panel respondent identified with the Conservatives on the four occasions when they were interviewed—in 1991, 1992, 1993, and 1994. Thus our dependent variable varies between 0 and 4. Our independent variables were all measured in 1991. In other words, our strategy is to use information from the first wave of the BHPS in 1991 to see if we can 'predict' the extent to which respondents identify with the Conservative Party in the subsequent years.

The independent variables in the analysis are listed in Table 3.1.[9] We also indicate, in the second column of the table, the sort of effect—positive or negative—that each variable is expected to exert on Conservative support. The remaining four columns in Table 3.1 report the results from testing a formal model. But before examining the results, a word about the selection of variables, which reflects a compromise between our desire to operationalize the main hypotheses about partisan identification and the constraints of the BHPS data.

The independent, or exogenous, variables fall into three main categories. The first group identifies the socio-demographic characteristics of respondents. Previous research has shown that these variables are related to voters' political preferences in fairly predictable ways: voters are more likely to support the Conservatives if they are older, female, middle class, home owners, not trades unionists, not university educated, and live in the south of England.[10] The second cluster of variables refers to the 'ideology and opinions' of respondents. With these variables, of course, there is a potential 'causality' problem. For example, does holding to a right-wing ideology 'cause' someone to identify with the Conservatives? Or does ideology reflect predetermined identification? Or are both identification and ideology caused simultaneously by something else? Given that we cannot explore these difficult questions here (indeed, it is quite possible that they are irresolvable), for the purposes of exposition we assume that the battery of 'ideology and opinions' variables we use are all genuinely exogenous; that is, that they are determined by variables outside the model. The final set of independent variables refers to the material circumstances of respondents. Here, we hypothesize that respondents enjoying relatively advantaged material conditions (higher income, better health, higher financial expectations, no housing payment problems, and so on) will be more likely to register high levels of support for the Conservatives; in short, they will be more likely, *ceteris paribus*, to want to preserve the political *status quo* that has produced their current (sense of) prosperity.

The formal model that we test is set out thus:

$$\text{Conservative support} = a + \Sigma\, b_{1\ldots14}\ \text{socio-demographic characteristics}$$
$$+ \Sigma\, b_{15\ldots22}\ \text{ideology and opinions}$$
$$+ \Sigma\, b_{22\ldots29}\ \text{material conditions} + e \qquad (4)$$

The estimated effects of each of our independent variables on the level of support for the Conservatives, shown in Table 3.1, broadly confirm our expectations. Note, first, how the signs on most of the independent variables are as predicted. For example, the positive sign on the age variable confirms the expectation that older respondents are more likely to score highly on the scale for Conservative support; the negative sign on the post-materialist variable confirms that post-materialists are less likely to be consistent Conservative supporters; and so on. Secondly, note that most of the estimated coefficients are more than twice as large as their respective standard errors. Recall our earlier point that, under these conditions, the null hypothesis of 'no effect' can be rejected. Indeed, the p values associated with most of the coefficients show that the null can be rejected at a probability greater than 95 per cent. The $p < 0.00$ for the variable 'left-wing ideology', for example, means that we can be at least 99.9 per cent sure that we can reject the null hypothesis that left-wing opinions do not affect Conservative support.[11]

Perhaps the most interesting feature of Table 3.1, however, is the magnitude of the coefficients reported. Recall that the coefficients in ordinary least squares regression measure the predicted change in Y given a unit increase in X_k, controlling for the effects of all the other variables in the model. For example, the coefficient of -0.33 on the dummy variable 'NHS concern' means that, after controlling for the effects of the other variables in the model, someone who is concerned about the National Health Service in Britain will, on average, score 0.3 points less on the Conservative-support scale (0–4) than someone who is not concerned about the NHS. Similarly, the coefficient of $+0.1$ on the age variable means that for each year that a person lives, *ceteris paribus*, their score on the Conservative support scale will increase by 0.1. Note that, in this specification, this effect applies across the entire age range: whatever age respondents are now, one more year adds the same increase in their predicted score for Conservative support.

Finally, Table 3.1 reports an R^2 value of 0.39. (Recall that R^2 is the square of the correlation between the observed values of the dependent variable and the predicted values derived from knowing the values of the independent variables and the coefficients of the model.) The R^2 statistic is sometimes converted into percentage terms and referred to as 'the percentage of explained variation'. This implies that the model shown in Table 3.1 'explains' 39 per cent of the variation in the Conservative-support scale. It is, of course, difficult to know what this means in substantive terms. Whether 39 per cent is 'high' or 'low' depends upon the context of the analysis. Previous analyses of individual-level partisan preferences typically produce R^2 values even lower than the 0.39 reported here. In this sense, the overall fit of the model, as measured by R^2, is quite good.

Alert readers may have noticed one or two anomalies in the analysis of Conservative support just presented. First, although it is not possible for a respondent to score a non-integer value on the Conservative-support scale, it is evident that some of the predicted values from the equation underlying the results shown in Table 3.1 are almost certain to be between 0 and 1, between 1 and 2, and so on. It is also possible that, for some individuals, their predicted values on the Conservative-support indicator could be either greater than 4 (the highest point on the observed scale) or less than zero (the low point). Secondly, in theoretical terms, we may be primarily interested in what differentiates Conservative supporters from non-supporters at a particular point in time, rather than the number of times that people identify with the Conservatives over a four-year period. In these circumstances, even though it fails to resolve the non-integer problem (although it does simplify it), the use of a simple dummy dependent variable model or 'linear probability model' commends itself.

In the current context, based on (4) above, the linear probability model approach involves defining the dependent variable as: Conservative

Table 3.1 Ordinary least squares regression with number of times respondents identified with the Conservative Party as the independent variable

	Predicted relationship	Parameter estimates	Standard error	t-values	Probability
constant		-1.67	0.12	-13.4	<0.01
Demography and class					
Age	+	0.01	0.001	7.4	<0.01
Male	-	0.09	0.03	2.7	0.01
Service class	+	0.10	0.05	1.9	0.06
Routine non-manual	+	0.27	0.05	5.0	<0.01
Petty-bourgeois	+	0.40	0.07	5.5	<0.01
Skilled manual	+	0.13	0.05	2.4	0.02
No occupation	none	0.18	0.06	2.9	<0.01
No class perception	none	0.00	0.04		
Middle-class perception	+	0.18	0.04	5.0	<0.01
Father middle class	+	0.16	0.04	4.4	<0.01
Union member	-	-0.08	0.04	-1.8	0.06
Homeowner	+	0.12	0.04	3.2	<0.01
Bought council home	+	0.03	0.06	0.5	0.65
Lives in south	+	0.13	0.03	4.1	<0.01
Has degree	-	-0.09	0.02	-3.7	<0.01

Ideology and opinions					
Reads left-wing paper	−	-0.56	0.04	-13.4	<0.01
Religious	+	0.15	0.03	4.2	<0.01
Interested in politics	+	0.24	0.03	6.3	<0.01
Concern about unemployment	+	-0.42	0.03	-13.6	<0.01
Left-wing ideology	−	-0.93	0.04	-26.1	<0.01
Concern about NHS	−	-0.33	0.03	-10.2	<0.01
Post-materialist	−	-0.29	0.03	-9.1	<0.01
Material circumstances					
Has good health	+	0.12	0.03	3.5	<0.01
Wants work	−	-0.15	0.05	-3.2	<0.01
Home cost problems	−	-0.12	0.05	-2.6	0.01
Room home density	+	0.01	0.02	0.3	0.74
Has investment income	+	0.18	0.04	4.9	<0.01
Optimistic living standards	+	0.12	0.04	3.2	<0.01
Consumer durable purchases	+	0.15	0.04	3.8	<0.01
Household income (k)	+	0.10	0.02	4.2	<0.01
N	6757				
R^2	39%				

identifier = 1; not a Conservative identifier = 0. The fitted Y values from such a model can be regarded as estimates of the probability that a given respondent will identify with the Conservatives at that particular time-point. In this instance, we focus on identification with the Conservative Party in the first wave of the panel survey, in 1991. Fitted Y values above 0.5 imply that a respondent is predicted to be a Conservative identifier; values below 0.5 indicate that a respondent is predicted not to be a Conservative identifier. Obviously, the closer the degree of correspondence between the observed and the fitted values of Y, other things being equal, the better is the model. The results from using a dummy dependent variable model of this sort are reported in Table 3.2.

The results here are broadly consistent with those shown in Table 3.1. The signs on all the independent variables are identical in both tables and the significance levels of the variables are very similar. Unfortunately, the simple OLS linear probability model typically exhibits a number of serious deficiencies. The most important of these is that the linear probability model generally yields residuals that are non-random. In particular, the residuals exhibit heteroscedasticity, that is, they tend to vary in magnitude systematically with the level(s) of the independent variable(s). Ordinary least squares estimation, however, assumes that residuals are homoscedastic. The difference between these patternings of the residuals are illustrated in Fig. 3.5.

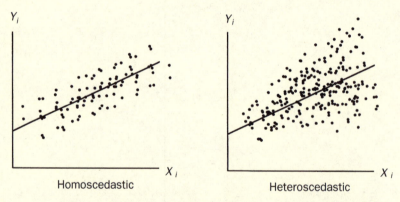

Fɪɢ. 3.5 Representation of homoscedastic and heteroscedastic residuals

If the residuals are, indeed, heteroscedastic, then the estimated coefficients, although they remain unbiased, do not possess the smallest possible sampling variances. As a result, significance tests conducted on the coefficients are highly misleading.[12] For this reason, OLS linear probability estimation is not recommended for models with a dichotomous dependent

Table 3.2 Ordinary least squares regression comparing Conservative identifiers and not–Conservative identifiers (1991 wave only)

	Parameter estimates	Standard error	t-values	Probability
constant	1.33	0.03	47.1	<0.01
Demography and class				
Age	0.07	0.01	6.1	<0.01
Male	0.02	0.01	2.1	0.03
Service class	0.05	0.02	3.2	<0.01
Routine non-manual	0.08	0.02	5.3	<0.01
Petty-bourgeois	0.09	0.02	3.8	<0.01
Skilled manual	0.03	0.02	1.7	0.09
No occupation	0.05	0.02	2.3	0.02
No class perception	0.00			
Middle-class perception	0.06	0.01	5.2	<0.01
Father middle class	0.04	0.01	3.9	<0.01
Union member	−0.03	0.01	−2.4	0.01
Homeowner	0.05	0.01	3.9	<0.01
Bought council home	0.01	0.02	0.5	0.63
Lives in south	0.05	0.01	4.6	<0.01
Has degree	−0.03	0.01	−3.7	<0.01
Ideology and opinions				
Reads left-wing paper	−0.15	0.01	−11.6	<0.01
Religious	0.04	0.01	3.7	<0.01
Interested in politics	0.11	0.01	11.2	<0.01
Concern about unemployment	−0.14	0.01	−13.6	<0.01
Left-wing ideology	−0.23	0.01	−21.0	<0.01
Concern about NHS	−0.11	0.01	−10.6	<0.01
Post-materialist	−0.07	0.01	-6.6	<0.01
Material circumstances				
Has good health	0.05	0.01	4.4	<0.01
Wants work	−0.05	0.01	−3.4	<0.01
Home cost problems	−0.04	0.01	−3.0	<0.01
Low home density	0.02	0.01	1.4	0.17
Has investment income	0.05	0.01	4.6	<0.01
Optimistic living standards	0.03	0.01	2.5	0.01
Above average durables	0.04	0.01	3.4	<0.01
High household income	0.03	0.01	2.1	0.04
N	6757			
R^2	31%			

variable. Rather, a technique known as logistic regression, which is expressly designed for the analysis of categorical data, is much the preferred choice of most contemporary analysts. The logistic regression model is considered in the next section.

Logistic Regression

There are many outcomes which social scientists view as binary; at the individual level, for example, decisions to get married (or not), to leave school, take a job, to vote for one party rather than another (or to vote rather than not vote), and so on. It is inappropriate to model these outcomes using ordinary least squares regression because such outcomes are always discrete and in no way mimic the interval-level dependent variable which OLS analysis requires. One of the standard techniques in these situations is logistic regression. This requires a categorical dependent variable which is usually dichotomous (a choice of two outcomes) but which may be multinomial (a choice of more than two). The discussion here is limited to the first situation, where the dependent variable is, in effect, a 0–1 dummy.[13]

A second major difference between ordinary least squares and logistic regression is that while OLS models the impact of an increase in one unit in one variable on another, logistic regression is based on the impact of an increase in one variable on the probability that the outcome under analysis will occur. This is an important distinction. It means that the technique is more indirect than OLS as it predicts the *probability of change* rather than the *amount of probable change*. Indeed, logistic regression can be seen as a compromise between standard ordinary least squares and log-linear modelling methods. Log-linear models are based on straightforward cross-tabulations (see McCutcheon and Mills, this volume). Consider, for example, the relationship between gender and vote. The probability of a woman voting Labour derives from the relationship between the marginal distributions (the proportion of the sample who are female, and the proportion who vote Labour) and their combination (the proportion of women who vote Labour). In log-linear modelling, however, the probabilities relate to the cell distributions (for example, the proportion of women who vote Labour) rather than the individual outcomes (the probability of any particular woman voting Labour).

While logistic regression is ultimately based on the notion of probabilities, its equations—as in log-linear models—make use of odds: the probability of an event occurring over the probability of it not occurring. Thus, if the probability of a woman voting Labour is 0.4, the probability of her not doing so is 0.6; thus, the odds of her doing so are 0.66 (0.4/0.6), while the odds of her not doing so are 1.5 (0.6/0.4). Equal probabilities produce odds of one. The binary nature of the dependent variable is explicit in these odds: the probability that the specified outcome will occur relative to the probability that it will not.

One further adaptation of the ordinary least squares structure is needed; this again is derived from the general log-linear model.The standard OLS equation is linear, but this does not apply to logistic regression. For example, the impact of income on the probability that someone will or will not vote for a particular party is not the same as the impact, say, of income on consumption (which is linear, at least over certain ranges of income). For the simplest equation where the probability $P(Y) = f(X)$, a graph of $P(Y)$ against X will have an S-shaped curve ranging from $P = 0$ to $P = 1$. Linearity is introduced through conversion to natural logs. Thus, the odds of the outcome become the log odds. The dependent variable is now linearly related to the predictors (in a well-determined model). It is also, by the same transformation, continuous. This means that we can interpret the coefficients in much the same way as in ordinary least squares: an increment of a predictor increases or reduces the odds of an event by a fixed amount over the entire range of that predictor. The final logistic regression equation is quite simple:

$$\log \text{odds}\,(Y) = B_0 + B_1 X_1 + \ldots B_n X_n \ldots + u \tag{5}$$

where u is a random error term. This reads pretty much like the standard ordinary least squares equation but its interpretation in terms of changes to the log odds is far less clear. The dependent variable can be converted to actual odds through exponentiation (that is, converting the logs). However, while this procedure produces an outcome which is more easily understood, the equation is multiplicative rather than additive. It is, therefore, generally less readable. Nevertheless, it can be used to recover the actual odds. This is shown in the following example with a single predictor:

$$\text{odds}(Y) = e^{B_0} \cdot e^{B_1} \cdot e^u \tag{6}$$

Equation (5) is the logit transformation of equation (6), in which the logit is a critical link function between the predictors and the dependent variable. Equation (6) clearly demonstrates the non-linear nature of the estimation process. This comes out yet more clearly when we try to recover the actual probability (rather than the odds) of the outcome, which is derived through the following equation:

$$P(Y) = \frac{1}{1 + e^{-(B_0 + B_1 X_1 + \ldots B_n X_n)}} \tag{7}$$

The expression in brackets is, in fact, our regression equation, and the formula is the basis of the estimation process which produces the values for the parameters. As we know $P(Y)$, in much the same way as we know the probability of an outcome in a log-linear model (by reference to the marginal distributions), the estimation process works by fitting the parameters to the actual data. Given that the relationship expressed in the equation is extremely non-linear, the least squares method of estimating the parameters is not applicable. The parameters are fitted through an iterative process in which the algorithm makes an initial 'guess' at the parameters which might fit the data, and then, in subsequent iterations, proceeds to improve them until the best fit is obtained. The fitting process is called *maximum likelihood*.

Testing the Efficacy of the Model

As in ordinary least squares, there are several aspects to model testing in logistic regression. At the minimum, logistic regression provides t-tests for individual coefficients, so it is possible to be fairly sure whether or not a given independent variable has an effect on the dependent variable in question. However, it is much harder to test the overall adequacy of the model. One method is simply to test the null hypothesis that the coefficients sum to zero (that is, that the model is redundant). This, in itself, is often not a very useful test. Nonetheless, this type of test—designed to tell us whether or not the dependent variables tell us anything more than a model which includes only the intercept—is central to model-fitting where different models are compared through the addition or subtraction of exogenous variables.[14]

One measure used to test the overall effectiveness of the logistic regression model is, again, based on the probability that the outcome will occur. All logistic regression packages give standard measures of the change in probability provided by the model. The probability is given as the *log likelihood (LL)* and is conventionally multiplied by -2 (to give $-2LL$). This means that the more the model explains, the more the value for this statistic, $-2LL$, will fall. While, as stated, a significance test for the whole model means rather little in itself, it might be necessary to know whether addition or subtraction of a variable, or a block of variables, has a significant impact. Thus, if $-2LL$ falls following the addition of a variable, and this change is significant (relative to one degree of freedom), the addition is valid.

These 'global' tests of different models will still not tell us whether the final model has good explanatory power. In ordinary least squares, R^2 is a straightforward measure of the explanatory power of a model, but this is inappropriate in logistic regression because we are not dealing with variation relative to the mean. A replication of R^2 does exist, and again it uses $-2LL$. The measure, however, is far less reliable than its OLS equivalent. It is based on the notion that the increase in likelihood provided by the model compared to a rival model, based solely on the constant, is equivalent to 'explained' variance. When this increase in likelihood (or reduction in the case of $-2LL$) is taken as a proportion of the total variance (defined as the value for $-2LL$ using just the constant) the equivalence with R^2 is complete. However, this 'pseudo-R^2' is not the same thing as R^2 (and its values are typically lower), as we are still not dealing with variations around a mean. Pseudo-R^2 measures should be treated with caution and their interpretation only makes sense in terms of comparisons between rival models.

In sum, while logistic regression provides a very useful means of testing the impact of one or more variables on a dependent variable, it is generally not possible to be sure that a final model is truly effective. And this is so even if we can be sure from global tests that the sample model is unlikely to be significantly different from the population model. This is hardly surprising given that we are trying to assess the probability that an outcome will occur, and that many of our predictors—as well as the dependent variable—are not continuous (a fact which entails a loss of accuracy in estimation). Above all, this means that the interpretation of coefficients must be undertaken with considerable care.

A Logistic Regression Model of Partisan Identification

The results shown in the third column of Table 3.3 are derived from the same model as reported in Table 3.2—based on (4) above—but arrived at by using logistic regression rather than OLS. Table 3.3 also reports the results of entering, first, 'material circumstances', and then 'ideology and opinions', as exogenous variables in discrete blocks. This procedure is frequently used in logistic regression in order to compare the resulting reduction in the $-2LL$ statistic. The dependent variable is the log odds of voting Conservative (rather than any other outcome) and, again, uses data from the first wave of the panel study. The number of independent variables in each model is given in parenthesis after the chi-square statistic.

How do we interpret the coefficients shown in the table? Each coefficient represents the increase or reduction in the log odds of the dependent variable occurring. Thus, in the case of a simple dummy such as gender, the effect on Conservative identification relates to being male rather than female. In the third column of Table 3.3 the coefficient for 'male' is 0.1. This means that if all the women in the sample were replaced by men, the log odds of each individual being a Conservative identifier would rise by 0.1. In other words, the coefficient can be seen as the effect produced by the average man. The actual odds are simply the exponentiated coefficients.[15] The exponentiated coefficient indicates how much the odds, rather than the log

Table 3.3 Logistic regression comparing Conservative identifiers and not-Conservative identifiers (1991 wave only)

	Model 1 class	Model 2 class material circumstances	Model 3 class material circumstances ideology and opinions
constant	–2.3	–2.40	–1.0
Demography and class			
Age over 40	0.6**	0.5**	0.4**
Male	–0.1	0.00	0.1*
Service class	0.8**	0.7**	0.3**
Routine non-manual	0.8**	0.7**	0.6**
Petty-bourgeois	1.0**	0.8**	0.5**
Skilled manual	0.3**	0.3**	0.3*
No occupation	0.3**	0.5**	0.3*
No class perception	0.1	0.1	0.00
Middle-class perception	0.6**	0.5**	0.3**
Father middle class	0.4**	0.4**	0.2**
Union member	–0.4**	–0.5**	–0.2*
Homeowner	0.7**	0.5**	0.3**
Bought council home	0.2*	0.1	0.1
Lives in south	0.3**	0.3**	0.3**
Has degree	–0.1*	–0.2**	–0.2**
Ideology and opinions			
Reads left-wing paper			–1.3**
Religious			0.2**
Interested in politics			0.7**
Concern about unemployment			–0.8**
Left-wing ideology			–1.7**
Concern about NHS			–0.6**
Post-materialist			–0.4**
Material circumstances			
Has good health		0.3**	0.3**
Wants work		–0.4**	–0.3**
Home cost problems		–0.3**	–0.3**
Low home density		0.2**	0.1
Has investment income		0.4	0.3**
Optimistic living standard		0.2**	0.2*
Above average durables		0.2**	0.2**
High household income		0.2*	0.1
N	6886	6816	6757
Initial –2*LL*	8779	8693	8627
Final –2*LL*	7890	7643	6165
Model	889 (15)	1050 (23)	2462 (30)
'Pseudo' R^2	10%	12%	36%

* $p<0.005$ ** $p<0.01$

odds, of the outcome either increase or decrease as a result of a one unit change in the predictor variable. Exponentiation of the gender coefficient of 0.1 produces a change in the odds of 1.1. Given that odds of 1 signify no change, this means that the odds of a Conservative rather than a non-Conservative outcome increase by 10 per cent. Where there are multi-category dummies, the reference category must be taken into account more explicitly. For example, in the case of occupational class in Model 3 in the table, the log odds of someone in the service class identifying with the Conservatives are 0.3 higher than for a semi-skilled or unskilled worker. Similarly, the 0.6 increase in the log odds for a routine non-manual worker relative to a less skilled worker is twice as large as the effect for the service class.

The models shown in Table 3.3 clearly improve as we add more variables. Only demographic and class variables are entered in Model 1. All have the expected effect on Conservative identification. The set of occupational categories shows that all groups, even skilled manual workers, tend to be more Conservative than the semi-skilled or unskilled; the service class, routine non-manual workers, and the petty-bourgeois groups are the most Conservative. This class effect is confirmed by other class-related measures. Class perceptions, class background, union membership (which reduces the odds of identifying with the Conservatives), housing tenure (council-house purchasers are more likely to be Conservative than tenants, but not as likely as homeowners), region, and education all clearly affect the odds of identifying with the Conservatives.

Note, however, that in terms of explanatory power, Model 1 is not particularly good at predicting which individuals are likely to identify with the Conservatives and which are not. While most of the coefficients achieve statistical significance, the $-2LL$ does not reduce very much from the simple constant model. When we add controls for material conditions in Model 2, there is some increase in the effectiveness of the specification, although this is not great. Model 2 also shows that the inclusion of variables for material circumstances does not have much impact on the class coefficients. This suggests that, thus far at least, the effects of class are correctly represented by the model. Overall, Model 2 clearly shows that, regardless of social class, people who are better off—or who feel better off—are more likely to support the Conservative Party.

While most of the variables measuring demographic and material circumstances are significant in Model 2, we obtain a far better determined and more effective model when we introduce attitudinal and ideological variables in Model 3. The coefficients for this latter group of variables are almost all substantial. They show that those respondents who have left-wing views, or who read a left-wing newspaper, are significantly less likely to identify with the Conservatives, while those who claim a religious affiliation are more likely to do so. Those who are interested in politics are also more likely to be Conservative, but here we must recall the construction of the dependent variable. The contrast is between Conservative support or not. Those not supporting the party include a large number of people with no political affiliation and who are, probably, less likely to be interested in politics.

These are hardly surprising findings. Perhaps the chief substantive significance of the analysis lies in the relative weights of the three blocks of variables, which show that ideological factors, despite claims about the 'end of ideology', remain powerful predictors of partisan identification. More important, however, is the effect that the addition of the ideological variables has on the coefficients reported for Model 1 and Model 2 in Table 3.3. While the effects of material circumstances change little between Models 2 and 3, the impact of the class variables reduces significantly between Models 2 and 3, with most of the change clearly deriving from the effects of the attitudinal variables. For example, in Model 3, members of the service class are no different from skilled workers in their propensity to identify with the Conservatives. This suggests that the service class effect shown in Model 1 reflects, in part, the strong tendency for the service class to hold right-wing views. Once these views are controlled for, as they are in Model 3, the propensity of the service class to support the Conservatives is much reduced. In short, while social class is still a significant predictor of partisan identification, ideology—which may cut across social class—is a more effective predictor.

Assessing the Models

The primary statistical objective in ordinary least squares models is to minimize Σe_i^2, that is, the sum of squared differences between the observed and predicted values of Y_i. Logistic regression, in contrast, makes use of maximum likelihood estimation, where the main statistical objective is to specify those coefficient estimates which maximize the probability of predicting the observed pattern of Y_i. One crucial feature of the logistic specification is that it is multiplicative or non-linear. In ordinary least squares regression, as we noted earlier, the predicted change in Y_i given a unit increase in X_i is the same whatever the current level of X_i. (Recall that, in Table 3.2, one additional year of life increased the average respondent's score on the Conservative support scale regardless of the respondent's current age.) With logistic regression, however, the multiplicative character of the specification means that the effect that X_{i1} has on Y_i depends both on the current levels of $X_{i2}, X_{i3} \ldots X_{ik}$ and on the current probability of Y_i. This, in turn, implies that the magnitudes of logistic regression coefficients cannot be interpreted in a straightforward manner. Formally, logistic estimates show the effects exerted by each independent variable on Y_i with all variables set equal to their respective means.

That said, logistic regression methods are enormously useful in models with a dummy dependent variable for determining whether or not coefficients have the correct (that is, theoretically predicted) signs, and in ascertaining whether or not a particular exogenous variable exerts a statistically significant effect on some Y_i. As in ordinary least squares, logistic coefficients have estimated standard errors; and, as in OLS, the null hypothesis of no effect can, in general, be rejected if a coefficient is more than twice its own estimated standard error. In this sense, interpreting the significance of logistic regression results is identical to interpreting the results from ordinary least squares regression.

What is intriguing about the results reported here is the strong similarity between the substantive conclusions that would be derived from the full logistic regression model shown in Table 3.3 and from the OLS linear probability model shown in Table 3.2. As noted above, the signs and significance levels of almost all the exogenous variables are identical in both tables. Of course, it could be argued that where there are minor differences between the two sets of results, it is the linear probability model that is misleading and the logistic regression model that is 'correct' because the estimates for the linear probability model are based on assumptions that are almost certain to be violated. In relation to our data, this would imply that, contrary to the results for the OLS linear probability model shown in Table 3.2, skilled workers are fractionally more likely than unskilled workers to identify with the Conservatives (see the significant coefficient for the skilled manual variable in Model 3 of Table 3.3). Note, however, that the other twenty-nine coefficients shown in Table 3.2 and Table 3.3 (Model 3) all yield identical substantive conclusions: their signs, significance levels, and relative magnitudes display a remarkable degree of consistency across the two tables.

As the patterning of the coefficients is the same, ordinary least squares and logistic regression lead to the same general interpretation. It might, therefore, be asked why one technique should be used rather than another? The answer is that OLS might, indeed, do just as well as logistic regression for exploratory analysis. In addition, the coefficients are easier to read. After all, in the case of logistic regression, what exactly are the log odds that an event will occur following a shift in the value of an explanatory variable? The figure has no immediate, common-sense interpretation. For that, we have to recover the actual odds (or probabilities). In the case of OLS, interpretation is very simple. Taking a different example, for instance a linear consumption equation, then a unit increase in income leads to an increase in consumption. The coefficient indicates the amount by which consumption rises.

Unfortunately, in the case of ordinary least squares, a binary dependent variable has no such interpretation. The dependent variable in our case is not the probability of supporting the Conservatives, which can vary continuously, but actual support. It makes no sense trying to interpret OLS coefficients as the proportion of change the explanatory variable makes to a dependent variable which, unlike the log odds, has only two states.

Nevertheless, the fact remains that where the sample is random and large, the two techniques will, when merely eye-balled, yield much the same picture. On what grounds, then, is one technique to be preferred to the other? On the one hand, on purely statistical grounds, logistic regression is undoubtedly the correct approach when using a dummy dependent variable. Moreover, it is likely that the robustness of ordinary least squares diminishes with smaller sample sizes for data of this nature, and ultimately the analyst must be able to justify the interpretation of the results on statistical grounds. On the other hand, the sheer proliferation of numbers in a logistic regression, and their associated intepretation, mean that it is rather difficult to make comprehensive and unambiguous statements about the effects of the independent variables on the dependent variable. Indeed, precise estimates are often of less value in this field than the overall picture. These considerations lead us to suggest that the OLS linear probability model should not automatically be discarded by analysts searching for a plausible but parsimonious explanation of some phenomenon. Equally, in the case of analyses where the results yielded by the two techniques are very different, then, clearly, the logistic estimates should be reported.

Notes

1. *Explicandum* is that which is to be explained; *explanans* is that which explains.
2. The best expositions of regression techniques are to be found in Beck (1980), and Berry and Feldman (1985).
3. The equations are: $a = Y - bX$; $b = \Sigma(x_i y_i)/\Sigma x_i^2$; where $x_i = (X_i - X)$ and $y_i = (Y_i - Y)$ and where Σ (sigma) means 'add up everything that follows'. To appreciate what this notation implies, consider the following variable, which is measured for 5 cases:

Obs	X_i	$X_i - X = x_i$	$(X_i - X)^2$
1	5	−10	100
2	10	−5	25
2	15	+0	0
4	20	+5	25
5	25	+10	100
	(Mean of X_i is 15)		$\Sigma x_i^2 = 250$

4. Formulae for computing standard errors vary according to the character of the data under analysis. In the simplest OLS case, however, the estimated standard error of b is given by $\Sigma e_i^2 / \Sigma x_i^2$ where the numerator, in effect, measures the size of the error term in the model and the denominator measures the degree of dispersal of the independent variable. The greater the size of the error term, *ceteris paribus*, the higher the estimated standard error of a given coefficient; and therefore the less likely it is that the observed coefficient will be significant at the required level. Similarly, the greater the dispersal of the independent variable, *ceteris paribus*, the smaller the estimated standard error of b; and therefore the more likely it is that b will be statistically significant.

5. To appreciate what is meant by the sampling distribution of a coefficient, consider a population of 50 million people. We can draw random samples of 1,000 from this population and measure each person we sample in terms of two attributes, X and Y. Suppose that we draw 150 samples of 1,000 from the population. For each sample, we can calculate b, the effect of X on Y. The values of b that we calculate would be likely to vary across the different samples. Taken together, the 150 b values could be arrayed in the sort of distribution described in Fig. 3.4; this would be the sampling distribution of b.

6. Obviously, the constant does not have the same geometric interpretation as before. As in the bivariate case, however, it continues to indicate the 'starting point' for Y_i before the effects of X_{1i}, X_{2i}, and X_{3i} begin to operate. The computing equation for the constant and the coefficients continues to minimize Σe_i^2 and is given by the (matrix algebra) equation of $b_k = (X'X)^{-1} X'Y$.

7. The work reported here is part of the scientific programme of the ESRC Centre on Microsocial Change in Britain. The support of the ESRC and the University of Essex is gratefully acknowledged. We are also grateful to Dr Nick Buck of the Research Centre for comments on a draft of this chapter.

8. The concept of party identification is central to many accounts of voting patterns. Voters are alleged to exhibit stable and enduring affective attachments to particular parties. These attachments act as both filters in the interpretation of political information and predispose voters towards voting for the party with which they identify. Party identification is measured here using responses to the 'standard' question: 'Generally speaking, do you think of yourself as Conservative, Labour, Liberal (in Scotland, Scottish Nationalist; in Wales, Plaid Cymru), or what?'

9. Note that all the variables are created as dummies. Most of them are 0–1 dummies where the coefficient represents the effect of being in one category rather that another; e.g. male rather than female. Therefore, the missing category is simply the opposite of the designation given in the table. However, three variables are not transformed into simple dummies, so the 'missing', or reference category, is less obvious. The first of these variables is occupational class, e.g. service class, which has six categories and is a slightly reduced version of the Goldthorpe scheme. The missing category is semi- and unskilled occupations. The second variable is class perceptions, where the base category is working

class, but people who do not see themselves as members of a class are entered as a distinct group. The third variable is housing tenure, which has three categories; the missing category is private sector tenants. For each of these three variables, the coefficient reported represents the effect of being in the category relative to the missing or base category.

10. See Butler and Stokes (1969); Heath *et al.* (1985, 1991, 1994); Särlvik and Crewe (1983).

11. Standard errors can also be interpreted as 'confidence intervals' around the 'point estimate' of the effect of X on Y that is represented by the estimated coefficient. For example, the coefficient of 0.3 for 'lives in south' has a standard error of 0.1. This means that, at the specified probability level shown in column 4, we can be confident that the true population parameter lies between 0.3 plus or minus 0.1 (i.e. between 0.2 and 0.4). From our data, 0.3 is the best guess.

12. Even OLS-based techniques such as weighted least squares, which explicitly seek to correct for heteroscedastic residuals, typically produce distorted estimates of coefficients and standard errors. This is because they continue to be based on assumptions of linearity, which are rarely appropriate with a dichotomous dependent variable.

13. The most accessible introduction to logistic regression is Aldrich and Nelson (1984).

14. Note that in these circumstances we might also be interested in the substantive impact of this change on the coefficients. Suppose, for example, that a model shows that voting is dependent on social class (defined by occupation). Suppose further, however, that when we add income to the equation it not only produces a statistically significant improvement to the model but also substantially reduces the coefficients for class. This implies a strong relationship between class and income. While the correlation between them means we cannot be sure which variable has the primary effect (the problem of 'multi-collinearity'), it will be reasonable to assume that at least some of the class effect works, in fact, through income rather than either the social status or community identity aspects of occupation.

15. The exponentiated coefficients are usually given in the printout for logistic regression. In *SPSS*, they are labelled Exp(*B*); in *SAS*, as the odds ratio.

4

LINEAR STRUCTURAL EQUATION MODELS
STEFFEN KÜHNEL

Linear structural equation modelling is widely used in the analysis of social science data. In this chapter, the approach is applied to analysing survey data about voting turnout. The basic concepts of the approach are presented in the first section. Next, hypotheses about voting turnout are discussed, based mainly on rational choice arguments. All the empirical material comes from a turnout study conducted in the context of the 1995 North Rhine-Westphalian state election. The design of the study and the operationalization of the theoretical concepts used in the analysis are discussed in the third section. The results of the analysis are presented in the fourth section. The chapter concludes with a discussion of the substantive and methodological implications of the analysis.

Basic Concepts

In essence, structural equation modelling is no more than an extension of the well-known linear regression model to a set of regression equations. In linear regression, a dependent variable is viewed as a linear function of one or more independent, or explanatory, variables and a residual variable which is uncorrelated with the explanatory variables. These relations can be represented, graphically, by a path diagram in which the variables of interest are symbolized by boxes and the linear relations by arrows connecting them (see Fig. 4.1). In a path diagram, covariances, or correlations, are symbolized by double-headed arrows, and regression coefficients by single-headed directional arrows.

There is one conceptual difference between classic linear regression and regression in structural equation modelling, however. In the linear regression model, only the residual variable is thought of as a random variable whilst the explanatory variables are thought of, or conceptualized, as given

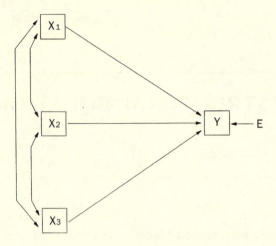

FIG. 4.1 Linear regression

values, or fixed numbers. But in structural equation modelling all the variables are usually viewed as random variables. This difference has consequences for the parameters of the model. In the linear regression model, the only parameters are regression coefficients and the variance of the residual variable. In the structural equation approach there are additional parameters, which are the variances and covariances (and, in some models, also the means) of all exogenous variables.

The distinction between exogenous and endogenous variables is important to the logic of linear structural equation modelling. A variable is exogenous if, and only if, the variable is not a dependent variable in any of the equations for the model. Any variable that is a dependent variable in one equation is endogenous even if that variable is an explanatory variable in another equation. For example, in the path diagram shown in Fig. 4.2, the variables F_2, F_3, and Y_1–Y_9 are endogenous variables, and the variables F_1, D_2, D_3, and E_1–E_9 are exogenous variables. The variances and covariances of all endogenous variables can be deduced as functions of the variances and covariances of the exogenous variables and the regression coefficients.

The linear regression model is the simplest structural equation model. Usually there is more than one regression equation in a single linear equation model. Moreover, it is not necessary for all dependent and explanatory variables to be actually measured. In the general case, some variables may be latent, as in factor analysis. In path diagrams, the latent variables of interest are usually symbolized by ovals whereas the observed variables are symbolized by boxes. In the example shown in Fig. 4.2 there are three latent variables (F_1, F_2, and F_3), and nine observed variables (Y_1–Y_9). Additionally there

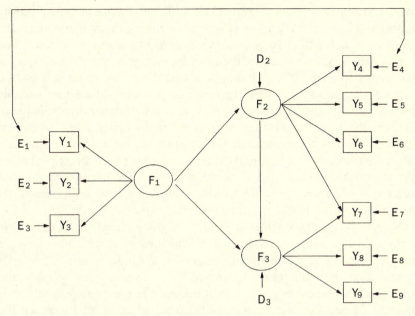

Fɪɢ. 4.2 Example of a linear structural equation model

are eleven residual variables, one for each of the dependent variables. Residual variables are also latent, by definition. In Fig. 4.2, E denotes the residual of an observed dependent variable Y, and D denotes the residual of a latent variable (or factor) F. This convention is suggested by the Bentler–Weeks representation of a linear structural equation model.[1]

One may wonder how it is possible to analyse relations between variables which are not actually observed. The answer is based on a fundamental statistical fact: linear dependencies between variables affect their means, variances, and covariances. Or, to put it another way, means, variances, and covariances contain all the information necessary to estimate the parameters of a linear model. According to statisticians (Casella and Berger 1990: 247), means, variances, and covariances are sufficient statistics for any linear model. Hence, if the latent variables are linearly related, and if these latent variables are also linearly related to the observed variables, then the relations between the observed variables and the relations between the latent variables will have consequences for the values of the means, variances, and covariances of the observed variables. Therefore, one can try to estimate the parameters linked to latent variables from the statistics for the observed variables.

An advantage of specifying latent variables is that we can control for random measurement errors. It is well known that measurement errors may distort relationships (Bollen 1989: 151–75). If measurement errors can be controlled for, there is a greater chance of analysing the true relationships. However, there is a price to be paid. Measurement errors can be controlled for only if there is more than one indicator for each property to be measured. This means, in terms of a path diagram, that there have to be at least two observed variables that can be regressed as indicators of a latent variable which is free of measurement error.[2] There is yet a further disadvantage to this approach: by definition there is no access to the actual values of a latent variable. One may try to estimate such values, but estimations are not the same as true values. Consequently, it is not possible to see directly whether there is a positive or negative relationship between the latent variables, nor if there is any relationship at all. All conclusions have to be drawn indirectly by examining relationships between observed variables.

To estimate the parameters, a model has to be *identified*. Identification means that the data at hand—that is, the observed variables—contain enough information to estimate all parameters in a unique way. If a model is not identified, then different values for at least one parameter will have the same empirical effects. In which case, it makes little sense to say that there is a positive or negative relationship, or no relationship at all. However, if a model is *over-identified*, it is possible to test whether or not the model fits the data because the model implies empirical restrictions which can be fulfilled, or not, by the data.

We noted above that means, variances, and covariances are sufficient for estimating linear models. These statistics, however, are meaningful only for continuous, or metric, variables. The variables used in social science analyses, however, are often categorical. Moreover, there may be doubts about whether differences between the categories can be interpreted substantively. In which case, linear models are inadequate. This problem can be solved if we can assume that the categorical variables are rough measures of underlying unobserved continuous variables, and that the relationship between the underlying variable and its rough measure can be modelled as a *threshold model* (see Fig. 4.3). A threshold is a cutting point that separates two adjacent regions of an unobserved continuous variable. If a value is below or equal to the threshold, the lower category will be observed; if a value is above the threshold, the higher category will be observed.

Under the assumptions of a threshold model, it is possible to estimate correlations across underlying continuous variables from the contingency tables of the rough measures. These estimations are called polychoric correlations. Additionally, the standard errors of the polychoric correlations, and the covariances between them, can also be estimated from the contingency tables (Jöreskog 1994). Then, in a second step, all the unknown parameters of a model will be estimated simultaneously by the generalized least squares

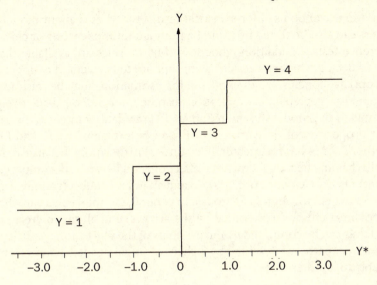

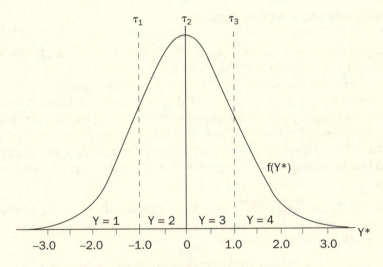

Fig. 4.3 Threshold model

method.[3] The computations are mathematically complicated, but, with modern programs, that is no problem. The models presented below are estimated using the programs *PRELIS* 2 (for the first step) and *LISREL* 8, developed by Jöreskog and Sörbom (1993a,b).

Different measures are available to evaluate a linear structural equation model. Standard errors of the estimations and correlations between the estimations can be used for statistical tests. Hypotheses about model parameters can also be tested by using Lagrangian multiplier tests or chi-square difference tests. In addition, goodness-of-fit statistics are available that can help to decide whether a model is appropriate to the data. If a model is not appropriate, conclusions drawn from the estimations may be misleading. If a model is acceptable, its implications can be interpreted substantively. For example, if the model shown in Fig. 4.2 fits the data of interest, we can see what proportion of the variance of F_3 can be explained by F_1 and F_2, and whether F_1 or F_2 has the greater effect on F_3. Furthermore, because F_1 in Fig. 4.2 also has an effect on F_2, the total effect of F_1 on F_3 can be decomposed into a direct effect (the path from F_1 to F_3) and an indirect effect (running from F_1 to F_2, and then, through F_2, on to F_3). In general, the total effects are the sum of the direct effects (represented by the arrows) and all the indirect effects. The latter can be computed by the products of the regression coefficients for the indirect paths, represented by a chain of single-headed arrows from one variable to another.

Hypotheses about Voting Turnout

Voting turnout has recently declined in several western democracies. Although this development has stimulated considerable interest among researchers (see Niemi and Weisberg 1993), the basic puzzle about voting and non-voting has not been resolved. We still do not know why many people participate in elections whereas others do not; nor why the proportions of voters and non-voters are so different as between regions, over time, and at elections for different levels of government. Labelling voting as a low-cost, low-benefit situation, Aldrich (1993: 274) came to a pessimistic conclusion:

[I]t is very difficult, practically impossible, to explain just who does and who does not vote in some absolute sense, precisely because marginal, small forces, can be just enough to make the difference.

But this does not mean that voting or non-voting are instances of idiosyncratic behaviours which are not open to social science explanations. There are regularities in the pattern of voting and non-voting, and these regularities have to be explained.

Some of the oldest and most prominent explanations about electoral participation are based on rational choice theories. The basis of rational choice is the simple postulate that no one chooses an alternative if they know there is a better one. Consequently, citizens will vote if, and only if, the benefits of voting are higher than the benefits of abstention. But what are the benefits from these two alternatives? According to Downs (1957: 40), the benefit of voting is 'the difference between the utility income' derived from voting for one party rather than another. But this so-called 'party differential' has to be weighed against the probability that their vote is decisive to the outcome. As this probability is very small, the benefit derived from voting is not great. Moreover, there are costs attached to voting, and there may be benefits from not voting; for example, an elector may drink a beer instead of casting a vote. In the language of rational choice, this is the 'opportunity cost' of voting. But if voting entails costs and almost no benefits, nobody would vote! To escape from this paradox, Downs (1957: 267) introduces a further motivation to vote:

Rational men in democracy are motivated to some extent by a sense of social responsibility relatively independent of their own short-run gains and losses.

In short, one of the benefits of voting is the fulfilment of what we call 'citizen duty': we all want to live in a democracy but if nobody votes democracy will collapse, so it is our duty to vote. Thus, electors are under an obligation to vote, independently of whether or not their preferred party will win.[4]

The problem with the 'citizen duty' argument is that democracy is a collective good: non-voters cannot be excluded from the benefits of a democratic system. However, as Olson (1965) argued, rational actors will tend to 'free-ride' in the production of collective goods. One way to solve this collective good problem is to create a social norm—in this instance, voting—which was Coleman's (1990: 289–92) solution to the paradox of voting. Within the framework of social norms, we can distinguish between two aspects. One is that acting against a norm may lead to social sanctions by other people. The other is that a norm can be internalized, so acting against it may lead to pangs of conscience.

A further argument is discussed at length by Brennan and Lomasky (1993) who propose a theory of expressive voting. Although a single vote is probably not decisive, electors may, even so, feel proud if their party wins the election. Just as football fans do not believe that they contribute decisively to their team's victories but nevertheless feel good in supporting the team, so, similarly, citizens may vote for a party without believing that their vote will lead to victory for their party. Obviously, expressive voting of this kind assumes that electors perceive some difference between the parties or candidates in ideological or emotional terms.

These different arguments are summarized in the theoretical model shown as a path diagram in Fig. 4.4. A plus sign indicates an expected positive effect; a minus sign an expected negative effect. The path diagram suggests that 'expressive utility', 'social pressure', and 'internalized norm' are assumed to have not only direct effects on 'vote intention' but also indirect effects. That is, 'duty', 'influence on outcome', 'party differential', and 'opportunity cost' are influenced by the other variables. Moreover, 'internalized norm' is not thought of as entirely stable but is supported by 'expressive voting' and 'social pressure'. One assumption of the rational choice approach, however, is missing: the interaction effect between 'influence on outcome' and 'party differential' is not specified. Such an effect cannot be specified in the context of linear structural equation modelling based on ordinal variables. The omission of an interaction term, however, is based on a preliminary probit regression analysis in which vote intention was regressed on all indicators, including an interaction term, which showed that the interaction effect is not significant.

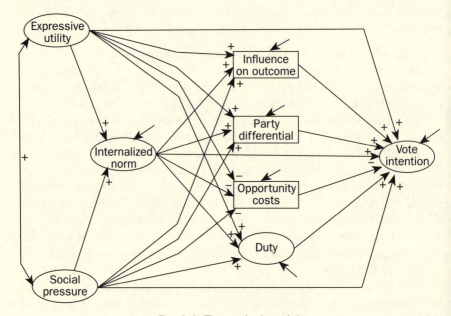

Fig. 4.4 Theoretical model

Other influences on voting turnout have emerged from research which is not rooted in rational choice theory. Some of these influences are incorporated in the model in a second step of the analysis. Age, gender, education, and other socio-economic variables are assumed to affect voting intention only indirectly, via psychological factors. The focus of the following analysis is on three attitudes: party identification, political dissatisfaction or political alienation, and interest in politics. The effects of these factors on voting turnout have been shown by other researchers (*cf.* Kleinherz 1995).

The Turnout Study

The analysis reported in this chapter is based on some of the early findings from a study of voting turnout undertaken in 1995. The fieldwork was conducted shortly before the state elections for North Rhine–Westphalia in May 1995. About 1,000 randomly chosen electors were interviewed during the week before the election; the interviews were conducted, by telephone, by professional interviewers using a standardized questionnaire. Nearly 73 per cent of the people interviewed before the election were re-interviewed in the week after the election.[5] Only two questions were asked in the second survey: one on voting behaviour, and one on 'regret'.

In the path diagram shown in Fig. 4.4, some of the variables are denoted within ovals and others within square boxes. This follows from the number of indicators used to measure the theoretical concepts underpinning the study. We set out to formulate at least one survey question to measure each of the concepts found in hypotheses about voting turnout derived from rational choice theory. In some instances, two questions were formulated. Thus, some concepts were measured by two indicators, others by only one. Concepts measured by two indicators are modelled as measurement error-free latent variables (shown in the ovals); concepts measured by one indicator are modelled as observed variables (shown in the boxes). The only major problem with these indicators arose with the operationalization of 'social pressure'. We asked, first, whether respondents expected to encounter disapproval if they decided not to vote. However, this question appears not to have worked, so more indirect measures were used, based on asking whether or not relatives and friends intended to vote. All the indicators are measured as ordinal scales. The question wording, translated from German, is given in the appendix to this chapter. Responses are coded such that higher numbers correspond to the labels of the variables given in the path diagrams (Figs. 4.4–4.9).

Analysis and Findings

In the first step of the analysis, the parameters of the theoretical model shown in Fig. 4.4 are estimated. The hypothesis being tested postulates that all over-identifying restrictions will hold in the population. One important indicator of the appropriateness of a model is the chi-square goodness-of-fit statistic which gives the result of a chi-square difference test. The test statistic is 80.52 (not shown here), with 914 cases in the analysis. If the hypothesis were true, the test statistic would be distributed as a central chi-square statistic with 46 degrees of freedom. As the level of significance is less than 0.01, the hypothesis is rejected.[6] The model does not fit the data.

To improve the model, modifications are specified step by step. A Langrangian multiplier test suggests that an additional path should be specified from 'duty' to 'opportunity cost'. Furthermore, a covariance should be estimated between the measurement error for the second indicator of 'duty' and the second indicator of 'internalized norm to vote'. Paths not significant at the 5 per cent level are deleted.

The results after making these modifications are presented in the path diagram shown in Fig. 4.5. The modifications have increased the fit remarkably. The chi-square statistic is now 70.79, with 53 degrees of freedom, which is equivalent to a probability of 0.05. A first substantive interpretation is therefore possible. The values shown for the paths are the estimated standardized regression coefficients. There are no effects on vote intention from 'party differential' or 'opportunity cost'. Remember that, according to rational choice theory, the effect of 'party differential' is weighted by the low probability that a single vote is decisive. Thus, this effect can be ignored. But 'opportunity costs' should, according to the theory, have an impact on 'vote intention'. Respondents do not seem to recognize that voting costs time: altogether about 92 per cent of respondents did not agree with the statement that 'Casting my vote keeps me from doing something more important.' In the model, 'opportunity cost' is no more than a poor negative indicator of 'duty'.

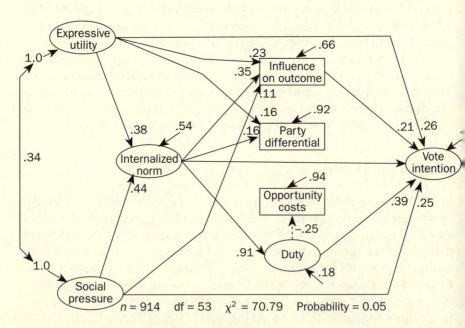

Fig. 4.5 Modified theoretical model

Only someone who does not feel an obligation to vote recognizes opportunity costs.

It is also interesting that voting as an internalized norm has no direct effect on turnout. This is because 'duty' has a very strong effect on the intention to vote, and voting as an internalized norm has a nearly perfect effect on 'duty'. The variable 'influence on outcome' also has a remarkable effect on vote intention. This result may be due to a misperception of the real influence of a single vote. Nearly 40 per cent of respondents thought their vote would have a strong influence on the outcome of the election; only 10 per cent thought their vote would have no influence at all, or almost none. This finding might be interpreted as a rationalization: people who have internalized voting as a norm, and who experience expressive utility in voting, may tend to overestimate the importance of their vote.

In a further step in the analysis, the model is extended to include concepts that are peripheral to the rational choice approach. The results of this extended model are shown in Fig. 4.6. It is clear that none of the additional variables has a direct effect on voting turnout. Party identification seems to be an additional indicator of 'expressive utility', and 'internalized norm' (to vote) has a small effect on 'party identification'. Political interest is influenced by an internalized voting norm and by expressive utility, and has some influence on 'party differential'. Lastly, 'political satisfaction' is an intermediate variable between 'expressive utility' and 'social pressure', on the one

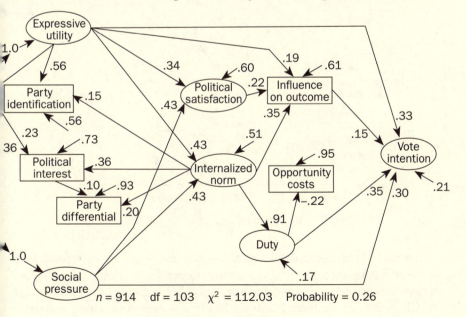

FIG. 4.6 Extended model

hand, and 'influence on outcome' on the other. The fit of the model is quite good: with 103 degrees of freedom, the chi-square statistic of 112.03 corresponds to a probability of 0.26.

The path diagram in Fig. 4.6 displays only the structural part of the model, without the measurement relations between the indicators and the latent variables. The whole model, including the measurement model, is presented in Fig. 4.7. The path diagram here looks much more complicated. Nevertheless, all the indicators (denoted in the square boxes) load on only one latent variable (denoted in the ovals) each. As noted above, there is also a covariance between the measurement errors of one indicator for 'duty' and one indicator of 'internalized norm'. To summarize our findings: it was not necessary to introduce major changes to the assumed measurement structure of the model in order to fit the data. All in all, the model looks very reasonable.

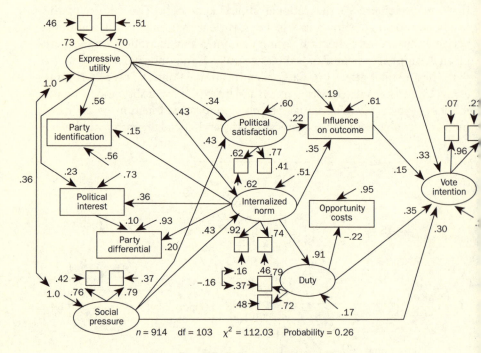

Fig. 4.7 Full extended model

In a next step in the analysis, actual turnout (measured in the second wave of the survey) is incorporated as a further dependent variable. The number of cases is now reduced to 668 due to attrition between the two waves. In this 'recall model', as we term it, shown in Fig. 4.8, reported voting is directly influenced only by vote intention. The fit of the recall model is acceptable

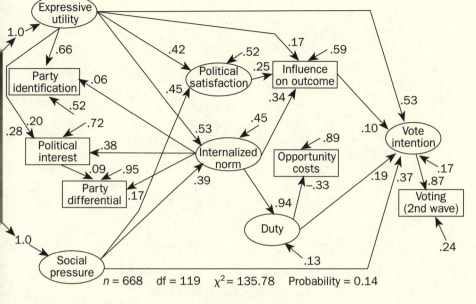

Fig. 4.8 Recall model

although it is not as good as for the model shown in Fig. 4.7. Moreover, there are some hints that the model could be improved. The paths from 'influence on outcome' to 'vote intention', and from 'internalized norm' to 'party identification', are not significant. After deleting these paths, univariate Lagrangian multiplier tests of possible effects indicate that additional paths from 'political satisfaction' to 'vote intention', and from 'social pressure' to 'voting' would improve the model. After making these modifications, the fit of the model is very good: the chi-square statistic is 126.39 with 119 degrees of freedom, which corresponds to a probability of 0.30. The modified recall model is shown in Fig. 4.9.

Summary results of the analyses are reported in Table 4.1, which shows the total effects of the different concepts about voting intention and voting recall. It is clear from the table that 'expressive utility' has the largest total effect on voting, followed by 'social pressure'—as measured by respondents' perception of other voters. The total effects of an 'internalized norm' to vote and 'duty' are almost the same, which is not surprising as the two concepts are highly correlated. It is only in the intention model that 'influence on outcome' has an effect. In the last model, political satisfaction substitutes for this effect. All the factors taken together determine a high proportion of the variance in vote intention and vote recall. Between 78 per cent and 81 per cent of the variance in all three models can be explained by the variation in the explanatory variables.

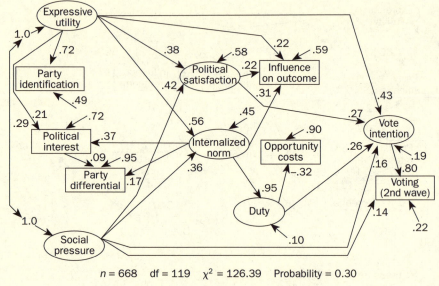

$n = 668$ df = 119 $\chi^2 = 126.39$ Probability = 0.30

Fig. 4.9 Modified recall model

Discussion

All in all, the analyses show that both vote intention and actual vote (based on the recall vote question) can be explained to a very high degree by only a few concepts. As the data being analysed are ordinal, however, these results are related to the levels of the unobserved continuous variables. Thus, the models cannot be used for individual predictions. Even so, the analysis tells us how the theoretical concepts are interrelated. For example, we can see that social pressure is an important determinant of electoral participation. Thus, if increasing individualization in modern societies results in less social cohesion, we might expect further declines in turnout rates in future elections.

The analyses reported in this chapter are based on rational choice hypotheses. Following this perspective, it is interesting to note that the 'soft' utility arguments implied in notions such as 'expressive voting' and an 'internalized voting norm' are important determinants of voting turnout, whereas 'hard' utility arguments such as the costs of voting and expected benefits from government actions are not.[7] On the other hand, the analyses do not imply that 'hard' rational choice arguments are not at all important in explaining voting turnout. Voting costs may be important, for example, in explaining differences in electoral participation rates across different democracies. Within any given political setting, however, variations in individual decisions to vote—or not—seem to be based only on 'soft' utility arguments.

Table 4.1 Total effects on voting

	Expressive utility	Social pressure	Internalized norm	Duty	Influence on outcome	Political satisfaction	Total (R^2)
Extended intention model							
Vote intention	0.53	0.47	0.37	0.35	0.15	0.03	79%
indicators:							
state election	0.51	0.45	0.36	0.34	0.15	0.03	
general election	0.47	0.42	0.33	0.31	0.13	0.03	
Modified recall model							
Vote intention	0.68	0.36	0.25	0.26	—	0.27	81%
indicators:							
state election	0.65	0.35	0.24	0.25		0.26	
general election	0.62	0.33	0.23	0.24		0.25	
Reported vote	0.54	0.43	0.20	0.21	—	0.22	78%

Turning to methodological questions, the analyses presented in this chapter are an example of the primacy of theory in social science research. Without theoretical grounding, empirical research can easily become lost in the plethora of significant but small correlations between the measured attributes, for which several *post hoc* explanations can be found. The primacy of theory is especially necessary when using structural equation modelling. Without a reasonable model from which to start, this approach is usually a hopeless enterprise.

Although the analyses yield very satisfactory results, one weakness is that incorporating voting recall led to a change in the model. This change may be a consequence of systematic panel attrition. Moreover, even for the model which excludes voting recall, it is possible to specify an alternative model with nearly the same fit. If, for example, in the extended intention model (Fig. 4.7) the effect of 'duty' on vote turnout is interchanged by a path from 'internalized norm' to 'vote intention', the chi-square goodness-of-fit statistic only increases from 112.03 to 113.72. That is, there is almost no empirical discrimination between these two specifications. It is often possible in linear structural equation modelling to specify different models with nearly the same or just the same fit.[8] In short, linear structural equation modelling is a powerful method for testing causal hypothesis: the analysis will tell you if a hypothetical model is wrong; and, if a model fits, it may mirror true causal relations. There is no guarantee that a linear structural equation model gives a 'true' and complete picture of social reality, but the method allows social scientists to put to the test their hypotheses about reality.

APPENDIX
Operationalization of the Concepts in the Survey Questions

Vote Intention (Indicator 1): 'Next Sunday will you vote; will you not vote; or have you not decided yet?'

Vote Intention (Indicator 2): 'If there was a general election on 14 May, would you certainly vote; probably vote; or certainly not vote?'

Influence on outcome: 'What do you think about the importance of your vote on the outcome of the state election on 14 May? Will your vote have a strong influence; a reasonable influence; little influence; nearly no influence; or no influence at all?'

Party differential: 'Do you think that your personal situation would differ depending on the party which governs North Rhine–Westphalia?' Yes; No.

Opportunity cost: 'Casting my vote keeps me from doing something more important.' Perfectly correct; partly correct; definitely wrong.

Duty (Indicator 1): 'Citizens are obliged to vote in a democratic system'. Agree strongly; agree partly; do not agree.

Duty (Indicator 2): 'A low voting turnout may put at risk the existence of the democratic system.' Agree strongly; agree partly; do not agree.

Internalized norm to vote (Indicator 1): 'I would feel guilty if I had not voted'. Perfectly correct; partly correct; definitely wrong.

Internalized norm to vote (Indicator 2): 'Not to vote would be against my nature.' Perfectly correct; partly correct; definitely wrong.

Social pressure (Indicator 2): 'Will most of your family or your near relatives vote; will most not vote; or don't you know?'

Social pressure (Indicator 2): 'And what about your friends? Will most of your friends vote; will most not vote; or don't you know?'

Expressive utility (Indicator 1): 'Is there a party that represents your political feelings and interests?' Yes; No.

Expressive utility (Indicator 2): 'Is there a party which can cope better with the problems in North Rhine–Westphalia?' Yes; No.

Party identification: 'There are many people in the Federal Republic who are inclined towards one of the parties. Nevertheless, sometimes they give their vote to another party. What about you? Are you inclined towards one of the parties or are you not inclined?'

Political satisfaction (Indicator 1): 'What do you think about the way democracy runs in the Federal Republic? Are you strongly satisfied; more or less satisfied; more or less dissatisfied; or strongly dissatisfied?'

Political satisfaction (Indicator 2): 'The political parties are interested only in the votes but not in the opinions of the voters.' Agree strongly; agree partly; do not agree.

Interest in politics: 'How is your interest in politics? Very strong; strong; somewhat; little; or none at all?'

Notes

1. Another, often used, representation of linear structural equation models is the Jöreskog–Keesling–Wiley model, in which all explanatory variables are modelled as latent. To allow for effects from observed variables, any observed independent variable has to be set equal to a corresponding latent variable. The Jöreskog–Keesling–Wiley model is available in the *LISREL* program (Jöreskog and Sörbom 1989). The Bentler–Weeks model is available in the *EQS* program (Bentler 1995).

2. In some very specific models, it is possible to estimate measurement error variables and measurement error-free latent variables with only one indicator for each factor (see Jagodzinski and Kühnel 1987).
3. If the analysis is based on metric data, the estimation can be realized in one step. Then different estimation methods are available. Estimation methods and statistical inferences for linear structural equation models are discussed in Bollen (1989).
4. A more formal version of this argument is set out in Riker and Ordeshook (1968).
5. All the fieldwork was done by the German field research institute FORSA. The study was sponsored by the Fritz Thyssen Stiftung.
6. The probability here should be high, because in the goodness-of-fit test we are interested in demonstrating that the model fits. In other words, the logic is just the opposite of the classical significance test.
7. Whiteley et al. (1993) in a paper on activism amongst members of the British Conservative Party report a similar result.
8. Linear models are called equivalent if they are different but have the same empirical consequences for the sufficient statistics. The consequences of equivalent and near-equivalent models are discussed by Williams et al. (1996).

5

CATEGORICAL DATA ANALYSIS: LOG-LINEAR AND LATENT CLASS MODELS

ALLAN McCUTCHEON AND COLIN MILLS

In this chapter we discuss some of the most recently developed methods for the analysis of categorical data.[1] The first half of the chapter introduces some necessary notation and then goes on to discuss log-linear models for contingency tables. Only some ten years ago such models were considered somewhat obscure and unduly difficult to apply. Today, their application to contingency table problems is routine and log-linear modelling programs are included in all the popular statistical packages. In the second half of the chapter we show how the log-linear model can be extended to include latent as well as manifest (observed) categorical variables. This new development in categorical data analysis has brought together two approaches to the analysis of association in contingency tables which, although often discussed in conjunction (Goodman 1978; Haberman 1978), have only recently been brought within a single unified framework (Hagenaars 1990, 1994). These are the latent class analysis (LCA) approach to the measurement of latent variables, and the log-linear modelling approach to testing structural models of relationships between manifest categorical variables. The outcome of this synthesis is the possibility of simultaneously formulating structural models for both latent and manifest categorical variables.

Throughout the chapter we use one dataset to illustrate the models we discuss. It is taken from the 1991 British Social Attitudes Survey and contains information about environmental and ethical awareness in the purchasing habits of a random sample of 1,347 men and women (Brook *et al.* 1992). The data tell us whether respondents 'always', as opposed to 'sometimes' or 'never', purchase each of four types of products: phosphate-free washing powders; CFC-free aerosols; cosmetics not tested on animals; and products that use recycled materials. In addition, we know the gender, age, and educational level of respondents. The variables for age and education are banded into three categories, or levels. We assume that we do not have access to the original, individual-level data, and so have to work with the categorizations as given. The univariate response distributions are given in Table 5.1.

Table 5.1 Percentage distributions for variables used in log-linear and latent class models

Buys recycled-source products	
Always	24.2
Sometimes/never	75.8
Buys non-phosphate washing powders	
Always	31.6
Sometimes/never	68.4
Buys non-animal tested cosmetics	
Always	34.0
Sometimes/never	66.0
Buys non-CFC aerosols	
Always	55.5
Sometimes/never	44.5
Gender	
male	42.1
female	57.9
Age	
18–35	33.6
36–60	40.8
over 60	25.5
Education	
No qualifications	39.7
Intermediate	40.7
Higher	19.6
$N = 1,347$	

Source: *British Social Attitudes Survey*, 1991.

Anatomy of a Contingency Table

Probabilities: conditional and marginal

Before discussing models, we start with some simple terms and descriptive material. Table 5.2 presents four versions of the cross-tabulation of gender, G, by whether or not a respondent buys products made of recycled materials, R. The observed frequencies found in each cell, f_{ij}, are set out in Panel 1. These frequencies are expressed as an observed cell probability, p_{ij}, in Panel 2. The probability of being in one or other category of R conditional on respondent's gender, $p_{i|j}$, is given in Panel 3. And Panel 4 gives the probability of being male or female conditional on the purchasing behaviour, $p_{j|i}$, of respondents.

Table 5.2 Whether respondent always buys versus sometimes/never buys products made of recycled materials by gender

Panel 1	Male	Female	
Always	103	223	326
Sometimes/Never	464	557	1021
	567	780	1347

Panel 2	Male	Female	
Always	0.076	0.166	0.242
Sometimes/Never	0.344	0.414	0.758
	0.420	0.580	1.0

Panel 3	Male	Female	
Always	0.182	0.286	0.242
Sometimes/Never	0.818	0.714	0.758
	1.0	1.0	

Panel 4	Male	Female	
Always	0.316	0.684	1.0
Sometimes/Never	0.454	0.546	1.0
	0.420	0.580	

Panel 1 shows just our raw data. It is rarely helpful to present data in this way. Panel 2 is a standardized version of Panel 1, in which the marginal distributions are the probabilities for the rows ($326/1347 = 0.242$; $1021/1347 = 0.758$) and the columns ($567/1347 = 0.420$; $780/1347 = 0.580$). Examining the marginal distributions, or probabilities, we can see that (i) comparing rows, the bulk of the observations tend to be in the second rather than the first row; (ii) comparing columns, a greater proportion of observations lie in the second column rather than the first. Interesting as this is, neither of these facts tells us anything about the degree of association between gender and purchasing behaviour. To examine this we have to look at Panels 3 and 4. Each of these gives us a different, but complementary, impression about whether or not the rows and columns are associated. Which of these it is most appropriate to present will depend on non-statistical considerations. If we believe that gender is causally related to buying behaviour, it might seem most natural to examine Panel 3. Doing so, we notice that there is a 10 percentage point difference between men and women in whether or not they always buy recycled products. Another clue would be to compare the conditional probabilities in Panel 3 with the row marginal probability: for instance, compare 0.182 and 0.818 with the corresponding row margin entries 0.242 and 0.758. If the conditional probabilities and the row marginal probabilities are equal, then there is no association between the rows and the columns. Panel 4, again, speaks to the existence of row-by-column association, but it gives us the answer to a slightly different substantive question. It would be the appropriate table to present if you were interested in the gender composition of, say, those who always purchased recycled products (you might be an advertising executive who wants to know what the consumer profile looks like). Comparing conditional probabilities, or conditional probabilities with column marginals, will tell you that the rows and columns are associated.

Odds and odds ratios

We now introduce a measure of association with some statistical properties that make it more attractive than the difference between two conditional probabilities: the *odds ratio*. It is the keystone of log-linear models. To avoid compounding rounding errors, we will work with the observed frequencies shown in Panel 1. We can calculate from these data two marginal odds: the marginal odds of being male rather than female ($567/780 = 0.727$) and the marginal odds of always, rather than sometimes or never, buying recycled products ($326/1021 = 0.319$). We can also calculate two sets of conditional odds: conditioning on gender ($103/464 = 0.222$ and $223/557 = 0.400$); and conditioning on purchasing behaviour ($103/223 = 0.462$ and $464/557 =$

0.833). Looking at the first set of conditional odds, each one indicates that a respondent is less likely to be found at the first rather than the second level of purchasing behaviour. However, women appear to be relatively more likely than men to be found at that level. We can measure this relative propensity by dividing one conditional odds by the other to give us an odds ratio. This ratio has a lower bound of zero and an upper bound of positive infinity. If the odds ratio is equal to unity, it means that there is no association between the rows and columns of the table; if the two conditional odds are equal, then this ratio will be 1. In this instance, it takes the value 0.554 (0.222/0.400). But what about the other set of conditional odds? If we perform the same exercise on those, we also get an odds ratio of 0.554 (0.462/0.833). In fact, all of the following expressions will give the same odds ratio, which we denote Ω:

$$\Omega = \frac{f_{11}/f_{21}}{f_{12}/f_{22}} = \frac{f_{11}/f_{12}}{f_{21}/f_{22}} = \frac{f_{11} \cdot f_{22}}{f_{21} \cdot f_{12}}$$

What happens if, instead of calculating the conditional odds on the first level of a dichotomy compared to the second, we calculate the conditional odds of the second compared to the first? This just gives us the reciprocal of the odds ratio already calculated: that is, $1/0.554 = 1.804$. It can be inconvenient to work with a measure of association like the odds ratio that has asymmetric bounds. This can be fixed very easily by working with the natural log of the odds ratio: the *log odds ratio*. This has lower and upper bounds of, respectively, negative and positive infinity. A value of zero means that there is no association between the rows and columns.

The Log-linear Model

How can we build a model for the frequencies in Table 5.2? This task can be viewed as breaking down and then putting back together the observed frequencies in the table. To do this, we need to take account of four things: the absolute number of observations in the table; the relative propensity to be in one row rather than the other; the relative propensity to be in one column rather than the other; and the relative propensity to be in one row and column (in other words a cell of the table) rather than any other. This suggests a multiplicative model of the following form:

$$F_{ij} = \eta \, \tau_i^R \, \tau_j^G \, \tau_{ij}^{RG} \tag{1}$$

If we take the logarithm of both sides of (1), we have a log-linear model for the estimated expected frequencies. We adopt the common convention of denoting the log of the η (eta) and τ (tau) terms in the multiplicative model with μ (mu) and λ (lambda) respectively. This gives a model of the form:

$$\log(F_{ij}) = \mu + \lambda_i^R + \lambda_j^G + \lambda_{ij}^{RG} \tag{2}$$

Equation (2) looks much like the kind of formulation which may be familiar from two-way analysis of variance. The left hand-side (the observed cell frequency) is decomposed into the sum of the right-hand side components: an overall size effects (constant or grand mean), a row effect, a column effect, and a row-by-column association effect.

This looks like an extremely complicated way of making an inference about a two-way contingency table. Indeed, it is. However its power comes from our ability to use this approach to evaluate both more simple and more complex models. Consider the following model:

$$\log(F_{ij}) = \mu + \lambda_i^R + \lambda_j^G \tag{3}$$

This says that the estimated expected cell frequencies (F_{ij}) are a function of an overall size effect, a row effect, and a column effect. Note that the parameter for the row-by-column association has been set to zero, by dropping it from the model. This is simply the log-linear model that is implicit in the calculation of expected values for the familiar Pearson chi-square test for row-by-column independence. Setting the association parameter to zero tests the hypothesis that the log of the odds ratio is equal to zero, or the odds ratio is equal to one. If this is the case, then we know, by definition, that there is no row-by-column association in the table of expected frequencies.

Now consider an enlarged contingency table consisting of the cross-tabulation of purchasing behaviour (R), gender (G), and educational level (E). A fully saturated model—that is, it contains all possible parameters for this three-way table—would look like this:

$$\log(F_{ijk}) = \mu + \lambda_i^R + \lambda_j^G + \lambda_k^E + \lambda_{ij}^{RG} + \lambda_{ik}^{RE} + \lambda_{jk}^{GE} + \lambda_{ijk}^{RGE} \tag{4}$$

We now have three sets of marginal effects, three sets of two-way association parameters, and one set of three-way interaction parameters. The additional one-way marginal effect simply allows for the fact that the observations may be differentially distributed over the levels of the additional variable we have introduced. In addition, by extension, we need to take account of the possible association between each pair of variables. This is what the two additional association parameters allow for. But what is the meaning of the three-way interaction term? Formally, this allows the odds ratio (or set of odds ratios) measuring the association between any pair of variables to vary in magnitude across each level of the third variable. So, for instance, it allows us to evaluate whether or not a hypothesized association between level of education and purchasing behaviour varies by gender. Perhaps education makes no difference to the purchasing behaviour of men but has the effect of making better-educated women, compared to less-educated women, more likely to buy recycled goods. If our hypothesis is that there should be no difference between men and women with regard to the impact of education, then we would test a model with the three-way interaction parameter set to zero:

$$\log(F_{ijk}) = \mu + \lambda_i^R + \lambda_j^G + \lambda_k^E + \lambda_{ij}^{RG} + \lambda_{ik}^{RE} + \lambda_{jk}^{GE} \tag{5}$$

If the estimated expected frequencies from model (5) are close to the observed frequencies, then we would have evidence supporting our hypothesis. We can test hypotheses about the other model parameters by making similar restrictions. But there is one proviso: within the class of models we are considering here—hierarchical log-linear models—we cannot restrict the values of lower-order parameters to equal zero if we simultaneously include a higher-order relative in the model. Thus the inclusion of a three-way interaction in a model implies that all the two-way interactions encompassed by it are also included:

$$\lambda_{ijk}^{RGE} \Rightarrow \lambda_{ij}^{RG}, \lambda_{ik}^{RE}, \lambda_{jk}^{GE}, \lambda_i^R, \lambda_j^G, \lambda_k^E$$

Model Fit

The fit of the model to the data can be evaluated by calculating a test statistic with a known asymptotic distribution. The most widely used test statistic for log-linear models is the likelihood ratio chi-square, L^2. For a two-way table this is given by:

$$L^2 = 2 \sum_{i=1}^{I} \sum_{j=1}^{J} f_{ij} [\log(f_{ij} / F_{ij})] \tag{6}$$

which, in words, means: for each cell in the table, take the natural logarithm of the ratio of the observed to the expected frequency and multiply this by the observed frequency, sum the result for each cell, then multiply the sum by two.

Normally L^2 will have degrees of freedom equal to the number of cells in the table minus the number of non-redundant estimated parameters. Tests for specific sets of parameters can also be carried out provided we nest models within each other. Consider the following pair of models:

$$\log(F_{ijk}) = \mu + \lambda_i^R + \lambda_j^G + \lambda_k^E + \lambda_{ij}^{RG} + \lambda_{ik}^{RE} + \lambda_{jk}^{GE} \tag{7}$$

$$\log(F_{ijk}) = \mu + \lambda_i^R + \lambda_j^G + \lambda_k^E + \lambda_{ij}^{RG} + \lambda_{ik}^{RE} \tag{8}$$

Model (8) is simply a special case of model (7) in which the gender/education (*GE*) parameter set has been constrained to take a zero value. To evaluate whether this is a reasonable restriction, we can carry out a conditional test. The difference between the L^2 statistics for the two models also has (asymptotically) a chi-square distribution with the degrees of freedom equal to the difference in the degrees of freedom between the models.

Model Specification

Finding a well-fitting model does not imply that one has discovered the correct model, even though it may be a good smoothed representation of the data in a particular sample. Making sure that the right variables are included is crucially important but it is an extra-statistical task. If the correct variables are not included, the model is mis-specified and will probably be of little scientific value. A related consideration is the decision about whether or not to consider some marginals in the model as fixed by design. Log-linear modelling is a symmetrical technique in the sense that it does not assume a rigid separation of variables into dependent and explanatory sets. The dependent variable in the model is the (logged) frequency distribution across the cells defining the table. Compare, for instance, the structure of the familiar multiple regression. An asymmetrical relationship is built into the structure of the model. The correlations between explanatory variables in the model are automatically taken account of, and the focus is on the net effect of each explanatory variable on the dependent variable. There is nothing in a log-linear model that will automatically impose this structure. Sometimes it is not even required.

Consider a table defined by the four purchasing behaviour variables in our data. We might be interested in the associations between these variables (the second half of this chapter deals precisely with this case) but be unable to make a sensible distinction between what is dependent and what is explanatory. In this case, a symmetrical treatment would be most appropriate. Alternatively, we might be interested in how the demographic characteristics—gender, age, and education—influence one of the purchasing behaviours. In this case, it is we, the researchers, who nominate one of the variables as dependent. It then becomes sensible to work only with models that, a priori, include the three-way interaction between the demographic explanatory variables. This leads to models which are analogous to those usually estimated within the framework of a regression analysis.

Another circumstance in which some thought must go into model specification is when the data have been generated by an experimental design. This usually implies that some marginals have been fixed by design and should not be estimated because they are not free to vary. Again, the logic of this kind of analysis compels one to include the highest-order interaction between the set of variables fixed in the experimental design. The bottom line here is that it is always necessary to think about the structure of the problem and the constraints imposed by the scheme used in collecting the data. This is something that we, as researchers, should be good at. It is not something that computer-automated, stepwise model-selection procedures are able to do.

Log-linear Models of Green Consumer Behaviour

In this section we examine the four-way table defined by age group (A), gender (G), education (E), and whether the respondent always buys recycled products (R). A good model should be based on informed judgements about its likely structure. It is rare to have no knowledge whatsoever about which variables are likely to be associated and which interactions are plausible. In principle, it is possible to search through every model to select the 'best' one. However, practitioners of this sort of inductive approach rarely make the appropriate adjustment to the probability values at which they accept or reject models in a *post hoc* analysis. Capitalizing on chance in a single sample is not a good way to evaluate a model. What one is trying to achieve is a simplified representation of the data that, at one and the same time, contains all the important substantive 'effects' and will withstand out-of-sample validation. Table 5.3 presents the raw data, and Table 5.4 gives the fit statistics for several different log-linear models.

The first thing to notice is that the structure of the data suggests an asymmetric approach. This implies that it will be convenient if all models contain the three-way (GAE) marginal, thus making model simplification easier. Attentive readers will notice that, in a subsequent section, we relax this restriction. Model H_1 is the most restrictive. In addition to the (GAE) interaction, it allows the proportions in the first and second level of the response variable to differ. Omitting the (R) term implies a restriction which forces the proportions to be equal. Notice that H_1 implies that there are no associations between any of the explanatory variables and the response variable. Model H_2 is a very general model, allowing for all possible three-way interactions. Model H_1 does not fit the data, but model H_2 fits very well. The question

Table 5.3 Observed cell frequencies for log-linear models

Age	Education	Buys recycled products			
		Men		Women	
		Always	Sometimes/ Always	Always	Sometimes/ Always
18–35	No qualifications	5	22	7	52
36–60	No qualifications	14	82	28	107
over 60	No qualifications	16	64	22	116
18–35	Intermediate qualifications	18	97	47	104
36–60	Intermediate qualifications	17	67	41	80
over 60	Intermediate qualifications	2	38	9	28
18–35	Higher qualifications	11	30	33	27
36–60	Higher qualifications	13	46	27	28
over 60	Higher qualifications	7	18	9	15

Table 5.4 Fit statistics and conditional tests for log-linear models

Model	L^2	df	p
H_1: (GAE) (R)	89.58	17	0.00
H_2: (GAE) (GAR) (GER) (AER)	5.04	4	0.28
H_3: (GAE) (GR) (AR) (ER)	22.50	12	0.03
H_4: (GAE) (GAR) (GER)	10.26	8	0.25
H_5: (GAE) (GAR) (AER)	13.71	6	0.03
H_6: (GAE) (GER) (AER)	5.74	6	0.45
H_7: (GAE) (GER) (AR)	11.09	10	0.35
H_8: (GAE) (GER)	13.08	12	0.36
Conditional tests			
H_2 vs. H_3	17.46	8	0.03
H_2 vs. H_4	5.22	4	0.27
H_2 vs. H_5	8.67	2	0.01
H_2 vs. H_6	0.70	2	0.71
H_6 vs. H_7	5.35	4	0.25
H_7 vs. H_8	1.99	2	0.37

now is: can we find a model which is more parsimonious than H_2 but which still fits the data adequately? Model H_3 is our first stab at this. It includes all possible two-way associations between the explanatory variables and the response variable. It does not fit well; moreover, the conditional test of model H_2 versus model H_3 suggests that it is necessary to include at least one other three-way interaction apart from (GAE). Models H_4, H_5, and H_6, in turn, drop one of the candidate three-way interactions. The effect of doing this is evaluated by the conditional tests of these models against model H_2. There is evidence that dropping the (GER) interaction—in models H_3 and H_5—leads to significant model deterioration, but that neither of the other two interactions is important. This leads us to model H_7 which fits the data well. Finally, we evaluate whether it is necessary to include the (AR) association. The conditional test of model H_8 against model H_7 suggests that we do not. Thus our final model for these data is H_8. We must now interpret it.

The meaning of model H_8 is illustrated in Fig. 5.1, where the estimated odds of always buying recycled goods are plotted. The estimated odds can be calculated either from the maximum likelihood estimates of the lambda parameters or from the fitted cell frequencies. These are provided, often automatically, by all the major log-linear modelling programs. The interpretation of Fig. 5.1 is very straightforward and has a surprising twist. It appears to be the case that relatively uneducated men and women are rather similar in their aversion to recycled goods; and that more highly educated men are only a little more enlightened. However, education seems to have a relatively large impact on women's purchasing behaviour. This is the substantive interpretation of the three-way interaction effect (GER).

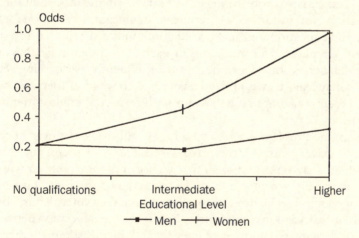

Fig. 5.1 Odds on always buying recycled goods

We could go on and repeat this exercise for each of the other three consumption items, but this would be a long-winded way to proceed. A more parsimonious approach might be to simultaneously model the determinants of all four consumption items. This is perfectly possible, at least in principle, within a log-linear modelling framework but it is unlikely that a simple model would fit the data. A moment's reflection suggests that the structure of the association between the four dependent variables is unlikely to be fully accounted for by their joint dependence on the explanatory variables. In other words, they will not be conditionally independent of each other. The most likely reason for this is that responses to each consumption item reflect a generalized pattern of behaviour, or attitude, among respondents. In other words, we might surmise that there exists a latent typology of behaviour of which the four items are manifest indicators. It is this latent typology that accounts for the structure of association amongst the items. We need, then, to extend our log-linear models to include such latent variables. This is what we now do.

Latent Class Analysis

Frequently we have several variables that measure the phenomenon we wish to study. In the present case, as we noted earlier, we could choose to perform four separate analyses, analysing each of the four variables in turn. In addition to increasing the total work load, this approach introduces two serious problems. First, the four analyses are very likely to yield differing values for the association amongst the variables in the model. In the previous section, for instance, we report a significant interaction between gender and education for the recycled goods indicator; this pattern may or may not be replicated for models using each of the other indicators of environmentally conscious consumerism. Consequently, performing separate analyses may leave us with mixed answers as to whether men and women differ in their consumption behaviour with respect to environmental consciousness.

The second problem is *measurement error*. All measures, even very good measures, have measurement error associated with them; for example, respondents may report answers that conform more closely to what they believe is socially acceptable, a student may guess the right answer in an exam, or people may incorrectly recall for whom they voted. Thus, observed measures of association result from two sources: the association between the actual, underlying phenomena of interest; and the measurement error associated with the observed measures, including phenomena we may not be interested in investigating (such as social desirability, for example). Performing separate analyses on the four observed indicators compels us to assume that each is a perfect indicator, ignoring the contribution of measurement error to observed associations. Since latent variable models allow the researcher to utilize a single analysis, social researchers are increasingly choosing latent variable approaches for data analysis. The approach reduces the problem of incorrect inference due to measurement error.

When we have observed multiple *categorical* indicators for the same underlying phenomenon, we can use latent class analysis to examine the issue of measurement error, as well as to guide us in our efforts at data reduction.[2] By analysing the pattern of association among the observed indicator variables, the latent class model (LCM) may enable us to characterize a categorical *latent* variable which focuses attention solely on the phenomenon of interest, net of measurement error. We turn now to this approach.

As we see in Table 5.5, the four indicators of environmentally conscious consumerism are clearly associated with one another in the 1991 sample of the British public. Of the 16 possible response patterns, nearly 43 per cent (139 + 436) of the 1,347 respondents gave one of the two possible consistent response patterns (that is, YYYY or NNNN). An additional 38 per cent (42 + 14 + 86 + 45 + 43 + 23 + 221 + 40) were consistent in three of their responses, while fewer than 20 per cent (12 + 68 + 19 + 42 + 11 + 106) split their responses evenly between 'regularly' and 'not regularly'. Moreover, the Pearson chi-square of independence (1196.92 with 11 degrees of freedom) suggests that these responses are highly interdependent. We do not suspect that these four items are causally related; for example, we do not suspect that buying recycled source products 'causes' a respondent to buy non-CFC aerosols. Instead, we are inclined to believe that the associations among these four items are due to a mixture of types, that is, that all of these items measure some unobserved (that is, latent) pattern of environmentally conscious consumerism. Thus, we might believe that among the British public there are those who are inclined to buy 'green' and others who are not inclined to do so. If we could 'unmix' the population into the constituent groups, we might find that the associations among the indicator variables are wholly accounted for; we might, for instance, find one class of respondents which is highly likely to 'buy green' regularly, and another class which is highly unlikely to do so.

Table 5.5 Regularly buys environmentally conscious products

Washing powders	No animal-tested cosmetics	Recycled source products			
		Yes		No	
		Non-CFC aerosols			
		Yes	No	Yes	No
Yes	Yes	139	42	43	42
Yes	No	14	12	11	23
No	Yes	86	68	106	221
No	No	19	45	40	436

The idea of mixtures is important and merits more discussion. Imagine the following: in the palm of your hand, you have mixed together a pinch each of salt, sugar, black pepper, and sand. Within this population of objects, the 'variables' of size, flavour, colour, and edibility will be associated; for example, colour will be associated with edibility since all the black objects (pepper) will be edible whereas some of the white objects are not (sand). If we test the simplest hypothesis that the population can be separated into two homogeneous classes (that is, $T = 2$), we may unmix the population into edible and inedible piles. But we would still have an unsatisfactory solution since our edible pile would remain a heterogeneous combination of salt, sugar, and pepper. Rejecting the solution that $T = 2$, we might further ask if we can successfully separate the objects into three types (that is, $T = 3$). In this instance, we might unmix the piles into inedible, white edible, and black edible. Still, this solution would be less than satisfactory, since the white edible pile would remain a heterogeneous mixture of salt and sugar. It would not be until we tried $T = 4$ that we reached a satisfactory solution. When $T = 4$, the variables would no longer be associated: crystals of sugar would still be sweet, no matter what their size or shade of white; flakes of pepper would remain the darkest in colour no matter how sharp in flavour or large in size any given flake might be. Thus, while there might still be variation within any given pile or class, the really significant variation is accounted for by unmixing the total, heterogeneous population into its four, internally homogeneous sub-populations (or classes).

This example also illustrates the issue of *local independence*. The latent class model, like all latent variable models (such as, factor analysis, structural equation models, latent trait models), relies on the principle of local independence to resolve the 'unmixing' problem. The central idea of local independence is quite simple. If we have a set of observed indicator variables (such as flavour, size, colour, edibility), all of which measure an unobserved (latent) set of classes, the indicator variables will exhibit observed associations amongst themselves. Once we 'unmix' the population into its component classes, however, the variables exhibit no associations within the class; the variables are said to be locally, or conditionally, independent with respect to the classes. Note that this is the criterion for defining the appropriate number of classes.

In our example of environmentally conscious consumerism, we have four survey responses as indicator items. Since we observe significant associations among the indicator variables, we may believe that the associations are due to the mixing of two (or more) types of consumers (classes), and that the probability of buying these four categories of products is high among the first type (the environmentally conscious, say) and low among the second type (the environmentally unaware). These observed associations, however, are due to the association of each indicator with the unobserved, latent variable—environmentally conscious consumerism. If we can characterize the latent variable, controlling for it should diminish the observed associations among the indicator variables to levels which are no greater than what may be expected by chance (that is, statistical non-significance). We can illustrate this idea, as shown in Fig. 5.2. As this illustration shows, when the latent variable (X) is included, the indicator variables (A, B, C, D) are found to be unassociated. Thus, we say they are locally independent; that is, independent within the classes of the latent variable.

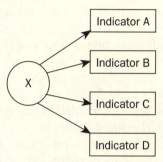

Fɪɢ. 5.2 Local independence

The basic idea of latent class analysis was first suggested in the early 1950s by Paul Lazarsfeld (1950a,b), although reliable and efficient procedures for actually estimating the latent class model were not presented until the mid-1970s by Goodman (1974) and Haberman (1979). Since that time, there have been several important extensions to the latent class model (see McCutcheon and Hagenaars 1997). We first focus our attention on the basic model, then, in the next section, examine a particularly important extension of the latent class model: log-linear models with latent variables.

The latent class model is formally expressed as the product of two types of parameters: the latent class probabilities π_t^x), which tell us the likelihood that a respondent will be in a specific class, and the conditional probabilities (for example, $\pi_{it}^{A|X}$), which tell us the likelihood that a respondent in a specific class will give a specific response on an indicator variable. For instance, in our environmentally conscious consumerism example, the latent class probability for the 'green-consumer' class (that is, π_1^x would tell us our estimate of the proportion of the sample who are inclined to buy environmentally friendly products regularly. A conditional probability, on the other hand, tells us the likelihood of a respondent in a given class responding to a specific indicator item, for example, the likelihood of getting a 'buys recycled source products regularly' response given that the respondent is a 'green consumer' (that is, $\pi_{11}^{A|X}$). Thus, the latent class model for the sixteen consumer response patterns reported in Table 5.5 would be expressed as:

$$\pi_{ABCD} = \Sigma_t \, \pi_t^X \, \pi_{it}^{A|X} \, \pi_{jt}^{B|X} \, \pi_{kt}^{C|X} \, \pi_{lt}^{D|X} \qquad (9)$$

What equation (9) says is that we obtain the estimated cell probabilities in the manifest table by summing (over latent classes) the product of the estimated latent class probability and the relevant conditional probabilities for each item response category, given membership of a latent class. So equation (9) shows that we have a latent variable with T classes, and four indicator variables regarding the respondents' reported regularity of purchase (A, B, C, D).

Consider the observed distribution reported in Table 5.5. These data represent the actual counts for each of the sixteen response patterns derived from the four dichotomous indicator items in our 1991 sample of the British adult public. In the absence of a well-developed theory, we investigate, first, the most parsimonious, or simplest, model. In this instance, the most parsimonious model is one which suggests that the observed distribution is the result of mixing together two types of sample respondents: those who are environmentally conscious consumers and those who are not. In the terms of the formal model, we are exploring the hypothesis that $T = 2$. Setting aside the issue of how the estimates for the formal latent class model represented in equation (2) are derived, we should note that there are now several publicly available programs for estimating latent class models. Nearly all of these programs use some variant of the expectation-maximization (EM) algorithm which provides maximum likelihood estimates for such models (Dempster *et al.* 1977).[3] Throughout this chapter, we use two of the more widely used programs—*LCAG* (Hagenaars and Luijkx 1987) and *LEM* (Vermunt 1993)— although there are other excellent programs for the estimation of many of the models presented here. We say something more about software for estimating these kinds of models at the end of the chapter.

To test the model that $T = 2$, indeed to test any model, we require a set of model evaluation criteria. By multiplying the left-hand side of the model specified in (9) by the total number of observations in our sample (N), we obtain an expected frequency count for each of the sixteen response patterns. Since we have both the observed count (reported in Table 5.5) and an expected count from (9), we can use the chi-square statistic to evaluate the model. As we see from the information reported in Table 5.6, we must reject the hypothesis that $T = 2$; that is, that we can explain the distribution in Table 5.5 as the result of two homogeneous classes.

Typically, when we reject the hypothesis that $T = 2$, we move directly to the hypothesis that $T = 3$, since the latter is the most parsimonious hypothesis given the rejection of the former. An investigation of the residuals (the observed frequencies minus the estimated expected frequencies—not shown here) for the hypothesis that $T = 2$ indicates, however, that the $T = 2$ model greatly under-estimates the number of respondents saying YYYY; many more were actually observed than estimated. This pattern suggests a situation first noted by Duncan (1979; Duncan *et al.* 1982) in which some respondents are likely to exhibit very high levels of response consistency. Duncan refers to such respondents as 'ideologues', and notes that they are likely to have a probability of 1.0 when agreeing (or disagreeing) to an item in their responses. In other words, it appears that our sample may contain a group (or class) which has a 'perfect' likelihood (1.0) of saying that they regularly buy each of the four categories of consumer products. Thus, when we estimate the model with $T = 3$, we include the provision that one of the classes has conditional probabilities of 1.0 for all four categories of products (that is, $\pi_{11}^{A|X} = \pi_{11}^{B|X} = \pi_{11}^{C|X} = \pi_{11}^{D|X} = 1.0$), while the conditional probabilities for the other two classes are allowed to vary freely. As the information reported in the bottom line of Table 5.6 indicates, this restricted 3-class model fits the observed data very well.

In Table 5.7 we report the conditional and latent class probabilities for

Table 5.6 Evaluation statistics for latent class model of four environmentally friendly consumer products

Model	L^2	X^2	BIC	AIC	df
H_1: unrestricted 2-class model	32.49	32.58	−10.69	20.58	6
H_2: restricted 3-class model	5.32	5.34	−30.74	−4.68	5

each of the three classes of environmentally conscious consumerism. As we see in the first column of Table 5.7, Class I respondents are absolutely likely to buy all four categories of consumer products, since they have a probability of 1.0 of responding regularly to each indicator item. Moreover, on the basis of our sample, we would estimate that approximately 1 in 15 (0.07) adult members of the 1991 British public were among these consistently 'green' consumers. At the other extreme, we see that Class III respondents were highly unlikely to report buying any of these products 'regularly'. As the conditional probabilities in the third column indicate, Class III respondents are estimated to have a probability of between 0.03 and 0.06 of responding 'regularly' for three of the products, although about 1 in 4 (0.27) appears to respond 'regularly' to the 'no animal-tested cosmetics' item. Consequently, Class III respondents appear to report very low levels of environmentally conscious consumer behaviour. We estimate this type of

respondent to represent about one-half (0.49) of the 1991 British adult public. Between these two extreme groups (that is, those consumers who are,
and are not, environmentally conscious in their purchasing behaviour) are
the Class II respondents. This intermediate class of respondents are estimated to have probabilities of between 0.36 and 0.81 of responding 'regularly' to these four items, and appear to represent about 9 in 20 (0.44)
members of the 1991 British adult public.

Before proceeding to our next analysis, we should make two remarks

Table 5.7 Latent class and conditional probabilities of responding 'regularly purchase'
to four environmentally friendly products

Indicator item	Class		
	I	II	III
Recycled-source products	1.00	0.49	0.06
Non-phosphate washing powders	1.00	0.36	0.03
No animal-tested cosmetics	1.00	0.81	0.27
Non-CFC aerosols	1.00	0.57	0.04
Latent class probabilities	0.067	0.443	0.490

regarding the information in Table 5.7. First, with respect to its measurement properties, the 'no animal-tested cosmetics' item appears to differ
from the other three items in that its 'error rate' for Class III is much higher
than the other three items. This is evident from comparing the conditional
probability of 0.27 with that for the other three items: none of them is larger
than 0.06. Its 'error rate' for Class II also appears to be quite high. Moreover,
there are substantive grounds for excluding this item from our measure: we
are attempting to measure environmentally conscious consumerism,
whereas the cosmetics item appears to include a dimension of empathy for
animals which is not included in any of the other items, and which is not the
issue of interest. Consequently, we exclude this item in our subsequent
analysis. Secondly, whereas Class I type respondents appear to be quite committed, and Class III type respondents totally indifferent, to environmentally
conscious consumerism, Class II type respondents may well be those most
susceptible to persuasion. Thus, public education campaigns, for example,
might wish specifically to target those most likely to be found in Class II.

Log-linear Models with Latent Variables

Who are the respondents most likely to be found in each of the three classes? This question can be addressed by integrating the new, three-category, latent variable into a log-linear model which includes the demographic variables considered earlier. Graphically, we can represent our model of interest as depicted in Fig. 5.3. Here we see that the variables age and gender are assumed to be causally prior to education, and that all three variables are viewed as causally prior to the latent variable (X). As in the latent class analysis presented above, the variable X is a three-category latent variable reflecting the three latent types of environmentally conscious consumers.

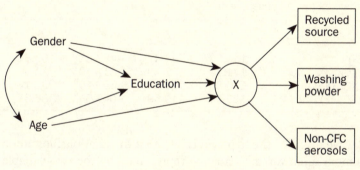

FIG. 5.3 Path model

The first hypothesis we examine is whether the same three-category latent variable found in our earlier analysis appears to be a plausible representation for all possible combinations of age, gender, and education. This amounts to assuming that, as in Fig. 5.3, the three exogenous predictor variables are associated with the three indicator variables only through the latent variable X. This hypothesis (H_1) is the first one explored. Remembering that a reasonable rule of thumb is to regard models that return an L^2 close to their degrees of freedom as well fitting, the first line of information in Table 5.8 indicates that we can accept this hypothesis, since the likelihood-ratio and Pearson chi-squares are modest relative to the degrees of freedom in the model ($L^2 = 100.39$ with 84 degrees of freedom).

The next hypothesis (H_2) is whether the relationship of each of the (prior) demographic variables with the latent consumerism variable can be considered independently of the other demographic variables. Here, we introduce two test statistics: BIC (Raftery 1986a,b, 1995) and AIC.[4] Models with a BIC lower than zero should, according to the approach underlying the statistic, be preferred to the saturated model; in other words, the model to choose is that with the most negative BIC. Similar reasoning applies to the AIC statistic: the model returning the most negative value should be preferred.

In this instance, the BIC and AIC statistics reveal a somewhat mixed story. Both the BIC and AIC indicate that H_2 is preferred to H_1, since each is considerably more negative (the preferred state) for H_2 than for H_1. The conditional L^2 suggests caution, however, since this value is 41.31 (141.70 − 100.39) with 24 (108 − 84) degrees of freedom; a chi-square value of 41.31 with 24 degrees of freedom exceeds the criterion alpha level (that is, $p < 0.05$). Thus, once again, we examine the hypothesis that education and gender interact with respect to consumer behaviours (H_3), and find that all three evaluation criteria recommend acceptance of H_3 relative to either H_1 or H_2.

Table 5.8 Fit statistics for log-linear models with latent environmentally conscious consumerism as the dependent variable

Model	L^2	X^2	BIC	AIC	df
H_1: (GAEX)	100.39	97.47	−483.81	−67.61	84
H_2: (GAEX)(GX)(AX)(EX)	141.70	137.43	−615.59	−74.30	108
H_3: (GAEX)(GEX)(AX)	120.88	111.14	−629.20	−87.12	104
H_4: (GA)(GE)(AE)(GEX)(AX)	129.39	119.59	−649.54	−86.61	108

Finally, we examine the hypothesis (H_4) that the relationships among the three demographic variables may be represented by the two-variable relationships, as depicted in Fig. 5.3. Since we previously concluded that H_3 is preferable to either H_1 or H_2, we now evaluate H_4 relative to our currently preferred model (H_3). In this comparison, only the BIC suggests a clear preference for H_4; the BIC for H_4 (−649.54) is clearly more negative than the BIC for H_3 (−629.20). The conditional L^2 test suggests that we might accept H_4, since this test results in a value of 8.51 (120.88 − 129.39) with 4 (104 − 108) degrees of freedom, although this value is only slightly below the criterion value of 9.51 at the 0.05 alpha level. Thus, while the purist could claim that the conditional L^2 allows acceptance of H_4 over H_3, we should remain cautious not to overstate this preference. The final evaluation statistic, the AIC, is also quite ambiguous since the value for H_3 is actually slightly more negative than the value for H_4.

We might pause at this juncture to note that all modelling requires attention to issues of substantive interpretation as well as strictly statistical criteria. The model posed by H_3 suggests that the relationship between gender and education changes across the three age groupings. This is plausible, given that there might well be greater gender equality among more recent, younger cohorts. The model posed in H_4 suggests that this age-related difference between gender and education is not so large as to play a significant role in our model; the association between gender and education does not differ significantly over the three age groupings. Thus, we will accept the model represented by H_4 on three grounds: there appears to be sufficient statistical justification for choosing H_4; the relationships among the three demographic variables are not our primary interest; and model H_4 is extremely close to the model we had hypothesized, as illustrated in Fig. 5.3. Thus, only the relationship between gender, education, and the latent consumerism variable (X) requires a three-variable interaction.

Although each of the associations specified in model H_4 are significant, our interest is primarily in those associations which include the latent consumerism variable (that is, GEX and AX). The log-linear coefficients for each of these associations are reported in Table 5.9. The interpretation of the coefficients regarding the age-by-latent variable association is fairly straightforward; the large, positive coefficient for younger people and Class I (0.3223) indicates that younger people are much more likely to be found among ideologically committed 'regular' consumers of environmentally conscious products. Note also that the coefficients for the young consumers (and for the other age groups as well) sum to zero across the three classes of consumers. This is logical, since saying that younger people are more likely to be found in Class I necessarily implies that they are less likely to be found in the other classes. Also, we note that the coefficients for Class I (as well as for

Table 5.9 Log-linear (lambda) coefficient estimates for associations with latent environmentally conscious consumerism as the dependent variable

Class	I	II	III
18–35 years	0.3223	−0.0838	−0.2385
36–60 years	0.1413	0.0359	−0.1773
over 60	−0.4637	0.0479	0.4158
Men	−0.4042	−0.1112	0.5154
Women	0.4042	0.1112	−0.5154
No qualifications	−0.4477	−0.2167	0.6644
Intermediate	0.0148	−0.0266	0.0118
High	0.4328	0.2433	−0.6761
Men			
No qualifications	0.2712	0.0319	−0.3031
Intermediate	−0.0194	0.0585	−0.0391
Higher	−0.2518	−0.0904	0.3422
Women			
No qualifications	−0.2712	−0.0319	0.3031
Intermediate	0.0194	−0.0585	0.0391
Higher	0.2518	0.0904	−0.3422

the other classes) sum to zero across the three age groups. Again this is logical, since saying that Class I is disproportionately comprised of young people necessarily implies that some other groups are less likely to be found there; note, for example, the −0.4637 coefficient for respondents older than 60. Thus, the information in Table 5.9 indicates that, even when we control for gender and education, younger people are more likely to be 'green' consumers (Class I), somewhat less likely to be among those who are infrequent 'green' consumers (Class II −0.0838), and a good deal less likely to be found among those who appear to be resolutely unlikely to buy 'green' products (Class III). On the other hand, older respondents appear to be substantially less likely to be Class I consumers (−0.4637) and substantially more likely to be Class III consumers (0.4158).

Unlike the interpretation of the effects of age-by-'green consumerism', the influence of gender and education on environmentally conscious consumerism is confounded by the three-variable interaction presented in the lower section of Table 5.9. The three-variable interaction requires that we include the effects of education when we interpret the impact of gender on consumerism. For example, it appears that, on average, men are less likely to be found in Class I (−0.4042); respondents with no qualifications are also less likely to be found in Class I (−0.4477); and men with no qualifications are less likely to be found in Class I. However, they are not so unlikely as the simple sum of the two main effect coefficients would suggest: the interaction coefficient must also be included (i.e. −0.4042 + [−0.4477] + 0.2712 = −0.5807). Thus, we can interpret each of the probabilities of the gender-by-education combination found in each of the three classes of consumerism. It is somewhat easier to display these probabilities graphically, which is shown in Fig. 5.4.

As the two lower lines in Fig. 5.4 indicate, education appears to have a large impact on women's probability of being in Class I, although it appears to have almost no effect on the probability of men being in Class I. Among women, the probability of being in Class I rises from about 7 per cent to 20 per cent over the three education categories, while the increase for men is much more modest—from 5 per cent to 7 per cent. Similarly, education has a large influence on the probability of women being in Class III, and a far more modest influence among men. The decline for women across the three education categories is from about 44 per cent in the lowest category to about 6 per cent in the highest; for men, the decline is from about 58 per cent in the lowest category to about 33 per cent in the highest. Interestingly, it is only for Class II type respondents that education appears to have a similar influence for both men and women; the 12–14 per cent difference between women's and men's probabilities appears to remain relatively constant over the three education groups (50 per cent as against 38 per cent for no qualifi-

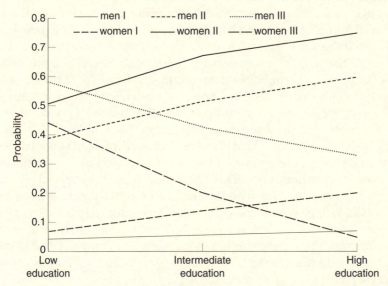

Fɪɢ. 5.4 Estimated class types by gender and education

cations; 74 per cent as against 60 per cent for high education). Thus, as the significant three-way interaction tells us, education has a differential impact on men and women, depending on the class of respondents we are considering.

Conclusion

In the past two decades, there have been a number of new developments in the analysis of data which are categorically scored. Recent extensions of the latent class model to allow the inclusion of latent variables in log-linear models provides one of the most exciting of these new developments. Such models allow researchers to combine efficiently the information available in multiple measures of the same phenomenon; and while measurement error is inevitable in all research, these methods enable analysts to reduce the overall amount of measurement error when multiple indicators are available. Moreover, there are now reliable and efficient computer programs available for such analyses.

We have briefly examined one example of how a set of categorically scored data could be analysed. As we have seen, a three-class model best explains the mix of consumer types in the 1991 British adult population: those who report 'regularly' purchasing environmentally conscious consumer items (Class I); those who have a more sporadic, although relatively high probability of 'regularly' buying such products (Class II); and those who have a near-zero probability of 'regularly' purchasing these items (Class III). If the age effects we find are attributable to cohort differences, it is plausible that cohort replacement will eventually result in a preponderance of Class I and II type respondents among the British public. If these age effects reflect life-cycle differences, however, we might expect that members of the two younger age groups will become less inclined towards environmentally conscious consumerism as they age.

Log-linear models of the kind discussed in this chapter are now easily estimated using any of the major software packages. *SPSS* allows for the estimation of a very general class of log-linear model, and has a special program for rapidly estimating hierarchical models. The *GLIM* program has a very nice model-fitting syntax which greatly facilitates interactive analysis. Although latent class analysis has yet to be incorporated into the major software packages, there are a number of excellent and easily obtainable specialized programs, such as the *LCAG* and *LEM* programs used for the analyses in this chapter.

Notes

1. Work on this chapter was supported by the ESRC under the initiative Analysis of Large and Complex Data Sets (H51944500495), the Methodology Institute of the London School of Economics, the Fulbright Program, and the Work and Organizations Research Centre of Tilburg University, The Netherlands. Data were supplied by the ESRC Data Archive at the University of Essex.
2. In addition to the issues of data reduction and measurement error, latent class models may be used to explore issues related to missing data. This issue is not addressed in this chapter, but we recommend that interested readers should consult Winship and Mare (1989), and Hagenaars (1990).
3. For further information about how these estimates are derived via the expectation-maximization (EM) algorithm, see McCutcheon (1987: 21–7).
4. BIC is calculated as L^2 – degrees of freedom (log N). The AIC statistic is calculated as $L^2 + 2p$ where p is the number of parameters estimated.

6

MODELLING CONTEXT AND HETEROGENEITY: APPLYING MULTILEVEL MODELS

KELVYN JONES AND CRAIG DUNCAN

Multilevel models are a useful tool for quantitative analysis when the problem under investigation has a multilevel structure, when a process is thought to operate at more than one level or scale, or when the researcher is particularly interested in variability and heterogeneity and not just overall average values. Many social science research questions have this form. Fig. 6.1*a* shows a two-level structure in which many Level 1 units are nested within a smaller number of Level 2 units. In this example, Level 1 consists of pupils and Level 2 consists of schools. The researcher may be interested in accounting for pupil attainment and whether this is influenced by the characteristics of pupils or the characteristics of schools, or, indeed, an interaction between them. For example, do girls have a higher attainment than boys? Do single-sex schools have a higher overall attainment? Do girls perform particularly well in all-girl schools?

The key feature of these examples is that there are potentially different processes operating at each level, but they may also operate in combination. We know from a great deal of empirical research that once groupings are created, even if their origins are essentially random, they will tend to become differentiated, with individuals being influenced by membership of the group. While the impetus for multilevel modelling arose in educational work (Aitkin and Longford 1986), Level 2 could be any organizational setting, such as a firm, a primary health-care practice, or a hospital. Other researchers have used multilevel modelling to examine voting behaviour in which Level 1 is the individual voter and Level 2 is the constituency in which the vote is cast. They are interested in whether or not, for example, voters of a lower social class are more inclined to vote for a right-wing party in places with a high percentage of voters of higher social class. Fig. 6.1*b* shows a three-level structure in which many Level 1 units are nested in fewer Level 2

(a) Two levels

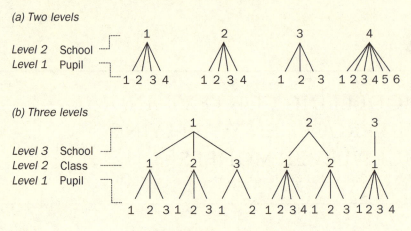

(b) Three levels

Fɪɢ. 6.1 Multilevel structures

units and even fewer Level-3 units. Examples would be pupils in classes in schools, or voters in households in constituencies.

These are examples of what are called 'naturally occurring hierarchies'. Such a multilevel structure may also arise, however, as a result of study design. For reasons of cost and efficiency, many large-scale surveys adopt a multi-stage design. For example, in the analysis of voting behaviour, this could involve a three-stage design, so that constituencies are selected first, then wards, and only then individuals. A design of this kind generates a three-level hierarchical structure with individuals at Level 1, nested in wards at Level 2, which are, in turn, nested in constituencies at Level 3. However, individuals living in the same ward can be expected to be more alike than they would be if the sample was truly random, that is they are autocorrelated. As a consequence, such 'clustered' samples do not contain as much 'information' as simple random samples of similar size. It is well known (Skinner *et al.* 1989) that ignoring this autocorrelation results in an increased risk of finding differences and relationships where none, in fact, exist. It can also result in building unnecessarily complicated models. From this sampling perspective, the convenience of a hierarchical design becomes a nuisance in the analysis, and much effort has been spent in both measuring this 'design effect' and correcting for it.

From a multilevel perspective, however, this hierarchical structure is seen not as a result of multi-stage sampling, but, rather, the population itself is conceptualized to have a complex—often hierarchical—structure. Individuals, wards, and constituencies are seen as distinct structures in the population which may be measured and modelled. The differing levels are then seen as an integral part of the population structure that needs to be properly modelled. Such an approach is able to model not only between-individual variation (at Level 1) but also between-context variation (between-ward and between-constituency variation at Levels 2 and 3 respectively). Consequently, this higher-level variation is not a nuisance but of potential substantive importance: individuals vary, but so may contexts.

Much of the published multilevel literature, to date, has been limited to Level 2 and Level 3 structures (partly due to software limitations), but now one software package (called *MLwiN*) can analyse *n* levels where *n* depends on the RAM of the computer platform. The originator of this package, Harvey Goldstein, was chided for having a Monty Python attitude in introducing such complexity (de Leeuw and Kreft 1995*a*). However, the need for many levels is not just an extension of the number of settings (such as voters in households, in neighbourhoods, in constituencies), but because a wide range of problems can, with advantage, be recast as multilevel structures, and these may combine to form a structure with many levels.

Fig. 6.2*a* recasts an approach known as a repeated cross-sectional design as a multilevel structure. Level 4 is the local education authority, Level 3 is the school, Level 2 is the year, and Level 1 is the pupil. Level 2 represents repeated measurements on the school. Such a structure allows researchers to model changing school performance as different cohorts of pupils pass through a school. Fig. 6.2*b* shows a repeated measures or panel design in which Level 1 is the measurement occasion, Level 2 is the voter, Level 3 is the household, and Level 4 is the constituency. Voters are measured at successive elections so that it becomes possible to model their changing voting behaviour. Thus, a model of this kind could be used to discover what sort of individuals and what sort of constituencies have changed their voting patterns. Moreover, in comparison to conventional repeated measures methods (Ware 1985) which require a fixed set of repeated observations for all persons, it is not necessary for all voters to be measured on every occasion. Both the number of observations per person and the spacing among the observations may vary. Repeated measures data are likely to generate a strong hierarchy in that, in general, there is likely to be greater variation between individuals (at Level 2) than between occasions within individuals (at Level 1). This marked autocorrelation needs to be explicitly modelled.

Fig. 6.2*c* shows a multivariate multilevel model in which Level 1 is a set of response variables measured on individuals at Level 2, in schools and in local education authorities at Levels 3 and 4 respectively. Thus, there may be two measures of performance (unseen examination or continuous assessment) for each pupil in each class in each school. In substantive terms, two main benefits arise from this approach. First, the responses are directly comparable in terms of how each is related to individual-level characteristics. Answers to complex questions can be given: for example, are the differences

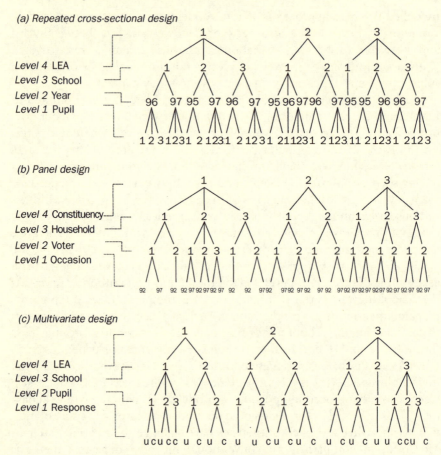

(a) Repeated cross-sectional design

Level 4 LEA
Level 3 School
Level 2 Year
Level 1 Pupil

(b) Panel design

Level 4 Constituency
Level 3 Household
Level 2 Voter
Level 1 Occasion

(c) Multivariate design

Level 4 LEA
Level 3 School
Level 2 Pupil
Level 1 Response

FIG. 6.2 More complex multilevel structures

between boys and girls the same for unseen examinations as for continuous assessment? Second, the covariance between the set of responses can be estimated at any level, so that it is possible to assess the 'correlation' of performance both between individuals and between schools. A technical advantage is that it is not necessary for measurements to be made for all pupils on both responses. Indeed, this multilevel approach can handle a matrix sample design in which all respondents are asked a set of core questions but additional questions are asked of random subsets of the total sample.

A number of other types of multilevel structure are becoming increasingly important as a result of improved estimation procedures and subsequent software implementation. Survival models are concerned with the timing of an event. An example would be the length of time since the beginning of a study that a respondent lived before dying. We would then be interested in the characteristics of individuals (Level 1) and places (Level 2) that are related to this survival. In this instance, special methods are needed to deal with censoring. For example, even if twenty years have passed since the start of the study, many respondents may still be alive. While we know that they have lived for twenty years, their complete survival time is unknown or 'censored'. Such survival models are a special and simple case of event duration models in which researchers are interested in the time until an event but, unlike the death example, the event can be repeated. For example, the event could be the change of state from unemployment to working. The multilevel model with a repeated measures structure, with periods taking the place of occasions, could then be used to relate the time spent in unemployment to individual and labour market characteristics. These models can include unchanging predictors such as a person's social origins or sex, and also time-dependent factors such as qualifications and number of dependants.

All the previous examples have been strictly hierarchical in that all Level 1 individuals that form a Level 2 group are always in the same group at any higher level. In contrast, in the cross-classified structure shown in Fig. 6.3, pupils at Level 1 are nested in schools at Level 2, and they are also nested in neighbourhoods again at Level 2. However, schools and neighbourhoods are not nested, but are *crossed*. Individuals are then seen as occupying more than one set of contexts, each of which may have an important influence. Such structures, which until recently have been computationally intractable, are likely to be very common, particularly in a panel study. People do not stay in a single setting, be it a household or labour market, but move from one context to another. Consequently, their higher-level units will be crossed not nested. If we make our models realistically complex (Best *et al.* 1996), we may anticipate that a combination of multivariate, repeated measures, and cross-classified structures will be needed.

Finally, we should also mention multilevel time-series models with 'extra' temporal autocorrelation at Level 1 (Goldstein *et al.* 1994), spatial models with complex geographical patterning (Langford *et al.* 1996), and multilevel

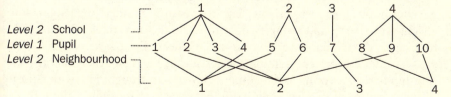

FIG. 6.3 Cross-classified multilevel structures

meta-analysis which is concerned with synthesizing a number of previously published research findings (Bryk and Raudenbush 1992). In addition, multi-level structural-equation models are currently being developed (Longford and Muthen 1992; McDonald 1994).

In the social sciences, there are many accounts of the (re)-discovery of the problems of scale and levels of analysis dating back (at least) to Thorndike (1939). Probably the best known of these is Robinson's (1950) paper on the ecological fallacy, in which he showed, empirically, through an analysis of data on race and illiteracy, that results derived at a higher-level, aggregate scale should not be applied to a lower, individual level. These results were extended by Alker (1969) who popularized the term 'atomistic fallacy': the invalid inference from individual results to a higher level. Consequently, social scientists were on the horns of a dilemma. They had to work at either the aggregate level or the individual level: the latter approach misses the context in which individual behaviour occurs; the former fails to recognize that it is individuals who act, not aggregates. The importance of multilevel modelling is that it allows the simultaneous analysis of data at the individual level and the ecological level.

Earlier multilevel models were restricted to 'balanced' data (the same number of observations in each higher-level unit), relatively small data sets, and simple two-level models (known as 'random effects ANOVA').[1] With the development, during the 1980s,[2] of a number of different algorithms for efficient computation, the situation changed rapidly, leading to a phase of enthusiastic but often uncritical use. This has given way, more recently, to a period of critical evaluation which Mason (1995: 221) believes will lead to the technique becoming incorporated in its appropriate place in the 'social science armamentarium'. Our intention in this chapter is to make these important developments accessible to as wide an audience as possible.

Varying Relations: Modelling Heterogeneity

One of the main attractions of multilevel models is their capacity to allow 'relations to vary over context'. To appreciate what this phrase means, we begin with a two-level structure, voters in constituencies. We discuss a single continuous response variable, a score measuring underlying support for a right-wing party, and a single continuous predictor variable, income. We have centred the income variable around its mean. Fig. 6.4 shows a range of possible models for representing these data. In Fig. 6.4a, the general relationship between voting and income is shown as a straight line with a positive slope: rich people generally vote for a party of the right. There is no context in this graph; voting is conceptualized only in terms of an individ-

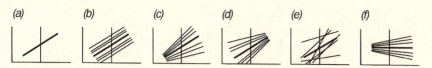

FIG. 6.4 Varying relationships between voting and income

ual's income, and place does not matter. This is remedied in Fig. 6.4*b*, in which the relationship in each of a number of places (six in this example, but normally many more) is represented by a separate line at a varying 'distance' from the general underlying relationship shown by the thicker line. The parallel lines imply that, while the relationship between voting and income in each constituency is the same, some places have higher rates of support for the right than others.

The situation becomes more complicated in Figs. 6.4*c* to 6.4*f* as the steepness of the lines varies from place to place. In Fig. 6.4*c*, the pattern suggests that place makes very little difference for the poor, but place matters when it comes to right-wing support among the rich. In contrast, Fig. 6.4*d* shows relatively large place-specific differentials in voting by the poor. The next graph, shown in Fig. 6.4*e*, with its criss-crossing lines, represents a complex interaction between income and place: in some places it is the poor who strongly support the right; in other places it is the rich. The final plot, Fig. 6.4*f*, shows that the poor are similar in all constituencies in terms of voting, but the intentions of the rich vary from place to place. This is similar to the relationship shown in Fig. 6.4*c*, but this time the difference is that some constituencies show a high rate of right-wing support from the rich, while in others it is the well-off who vote for a party of the left.

Another way of portraying these varying relationships is to plot the between-context heterogeneity, that is the variation at Level 2. This is done in Fig. 6.5. In Fig. 6.5*a*, all places show the same relationship; there is no between-place variation. In Fig. 6.5*b*, there are differences between places but this is unchanging in relationship to income. In Fig. 6.5*c*, the differences between places increase rapidly with income; they also do so in Fig. 6.5*f*, whereas in Fig. 6.5*d* they decline rapidly with income. The complexity shown in Fig. 6.5*e* is characterized by a between-context difference that is relatively large at all levels of income.

The differing patterns in Figs. 6.4 and 6.5 are achieved by varying the slopes and intercepts of the lines. The slope measures the increase in right-wing voting associated with a unit increase in income. As the horizontal axis in these graphs is centred at the mean of income, the intercept is the measurement of right-wing support for a person of average income. The key feature of multilevel models is that they specify the potentially different

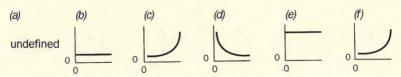

FIG. 6.5 Between place heterogeneity

intercepts and slopes for each context as coming from a distribution at a higher level. Figs. 6.6 and 6.7 show the higher-level distributions for the slope and intercept that correspond to the different graphs of Fig. 6.4. Fig. 6.6 shows a 'dot plot' for the distributions of the slopes and intercepts separately. Fig. 6.7 plots the 'scatter' of the joint distribution. These distributions concern places as contexts, not individuals, and result from treating constituencies as a sample drawn from a population.

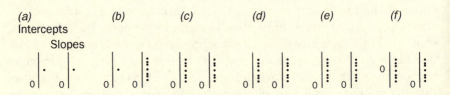

FIG. 6.6 Dot plots of the higher-level distributions underlying FIG. 6.4

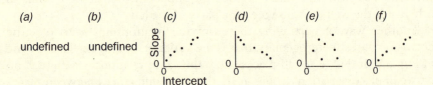

FIG. 6.7 Scatterplots of the higher-level distributions underlying FIG. 6.4

We can now see that the relationship represented in Fig. 6.4a, is the result of a single, or fixed, non-zero intercept and slope, whereas Fig. 6.4b has a single fixed slope but the intercepts are allowed to vary. In other words, the intercepts are treated as *random* terms. Figs. 6.4c to 6.4f, however, have sets of intercepts and slopes, that is, both the slopes and intercepts are allowed to vary. In other words, both the slopes and the intercepts are treated as *random* terms.

The different forms of the relationships represented in Figs. 6.4c to 6.4f are a result of how the intercepts and slopes are associated. In Fig. 6.4c, the relationship between voting and income is strongest in places where there is strong support for a right-wing party among people of average income; a steep slope is associated with a high intercept. Put another way, there is a positive association between the intercepts and slopes, as shown in Fig. 6.7c. In contrast, Fig. 6.4d shows that there is a relatively weak relationship between voting and income in places where there is strong support for the right-wing party. A high intercept is associated with a shallow slope. Consequently, Fig. 6.7d shows a negative association between the slopes and intercepts. The complex criss-crossing in Fig. 6.4e results from the lack of pattern between the intercepts and slopes shown in Fig. 6.7e. In this case, the degree of right-wing support from people on average income in a particular constituency tells us nothing about the marginal increase in right-wing voting with rising income in that community. The distinctive feature of the final plot, shown in Fig. 6.4f, results from the slopes varying around zero, so that in the 'typical' constituency there is no relationship between voting and income; in some constituencies the slope is positive, in others it is negative. In the latter case, a single-level model would reveal no relationship whatsoever between income and voting for a right-wing party. This 'average' relationship, however, would not occur anywhere.

Specifying Multilevel Equations

All statistical models have a common underlying structure, which we can represent as:

> Response = systematic component + fluctuations   (1)

or equivalently as:

> Response = fixed terms + random terms   (2)

In the single-level simple regression model, this becomes:

Response	*Systematic part*		*Random part*
right-wing support of each individual	= right-wing support for person of average income	+ change in support for unit increase in income	+ residual variation for each individual (3)
	Intercepts	*Slopes*	*Residuals*

This can be developed into a microlevel model for individual voters by having an intercept and a slope for each place:

Response	Systematic part			Random part	
right-wing support of each individual	=	right-wing support for person of average income in each place	+	change in support for unit increase in income in each place	+	residual variation for each individual	(4)
		Intercepts		*Slopes*	*Residuals*

We now need two macrolevel statistical models specified at the higher level to model the between-context variations in the intercepts and slopes:

Response	Systematic part		Random part	
right-wing support for person of average income in each place	=	national support for person of average income	+	place-specific differential support for person of average income	(5)

Response	Systematic part		Random part	
change in support for unit increase in income in each place	=	national change in support for a unit change in income	+	place-specific differential change for unit change in income	(6)

Specifying multilevel models can be seen, then, as a staged process. First, there is a microlevel model that represents the within-context equation. Then macrolevel models are developed in which the parameters of the within-context model are the responses. This is seen most clearly if we adopt a (fairly) standard notation, and rewrite (4), (5), and (6) as equations:

Micro-model: $\quad y_{ij} = \beta_{0j} + \beta_{1j}x_{ij} + \varepsilon_{ij}$ (4)

Macro-models: $\quad \beta_{0j} = \beta_0 + \mu_{0j}$ (5)

$\qquad\qquad\quad \beta_{1j} = \beta_1 + \mu_{1j}$ (6)

and then combine them into an overall multilevel model:

$$y_{ij} = \beta_0 + \beta_1 x_{ij} + (\mu_{1j}x_{ij} + \mu_{0j} + \varepsilon_{ij})$$ (7)

where y_{ij} is the response; a measure of right-wing support for individual i in place j;

$\qquad x_{ij}$ is the predictor; the income of person i in place j centred about the national mean for income;

$\qquad \beta_0$ is the overall intercept, representing national right-wing support from a person of average income;

β_1 is the overall slope, representing the national relationship between income and right-wing support; this overall slope and intercept are used to draw the thick 'general' line in Fig. 6.4;

( ) represents the random part which, in this model, consists of three elements:

μ_{1j} the differential slope for place j, a residual at Level 2;

μ_{0j} the differential intercept for place j, another residual at Level 2;

ε_{ij} the remaining individual differential after taking into account income and place; the residual at Level 1.

The novel features of a multilevel model are, of course, the random terms (μ_{1j}, μ_{0j}) at Level 2. It is the estimates of these terms that are plotted in Figs. 6.6 and 6.7. In fact, it is not their specific values that are estimated but their variances and covariances ($\sigma_{\mu 1}^2$, $\sigma_{\mu 0}^2$, $\sigma_{\mu 0 \mu 1}$) as well as the residual variance at Level 1, σ_{ε}^2 The total variance at Level 2 is the sum of two random variables at Level 2:

$$Var(\mu_{0j} + \mu_{1j}x_{ij}) = \sigma_{\mu 0}^2 + 2\sigma_{\mu 0 \mu 1}x_{ij} + \sigma_{\mu 1}^2 x_{ij}^2 \tag{8}$$

The graph of this quadratic function was shown earlier in Fig. 6.5. If the covariance is substantial and positive, we get the greater between-place differences for high income shown in Fig. 6.5c; if negative, we get the narrower between-place differences at high income shown in Fig. 6.5d. If the covariance is zero but the slope and intercept variances are large, we get the complexity of Fig. 6.5e. If the covariance and slope variances are close to zero but the intercept variance is not, we get the parallel lines shown in Fig. 6.5b, the 'random-intercepts' model. If all the higher-level variances are zero, the model reduces to the single-level of Fig. 6.5a; we do not need a multilevel model at all. Importantly, the presence of more than one random term in the model means that we cannot use standard ordinary least squares procedures to derive estimates.

Multilevel models require the simultaneous estimation of residuals at each level. Fig. 6.8a shows the case of a single-level model with ten observations. The general relationship for income and support for a right-wing party is shown, as well as the residuals, defined as the vertical distance to the general line. Fig. 6.8b shows that the ten observations belong to two groups; the general relationship is plotted, so is the specific line for each group (as if from a random intercepts model). It is clear that the Level 2 residuals (the μ_{0j}'s) are defined as the vertical distance to the general line. In contrast, Fig. 6.8c shows that the Level 1 residuals (the ε_{ij}'s) are defined as the vertical distance to their associated Level 2 context-specific lines. The Level 2 residuals estimate the 'differences' between contexts; the Level 1 residuals estimate the 'differences' between individuals within contexts.

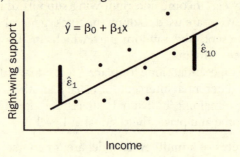

(a) Residuals from single-level model

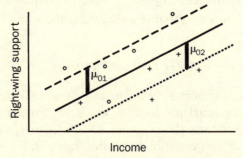

(b) Level 2 residuals from two-level model

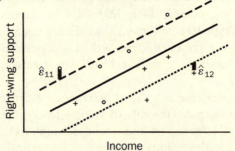

(c) Level 1 residuals from two-level model

FIG. 6.8 Residuals at various levels

In the two-level random intercepts model, a statistic known as the *intra-unit correlation* is defined as:

$$\rho = \sigma_{\mu 0}^2 / (\sigma_{\mu 0}^2 + \sigma_{\hat{\varepsilon}}^2) \tag{9}$$

That is, the ratio of the Level 2 variance to the total variance. If this is zero, there is no Level 2 variance, and the context-specific lines coincide with the general line. If the ratio is one, all the Level 1 residuals are zero and all the observations within a group will lie exactly on the group-specific line. When this autocorrelation statistic is zero, all the variation is between individuals; when it is one, all the variation is between the groups (that is, individuals within the group will be alike given their income). This statistic, therefore, represents the 'correlation' in right-wing support between two voters within the same context, conditional on their income.

A standard assumption of ordinary least squares regression analysis is that the residuals—that is, the response given the predictors—have a constant variance. As the variability about the fitted line is presumed to be constant, it can be summarized in a single variance term (σ_ε^2). The scatter around the line, such as in Fig. 6.8a, should show the same amount of variability at high, middle, or low levels of the predictor variable. If this is not the case, there is Level 1 heterogeneity. This is particularly important in multilevel analysis as there may be confounding across the levels, so what may appear to be higher-level, between-context heterogeneity is, in reality, between-individual, within-context heterogeneity (see Bullen *et al.* 1997). Fortunately, such heterogeneity can be readily modelled in a multilevel framework.

To continue our example with a single continuous predictor for income, we can specify a new microlevel model as follows:

$$y_{ij} = \beta_{0j} + \beta_{1j} x_{ij} + (\varepsilon_{0ij} + \varepsilon_{1ij} x_{ij}) \tag{10}$$

in which there are now two Level 1 random terms. The total variation at Level 1 is then a quadratic function of income:

$$Var(\varepsilon_{0ij} + \varepsilon_{1ij} x_{ij}) = \sigma_{\varepsilon 0}^2 + 2\sigma_{\varepsilon 0 \varepsilon 1} x_{ij} + \sigma_{\varepsilon 1}^2 x_{ij}^2 \tag{11}$$

A substantial positive estimate for $\sigma_{\varepsilon 0 \varepsilon 1}$ represents 'fanning out', in which higher-income individuals are not only more likely, on average, to vote for the right (a positive fixed effect, β_1) but they are also more variable. A sizeable negative estimate for $\sigma_{\varepsilon 0 \varepsilon 1}$ suggests 'fanning in' so that, at the individual level, the highest-income groups are the least variable in their support for the right. It is also possible to model what is known as the *constant coefficient of variation* model in this framework. Instead of the predictor variable being included in the Level 1 random part, the square root of the predicted response based on all (or part) of the fixed part is included (see Goldstein 1995: 50). The Level 1 variance will then be proportional to the predicted values, and will be greatest for the highest predicted values.

It can be seen, then, that multilevel analysis is not just concerned with the 'average', or fixed effect, but how people, groups, and higher-level units vary. Importantly, the ideas and estimation procedures originally developed for higher-level heterogeneity can be used routinely for complex variation at Level 1. Heterogeneity and difference are seen as the norm, not as an aberration.

Modelling Categorical Data

So far the discussion has solely concerned continuous data, but multilevel models can also readily analyse categorical variables, both as predictors and as responses. A categorical predictor can be included in the fixed part of the model, and it can be allowed to vary at any level. For example, individual voters could be categorized by sex as male and female. Then, inclusion of a relevant dummy in the fixed part would allow one sex to have higher average support for the right; the inclusion of the dummy in the random part at Level 1 would allow one sex to be more variable in its level of right-wing support; and inclusion of the dummy in the random part at Level 2 would allow there to be a differential 'map' of support for each sex. In some places, it may be women who give higher support to the right; in others, it may be men.

Returning to the income example, a higher-level categorical predictor variable, w_j, relating to the constituency not to the voter, could also be included in the model. This can be done through specification in the macrolevel models:

$$\beta_{0j} = \beta_0 + \alpha_0 w_j + \mu_{0j} \tag{12}$$

$$\beta_{1j} = \beta_1 + \alpha_1 w_j + \mu_{1j} \tag{13}$$

which results in the overall multilevel model:

$$y_{ij} = \beta_0 + \beta_1 x_{ij} + \alpha_0 w_j + \alpha_1 w_j x_{ij} + (\mu_{1j} x_{ij} + \mu_{0j} + \varepsilon_{ij}) \tag{14}$$

If this Level 2 categorical variable is a dummy, reflecting, say, whether or not the constituency is dominated by the service-sector, the multilevel model allows for assessing the extent to which the relationship between right-wing support and income differs in the two types of constituency.[3] If this dummy is included in the random part at Level 2, it allows constituency support to vary between the two types. If it is included in the random part at Level 1, this will allow different between-voter variances for each type of constituency. Moreover, there are no difficulties in dealing with sets of categorical predictors so that, at Level 1, voters could be categorized into several fractions of class, while, at Level 2, the classification of constituency types could be extended to include several categories. The only novel element of categorical predictors relates to predictors which are allowed to vary at the same level or at a lower level than the level at which they are defined. For example, as an individual voter cannot be in more than one category (simultaneously male and female, for example), it is not possible to estimate the full quadratic function for Level 1 heterogeneity (equation 10), but only a linear simplification of it (Goldstein 1995: ch. 3).

Very recently non-linear multilevel models have been developed for hand-ling a wide range of non-continuous responses (see Yang *et al*. 1996). In the case of a single predictor, it is now possible to model proportions and binary outcomes (as logit, log-log, and probit models), multiple categories (as multinomial and ordered multinomial models), and counts (as Poisson and negative binomial distribution models). These models work, in effect, by assuming a specific, non-normal distribution for the random part at Level 1, while maintaining the normality assumptions for random parts at a higher level. This means (and contrary to Duncan *et al*. 1993) that it is not possible to decompose the remaining variation into Level 1 and Level 2 proportions, as in equation (9). The estimation of non-linear models is the subject of active research. It has been shown that Goldstein's (1991) original proce-dures underestimate both the fixed and random parameters, especially when the number of observations in a higher-level unit is small. Improved esti-mates are, however, now available (Goldstein 1995: chs. 5 and 7).

To give an example, the response could be the number of days patients occupy a hospital bed which could be related to the characteristics of patients, wards, and hospitals. Such a count is often 'overdispersed' in that it has a greater than expected variance when compared to an exact Poisson dis-tribution; there is a tendency for a few patients to occupy a bed for a long period of time. This suggests that a negative binomial distribution (NBD), non-linear multilevel model would be needed for effective modelling. A multinomial multilevel model may be used to model a choice set of voting intentions (Labour, Conservative, Liberals, and 'other'). This may be extended to two choice sets representing party identification and actual vot-ing. As a result of the ability of multilevel models to handle multivariate structures, it is also possible to handle both sets of categorical responses and mixtures of categorical and continuous outcomes! Duncan *et al*. (1996) pro-vide an example of such a mixed-response multivariate model. The responses in this case are smoking or not (modelled by a binary logit model) and, if the respondent does smoke, the number of cigarettes consumed (modelled by a normal theory model). This approach ensures that the occur-rence of smoking can be separated from, yet considered simultaneously with, the quantity smoked. As a result, important questions concerning the concurrence of the two dimensions of behaviour can be answered at the level of both people and contexts. For example, are young people both more likely to be smokers and to smoke heavily? Are places with many smokers also heavy smoking places?

Fixed and Random Effects

Re-examining Fig. 6.4, it would appear that a multilevel analysis of the form we have so far considered could be undertaken using dummy (indicator) variables and interaction terms. This approach is known as (fixed effects) analysis of variance (ANOVA) and analysis of covariance (ANCOVA). Both types of models can be estimated by ordinary least squares (OLS). In the former, the 'parallel lines' graph shown in Fig. 6.4b is achieved by entering into the fixed part of the model a dummy variable as the indicator for each constituency. In the latter, which produces results akin to those shown in Figs. 6.4c to 6.4e, the fixed part additionally includes interactions between income and each and every dummy. Thus, if 200 constituencies have been sampled, 400 extra terms would have to be entered into the fixed part of the model! In terms of the estimated coefficients, this approach is equivalent to fitting a separate regression line to each constituency. In effect, 200 separate models are being fitted, not a single overall model. Consequently, very large sample sizes would be needed to obtain reliable estimates, and there would need to be a range of income values in each constituency for precise estimation. This approach is appropriate when there are relatively few higher-level units, a lot of within-unit observations, and when attention focuses on those specific units and not on generalization to a wider population. The latter point is most marked when the Level 2 units are individuals and the Level 1 units are repeated measures. If differentiating factors are placed in the fixed part of the model, the generalization is limited to the *particular* people examined in the study (Tom, Jane, and the like). In contrast, specification as random effects, as is done in a multilevel analysis, means treating individual respondents as 'nameless' versions of a general population of people. The contrasts with the multilevel approach, and consequent gains in efficiency, can be marked.

Multilevel modelling can be viewed as a two-stage procedure. At the first stage, the overall summaries (variances and covariances) of the higher-level distributions are estimated. As we have seen, a multilevel analysis would involve estimating only two fixed terms giving the average intercept and slope across all 200 places and three random terms summarizing the variability between constituencies. These terms would be estimated from the whole sample data set. Multilevel estimation is not, therefore, a separate estimation strategy but is based on 'pooling' all the information in the data in the combined estimation of the fixed and random part. It is this pooling that potentially allows more precise estimates of the differential intercepts and slopes. At the second stage, these summaries are combined with place-specific information in order to derive *predictions* of constituency-specific intercepts and slopes. If a particular constituency has a small number of observations, or if there is little variation in the predictor variable, the predictions for such a place will be 'down-weighted' or 'shrunk' towards the overall fixed relationship. A reliably estimated within-constituency relationship will, however, be largely immune to this shrinkage. In Bayesian terminology, these predictions are known as the *posterior residual estimates*.

To summarize: the multilevel estimates, unlike their traditional counterparts in ANOVA or ANCOVA, are 'precision-weighted' so as to reflect the number of observations on which they are based. Jones and Bullen (1994) provide a comparison of ANCOVA and precision-weighted estimates of the relationship between price and size of domestic properties for thirty-three London districts. Fig. 6.9 shows both sets of estimates. The ANCOVA results show a much greater tendency to vary. Moreover, the estimates for some districts are unlikely: their negative slopes indicate that larger properties cost less. One place, the borough of Sutton, has a very steep price–size relationship. The multilevel estimates are much more intuitively reasonable, and Sutton, which is based on only four properties (and only two sizes of property), is shrunk considerably towards the overall, fixed London relationship, which is, itself, a weighted average of all the district-specific estimates, weighted so as to emphasize the more precisely estimated relationships. The differences between the two approaches are marked here because of the small sample sizes for some districts.

There are non-trivial conceptual differences between treating the higher-level units as either fixed or random which can have important consequences in practice. The multilevel approach treats the higher-level units as a sample coming from a distribution. Consequently, in the case of the analysis of house prices, it is presumed that there is a general London housing market and information can be pooled across districts. However, this may be inappropriate for a particular district, such as Docklands for example, which may be operating in a national or international—rather than local—market. If that is the case, it would be unreasonable for the estimates for that place to be 'coerced' into shrinking to the price–size relationship found in the rest of the city. It is, of course, possible to have both fixed and random elements in an overall model. Thus, if we believed that a particular place (or set of places) was not part of a single 'overall' distribution but was in some way untypical, this could be accommodated by including appropriate dummies and interactions as fixed terms in the model, while still allowing the remaining districts to form a higher-level distribution. There would be no 'pooling' of information across the typical and untypical sets of places. In practice, this approach may be adopted when a particular place is an outlier, which, thereby, unduly inflates the size of the between-place variance.

(a) ANCOVA estimates

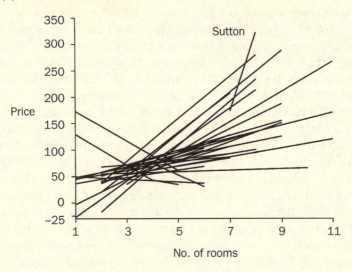

(b) Multilevel estimates

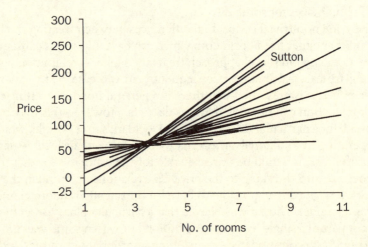

Fɪɢ. 6.9 Comparing ANCOVA and multilevel estimates: house prices in London

Testing, Exploring, and Measurement Error

As with other statistical procedures, it is possible to use a whole range of statistical hypothesis-testing procedures for the evaluation of a multilevel model, although we would stress the importance of confidence interval estimation rather than significance testing of null hypotheses. In particular, it is possible to test singly and simultaneously whether a particular coefficient differs from particular values, and whether a more complex model represents a significant improvement ('smaller deviance') over a simpler one. Care is needed, however, with the terms of the random part based on few units, and when non-normal data (especially binary outcomes; see Goldstein 1995: 86) are being modelled. Research is currently underway to develop bootstrapping procedures (Laird and Louis 1987, 1989) in which simple random resampling with replacement of the values of residuals is employed to generate a single bootstrap sample. This procedure is repeated a large number of times to produce a random sample and thereby to derive standard errors and confidence intervals.[4]

As with all modelling, it is important that the model is well specified and that the underlying assumptions are met. As yet, there have not been the major developments in multilevel diagnostics of the kind which are now routine in single-level regression analysis (Belsey *et al.* 1980). However, some useful procedures are to plot the Level 1 residuals against the predicted values for the response. Level 1 heterogeneity will be portrayed as a wedge-shaped plot; non-linearity will show as a curve; and Level 1 outliers will show up as isolated points. At higher levels, a plot of the residuals against their equivalent normal scores should result in a straight line with no outliers if the normality assumption is met. When there is complex heterogeneity at higher levels, a scatter plot of each pair of higher-level residuals will reveal bivariate outliers. More progress has been made with measurement error (see Goldstein 1995: ch. 10; Woodhouse *et al.* 1996). It is now possible to specify a range of plausible measurement errors for variables at different levels and to see what impact these have on the estimates.

Study Design for Multilevel Modelling

It is perhaps fair to say that detailed theoretical and empirical work on the relative costs of different designs has hardly begun. The key question to ask, however, is: what is the basic unit for comparative purposes? Is it the school or the pupil? If it is the school, then the students can be regarded as 'repeated measures' of effectiveness, and limited resources should be concentrated on measuring as many schools as possible. Indeed, Goldstein (1984) has argued that the multi-stage design is the most efficient one for studying contextual effects. To take an example, and using UK census wards as the higher-level unit, if a national study were conducted on 10,000 respondents chosen according to simple random sampling, we would anticipate that only one voter would be found on average in each of the wards. The within-ward variation would then be totally confounded with the between-ward variation, and no separate estimates of these distinct components would be possible. To obtain reliable estimates of both the within- and between-group variation, we need a compromise between the number of lower- and higher-level units. This, of course, is what is achieved by a multi-stage design. For a given total sample size, if we allow the number of higher-level units to increase, each unit will contain fewer individuals, and we approach the situation of a single-level model, where we are unable to model contextual effects. Moreover, we need 'adequate' samples at each level. For example, in the British Election Study only one ward is sampled in each constituency, so that the variation at these two distinct levels is confounded in the survey design.

To get reliable estimates of differences between places we need lots of places. Having many individual respondents provides information on the relationship between voting and income within a place, but many places are needed to assess the differences between places. While it is difficult to be specific about the required sample size (much depends on the magnitude of the higher-level random effects), there is some guidance from educational research, the area in which multilevel modelling has been most widely applied. Bryk and Raudenbush (1992: 203) found that with sixty students per school and 160 schools, it is possible to have a total of four variables random at the school level. Paterson and Goldstein (1992) suggest a minimum of twenty-five individuals in each of twenty-five groups to do useful work; by preference, 100 groups are needed. What is not appropriate, and yet this has often been the case, is hundreds of respondents in five or ten higher-level units. Moreover, when making judgements about the performance of schools or clinics, the numbers should be as balanced as possible, avoiding, for example, a sample of 100 in one unit and only two in the next.

Of course, in some situations it is impossible to follow this 'rule of 25', for example, when dealing with households and repeated measures of voting behaviour. In such cases, while it is vital that multilevel approaches are applied (because high levels of autocorrelation can be anticipated), it would be neither sensible nor useful to make inferences about particular households or individuals. That is, the higher-level variances (stage 1) can and should be estimated, but the *predictions* (stage 2) for specific individuals or households will have large confidence intervals. Finally, if there is a need to derive sample-based aggregate variables, then a higher degree of sample clustering than is normal practice may be employed. For example, if a researcher is interested in cross-level interactions between voting and individual and neighbourhood income, then a sample-based estimate of the latter would require a sizeable number of respondents in each neighbourhood.

Advantages of a Multilevel Approach

To conclude, we discuss the advantages of the multilevel modelling approach. We divide the discussion into technical and substantive benefits, giving some brief examples from our own research and that of other people. We would point to four major technical advantages. In the first place, missing observations are now allowable in a repeated measures design (see Raudenbush 1993) and in rotation designs (see Goldstein 1995: ch. 4). Secondly, the approach has advantages in dealing with autocorrelation. Ignoring autocorrelation results in incorrect estimates of precision, giving incorrect confidence limits and tests. For example, Aitkin *et al.* (1981), reanalysed an influential study of primary school teaching which had shown significant additional progress in reading when 'formal' teaching methods were used. Reanalysis of the data with multilevel modelling which recognized the structure of pupils in classes did not reveal a significant difference.

The third technical advantage of multilevel modelling relates to the analysis of higher-level variables. The variability of the higher-level differences—that is, the responses in macrolevel models such as those specified in equations (12) and (13)—is composed of two parts: the true parameter variance (the real differences between constituencies) and the sample variance (a consequence of working with a sample of individuals within each place). The former can potentially be accounted for by developing an appropriate macro-model, while the latter cannot be explained in terms of any predictor variables. Multilevel models distinguish between these two different levels of variation through the random parameters. The explanatory power of any predictors defined at the higher level is likely to be incorrectly estimated if a single-level model is used. Bryk and Raudenbush (1992) provide a number of examples of this.

Finally, in technical terms, multilevel modelling allows for precision-weighted estimation. Rubin (1980) compares ordinary least squares and multilevel approaches to analysing the relationship between the performance of students in their first year at eighty-two law schools and their assessment score on entry. With the ordinary least squares approach, with dummies for each law school, he found some negative slopes (worse student score on entry, better performance) which were difficult to interpret, and unreliable 'bouncing βs' over time. This was due to the lack of information in the predictor variable because of the restricted range of entry scores among students in some of the law schools. The precision-weighted multilevel estimates were both more interpretable and stable. Rubin calibrated a model for 1974, and used that to predict the 1975 results. Comparing the actual and the predicted performances, he found that the estimates derived from multilevel modelling were some forty times better than the estimates from the ordinary least squares analysis.

There are also four substantive advantages in adopting a multilevel approach. First, it allows variability to be assigned to the appropriate context, or level. Goldstein (1995), for example, reports a cross-classified multilevel model in which pupils are nested in primary schools which are crossed with secondary schools. A two-level analysis of pupils within secondary schools allowing for an intake score would lead to the interpretation that there are substantial differences in progress between the secondary schools. The cross-classified analysis, however, shows that most of these differences are attributable to the primary school level. This suggests that explanations for between-school differences need to look at more than the current school setting. Without such a complex model, we could be looking for an 'explanation' in the wrong place.

The second advantage is that multievel modelling allows relations to vary according to context. There are a growing number of examples where multilevel models have revealed contextuality and complexity which would have been hidden by standard procedures. Just two examples are briefly mentioned here. Jones *et al.* (1992) developed a three-level model of the Labour vote in the 1987 British general election. Fig. 6.10 shows one result of modelling the binary choice of Labour or Conservative for 2,281 individual voters in 250 constituencies in twenty-two regions. The explanatory variables at the individual level are a mixture of continuous and categorical variables recording respondents' age, occupational class, housing type, and employment status. At the constituency level, there are variables (from the 1981 census) for unemployment, employment change, and workers in the mining industry. The constituency-level relationship between mining and voting Labour is allowed to vary between regions. Traditionally, mining constituencies have been seen as Labour's heartland. That this is generally true is evident from the relationships plotted in Fig. 6.10; most of the slopes are positive. But there are some noticeable exceptions. The most marked contrast is between South Wales and the East Midlands. South Wales is a pro-Labour area, and support levels increase as the economy of the constituency is more involved with mining (in 1981). Quite the opposite is found in the East Midlands: the most anti-Labour areas are the coalmining constituencies. The other two notable relationships are in the North-East, which shows

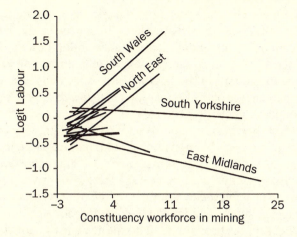

FIG. 6.10 Varying relations between Labour voting and mining constituencies

a relationship similar to that found in South Wales but from a lower base, and South Yorkshire which shows generally strong support for Labour that does not change radically in the coalmining areas. Thus, the relationship between mining and voting for the Labour Party is more complex than the simple notion that coalmining areas are 'natural' Labour strongholds.

The second example concerns educational attainment in London schools. Nuttall and his colleagues (Nuttall *et al.* 1990) examined progress in school using a three-level model: pupils in years in schools. The striking finding in the fixed part of the model is that, generally, pupils from 'ethnic' groups do better than English, Scottish, Welsh, or Irish pupils. On average, 'black' pupils progress to a higher score than 'white' pupils. It was also found that girls show more progress than boys; that, on average, there was improved attainment over the three years; and that pupils in single-sex and church schools outperform pupils in co-educational and voluntary schools. When a complex multilevel model was fitted, it was found that schools perform differentially, and that they cannot be readily ranked on a single dimension. Some schools narrow the gap between boys and girls, while some schools had not shared in the general improvement in attainment over the three years. The most marked differences between schools, however, were found for pupils with the highest ability on intake. It was also found that school results are somewhat 'unstable' over even just a three-year period.

The third substantive advantage of mutilevel models is that they can distinguish between contextual and compositional differences. There has been considerable debate on a number of social science questions over whether apparent contextual differences are really an artefact produced by differential composition. One such area of debate is the geography of voting. A map of voting patterns in Britain reveals marked differences in the Labour vote. However, it cannot be concluded that, because voting outcomes vary geographically, places or context must make a difference. For example, the strong support for Labour in the South Wales valley constituencies may be due to a high percentage of the population being low social-class voters who, irrespective of place, generally vote Labour.

Much research has been unable to address these questions because, in working at a single level, 'compositional' and 'contextual' effects are confounded. Fig. 6.11 demonstrates this point for aggregate analysis. The graphs show that exactly the same average level of right-wing support in a constituency can be achieved in a number of different ways. Constituency *a* is truly 'average' in support and income; constitutency *b* shows high underlying right-wing support brought down to the average by a low-income population; constituency *c* is a place with low support brought up to the average by high income; constituency *d* is a place where the average level of support is derived from strong support among the rich counterbalanced by weak support among the poor; while the average-level support in constituency *e* is an outcome of little differential support by income.

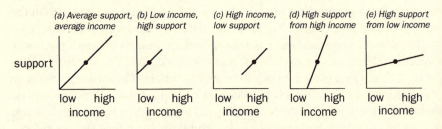

Fig. 6.11 Context and composition

In short, the crude constituency averages are composed of three distinct sources of variation: composition of the constituency, contextual difference, and the interaction between composition and context. In this instance, 'composition' refers to the make-up of the constituency in terms of the incomes of the people living there; the 'contextual' effect is the overall difference a constituency makes irrespective of income; and the interaction term represents the differential effect of a constituency in relation to the composition of its population. Thus, the crude averages obtained by conflating these distinct sources of variations are uninterpretable and meaningless. The contextual differences of 'strong' and 'weak' support are rendered 'average' by differing compositions in constituencies *b* and *c*, and by substantial interactions in constituencies *d* and *e*.

The multilevel approach, of course, is to model simultaneously at each level. Then the empirical questions concerning contextual variation become: (i) does the higher-level variation remain substantial and significant when a range of appropriate and relevant individual-level variables are included in an overall model? and (ii) do higher-level variables continue to have significant and substantial effects on the response in the presence of relevant individual-level variables? Even then, it is possible to argue that apparent contextual effects are a result of the mis-specification of individual effects (cf. Hauser 1970). However, if higher-level variation and/or effects remain substantial after taking into account 'many' individual factors, then it is not unreasonable to conclude (albeit, and always, provisionally) that there are genuine contextual differences. It is also possible that genuine contextual effects are masked by not taking account of individual-level variables (Jones and Bullen 1993). Such a result can occur, for example, when a place with a genuinely low level of right-wing support has a relatively large number of high-status individuals who, nationally, have a high probability of voting for the right.

Again we note two brief examples. Jones, Tonkin, and Wrigley (1996) analysed a two-level model—voters in constituencies—using survey data collected at the time of the 1992 British general election. They found that a strong ecology of voting remained after a wide range of demographic and socio-structural variables were included in the model. This ecology was most strongly related to the class character of a constituency, defined in terms of employers and managers. Where this group forms a sizeable proportion of the population, more or less everyone, irrespective of their individual class, voted Conservative. In other words, constituencies are more polarized politically than people. In contrast, Duncan et al. (1993), in an analysis of data from the 1984–5 British Health and Lifestyle Survey, found there was hardly any regional variation in smoking and drinking behaviour, once individual sociodemographic factors are included in the model.

Taking account of both contextual and compositional differences is particularly important in performance review. For example, family doctors in Britain are now differentially rewarded for achieving certain targets for childhood immunization (Jones and Moon 1991). The performance measure used for these targets is the percentage of children who are immunized. This measure may reflect not the clinic's contextual performance, but merely the composition of the clientele in different practices. A high value-added performance in a particular practice may be the result of a high proportion of middle-class parents who, across all practices, have high rates of immunization. Multilevel models, by simultaneously modelling at the level of the individual and the clinic, can get some purchase on which practices are performing well (given their client groups) and, thereby, develop a contextualized measure of performance.

The commonly found practice of confounding context and composition in the assessment of school performance is the subject of a withering attack by Aitkin and Longford (1986), who stress the need for a multilevel perspective. However, it must be emphasized that, even after careful modelling which adjusts for client composition and takes into account sample size, institution rankings can carry such large uncertainty bands that it is extremely difficult to isolate particular institutions. For example, Draper (1995), commenting on work by Goldstein and Thomas (1993) on school differences in pupil attainment, emphasizes that, when uncertainty is taken into account, the resulting categorization of performance is necessarily so broad that the majority of schools (70 per cent) can only be accurately located 'somewhere in the middle of a large grey area' (Draper 1995: 133). As Goldstein and Speigelhalter (1996) point out, problems of uncertainty such as this are greatest where there are few Level 1 units for each Level 2 unit.

A further substantive advantage of multilevel modelling is that it promotes linkage between survey-based, quantitative research, and intensive, qualitative research. Multilevel modelling is firmly rooted in the framework of using quantitative techniques to uncover patterns in large-scale data (Sayer 1984). Such analyses may, however, identify specific groups that need to be studied by intensive, qualitative methods. In particular, higher-level groups such as schools and clinics remain in the analysis as identifiable entities that are not lost in the statistical soup of aggregate analysis, or assumed away as in an individual-level analysis. In the immunization example, having found the clinics with the best 'value-added' performance, or the clinics that have the highest differential performance for lower-class parents, it is possible to study them intensively to uncover the processes used to achieve that success (Clegg 1993; Jones et al. 1991).

Finally, because multilevel modelling constitutes both a conceptual and a technical tool, it can influence the way we develop an approach to a social science problem. Skinner et al. (1989: 289) capture this well when they write:

[T]he issues raised are not mere technical issues which have only a marginal esoteric interest . . . On the contrary our experience suggests that the use of analytical procedures which take account of the population structure and the sample selection mechanism can change the objectives of the analysis and can have a substantial impact on the subsequent interpretation of the results.

Software

Multilevel modelling is such a recent development that it has not yet been implemented in all the well-known packages, although there are facilities in *SAS*, *GENSTAT*, and *BMDP*. Of the four original multilevel packages, *GEN-*

MOD is no longer generally available. *VARCL* handles complex heterogeneity for up to three levels and random-intercepts for up to nine levels. This program can also deal with Poisson and binomial variation at Level 1, but only simplified non-linear procedures that are known to underestimate the coefficients are implemented. *VARCL* is no longer being developed. *HLM* (Bryk *et al.* 1988) is undergoing development and a Windows version has been released; it is generally regarded as a package that is particularly straightforward to use. *MLwiN* is a complete package, with a high-level macroprograming language for the implementation of new procedures and general data manipulation, together with graphical facilities as well as multilevel estimation. Multilevel models can also be estimated by another approach called Markov Chain Monte Carlo, especially a particular variant called Gibbs Sampling. This is implemented in the *BUGS* software (Bayesian inference Using Gibbs Sampling; see Gilks *et al.* 1993) which is currently available for free. It is particularly useful in small samples (but can be incredibly time consuming when used to analyse medium-sized samples). This form of estimation can take account of uncertainty associated with the estimates of the random parameters. This is of especial importance when making the predictions for specific higher-level units. The *BUGS* and *MLwiN* software are able to fit (nearly) all the models discussed in this chapter, while McDonald's *BIRAM* deals with multilevel factor analysis. Kreft *et al.* (1994) provide a comparative review of the four original packages. Details of contact points for multilevel software packages are given in the appendix.

APPENDIX
Further reading

Three books provide a good starting point for embarking on multilevel modelling. Bryk and Raudenbush (1992) is practically orientated (based on educational research) and covers normal theory (continuous responses), and two-level and three-level models, and includes repeated measures. Longford (1993) is more theoretical but also has material on categorical responses, multivariate models, and factor analysis. Goldstein (1995) extends the first edition (1987), covering a very wide range of models in a remarkably short space. If you learn by doing, an excellent place to start is Woodhouse (1995), which is a step-by-step guide to a number of different models using the *MLwiN* package. The *ML* tutorial by Bullen *et al.* (1997) provides a detailed worked example of applying multilevel models when the predictor variables consist of a mixture of categorical and continuous variables. Hox and Kreft (1994), and DiPrete and Forristal (1994), provide up-to-date overviews; the latter also introduce an issue of *Sociological Methods and Research* devoted to multilevel modelling. We would also strongly recommend the *Journal of Educational and Behavioural Statistics*, 1995 (vol. 20, part 2), for interesting exchanges about the value of the multilevel approach; see, in particular, de Leeuw and Kreft (1995b) and Draper (1995).

Good overviews about applying multilevel models in substantive areas of research can be found in Raudenbush (1988), and Goldstein and Spiegelhalter (1996) for education; in Jones and Duncan (1996) for geography; in Leyland and Rice (1996) for health studies; and, for voting behaviour, Jones (1996). For discussions of the application of specific types of models, see Goldstein (1994), Rasbash and Goldstein (1994), and Jones et al. (1996, 1998) for cross-classified data; Duncan et al. (1995, 1996) for multivariate data; Duncan et al. (1993), Goldstein (1991), and Yang et al. (1996) for non-linear models; and Goldstein et al. (1994) for multilevel time-series.

Obviously, as you start using the approach there will be further questions. There is an e-mail discussion list with 800 members at the time of writing. To join the list, send a message to: mailbase@mailbase.ac.uk. The message should contain a single line, with a command of the form: join multilevel <firstname(s)> <lastname>. For example: join multilevel Jane Smith. You should also look at the home page of the Institute of Education's Multilevel Models Project: http://www.ioe.ac.uk/multilevel/index.html, or its mirror site at the University of Montreal:http://www.medent.umontreal.ca/multilevel. Another useful site is the Longitudinal and Multilevel Methods Project at Michigan State University: http://www.edcu.msu.edu/units/LAMMP.

Contact addresses

The software discussed above can be obtained from the addresses given here.

BIRAM: Professor R. P. McDonald, Dept. of Psychology, University of Illinois, 603 E. Danial St, Champaign, Ill. 61820, USA.

BMDP: BMDP Statistical Software Inc., 1440 Sepulveda Blvd. Suite 316, Los Angeles, Calif. 90025, USA.

BUGS: MRC Biostatistics Unit, Institute of Public Health, Robinson Way, Cambridge, CB2 2SR, UK. The e-mail address is bugs@mrc-bsu.cam.ac.uk; and the web site is http://weinberger.mrc-bsu.cam.ac.uk/bugs/.

GENSTAT: NAG Ltd Wilkinson House, Jordan Hill Road, Oxford, OX2 8DR, UK.

HLM and *VARCL* are distributed by both ProGamma and Scientific Software Inc. The contact address for ProGamma is Iec ProGAMMA, PO Box 841, 9700 AV Groningen, The Netherlands. The e-mail address is gamma.post@gamma.rug.nl; and the web site is http://www.gamma.rug.nl/. The postal address for Scientific Software Inc. is 1525 East 53rd St, Suite 906, Chicago, Ill. 60615, USA.

MLwiN is also distributed by ProGamma and by the University of London's Institute of Education. The web site for the Institute is http://www.ioe.ac.uk/multilevel. For technical information, contact the Multilevel Models Project, Mathematical

Sciences Centre, Institute of Education, 20 Bedford Way, London WC1H 0AL. The e-mail address is temsmya@ioe.ac.uk. *MLwiN* can be ordered from the Institute's Finance Dept. at the same address; the e-mail contact address is *mln*: order@ioe.ac.uk

SAS is available from SAS Institute Inc., SAS Campus Drive, Cary, NC 27513, USA.

Notes

1. Longford (1993) gives an account of the early history of the multilevel approach.
2. Four groups were particularly active at that time. The key publications and associated software are: Mason *et al.* (1984) and the *GENMOD* package; Raudenbush and Bryk (1986) and *HLM*; Longford (1987) and *VARCL*; Goldstein (1986) and *ML2*, then *ML3*, then *MLn* and now *MLwiN*.
3. These higher-level variables can, in general, be any measure. Thus, continuing the income example, it could be the proportion of the population in the constituency with income over £20,000 per annum, or the average income (mean or median), or the spread of income (standard deviation or midspread). Jones and Duncan (1995) use such higher-level variables in a multilevel analysis of morbidity.
4. Bootstrapping (and Monte-Carlo Markov chain estimation) have been implemented in the *MLwiN* software package.

PART II
ANALYSES ACROSS TIME

7

IT'S ABOUT TIME: MODELLING POLITICAL AND SOCIAL DYNAMICS

HAROLD D. CLARKE, HELMUT NORPOTH, AND PAUL WHITELEY

'Time is perhaps the most mysterious thing in a mysterious universe' (Kendall 1973: 1), thus one of the masters of time-series methodology opens his classic text on time-series analysis. Time is a concept that has befuddled philosophers, physicists, and mathematicians. No wonder the analysis of time-series data is an intimidating exercise for social scientists, too. Time does strange things to data, insinuating patterns that often prove illusory on closer examination.

Much of the work on time-series analysis in the social sciences was pioneered by economists, largely because of their long-standing interest in business cycles and other recurring changes in the macroeconomy (Morgan 1990). In the past two decades, however, time-series methods have become increasingly common in political science as analysts have sought to explain the dynamics of various political phenomena, and the kinds of data needed to use these methods have become more readily available. Time-series techniques have been used to understand the relationships between political support and the economy;[1] to analyse the dynamics of conflict processes at the global level;[2] to understand the way in which institutional and structural variables shape policy choices in democratic states;[3] and to examine the extent to which the policy choices of governments reflect the preferences of voters.[4]

A variety of related methods can be employed to model political and social dynamics. It is useful to classify them in relation to the number of time-points used in the analysis, and the level of aggregation of the cases. Aggregate-level data focusing, for example, on changes in public support for political parties over many time-points (months, quarters, years) generate one type of methodological approach, which might be described in very general terms as dynamic regression modelling (see Beck 1992). In this type of analysis, time-periods constitute the individual cases. A second, related approach, referred to as pooled cross-section and time-series analysis, involves aggregate analysis in which the cases consist of both time-points and groups (such as business firms or countries). Although pooled analyses use statistical models generally similar to those discussed here, the presence of both spatial and temporal dimensions in the data raises technical issues that do not arise when spatial variation is absent (see Beck and Katz 1995). A third type of dynamic analysis, but beyond the scope of this chapter, uses individual-level survey data and multiple observations over time as the cases. In such panel studies the observations are generated by repeated surveys of the same individuals (see Finkel 1995; Whiteley and Seyd 1997). The fourth group of models, also not considered in this chapter, are event history models in which the object of analysis is the frequency with which certain events occur over time (see Allison 1984; also Beck, this volume).

This chapter focuses on two classes of dynamic regression models: ARIMA intervention and transfer function models, and error-correction models. ARIMA models, pioneered by Box and Jenkins, gained prominence in the 1970s following the publication of their classic text *Time Series Analysis: Forecasting and Control* (1976). The authors developed a methodological strategy for identifying, estimating, and testing the adequacy of a very general class of univariate and multivariate time-series models. Their background in statistical theory and control engineering made them critical of the often simplistic econometric models of the time (Jenkins 1979), and their work represented a significant breakthrough in analysing time-series processes. An initial reluctance on the part of economists to embrace these methods gave way as a new generation of researchers adapted and built on the Box–Jenkins approach. This ultimately transformed econometric methodology, and analysts became more careful about imposing arbitrary assumptions and restrictions on models, and more willing to apply inductive methods to the development of theory. Since political methodology has a long tradition of inductive research, these techniques were adopted without any significant resistance among political scientists (see Whiteley 1979; Norpoth 1986, 1995).

Time-series analysis has not stood still since Box and Jenkins introduced ARIMA methods to social scientists two decades ago. Again, econometricians led the way. As one economist recently stated: 'At the moment, both economics and econometrics are going through a new type of revolution: the unit roots and cointegration revolution' (Rao 1994: 1).

In this chapter, we first review Box–Jenkins techniques. We then explain key concepts and methodological strategies associated with contemporary developments, and discuss the impetus they have provided for the specification and analysis of an important class of models called *error-correction models*. These models have attracted wide attention because of their ability to capture both short- and long-term relationships in a time-series of interest. Overall, the literature on time-series methodology is currently very lively and interesting, and the aim of the present chapter is to help social scientists to appreciate why this is the case. We begin with Box–Jenkins ARIMA modelling.

ARIMA, Intervention, and Transfer Function Models

Say we are interested in finding out what makes public support for a governing political party and its leader rise and fall, a topic that has attracted considerable scholarly attention. As an example, consider the popularity of Margaret Thatcher as British prime minister (1979–90). Fig. 7.1 charts her monthly popularity rating among the British public as measured in opinion polls by the percentage of people satisfied with her performance as prime minister. It is readily apparent that her appeal varied greatly, swinging from rejection to affirmation several times. Two broad causal forces, above all, come to mind as explanations of these patterns: international conflict and domestic prosperity.

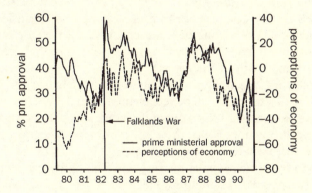

FIG. 7.1 Prime ministerial approval and perceptions of the economy, June 1979–December 1990

Fig. 7.1 also charts individual perceptions of the economy during the period when Margaret Thatcher was prime minister,[5] measured as the percentage who viewed the economy favourably minus the percentage who viewed it unfavourably. Here, too, one can spot some remarkable swings in British public opinion. In addition, Fig. 7.1 marks the timing of the Falklands War between Britain and Argentina in Spring 1982. This plot of government popularity alongside economic opinion, punctuated by a major international event, provides some clues to the discerning eye. But beyond eyeballing the data, we need proper analytical tools to deal with two things: the behaviour of a time-series itself; and the influence of external forces on that time-series. For these purposes, we introduce the Box–Jenkins ARIMA models, which stands for 'autoregressive, integrated, moving-average' (Box and Jenkins 1976). We begin with the properties of a single time-series such as prime ministerial popularity.

Univariate models

This section introduces a number of technical terms which sound arcane, but we will illustrate their meaning with examples. First, the idea of *white noise*. Life would be easy if something unfolding across time followed the rule of tossing a fair coin. Tossing a penny repeatedly produces outcomes— heads or tails—that form a white noise process. We know that for each toss, the probability of getting a head is the same as the probability of getting a tail, that is, 0.50, or 50 times in 100 tosses. In predicting the outcome of the next toss of the coin it makes no difference whatsoever whether the last flip was a head or a tail. Thus, even after a million heads in a row, the probability of getting another head with the next flip of a fair coin is still 0.5. The characteristic feature of a time-series generated by a white noise process is the total independence among observations, which is the case with tossing the coin. Any resemblance between one observation in the series and any past observation is purely coincidental.

In the following, we designate a white noise variable by the symbol u_t. Technically, such a series would be represented as an ARIMA (0,0,0) process. It has neither autoregressive nor moving-average components; nor is it integrated. We will say more about these concepts when we encounter examples of time-series where they are present.

Turning to our time-series of interest, can we say that prime ministerial popularity behaves like white noise? Does the public as a whole flip a coin each month to decide whether it approves or disapproves of the prime minister? The answer is clearly 'No'. So, what is the use of this idea? As so often in social science analysis, an implausible idea provides a convenient point of departure to finding a more plausible approach. While still tossing the coin repeatedly, consider a seemingly trivial modification of the operation, namely adding up the outcomes of the tosses (with heads counting 1 and tails −1). In so doing, we obtain a time-series that accumulates random events. We denote the value of the resulting time-series as z_t. For example, after two coin flips, the value of that time-series would be:

$$z_2 = u_1 + u_2 \tag{1}$$

After three coin flips, it would be:

$$z_3 = u_1 + u_2 + u_3 \tag{2}$$

And so on. A time-series formed by adding outcomes of the same random variable is called a *random walk*. It sounds very much like white noise, one event being as random as the other. It might be thought that random plus random is still random, just as 0 plus 0 is still 0. But the plot of a random walk does not look random at all, especially over short stretches. This can be seen by glancing in a newspaper at the chart of a stock market index like the Dow-Jones, which is a random walk (Malkiel 1973). A more formal way of making this point is by rewriting equation (2) as follows:

$$z_3 = z_2 + u_3 \tag{3}$$

Writing (3) in terms of a *general* time subscript gives:

$$z_t = z_{t-1} + u_t \tag{4}$$

Now it is clear that at any moment (t) the location of a random walk is fixed by its location at the previous moment ($t-1$), plus a new random shock (u_t). In terms of the ARIMA framework, a random walk is a (0,1,0) process; it is an *integrated* series of order 1.[6] The order of integration is determined by the number of differences required to transform the random-walk series into a stationary process. Subtracting z_{t-1} from both sides of equation (4) (taking the first difference) yields u_t, the stationary white-noise process.[7]

The idea of a random walk takes us closer to the reality of prime ministerial popularity. As far as our own opinion of an important politician is concerned, we all know that our opinion today typically is very much like the opinion we had yesterday. And the same applies to our evaluation of the economy. A random walk recognizes a basic fact of life: what happens today, provided nothing new has occurred, is a continuation of yesterday. The random-walk idea pushes this point to an extreme, since, as can be seen in equation (4), the past is preserved in its entirety. Like the Bourbon Kings of France, a random walk forgets nothing. When it comes to prime ministers or presidents, it is doubtful that we remember fully in September what we thought of them in August. The same is true of the economy.

It is the virtue of both autoregressive and moving-average models that they are capable of handling memory. Consider the *moving-average* variety, the MA part of ARIMA. The name does not tell us very much about the process, and some notational quirks confuse matters even more. The easiest way to grasp its essence is to go back once more to the idea of white noise (complete randomness). But instead of letting all past outcomes of random trials accumulate, we now call only for a portion of the last random shock (u_{t-1}) to carry over to the next period, with the size of that portion being determined by the parameter θ:[8]

$$z_t = u_t + \theta u_{t-1}; \quad |\theta| < 1.0 \tag{5}$$

As we can see, the moving-average model in (5) is only a short step away from pure randomness. Memory today (t) only extends to yesterday's news ($t-1$), not to any before then. It is like an exam where a student has to know some of the material covered in the previous exam. Such a model perhaps assumes too much forgetfulness to be applicable in many real-life time-series (other than the classroom).

Even though a moving-average model can be easily extended to accommodate a larger set of prior random shocks, say u_{t-2} or u_{t-3}, there soon comes the point where this model proves too cumbersome. A more practical way of handling the accumulated, although discounted, shocks of the past is by way of the autoregressive model. That takes us to the AR part of ARIMA, where:

$$z_t = \phi z_{t-1} + u_t; \quad |\phi| < 1.0 \tag{6}$$

In the AR(1) process, as shown in equation (6), the portion of the accumulated past that is carried over from one period to the next is governed by the parameter ϕ. This is unlike the MA(1) process, where only the previous random shock carries over. And it is also unlike the random walk, where the past carries over fully (the ϕ coefficient for the random walk model is 1.0). The autoregressive process requires some leakage in the transition from time $t-1$ to time t ($|\phi| < 1.0$). If ϕ is close to 1.0, a large portion of the past will be preserved across adjacent time-periods $(t-1$ to $t)$. But even in this case, something will be lost.

An AR(1) process has an invaluable quality which is absent in a random walk: *equilibrium*. The AR(1) has a fixed level to which observations gravitate after departing from it, just as the concept of gravity implies.[9] A random walk, on the other hand, has no such homing instinct; it is free at any moment to fly in any direction under the impact of a random shock, and then to fly off in any other direction when the next shock occurs. Hence another paradox: while looking very stable in the short run, with successive observations being spitting images of each other, a random walk does not have long-run stability.

Equilibrium is a concept which appears paradoxical. It does not mean standing still. There can be a lot of movement in the short run, possibly even more than in a random walk. But with equilibrium, all that (short-run) movement does not change the long-run balance. Like people riding a bicycle, who can only keep their balance by pedalling, a time-series in equilibrium keeps its balance by moving on. There is change, to be sure, but the changes over time do not upset stability. For a time-series to be 'weakly' stationary (stationary being just another word for referring to equilibrium), three requirements must be met. The series must have: (i) a constant mean level, around which observations fluctuate; (ii) a constant variance, within which those fluctuations occur; and (iii) a constant correlation (autocorrelation) between observations separated by k time-periods.[10]

Thus, a stationary time-series cannot experience long-term growth or decline (trends); nor is it free to explore unbridled movement in all directions like a random walk. The gravity of the mean is too strong to let any wayward movement get out of hand. Both AR(1) and MA(1) processes are stationary so long as the key parameters (ϕ, θ) are less than 1.0 in absolute size. In other words, stationarity is what the I in ARIMA refers to, although in an indirect way. For a stationary time-series, the count of I is zero ($I = 0$). If we think of I as the degree of non-stationarity, then I counts the number of times a series must be differenced to achieve stationarity. The standard procedure for turning a non-stationary time-series into a stationary one is to take differences, that is, to compute change scores for adjacent (t and $t{-}1$) observations:

$$\Delta z_t = z_t - z_{t-1} \tag{7}$$

One difference ($I = 1$) is sufficient for many economic and political series to turn them into a stationary series, in this case white noise.

Tools of the trade

Having introduced the terms used in time-series analysis, how can we tell which model best describes a real-life time-series such as prime ministerial popularity or economic opinion? Is it white noise, a random walk, autoregressive, or moving-average? Common sense, good theory, and lots of experience are the best guides. It is makes good sense, above all, to be wary of using short time-series, containing only a few observations; 'it takes time' for the dynamic process driving a particular time-series to reveal itself. The general advice is to observe a time-series long enough to be able to capture its characteristic variation. For an economic variable, for example, it would make no sense to follow it only during a stretch of good times. There are also technical reasons for preferring long time-series. In addition to having enough cases (degrees of freedom) to estimate the parameters in a model, the statistical theory justifying some important aspects of time-series analysis assumes we live in 'asymptopia'—that we have an infinitely large number of cases. Statisticians will quickly remind us that, in fact, we are residents of a 'finite sample land' where analyses based on a small number of cases (say less than fifty) may prove misleading.

There are good reasons not to expect any real-life time-series, short of extensive data surgery, to be white noise. Games may begin with a flip of a coin, but few are decided in that manner. We also know that many things in life follow powerful trends. They move, almost without exception, only in one direction. Prices, for example, always rise (as far as anyone can remember). Hence, we immediately seize on the change of prices and acquire a sense for the magnitude of change, called the inflation rate. Some believe that the popularity of any governing party is subject to a downward trend during its term in office because voters inevitably grow disenchanted with an incumbent government. Yet too many governments and their leaders manage to retain public confidence in a subsequent election to lend this law of political gravity much credibility. To be sure, there were periods when Margaret Thatcher appeared to be headed downhill in the popularity ratings (see Fig. 7.1), but she managed to regain the confidence of the British electorate in opinion polls as well as in general elections. Frequent ups and downs, a limited range of variation, and the absence of a long-term trend are tell-tale signs of a stationary time-series. With our British data, more powerful tests confirm that impression for both prime ministerial approval and economic evaluations.[11]

The next question is whether the dynamics of those time-series are autoregressive (AR), moving-average (MA), or both. To help us with that chore, we turn to the autocorrelations of these time-series. An autocorrelation indicates how strongly one observation is correlated with a previous observation of the same time-series. We are interested not only in the autocorrelation between observations separated by one time unit, although that is often the most telling one, but also in autocorrelations connecting more distant observations. It is only with the help of a string of autocorrelations that we can identify the data-generating process that drives a time-series. Fig. 7.2a depicts the autocorrelations up to a lag of twenty-four periods (months) for the prime ministerial approval series. We call such a diagram an *autocorrelation function* (ACF). This one has the typical shape of a stationary autoregressive process: a progressive decline to non-significant values. To decide if one autoregressive parameter is enough, we turn to the *partial autocorrelation function* (PACF) shown in Fig. 7.2b. Like a partial correlation in survey analysis, this lists the correlations between observations of the same variable over different time-points, with the influence of intermediate correlations partialled out. With only one PACF value being unequivocally significant, we conclude that only one is needed (hence the AR process for government popularity is of 'order' 1). Prime ministerial approval fluctuates in the manner of equation (6) above. That, however, will not do for the series tracking perceptions of the state of the economy. Although the ACF (Fig. 7.3a) for this series resembles the one for prime ministerial popularity, the PACF hints at greater complexity (Fig. 7.3b). The first two partial autocorrelations prove significant, prompting us to specify an autoregression of order 2. Furthermore, the significant value at lag 13 hints at the presence of a seasonal effect.

(a) Autocorrelation function

```
           -1.0 -0.8 -0.6 -0.4 -0.2  0.0  0.2  0.4  0.6  0.8  1.0
LAG   CORR. +----+----+----+----+----+----+----+----+----+----+
                                      I
  1   0.895                         +    IXXX+XXXXXXXXXXXXXXXXXXX
  2   0.782                     +        IXXXXXX+XXXXXXXXXXXXXX
  3   0.703                   +          IXXXXXXX+XXXXXXXXXX
  4   0.619                 +            IXXXXXXXX+XXXXXX
  5   0.543               +              IXXXXXXXXX+XXXX
  6   0.470               +              IXXXXXXXXX+XX
  7   0.405              +               IXXXXXXXXX+
  8   0.353              +               IXXXXXXXXX +
  9   0.279              +               IXXXXXXX   +
 10   0.189              +               IXXXXX     +
 11   0.146              +               IXXXX      +
 12   0.102              +               IXXX       +
 13   0.021              +               IX         +
 14  -0.069              +             XXI          +
 15  -0.140              +           XXXXI          +
 16  -0.205              +          XXXXXI          +
 17  -0.249              +         XXXXXXI          +
 18  -0.314            +       XXXXXXXXI            +
 19  -0.364            +     XXXXXXXXXI             +
 20  -0.380          + XXXXXXXXXXXI                 +
 21  -0.410          + XXXXXXXXXXXI                 +
 22  -0.436          +XXXXXXXXXXXXI                 +
 23  -0.443        + XXXXXXXXXXXXI                    +
 24  -0.447        + XXXXXXXXXXXXI                    +
```

(b) Partial autocorrelation function

```
           -1.0 -0.8 -0.6 -0.4 -0.2  0.0  0.2  0.4  0.6  0.8  1.0
LAG   CORR. +----+----+----+----+----+----+----+----+----+----+
                                      I
  1   0.895                         +    IXXX+XXXXXXXXXXXXXXXXXXX
  2  -0.099                         + XXI    +
  3   0.110                         +    IXXX+
  4  -0.088                         + XXI    +
  5   0.024                         +    IX  +
  6  -0.059                         +  XI    +
  7   0.016                         +    I   +
  8   0.005                         +    I   +
  9  -0.141                         XXXXI    +
 10  -0.114                         +XXXI    +
 11   0.159                         +    IXXXX
 12  -0.098                         + XXI    +
 13  -0.178                         XXXXI    +
 14  -0.129                         +XXXI    +
 15   0.002                         +    I   +
 16  -0.084                         + XXI    +
 17   0.062                         +    IXX +
 18  -0.192                         X+XXXI   +
 19   0.010                         +    I   +
 20  -0.001                         +    I   +
 21  -0.024                         +  XI    +
 22  -0.021                         +  XI    +
 23  -0.021                         +  XI    +
 24  -0.071                         + XXI    +
```

FIG. 7.2 Autocorrelation function (ACF) and partial autocorrelation function
(PACF), prime ministerial approval

(a)   Autocorrelation function

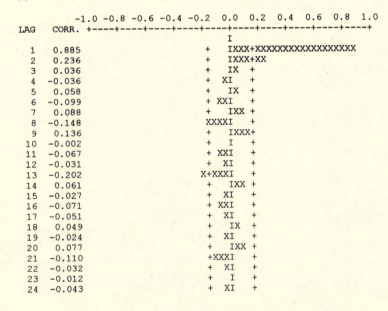

```
            -1.0 -0.8 -0.6 -0.4 -0.2  0.0  0.2  0.4  0.6  0.8  1.0
LAG   CORR. +----+----+----+----+----+----+----+----+----+----+
                                          I
 1    0.885                           +   IXXX+XXXXXXXXXXXXXXXXXXX
 2    0.834                       +       IXXXXXX+XXXXXXXXXXXXXXX
 3    0.780                    +          IXXXXXXX+XXXXXXXXXXXXX
 4    0.722                 +             IXXXXXXXX+XXXXXXXXX
 5    0.684               +               IXXXXXXXXX+XXXXXXX
 6    0.621             +                 IXXXXXXXXXX+XXXXX
 7    0.593           +                   IXXXXXXXXXXX+XXX
 8    0.525           +                   IXXXXXXXXXXX+X
 9    0.505         +                     IXXXXXXXXXXXX
10    0.474         +                     IXXXXXXXXXXXX+
11    0.426         +                     IXXXXXXXXXX  +
12    0.394         +                     IXXXXXXXXXX   +
13    0.313       +                       IXXXXXXXX        +
14    0.284       +                       IXXXXXXX         +
15    0.233       +                       IXXXXXX          +
16    0.183       +                       IXXXXX           +
17    0.135       +                       IXXX             +
18    0.093       +                       IXX              +
19    0.066       +                       IXX              +
20    0.038       +                       IX               +
21    0.010       +                       I                +
22   -0.028       +                      XI                +
23   -0.061       +                     XXI                +
24   -0.092       +                     XXI                +
```

(b)   Partial autocorrelation function

```
            -1.0 -0.8 -0.6 -0.4 -0.2  0.0  0.2  0.4  0.6  0.8  1.0
LAG   CORR. +----+----+----+----+----+----+----+----+----+----+
                                          I
 1    0.885                           +   IXXX+XXXXXXXXXXXXXXXXXXX
 2    0.236                           +   IXXX+XX
 3    0.036                           +   IX  +
 4   -0.036                           +  XI   +
 5    0.058                           +   IX  +
 6   -0.099                           + XXI   +
 7    0.088                           +   IXX +
 8   -0.148                         XXXXI     +
 9    0.136                           +   IXXX+
10   -0.002                           + I     +
11   -0.067                           + XXI   +
12   -0.031                           + XI    +
13   -0.202                         X+XXXI    +
14    0.061                           +   IXX +
15   -0.027                           + XI    +
16   -0.071                           + XXI   +
17   -0.051                           + XI    +
18    0.049                           + IX    +
19   -0.024                           + XI    +
20    0.077                           +   IXX +
21   -0.110                          +XXXI    +
22   -0.032                           + XI    +
23   -0.012                           + I     +
24   -0.043                           + XI    +
```

Fig. 7.3 Autocorrelation function (ACF) and partial autocorrelation function
(PACF), perceptions of the economy

The economy is largely a seasonal business, and many economic series are corrected for such effects, and are then reported as 'seasonally adjusted'. With monthly observations, a seasonal effect would manifest itself in pronounced correlations at lags near 12, 24, 36 months, and so on. The modest partial correlation at lag 13 is consistent with a moving-average model for seasonality. Hence for the economic series, we propose the following model:

$$z_t = \phi_1 z_{t-1} + \phi_2 z_{t-2} + \theta_{12} u_{t-12} + u_t \tag{8}$$

This model has two autoregressive terms, z_{t-1} and z_{t-2}, operating at lags 1 and 2, and one moving average term, u_{t-12}, operating at lag 12. The parameter estimates and standard errors for the model are:

$$z_t = 0.67 z_{t-1} + 0.22 z_{t-2} + 0.29 u_{t-12} + u_t \tag{9}$$
$$\quad (0.08) \qquad (0.08) \qquad (0.10)$$

For the Thatcher popularity model, the parameter estimates are:

$$z_t = 0.90 z_{t-1} + u_t \tag{10}$$
$$\quad (0.04)$$

Recall that in both instances the overall mean of the respective series (equilibrium estimate) has been subtracted from all observations. All parameter estimates are consistent with the assumption that the government popularity series and the economic series are stationary. Also, these estimates are at least twice the size of their respective standard errors and, hence, are significant beyond the 0.05 level. These are encouraging results, but conclusions about the adequacy of these ARIMA models for representing the processes generating the dynamics of the time-series depends on another diagnostic. We have to establish that the model residuals behave like white noise (u_t) to conclude that no dynamic forces have been overlooked.

A standard summary test with a chi-square distribution is the Ljung–Box Q. The Q-test statistic is calculated using autocorrelations for model residuals over several time lags. Quite understandably, significant residual autocorrelations hint at the presence of additional autoregressive or moving-average components that must be specified to provide an adequate model of the dynamics of the series. Hence, a statistically significant Q is a bad sign for the model being estimated. It compels us to reject that model and specify an alternative, typically a more comprehensive one. In contrast, an insignificant Q affirms that the model as specified is adequate. The models in expressions (9) and (10) each pass the Q-test, based on the first twenty-four autocorrelations. For prime ministerial approval, $Q(df = 23) = 30$, $p > 0.10$ and, for economic evaluations, $Q(df = 21) = 15$, $p > 0.70$.

With these satisfactory diagnostics, we can close the book on coming to grips with the dynamic behaviour of the series for Thatcher popularity and economic perceptions. However, for social scientists, building explanatory (structural) models of public support for a governing party or its leader is often the compelling objective. That calls for multivariate time-series analysis, to which we now turn. We will first consider the effect of a discrete event, called an *intervention,* on a time-series of interest.

Intervention effects

There are events, broadly speaking, that have the potential to jar an ongoing time-series with the force of an earthquake. Unlike earthquakes, however, some of those effects are intended to happen. Government policies, for example, dealing with drinking, speeding, smoking, or other hazardous activities, deliberately aim at reducing fatalities. Whether particular policies succeed in their objective is often a matter of dispute. Regarding government popularity, it is commonly assumed that international crises create 'rally round the flag' effects, with governments all too happy to wrap themselves in the national flag. Their popularity surges when crises occur, but the boost may prove short-lived. Time-series analysis can be employed to measure the surge and how it evolves over time. Moreover, time-series techniques can be marshalled to help us assess rival explanations of the hypothesized effect.

To assess the impact of an international event on government popularity, we rely on an intervention model that allows for a shift of popularity when the event first occurs and a systematic decrease (or increase) in the effect in subsequent periods (Box and Tiao 1975; McCleary and Hay 1980). For this exercise, consider the Falklands War between Britain and Argentina. Some analysts (Clarke *et al.* 1990; Norpoth 1987, 1992; but *cf.* Sanders *et al.* 1987) have argued that Britain's success in this war did much to restore public confidence in the British prime minister, Margaret Thatcher, and the governing Conservative Party. The two parameters of a model of the 'Falklands effect' on public support for Prime Minister Thatcher are denoted by omega (ω) and delta (δ), and is stated thus:

$$y_t = \omega/(1 - \delta B)\ I_t + N_t \tag{11}$$

in which y_t = Prime Minister Thatcher's popularity in the I-th month,

$\quad\quad I_t$ = the intervention variable (1 during the Falklands War and 0 elsewhere),

$\quad\quad \omega$ = the step change associated with the intervention variable,

$\quad\quad \delta$ = rate of decay of the step change,

$\quad\quad B$ = a backward-shift operator (such that, for example, $BI_t = I_{t-1}$),

$\quad\quad N_t$ = an ARIMA or 'noise' model.

As specified, this model neither presumes that the impact of the intervention alters the popularity level permanently, nor that the impact is gone the moment the intervention is over. Instead, we stipulate a decay or 'adjustment' process, not unlike radioactivity. While lingering, the popularity shift diminishes at a constant rate over time.

This 'pulse-decay' model strikes us as the most plausible model for a phenomenon like government popularity, but it represents only one of a larger family of intervention models that can be estimated using the ARIMA methodology (see Box and Tiao 1975). There are numerous ways in which an alleged intervention impact could be confounded with other effects. ARIMA models can help us weed us out some, although not all of them, by specifying the dynamic properties of a time-series. Once a time-series has been passed through the appropriate ARIMA filter, a purely random series is left, namely white noise. Such a randomization would preclude the possibility of mistaking a trend for an intervention effect. In other words, we estimate the impact of the Falklands intervention while holding constant the autoregressive nature of prime ministerial popularity as revealed by our previous ARIMA modelling exercise for this series. According to equation (10), this variable behaves like an AR(1) process, and that is what we use as the 'noise model' in equation (11). The results in Table 7.1, Model 1, indicate that the Falklands War raised Thatcher's approval ratings by a large and very significant amount (15 points). The very large δ-estimate (0.98), moreover,

Table 7.1 Intervention/transfer function models of prime ministerial approval in Britain, June 1979–December 1990

Predictor variables	Model 1		Model 2	
	Coef.	s.e.	Coef.	s.e.
Constant	34.3	4.0***	42.1	3.7***
Falklands War				
ω	15.5	3.1***	13.5	3.0***
δ	0.98	0.01***	0.94	0.06***
Economic opinion				
ω	X	X	0.11	0.03***
δ	X	X	0.53	0.18***
AR(1)	0.86	0.04***	0.86	0.04***
MA(12)	X	X	0.19	0.10*
Model diagnostics				
Ljung–Box Q	27		27	
df	23		22	
p	>0.20		>0.20	
Root mean square error	3.21		3.00	

*** $p \leq 0.01$; ** $p \leq 0.05$; * $p \leq 0.10$. One-tailed test.

Notes: X indicates that the variable is not included in the model.

Source: Monthly MORI surveys. $N = 139$.

suggests that the Prime Minister's newly acquired popularity decayed at an extremely slow pace, and a substantial part of it was still intact a year later when she called a general election.[12]

As with any intervention analysis of this kind, some will question the claim that it was the intervention of the war that did it. Given the precautions taken here in 'randomizing' the popularity series, we are quite confident about our estimates. There are no plausible rivals that could account for the massive surge of popularity coming on the heels of the military action. Yet it is debatable whether Thatcher's high ratings in the aftermath of the war are largely attributable to it. Others, such as Sanders *et al.* (1987), have proposed an alternative explanation focusing on the economy. To test this hypothesis, we require an analytic technique suitable for multiple time-series. Box and Jenkins (1976) call it *transfer function analysis*. It enables us to analyse relationships among several time-series in the presence of an ARIMA noise model.

Transfer functions

According to Harold Wilson, one of Margaret Thatcher's predecessors, 'the standing of a Government . . . depend[s] on the success of its economic policy'. And she would probably have agreed on this point; many students of elections certainly do, judging by the extent of research on 'economic voting'. The ups and downs of the economy provide the perfect foil for the ups and downs of the popularity of governing parties and their leaders.

To keep things simple, consider a single economic time-series, x_t, as it impinges on a prime ministerial popularity series, y_t. Since both variables have a t-subscript, the relationship between them may not be captured by a single correlation or regression estimate. Not only does time create dependence in manifold ways, as we have seen above, but it also 'takes time' for some effects to materialize. We must reckon with the likelihood that it is not simply today's economy that shapes our judgements of political leaders today, but also yesterday's economy, and the one before that, although to a lesser extent.

How far does the public's memory extend? How many lags, technically speaking, require attention? Unfortunately, while the time dimension opens this door of inquiry, it also slams it in our faces. Time-series data, in themselves, cannot answer those questions. If X and Y are time-series worth the name, each is bound to be so heavily autocorrelated as to obscure any clues about their correlation with each other. How can we separate the one kind of correlation from the other?

Box and Jenkins (1976) offer a rather drastic-sounding strategy, which calls for the removal of the ARIMA dynamic inherent in the exogenous time-series (X). The X-series is thereby transformed into white noise. Then the same operation is performed on the dependent series (Y), again using the ARIMA model for the X variable. Think of this as a rigorous way of controlling for the dynamic of the input series. It is only time-series transformed in this fashion, according to Box and Jenkins, that yields usable clues about possible causal relationships between the two series of interest (Norpoth 1986).

```
            -1.0 -0.8 -0.6 -0.4 -0.2  0.0  0.2  0.4  0.6  0.8  1.0
  LAG   CORR. +----+----+----+----+----+----+----+----+----+----+
                                      I
  -12   0.099                     +   IXX +
  -11   0.000                     +   I   +
  -10   0.046                     +   IX  +
   -9   0.097                     +   IXX +
   -8  -0.020                     +  XI   +
   -7   0.023                     +   IX  +
   -6  -0.002                     +   I   +
   -5   0.004                     +   I   +
   -4  -0.146                   XXXXI   +
   -3   0.002                     +   I   +
   -2   0.336                     +   IXXX+XXXX
   -1   0.153                     +   IXXXX
    0   0.233                     +   IXXX+XX
    1  -0.077                   + XXI   +
    2  -0.017                     +   I   +
    3   0.001                     +   I   +
    4   0.042                     +   IX  +
    5   0.129                     +   IXXX+
    6   0.011                     +   I   +
    7  -0.068                   + XXI   +
    8  -0.097                   + XXI   +
    9   0.087                     +   IXX +
   10  -0.016                     +   I   +
   11   0.035                     +   IX  +
   12   0.047                     +   IX  +
```

FIG. 7.4 Cross-correlations, prime ministerial approval, and perceptions of the economy

Notes: For correlations –1 to –12, perceptions of the economy lag prime ministerial approval; for correlations 1 to 12, prime ministerial approval lags perceptions of the economy.

In the case at hand, we can take advantage of the ARIMA work done above for the economic series in (9) and *pre-whiten* that time-series. Then we use the same ARIMA model to purge the popularity time-series. Fig. 7.4 depicts the correlations between those transformed time-series, each lagged up to twelve time-periods (months). Such cross-correlations speak to the nature of the relationship between the variables without the confounding effect of autocorrelations. In our example, there are three consecutive significant cross-correlations between lagged economic perceptions and prime ministerial approval, but none between lagged approval and economic perceptions. This suggests that economic opinion influences prime ministerial popularity in the manner of a distributed-lag model:

$$y_t = \omega/(1 - \delta B)x_t + e_t \quad |\delta| < 1.0 \tag{12}$$

Readers will notice that (12) looks just like the intervention model in (11) with parameters ω and δ appearing here as well. That is deceptive, however, since X is not a variable that comes to life only on rare occasions. With X taking on values throughout the entire time-period under consideration, ω and δ describe an influence constantly at work. The moment X moves, Y does too, with a magnitude set by the ω–parameter. Then a moment later, that movement of X triggers yet a further reaction in Y, according to the δ-parameter, and so on. Equation (12) is a terse way of summarizing a lengthy process of after-effects.[13] The behavioural assumption of this model is that the public adapts its opinion of the prime minister (Y) in response to changes in its opinion about the economy (X). A large estimate for δ (i.e. $\delta \rightarrow 1.0$) implies that the public reacts very slowly to such changes while a small estimate (i.e. $\delta \rightarrow 0.0$) implies rapid adjustment.

It would not be wise to assume that the errors in (12) are white noise. Our close examination of the popularity series above has revealed its autoregressive nature, and it would be surprising if that were no longer present when we relate economic opinion to prime ministerial popularity. Besides specifying an AR(1) process for the errors, we also provide for the possibility of an MA(12) effect owing to the seasonal nature of economic opinion. Model 2 in Table 7.1 presents the full set of estimates for the multivariate transfer function intervention model of prime ministerial popularity with this ARIMA noise model.

There is evidence indeed for a distributed-lag model of economic opinion. The British public not only factors today's economy into their popularity judgements, but also the economy of yesterday and before, although to a lesser degree. The estimates indicate that a 20 per cent upward shift in the balance of opinion regarding the state of the economy (on a scale ranging from -100 to $+100$) is sufficient to raise the prime minister's approval rating immediately by 2.2 per cent (0.11×20). The long-run impact is larger; calculated as $\omega/(1 - \delta)$, the parameter estimates indicate that such a shift in evaluations of the economy will eventually raise prime ministerial approval by 4.7 per cent ($2.2/(1 - 0.53)$).

However economic effects are not the whole story. To return to the dispute reviewed above, the analysis clearly shows that the favourable shift in opinion about the economy that occurred in Spring 1982 does not explain away the effect of the Falklands intervention. Controlling for the impact of economic evaluations, our multivariate transfer function intervention model reveals that the immediate impact of the war on Mrs Thatcher's approval rating was very large and statistically significant (13.5 points), and, as indicated by the large δ parameter (0.94), the effect lingered for many months after the war ended.

This extended example demonstrates the flexibility of Box–Jenkins models to deal with both discrete interventions and lagged relationships among time-series, while holding constant the dynamic nature of time-series. What these models do not do is to take into account any long-term equilibrium relationships between variables that are growing together over time, since they focus on short-term effects after such variables have been rendered stationary by differencing them. Next, we consider the problem of incorporating such effects.

Non-stationarity and Error-correction Models

In the preceding section, we introduced the distinction between stationary and non-stationary time-series. This distinction is very important because assuming time-series are stationary when, in fact, they are non-stationary, can produce very misleading results. The situation where both the dependent variable and the independent variables are non-stationary invites 'spurious regressions' in which regression coefficients appear statistically significant even when the variables are, in fact, wholly unrelated. Reviewing their Monte Carlo experiments with artificial data sets, Granger and Newbold (1986: 208) conclude: 'When random walks or integrated moving average processes are involved, the chances of "discovering" a spurious relationship using conventional test procedures are very high indeed, increasing with the number . . . of independent variables included in the regression.' Social scientists working with non-stationary data thus run a risk of 'getting it wrong'. Moreover, as many time-series are non-stationary, the risk is substantial. As Price describes (this volume), Hendry (1980) illustrated this problem in an amusing example in which he showed that inflation in Britain appeared to be strongly driven by cumulative rainfall!

Intuitions concerning the threat to inference posed by the spurious regressions problem are not new (cf. Keynes 1939), and, as observed above, Box and Jenkins emphasize that diagnosing data for non-stationarity should be the first step in ARIMA modelling. Their recommendation that analysts difference data which are believed to be mean non-stationary has long been standard practice. If a series is characterized by a *stochastic trend*, as is the case for a random walk, then differencing it will render it stationary.[14] However, there is a price to pay for differencing variables, namely that any long-run relationships between them are necessarily obfuscated (Beck 1992: 68–9).

Are we, then, bound to be caught between the methodological 'rock' of spurious regressions and the theoretical 'hard place' of ignoring long-term relationships? The answer is 'not necessarily'.

Following pioneering work by Sargan (1984) and other 'LSE' econometricians,[15] Engle and Granger (1987) have proved, via the Engle–Granger 'representation theorem', that it is possible to analyse non-stationary series that *cointegrate* using an *error-correction* model specification. Simply stated, cointegrated series are in a state of dynamic equilibrium such that they 'travel together' in the long run. For example, it appears that during the 1990s, party identification, voting intentions, and evaluations of the party leader were cointegrated for the Conservatives in Britain (Clarke *et al.* 1997). Thus, if some voters decide that they will not vote Conservative because, say, of some short-run political scandal affecting a backbench Conservative MP, much of this loss of support would eventually be restored if Conservative partisanship and support for the party leader among the electorate were not greatly affected by the scandal. These variables would, in effect, compensate for the loss of support and help to restore it after a period of time. We return to this example below.

Obviously, if two series are in equilibrium while growing over time, they will not drift apart or significantly diverge from each other. Thus cointegrated series have the property that a linear combination of them is a stationary variable. It is important to emphasize that cointegration cannot be assumed, but must be demonstrated empirically. If, however, one concludes that non-stationary series cointegrate, then they may be modelled in error-correction form.

These considerations suggest a straightforward approach for modelling two or more time-series suspected of being non-stationary:

1. Test the series to determine if they are non-stationary.
2(*a*). If all of the series are stationary, model them in level form.
2(*b*). If two or more series are non-stationary, test to determine if they cointegrate.
3(a). If the non-stationary series do not cointegrate, model them in differenced form.
3(*b*). If the non-stationary series cointegrate, model them in error-correction form.

This approach starts with testing time-series for non-stationarity. This may be done using *unit-root tests*. Over the past decade, econometricians have developed a variety of these tests (see Enders 1995: ch. 4). The most popular is the Dickey–Fuller test (Dickey *et al.* 1986) where the null hypothesis is that a series has a unit-root, that is, the coefficient for z_{t-1} in equation (4) is 1.0. Rejection of the null implies that the series is stationary. Although the

Dickey–Fuller test statistic is a simple t-ratio, note that the critical values for the test are non-standard, and vary depending upon whether one includes a constant or deterministic trend in the regression analysis that generates the unit-root test statistic. Appropriate critical values may be found in a number of the more recent econometric texts (for example, Charemza and Deadman 1992; Enders 1995). Some 'state-of-the-art' software packages automate the unit-root testing procedure, providing menus of tests and test options, and displaying critical values at given probability values for estimated parameters.

Assuming that unit-root tests prompt the inference that the series are non-stationary, the next step is to determine if they cointegrate. Engle and Granger (1987; see also Engle and Yoo 1991) suggest that a suitable procedure to test if two series, z_t and x_t, cointegrate is to regress one series on the other. The regression is:

$$z_t = c_0 + c_1 x_t \tag{13}$$

If z and x are cointegrated, it is expected that this regression will have a 'large' R^2, and the estimated coefficient c_1 will be statistically significant and properly signed. The next step is to perform a unit-root test on the residuals of (13)—a linear combination of z_t and x_t—to determine if they constitute a stationary series. This procedure is very straightforward, and is appropriate if there are only two series being tested for cointegration. However, if one is working with more than two series, this opens the possibility of multiple cointegrating relationships among these series. If one believes that the hypothesis of multiple cointegrating relationships among three or more variables is plausible, more sophisticated testing procedures developed by Johansen (1988) may be employed. These procedures are quite complicated, and explicating them is beyond the scope of this chapter (see Harris 1995: ch. 5; Price, this volume). As in the case of unit-root tests, some newer software packages include 'canned' versions of the Johansen tests.

If one concludes that the series of interest are non-stationary and cointegrate, it is appropriate to model them in error-correction form. Assuming we have two series, z_t and x_t, and hypothesizing that the former is a function of the latter, the error-correction model will be:

$$\Delta z_t = \beta_0 + \beta_1 \Delta x_t + \beta_2 \text{ECM}_{t-1} + u_t \tag{14}$$

where: Δ = difference operator (i.e. $x_t - x_{t-1}$),
  β_0 = constant,
  β_1, β_2 = regression coefficients,
  ECM = error-correction mechanism, $z_t - c_0 - c_1 x_t$, where c_0 and c_1 are
  estimated by the cointegrating regression (13),
  u_t = error term.

In (14), Δz_t and Δx_t are stationary variables (made so by differencing), and the short-term impact of x on z is estimated by β_1. The ECM also is a stationary variable (measured as the residuals of the cointegrating regression which have been tested for stationarity). The ECM operates with a lag of one period, and it captures the long-term relationship between z and x. In keeping with the idea that z and x are in dynamic equilibrium (they move together in the long run), it is expected that the ECM's coefficient in (14), β_2, will carry a negative sign and be less than 1.0 in magnitude. The negative sign implies that shocks to z at time t will be adjusted or 're-equilibriated' in subsequent periods by the cointegrating relationship between z and x. The adjustment rate is determined by the magnitude of β_2. For example, if $\beta_2 = -0.5$, it means that 50 per cent of a shock (from whatever source) to z at time t will be eroded at time $t + 1$. Fifty per cent of what remains of the shock at $t + 1$ will be eroded at $t + 2$, and so on into the future. If the error process, u_t, meets standard (Gauss–Markov) assumptions, the parameters in (14) may be estimated using OLS regression.

The Conservative crash

To provide an empirical example of constructing and testing an error-correction model, we analyse support for the governing British Conservative Party and the prime minister, John Major, over the period January 1992–November 1995. As Fig. 7.5 shows, shortly after the April 1992 general election, the percentage of people stating that they intended to vote Conservative in the next general election began to decline sharply. This was also true of the percentage thinking of themselves as Conservative party identifiers, and the percentage reporting that they approved of Major's performance as prime minister.[16] The correlations (r) between, on the one hand, Conservative vote intentions, and, on the other hand, prime ministerial approval and Conservative party identification, are +0.94 and +0.87, respectively. These strong correlations suggest the possibility that the three variables cointegrate. This possibility is consonant with recent studies of electoral choice in Britain (see Stewart and Clarke 1992, for example) suggesting that prime ministerial approval and party identification have important causal effects on vote intentions.

To determine if the three variables do cointegrate, we first perform unit-root tests to see if they are non-stationary. Table 7.2 shows that all three variables are non-stationary in their original level form, but become stationary when first-differenced, that is, they are $I(1)$, or integrated of order 1. Table 7.2 also displays the results of unit-root tests for personal economic expectations [17] and interest rates, two variables which have been prominent in widely cited models of the political economy of governing party support in

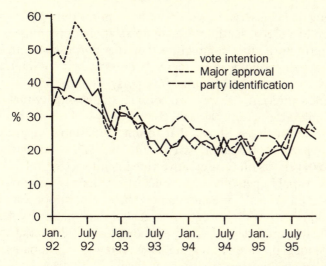

Fig. 7.5 Conservative trends, January 1992–November 1995

Notes: Vote intention and Major approval, $r = 0.94$; vote intention and party identification, $r = 0.87$; Major approval and party identification $r = 0.83$.

Britain developed by Sanders and his colleagues (Sanders 1993; Sanders *et al.* 1987). According to these models, interest rates have strong effects on personal economic expectations and, in turn, such expectations do much to drive the dynamics of governing party support. Like Conservative vote intentions, prime ministerial approval, and Conservative Party identification, personal economic expectations and interest rates are non-stationary in level form but are stationary when first-differenced.

Table 7.2 Unit-root tests for stationarity of Conservative vote intentions, prime ministerial approval, party identification, subjective economic evaluations, and interest rates, January 1992–November 1995

Variables	Original series	Differenced series
Conservative vote intentions	−1.86**	−8.84
Prime ministerial approval	−1.81**	−5.74
Conservative Party identification	−2.00**	−10.30
Personal economic expectations	−2.40**	−7.98
Interest rates	−2.51**	−4.61

Notes: ** fails to reject null hypothesis of unit root, $p \leq 0.05$ (critical value = −2.93). Tests conducted with constant but without trend. Tests with trend reject null hypothesis in all cases.

The finding that Conservative vote intentions, prime ministerial approval, and Conservative party identification are non-stationary permits us to proceed to determine if they cointegrate. For this purpose, we utilize the Engle–Granger methodology and regress Conservative vote intentions on prime minister approval and Conservative party identification. Also, given its prominence in recent research, we consider the possibility that the personal economic expectations variable cointegrates with these three series. The regression analyses show that prime ministerial approval and Conservative party identification have strong ($R^2 = 0.91$), statistically significant ($p \leq 0.001$) effects on Conservative vote intentions (see Table 7.3).[18] In contrast, the variable personal economic expectations is insignificant and negatively signed. As is required for cointegration, a unit-root test indicates that the residuals from these regression analyses are stationary. Based on these results, we conclude that vote intentions, prime ministerial approval, and party identification are cointegrated. It is therefore appropriate to model their interrelationships in error-correction form.

Table 7.3 Cointegrating regressions, Conservative vote intentions, prime ministerial approval, Conservative party identification, and personal economic expectations, January 1992–November 1995

	Model	
Predictor variables	A	B
Constant	0.05	−1.49
Prime ministerial approval (t)	0.45 (0.40)[a]	0.47 (0.42)[a]
Party identification (t)	0.48 (0.56)[a]	0.50 (0.56)[a]
Personal economic expectations (t)	X	−0.05 (−0.04)
R^2	0.91	0.91
Unit root test, residuals	−5.45**	−5.50***

Notes: Engle–Yoo 'three-step' estimates are shown in parentheses. a indicates that $p \leq 0.001$. ** rejects null hypothesis of unit root, 95% critical value = −3.93; *** rejects null hypothesis of the unit root, 95% critical value = −4.34. X indicates that the variable is not included in the model.

The error-correction model of Conservative vote intentions is specified as follows:

$$\Delta CVI_t = \beta_0 + \beta_1 \Delta PM_t + \beta_2 \Delta CPID_t + \beta_3 ECM_{t-i} + \beta_4 \Delta PERSEC_{t-i} + \beta_5 \Delta INTR_{t-i} + \beta_{6-k} SHOCKS_{t-i} + u_t \tag{15}$$

in which CVI = Conservative vote intentions,

        PM = prime ministerial approval,

        CPID = Conservative party identification,

        ECM = error-correction mechanism,

        PERSEC = personal economic expectations,

        INTR = interest rates,

        SHOCKS = various interventions that may have influenced Conservative vote intentions,

        u = error term ($\sim N(0,\sigma^2)$),

        Δ = differencing operator,

        β_0 = constant,

        β_{1-k} = regression coefficients,

        $t - i$ = time lag.

The error-correction mechanism (ECM) captures the cointegrating relationship among vote intentions, prime ministerial approval, and party identification, and is measured as the residuals from the cointegrating regression of Conservative vote intentions, prime ministerial approval, and Conservative party identification (Table 7.3).

Although theory does not specify the exact lags when the continuous variables (personal economic expectations, for example) influence Conservative support, it is plausible that their effects occur either contemporaneously or with only minimal delays. Accordingly, preliminary versions of model (15) were estimated with these variables operating at lags of 0–2 periods. These analyses also included various prominent interventions that may have affected Conservative support. Some of them—for example, the currency crisis in September 1992 and the re-election of John Major as Conservative leader in July 1995—proved insignificant.[19]

Parameter estimates for the final version of the model reveal that prime ministerial approval, Conservative party identification, personal economic expectations, and interest rates all exerted statistically significant effects on Conservative vote intentions (see Table 7.4). As anticipated, the effects of the first three of these variables are positive; for example, as prime ministerial approval increases so does the governing party's share of vote intention. In contrast, the impact of interest rate hikes are predictably negative; as rates increase, support for the governing party declines. Conservative vote intentions were also affected by various interventions, including the 1992 election, the Maastricht crisis, and the 1994 local elections-change in Labour leadership.[20] As expected, the impact of the first of these interventions was positive, whereas the impacts of the latter two were negative. Finally, controlling for all other predictor variables, the parameter estimate for the error-correction mechanism is significant and appropriately negative. The size of this parameter (−0.75) indicates the existence of a powerful cointegrating relationship between Conservative vote intentions, on the one hand, and prime ministerial approval and Conservative party identification, on the other.

As we can see from the table, shocks to vote intentions, from whatever source, in month *t* are adjusted (eroded) in subsequent months at the rate of 75 per cent per month by this cointegrating relationship. For example, if an intervention drove Conservative vote intentions up by 10 points in a given month, *ceteris paribus*, 7.5 of those points would evaporate in the following month. This strong tendency for the variables that comprise the cointegrating relationship to 'stick together' indicates the extent to which the long-term dynamics of Conservative vote intentions are governed by movements in levels of prime ministerial approval and the percentage of Conservative party identifiers in the electorate.

The story told by our error-correction model of the aggregate dynamics of Conservative vote intentions since 1992 is, thus, both straightforward and consistent with the results of recent individual-level analyses of British vot-

Table 7.4 Error-correction model of Conservative vote intentions, March 1992–November 1995

Predictor variables	β	s.e.
Constant	−0.30	0.21*
ΔPrime ministerial approval (*t*)	0.26	0.53***
ΔConservative party identification (*t*)	0.18	0.10**
Error-correction mechanism (*t*−1)	−0.75	0.10***
ΔPersonal economic expectations (*t*-1)	0.08	0.04**
ΔInterest rates (*t*)	−2.36	0.66***
Maastricht crisis (*t*)	−2.42	1.51*
1992 election (*t*)	4.49	0.96***
1994 local elections-Labour leader (*t*)	−3.24	1.00***
Model diagnostics		
R^2		0.80
s.e.e.		1.33
Serial correlation		
d		2.13
LM		16.62
Functional form		0.24
Normality		0.38
Heteroscedasticity		
General		6.63**
ARCH(1)		0.00

*** $p \le 0.01$; ** $p \le 0.05$; * $p \le 0.10$. One-tailed test.

Notes: The *LM* test, as well as the tests for functional form, normality, and heteroscedasticity are χ^2. Degrees of freedom are $LM = 12$; functional form = 1; normality = 2. Heteroscedasticity: general = 1; ARCH(1) = 1; * $p \le .05$.

ing behaviour (Stewart and Clarke 1992). But can we believe the story? Confidence in the model is enhanced by its explanatory power (adjusted R^2 = 0.80) and its satisfactory performance on an extensive battery of diagnostic tests for serial correlation, functional form, normality, and heteroscedasticity.[21] Such diagnostic tests are strongly recommended (Hendry 1995), and are easily performed using some of the newer econometric software packages.

Finally, it is important to note that we have thus far assumed that prime ministerial approval and Conservative party identification are weakly exogenous to Conservative vote intentions. This means that the former two variables affect the latter at time t, but not vice versa.[22] In a single equation analysis such as that presented above, weak exogeneity is required for making valid inferences about the effects of the hypothesized independent variables in a cointegrating relationship (here prime ministerial approval and party identification) and the dependent variable (vote intentions). If weak exogeneity does not obtain, then a more complicated multiple equation approach to analysing cointegrated series is required (see Harris 1995: ch. 5). Intuitively, if weak exogeneity does not apply, then simultaneous feedback mechanisms from the dependent variable to the predictor variables will distort the estimates, making statistical inference unreliable.

The weak exogeneity test for an error-correction model requires that we develop models for the hypothesized weakly exogenous variables. In the present case, these are models for prime ministerial approval and Conservative party identification.[23] The weak exogeneity test uses these models in a two-step procedure (Charemza and Deadman 1992: 255–6). The first step involves re-estimating the models of prime ministerial approval and Conservative party identification with the error-correction mechanism included as a predictor. If weak exogeneity exists (that is, prime ministerial approval and Conservative party identification are not contemporaneously influenced by Conservative voting intentions), then the coefficient for the ECM should be insignificant in these models. If so, then we can proceed to the second step, which involves entering the residuals from these models for prime ministerial approval and party identification (estimated without the insignificant ECM) as predictors in the error-correction model of interest, in this case the model of Conservative vote intentions (equation 15). Weak exogeneity also requires that these residuals are insignificant.

Applying this two-step testing procedure in our analysis of Conservative party support reveals that all coefficients of interest are insignificant ($p \geq$ 0.10), results which are consistent with the hypothesis that evaluations of the performance of the prime minister and party identification are weakly exogenous to vote intentions. Inferences regarding the effects of prime ministerial approval and party identification on vote intentions based on a single-equation analysis, such as that presented in Table 7.4, are thereby warranted.

Conclusion: It's Time to Model Political and Social Dynamics

For a novice, time-series analysis may appear as an arcane, obscure art, the mysteries of which are accessible only to the high priests of econometrics. This need not be the case. In this chapter, we have discussed procedures involved in the specification, testing, and diagnosis of transfer function/ intervention models and error-correction models. These procedures are logical and straightforward, and anyone with a solid grounding in basic regression methods should have no difficulty in applying them in their research. And anyone wishing to learn more about ARIMA and ECM modelling will find that the time-series literature now contains a number of excellent treatments of these techniques. We have referred to several of these works in this chapter, and we encourage readers to consult them. Equally important is the availability of user-friendly computer software. Programs implementing garden-variety OLS regression are, of course, legion, and they can be employed for a number of the analytic tasks discussed in this chapter. However, there are also several programs designed explicitly for time-series applications, and they contain 'canned' routines for graphing data, estimating the parameters of ARIMA models, conducting tests for unit-roots and cointegration, and performing post-estimation model diagnostics. The major features of some of these specialized time-series programs are described below.

Last, but certainly not least, are questions of data availability. In economics, the aggregate time-series data needed to estimate the parameters of a variety of theoretically important models have long been readily available. This has not been true in fields such as political science or sociology, but, fortunately, the time-series data required to address a range of theoretical controversies are now starting to come on line. An excellent example of the data unavailability problem in political science is the American 'macropartisanship' controversy, in which debates concerning the aggregate dynamics of party identification have been fuelled by the absence of data generated using conventional measures of that concept (see Clarke *et al.* 1997). In this regard, the party identification data used in the ECM analyses presented above were gathered precisely to make it possible to use time-series techniques to address long-standing theoretical controversies concerning the determinants of electoral choice in Britain. As additional time-series data become available, powerful procedures such as the ARIMA and ECM techniques discussed in this chapter will provide social scientists with the analytic leverage needed to address a variety of theoretically interesting problems.

Largely because dynamic analysis is so integral to the development of good social science theory, time-series methods are becoming increasingly central to understanding social and political processes. The fact that the statistical theory and applications are also rapidly developing in this area further serves to make this an interesting and stimulating topic for students of politics, the economy, and society.

Software

The computer software for doing the kinds of time-series analyses discussed in this chapter can be divided, broadly, into two categories. First, there are general statistical packages such as *BMDP*, *SAS*, and *SPSS* which incorporate modules for doing time-series analysis. These well-known packages are available for micro-, mini-, and mainframe computers, and can be used with several different operating systems. The time-series modules in *BMDP* and *SAS* contain the full set of univariate ARIMA and transfer function/intervention modelling routines described in this chapter.

A second category is comprised of specialized, and perhaps less familiar, time-series programs, written especially for use on microcomputers using DOS or WINDOWS operating systems. Four such programs are *EVIEWS*, *MICROFIT*, *PCGIVE/PCFIML*, and *RATS*. All these programs have very good-to-excellent graphics capabilities for displaying time-series data, and the first three are explicitly designed to facilitate unit-root and cointegration (including Johansen) tests. Error-correction models are easily specified in all four progams. *RATS* has a module for estimating univariate ARIMA and transfer function/intervention models, and a special add-on procedure (called *CATS in RATS*) for Johansen procedures. Consistent with the 'LSE' approach to econometrics (Gilbert 1990; Hendry 1995), all four programs enable one to perform extensive batteries of diagnostic tests. *EVIEWS*, *MICROFIT*, and *PCGIVE/PCFIML* automate many of these tests, whereas *RATS* makes a number of them available as 'third-party-written' sub-routines. All these programs incorporate a wide variety of 'canned' procedures, and *EVIEWS*, *PCGIVE/PCFIML*, and *RATS* have sophisticated programming capacities for users who wish to write their own code. Their menu-driven or 'point-and-click' interfaces make these programs extremely easy to use.

Notes

1. See e.g. Clarke and Stewart (1994); Clarke *et al.* (1997); MacKuen *et al.* (1992); Norpoth (1992, 1996).
2. e.g. Boswell and Sweat (1991), and Pollins (1996).
3. See Castles (1982); Hibbs (1987); Swank (1992).
4. e.g. Page and Shapiro (1983); Stimson *et al.* (1995); Wlezien (1996).
5. Strictly speaking, the economic opinion question ascertains perceptions about the future state of the economy. However, this is not the place to enter the debate concerning which kinds of economic evaluations (retrospective or prospective) have the largest effects on party support. On this debate, see Clarke and Stewart (1994); MacKuen *et al.* (1992); Norpoth (1996); and Sanders *et al.* (1987).
6. For now, think of 'integration' as addition. It is by adding (or integrating) random outcomes that we get from white noise to a random walk.
7. It is often a puzzle to students who meet this model for the first time to understand why the exercise of flipping coins creates a series which is non-stationary, when this most commonly implies that the series has no constant mean, but rather drifts upwards (or downwards) without limit. After all, if heads is equally as likely as tails, how can the proportion of heads (or tails) drift upwards over time? The answer is that a random walk has a constant mean but does not have a constant variance, so the magnitude of the latter grows larger as the series extends over time. In the technical jargon, a random walk is mean stationary and variance non-stationary.
8. It is very confusing that, for purely notational reasons, the moving-average parameter θ typically carries a negative sign in ARIMA representations; i.e. $z_t = u_t - \theta u_{t-1}$. To keep matters simple, we have assigned a positive sign to θ.
9. The values of z_t and z_{t-1} in equation (6) have been adjusted for that level, the overall mean (μ) of the time-series.
10. The autocorrelation for lag 1, for example, would be the correlation between the observation of a time-series at any time t and the observation of that series one unit earlier in time, i.e. $t-1$.
11. As discussed in the next section of this chapter, unit-root tests are a more compelling way to establish stationarity or its absence. For the two time-series considered here, we can reject the unit-root (random walk) hypothesis and conclude that both of these series are stationary.
12. To keep the model simple, we have limited the impact of the Falklands variable to just one month, May 1982, when most of the action occurred. For more complex intervention models that capture the varied effects of that war during its three-month duration, see Clarke *et al.* (1990), and Norpoth (1987, 1992).
13. This transformation is known in econometrics as a 'Koyck lag scheme' and it may be motivated theoretically by adaptive expectations and partial adjustment models. See e.g. Gujarati (1995: 592–612).

14. An example of a deterministic trend model is $z_t = \beta_0 + \beta_1 t + u_t$ where: β_0 and β_1 are coefficients, u_t is a error term ($\sim N(0, \sigma^2)$) and t takes on the values 1, 2, 3, etc. for successive time-periods. See Enders (1995: 166–85).

15. For a review of the work of the LSE econometricians, see Gilbert 1990.

16. These monthly survey data were gathered by Harold D. Clarke, Marianne Stewart, and Paul Whiteley with research funds provided by the National Science Foundation (grants nos. SES-9309018 and SES-9600018). Fieldwork for the surveys was conducted in Britain by Gallup under the direction of Robert Wybrow. Neither the NSF nor Gallup is responsible for the analyses and interpretations of the data presented in this chapter. For the wordings of questions measuring vote intentions, prime ministerial approval, and party identification, see Clarke *et al.* (1997: nn. 16, 17, 18).

17. The personal economic expectations data are generated from monthly Gallup surveys. For question wording, see Clarke *et al.* (1997: n. 27).

18. Since c_1 is biased in finite samples and has a non-standard distribution, Engle and Yoo (1991) have proposed a procedure for adjusting the estimated values of c_1 and its standard error (see Harris 1995: 56).

19. Additional analyses showed that the currency crisis and Major's re-election as Conservative leader exerted indirect effects on Conservative vote intentions by influencing prime ministerial approval and Conservative party identification. See Clarke *et al.* (1998).

20. This variable captures the compound effect of the political fallout following Conservative losses in the 1994 local elections, the death of John Smith, leader of the Labour Party, and the likely election of Tony Blair as the new Labour leader.

21. The only exception is the general test for heteroscedasticity. The Breusch–Pagan (1979) test reported in Table 7.4 is significant at the 0.05 level; an alternative test, proposed by White (1980), is insignificant.

22. If variable x is weakly exogenous to variable z, then z does not affect x contemporaneously, although it is possible that z affects x with a lag. If z does not affect x either contemporaneously or with a lag, x is said to be *strongly exogenous* to z. See e.g. Hendry (1995: ch. 5).

23. These models are discussed in Clarke *et al.* (1997).

8

COINTEGRATION AND MODELLING THE LONG RUN

SIMON PRICE

This chapter looks at an issue of tremendous importance to anyone intending to examine relationships between time-series data. The special focus is on *non-stationary*, usually trended, data. In many cases, this is the norm, rather than the exception. For instance, most macroeconomic time-series, such as GDP, unemployment, or prices are trended. It holds in other disciplines too; for example, government popularity tends to follow a long-run trend. Even where this is not the case, the variables that affect popularity (like unemployment and inflation) are often trended. The problem with these kinds of data is that the standard procedures can easily lead analysts hopelessly astray; nothing is easier than getting R^2's of over 0.95 and t-ratios well over 4 are equally easy to find. But these statistics will often be totally spurious (Granger and Newbold 1974). One example using real data makes the point. The log of GDP ly_t is regressed on labour costs lc_t, a constant, and a time trend t for the period from the first quarter of 1980 to the second quarter of 1996:

$$ly_t = \alpha + \beta_1 lc + \beta_2 t \qquad (1)$$

Presumably, higher labour costs reduce GDP but the economy still grows, so $\beta_1 < 0$ and $\beta_2 > 0$. Sure enough we find:

$$ly_t = 6.25 - 0.52 lc_t + 0.0068 t$$
$$(257.75)\ (-4.20)\ (16.61)$$

The 't-ratios' are pretty good! What is more, the coefficients show the right signs and 'plausible' magnitudes. The R^2 is 0.976. A clue that something is wrong, however, is given by the Durbin–Watson (DW) statistic, which measures first-order autocorrelation. It is a mere 0.174, only just above the lowest possible value. In fact, this regression is completely meaningless. The GDP data are for France, but the labour costs data are for Germany. Any connection is at best tenuous and certainly not reliable for policy; no policymaker in France would get far by assuming that higher costs in Germany will reduce French GDP. Even so, the regression seems to fit very well. The simple explanation is that both GDP and labour costs are heavily trended. The correlation is spurious. The lesson is that regression analysis becomes a minefield in the presence of trends or non-stationarity. However, the good news is that if a relationship does exist, powerful techniques are available to unearth it and estimate the parameters with great precision.

In this chapter, we build upon the discussion of time-series analysis, stationarity, and order of integration in the previous chapter. Our focus is on explaining how non-stationarity implies the possibility of long-run or *cointegrating* relationships between variables. If these exist, there are several ways of estimating them, which makes the econometrician's life simpler, as we are often mainly interested in long-run phenomena. But if there are in fact no such relationships, we may find ourselves profoundly misled by the standard techniques available. Thus, testing for cointegration is the vital first step in analysing non-stationary data. After showing how to do this, we discuss the important issue of *identification,* in which there are several long-run relationships at work. Although this complicates matters, it also enables us to shed light on the workings of the system of equations we are examining. Very little prior knowledge is assumed other than basic statistical concepts such as the expectations operator and the least squares estimator. Some of the concepts are introduced on a fairly cursory basis to avoid reiterating material presented elsewhere in this volume.

Non-stationarity, Spurious Regressions, and the Long Run

Stationarity and unit roots

A variable which is stationary (in mean) has a mean value which, in the long run, is constant. That is, no matter how large the sample, the unconditional mean of the sample tends to a constant value. This excludes many variables, especially anything that grows over time. As this covers most macroeconomic variables—such as GDP, unemployment in many countries, real consumption, real wages—economists have been concerned to understand the implications of non-stationarity.

An important class of non-stationary variables are those with a *unit root.*[1] To understand this rather technical term, consider a variable which can be described by a finite-order AR process,[2] such as:

$$y_t = \beta_0 + \beta_1 y_{t-1} + \beta_2 y_{t-2} + \ldots + \beta_n y_{t-n} + \delta_t \tag{2}$$

One way of thinking about this expression is that it is a *lag polynomial.* The lag operator $L^i(x_t)$ simply means that x is lagged i times. For many purposes, lag operators can be treated as if they were variables. In particular, the nth-order lag polynomial $\beta(L)$ has n solutions, or roots; if one of these is unity (one of $\beta_i = 1$), then we say that the process has a unit root. What this means is that (2) can be written with expressions like $(1 - L)$ in it, but $(1 - L)y_t$ is simply the first difference of y_t, usually expressed as Δy_t. In other words, a process including a unit root can be expressed in first-difference form without any loss of information.

The unit root also defines the borderline stability condition. If the roots of the equation have an absolute value greater than 1 (that is, they 'lie outside the unit circle'), the equation is stable in the sense that it has a well-defined long-run value to which it will converge. If any of the roots lie on, or within, the unit circle, the process is unstable. In the case where $n = 1$, the condition is very simple, as we shall see shortly.

We can explore the rather profound implications of a unit root by taking two simple examples of the form:

$$y_t = \alpha + \beta y_{t-1} + v_t \qquad (3)$$

In one case $\beta = 1$ and in the other $\beta < 1$. These two cases differ hugely in their properties; v_t here is the error term, not necessarily white noise but invertible. If $-1 > \beta < 1$ then the (single) root lies outside the unit circle (it is β^{-1}) and the process is stable. In particular, it has a well-defined long-run solution. To see this, let the long-run value of y, $y^\star$, be where:

$$y^\star = y_t = y_{t-i} \quad \forall_i \qquad (4)$$

and where the error is zero.[3] Then the long-run value of y is simply:

$$y^\star = \frac{\alpha}{1 - \beta} \qquad (5)$$

This can easily be generalized to richer lag structures, and (as we shall see later) to include other explanatory variables. Clearly, if $\beta = 1$, $y^\star$ is undefined. Less obviously, if $\beta > 1$, while $y^\star$ is now defined, the equation has an explosive solution. To make all this more concrete, we will look at a stationary series y_{1t} generated by the process:

$$y_{1t} = 5 + 0.95y_{1t-1} + v_t \qquad (6)$$

As the root lies outside the unit circle, this process is stationary.[4] Fig. 8.1 illustrates one realization. The long-run value is 100. Note how y_{1t} cycles round that value. There is a lot of persistence in the data, reflecting the high value of β, but y_{1t} tends to return ('revert') to the mean. It is pretty obvious that this variable is stationary.

By contrast, y_{2t} has a unit root:

$$y_{2t} = 0.5 + y_{2t-1} + v_t \qquad (7)$$

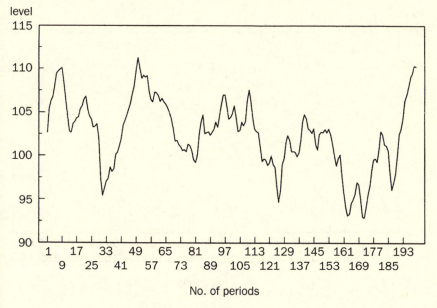

Fig. 8.1 A stationary series (equation 6)

As Fig. 8.2 shows, the series grows without limit. The reason is easy to see. The equation could be rewritten as:

$$\Delta y_{2t} = 0.5 + v_t \qquad (8)$$

This is an example of a random walk with drift. The 'drift' is the constant, which ensures that y_{2t} grows at an average of 0.5 per period. Thus, there is a well-defined long-run trend. But exactly where the series ends up is impossible to forecast, as the random error will have an effect which quite literally persists for ever. By contrast, in the previous case, any shock decays at a rate of 5 per cent per period.[5]

Nevertheless, this non-stationary series, by virtue of the unit root, can easily be transformed into a stationary series, as Fig. 8.3 shows. If there were two unit roots, then the series (such as the one illustrated in Fig. 8.4) is not only trended, but is rising at an increasing rate. In other words, the first difference is trended but the second difference is stationary.

We may now define the *order of integration* of a variable, which is the number of times a series needs to be differenced in order to induce stationarity. We refer to this as $I(J)$ where J is the order of integration. Thus, if $y_t \sim I(1)$ then Δy_t is stationary ($I(0)$). It should be clear from the plots above that the order of integration of a series is vital information. We can draw one conclusion straightaway. If we have two variables, say y_t and x_t, of different

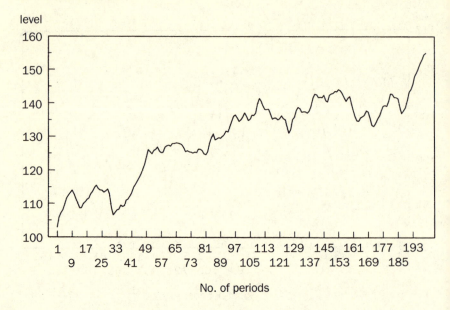

FIG. 8.2 A non-stationary series with one unit root (equation 7)

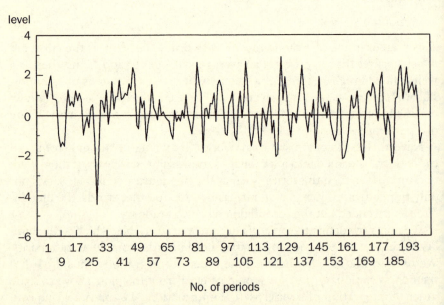

FIG. 8.3 The (stationary) first difference of a non-stationary series (equation 7)

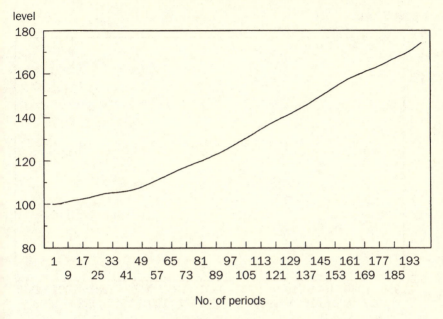

level

FIG. 8.4 A non-stationary series with two unit roots

orders of integration, and one (say y_t) is (say $I(1)$ and consequently trended while the other is stationary ($x_t \sim I(0)$)), then it is obvious that x_t, the stationary variable, cannot explain the long-run component of y_t. The simple reason for this is that y_t grows and x_t does not. This is a major insight which the reader should keep in mind.

Testing for unit roots

Often the order of integration of a variable is obvious from inspection. For example, Fig. 8.5 shows the log of UK GDP. It is clearly trended, but the first difference[6] is equally clearly stationary (see Fig. 8.6). By contrast, Fig. 8.7 plots real interest rates for the UK; while interest rates are generally higher after 1979, this does not look like a trended variable.

We also need formal tests, of course. There is a plethora of these, but the simplest, the Augmented Dickey–Fuller (ADF) test (Dickey and Fuller 1981), is also robust, according to the Monte Carlo evidence (see Banerjee *et al.* 1993). The key insight is that a test for non-stationarity amounts to a test for the existence of a unit root. Thus the obvious test, known as the Dickey–Fuller (DF) test, is formulated as the null H_0: $\beta = 1$ against the alternative H_a: $\beta < 1$ in:

log(1985 = 100)

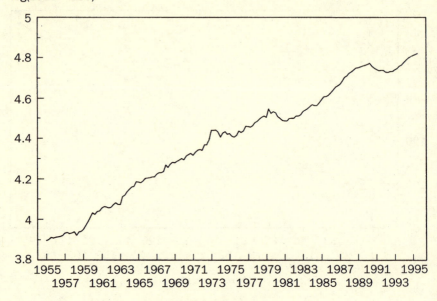

FIG. 8.5 UK GDP (log scale)

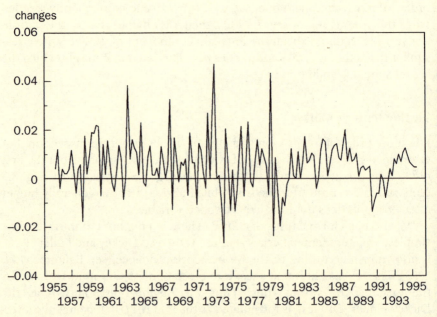

FIG. 8.6 Growth in UK GDP (change in log (GDP))

per cent

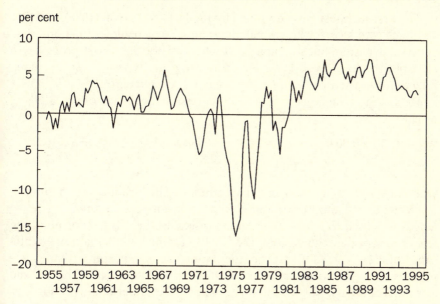

FIG. 8.7   Real UK interest rates (Treasury bill rate less RPI inflation)

$$y_t = \alpha + \beta y_{t-1} + v_t \tag{9}$$

Notice that y_t is non-stationary under the null. This means that standard t-ratios are invalid, as β is biased down and the standard errors have non-standard distributions. MacKinnon (1991) has tabulated the appropriate critical values. The main point is that instead of a critical value for the t of around -1.7, we require values of around -2.9. An easier way to estimate this statistic is to run the regression:

$$\Delta y_t = \alpha + \gamma y_{t-1} + v_t \tag{10}$$

Under the null, $\gamma = 0$; under the alternative, $\gamma < 0$, which is even easier to implement. As the error v_t is unlikely to be white noise, Dickey and Fuller proposed the augmented ADF version where extra lags in the dependent variable are added to 'mop up' the autocorrelation. The lag length on these extra terms is chosen either by some arbitrary criteria, or, more usefully, at the length necessary to whiten the residuals. The critical values are the same as for the DF test. This is a fully parametric test, although we are not interested in the effect of the lagged difference terms, which are 'nuisance' parameters.

Other proposed tests include various semi-parametric methods, where the standard error of γ is adjusted to take account of the autocorrelation in

v_t. The first such test was developed by Phillips and Perron (1988). Another approach is to look for 'fractional integration', which allows the borderline between persistent but stationary processes and non-stationary processes to be explored (see Sowell 1992a,b). There are other types of test, including fully non-parametric ones, but they are not discussed here.

To illustrate, the fourth-order ADF regression for the log of UK GDP (q_t) reveals:

$$\Delta q_t = 0.002 - 0.004q_{t-1} - 0.014\Delta q_{t-1} + 0.068\Delta q_{t-2} + 0.177\Delta q_{t-3} - 0.016\Delta q_{t-4}$$
$$(-1.10) \quad (-0.17) \quad\quad (0.85) \quad\quad (-2.24) \quad\quad (-0.20)$$

where the 't-ratios' are shown in parentheses. (The 't-ratios' are not, in fact, distributed with the t-distribution, hence the inverted commas.) The lag length is chosen to ensure white noise residuals; the LM test for up to the eighth order of autocorrelation is $X_8^2 = 10.21$, which has a marginal significance of 0.25. The ADF statistic, the 't-ratio' on q_{t-1}, is above (that is, less negative than) the critical value of -2.88. Thus we cannot reject the null and q_t is non-stationary. But we still do not know what order of integration it is. To establish this, we run the regression:

$$\Delta\Delta q_t = \alpha + \gamma\Delta q_{t-1} + \sum_{i=1}^{n} \zeta_i \Delta\Delta q_{t-i} + \delta_t \tag{11}$$

and proceed as before. We find the ADF statistic is now -5.01, which is comfortably below the critical value. So, we may conclude that Δq_t is stationary and $q_t \sim I(1)$.

These tests must be used with caution, however. They have low power in several important instances which, unfortunately, are very likely to be encountered; for example, when the true process is stationary but close to a unit root, or when the true process is stationary around a deterministic trend. In practice, it is safest to work on the assumption that the variables are non-stationary. If they are, in fact, $I(0)$, then the cointegrating techniques we spell out later will not lead to misleading conclusions. But if the variables are $I(1)$ and that is disregarded, the results may be extremely misleading.

Another instance demanding caution is when there is a break in the series, a common occurrence in macroeconomic data. The classic example is the 1974 oil crisis. Perron (1989) gives a test for such a structural break. The procedure is simple to implement, requiring only the addition of intercept, slope, and trend dummies to the ADF regression. The standard ADF critical values no longer apply, however. Perron has a fixed break date; Zivot and Andrews (1992) endogenize the break date.

Spurious regressions

At this point, there may be doubts about whether it really matters if the variables being examined are trended. It most emphatically does, for technical and commonsense reasons. Technically, the nice properties of least squares and many other statistical estimators are only valid under the assumption that the variables are stationary. If not, the moments of the relevant distributions are asymptotically unbounded. To understand what this means, take a simple random walk with drift. We know y_t will grow without limit, so that the first moment (the mean) is unbounded. Like Topsy, it just grows. Moreover, the second moment, the variance, is also unbounded. This is in contrast to the stationary case, where both moments converge to constants. The simple intuition is that as the sample lengthens, the variance of y_t becomes dominated by the trend. But this is true for *any* such variable. So any regression of one $I(1)$ variable on another over a sufficiently long sample is likely to give a good fit, as the variances are growing at the same rate. And that is so even if there is absolutely no causal relation between the two variables. To use an example similar to one used by Hendry, a regression of $\log(p_t) = \alpha + \beta \log(m_t)$ reveals:

$$\log(p_t) = -0.163 + 0.971\log(m_t)$$
$$(24.7)$$

with an R^2 of 0.86. The sample runs from the first quarter of 1965 to the second quarter of 1990. But while p is the Retail Price Index, m is not money, but cumulated Scottish hydroelectric output! Just as with the earlier example of German and French labour costs, it is quite impossible that there could be any genuine relationship between them. Despite this, we have a pretty good fit, judging from the R^2 and the sensationally high t-ratio on $\log(m_t)$. This kind of relationship was first discussed by Yule (1926), but was really brought to the fore by Granger and Newbold (1974), who introduced the term 'spurious regression' to describe such a situation. They put forward the rule of thumb: if the R^2 exceeds the Durbin–Watson statistic, beware.[7] In this case, the advice works: DW = 0.039.[8] The intuition here is that the trend dominates the variance, leading to the high R^2, while the autocorrelation revealed by the DW statistic is a sign that the equation is profoundly misspecified.[9]

So, running regressions using non-stationary data is a dangerous procedure. Luckily, there are circumstances in which such regressions are valid. If this is the case, then a simple, static regression like that above is very likely to provide accurate estimates. We now turn to this case.

Unique Cointegrating Vectors and the ECM

In this section we look, first, at the idea of a long-run (cointegrating) relationship between a set of variables. Then, secondly, we see how it relates to the idea of an error-correction mechanism.

Cointegration and the equilibrium error

The key word here is *cointegration*. The order of integration was defined above; and why two variables of different orders of integration cannot have a genuine long-run relation was also explained. But what if we have two or more non-stationary series of the same order of integration? In this case, there may be a valid long-run relation, but the difficulty is distinguishing it from the results of a spurious regression.

The key insight is that if there is a genuine long-run relation, then, although the variables will all rise over time, there will be a common trend binding them together.[10] Suppose we have a set of variables $\{y, x, z\} \sim I(1)$; that is, each variable is non-stationary, and needs differencing once to induce stationarity. For an equilibrium or long-run relation to exist, we require that a vector $\{\beta_1, \beta_2, \beta_3\}$ exists such that:

$$\beta_1 y_t + \beta_2 x_t + \beta_3 z_t = \varepsilon'_t \sim I(0) \tag{12}$$

In other words, there is a linear combination of $\{y, x, z\}$ which is stationary. If this were not true, then all the variables would drift away from each other over time in a completely unpredictable way. So why do we use the term 'cointegration'?

Integration refers to the method whereby a single non-stationary variable may be rendered stationary (by differencing); cointegration refers to the way in which a set of variables may jointly be rendered stationary (by linear combination). In these circumstances, $\{y, x, z\}$ is referred to as a cointegrating set, with an associated cointegrating vector $\{\beta_1, \beta_2, \beta_3\}$. Note that if $w_t \sim I(J)$, then $k_0 + k_1 w_t$ is also $I(J)$ for any arbitrary constant values k_0, k_1, where k_0 is simply a constant. So we can rewrite (12) in a more familiar form, normalizing on y_t. Then the relation looks like a conventional regression equation, as:

$$y_t = \alpha + \beta x_t + \gamma z_t + \varepsilon_t \tag{13}$$

or

$$y_t = y^\star + \varepsilon_t \tag{14}$$

where $y^\star = \alpha + \beta x_t + \gamma z_t$ can be interpreted as the long-run or equilibrium value of y_t (conditional on the values of x_t and z_t); ε_t is the equilibrium error (normalized to $E[\varepsilon_t] = 0$) and $\varepsilon_t \sim I(0)$. Note, for example, that $\gamma = -\beta_3 / \beta_1$.

This point about normalization is more significant than at first appears. By itself, the existence of a cointegrating relationship offers no information about the causal structure at work. In particular, just because we choose to normalize on y_t can, obviously, not be taken to imply that x_t and z_t cause y_t, although our theory might suggest this is the most sensible interpretation. But, as we shall see later, we can use other information to make statements about causality.

Engle–Granger cointegrating regression

We now consider how to test for the existence of cointegrating relationships and estimate the parameters. The remarkable conclusion that Engle and Granger (1987) reached is that both tasks can be performed with a simple OLS regression on the levels of the relevant variables. In other words, we simply run the regression specified, for example, in (13). If the variables form a cointegrating set, the parameter estimates will be *superconsistent*: that is, they will converge on the true values at a very fast rate. This follows from the fact that, once again, the variance is dominated by the trend; in this case, by the *common* trend.[11] Moreover, we can test for a cointegrating relationship very simply. From (13), if the variables cointegrate, then $\hat{\varepsilon}_t$ must be stationary. So testing for cointegration is the same as testing for a unit root, and we can apply an ADF test to the estimated residuals. The critical values differ from the standard DF levels, being more negative (typically around -3.5, and depending partly on the number of variables in the cointegrating set), but otherwise the tests are identical. If the ADF is less than the critical value, the null—that the variables are not cointegrated—can be rejected.

The error-correction mechanism

The notions of cointegration and the error-correction mechanism (ECM) are intimately linked, although this was not always appreciated. As noted by Clarke and his colleagues (this volume), the ECM was originally developed in an engineering control environment and first used in economics by Phillips (1954, 1957). It was subsequently used by Sargan (1964) in an influential paper on wage and price determination, and then popularized in a widely cited paper by Davidson *et al.* (1978). It was in this paper that Hendry began his crusade to introduce the ECM to the econometric public.

The ECM can be seen as a convenient reparametrization of the general linear Auto Regressive Distributed Lag (ARDL) model (Wickens and Breusch 1988). As we shall see, it is useful to think about it as a non-linear specification that focuses on the long-run and adjustment to it (Alogoskoufis and Smith 1991). Consider the general ARDL model with two variables y_t and x_t (the extension to more explanatory variables just requires a few more letters, but the algebra is the same):

$$y_t = \alpha + \sum_{i-1}^{n} \beta_i y_{t-i} + \sum_{i=1}^{m} \gamma_i x_{t-i} + \delta_t \tag{15}$$

This equation has a long-run solution, defined as the point where y_t and x_t settle down to constant steady state levels $y^\star$ and $x^\star$ as in (4) above,[12] so:

$$y^\star = A + Bx^\star \tag{16}$$

This means that we can define the long-run value of $y^\star_t$ conditional on the value of x at time t as:

$$y^\star_t = A + Bx_t \tag{17}$$

The link with the discussion on cointegration earlier should now be clear. Defining ε_t as the equilibrium error,[13] as before, we have:

$$\varepsilon_t \equiv y_t - y^\star_t = y_t - A - Bx_t \tag{18}$$

Now, very often we are only really interested in the long-run parameters, A and B. Clearly, they can be derived from (15), but the results are not transparent, and calculating the standard errors is a non-trivial problem as, for example, B is a complicated non-linear function of the underlying parameters.[14]

The ECM specification cuts through all these difficulties. Take the model:

$$\Delta y_t = a + \sum_{i=1}^{n-1} b_i \Delta y_{t-i} + \sum_{i=1}^{m-1} c_i \Delta x_{t-i} + dy_{t-1} + ex_{t-1} + \delta_t \tag{19}$$

This equation looks very different from the ARDL, but is, in fact, the same. It is simply a *reparametrization*, or linear transformation, of (15). To put it another way, each of the parameters in (15) may be identified in terms of the parameters in (19). The easiest way to see this is to expand (19) using the fact that $\Delta z_t \equiv z_t - z_{t-1}$, arrange all the terms in the levels, and match the parameters. A little algebra reveals that the long-run parameter is given by:

$$B \equiv -e/d \tag{20}$$

Thus the levels' terms in the ECM tell us exclusively about the long-run parameters. Given this, the most informative way to write the ECM is as:[15]

$$\Delta y_t = \sum_{i=1}^{n-1} b_i \Delta y_{t-i} + \sum_{i=1}^{m-1} c_i \Delta x_{t-1} - \lambda(y_{t-1} - A - bx_{t-1}) + \delta_t \tag{21}$$

This equation is non-linear in parameters, but can easily be estimated by any standard non-linear least squares algorithm. Using our expression for the equilibrium error, ε_t, we can now write:

$$\Delta y_t = \sum_{i=1}^{n-1} b_i \Delta y_{t-i} + \sum_{i=1}^{m-1} c_i \Delta x_{t-i} - \lambda \varepsilon_{t-1} + \delta_t \tag{22}$$

This emphasizes the importance of λ, which is mathematically related to a stability condition. But it also has a direct and intuitive interpretation: it tells us how much of the adjustment to equilibrium takes place in each period. In other words, how much of the (equilibrium) error is corrected. This is, of course, how the term 'error-correction mechanism' was derived. λ must be positive as otherwise the error is magnified.[16] If the error is too large (greater than 2), the equation is unstable as the error is 'overcorrected' and the variable is driven increasingly far away from equilibrium. If it is negative, the error never corrects; it just gets bigger. Fig. 8.8 illustrates the point.

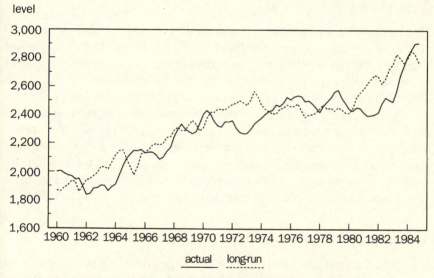

Fɪɢ. 8.8 Actual and long-run equilibrium values of a non-stationary series

The figure shows a (trended) [17] series with an associated long-run path, $y_t^\star$. So long as λ is positive, then positive (negative) errors ε_t will lead to falling (rising) y_{t+1}. This will tend to correct the error. If $\lambda = 1$, then all the adjustment (100 per cent) takes place within the period: adjustment is instantaneous. If λ is (say) 0.2, then 20 per cent of the adjustment takes place in each period.[18] If $\lambda \leq 0$, then no adjustment ever happens, and it is unclear what it means to say that y_t^* is the long-run path of y_t. Thus, to anticipate, the hypothesis that H_0: $\lambda = 0$ against the alternative H_a: $\lambda > 0$ amounts to a test for the absence of cointegration.

Put in this form, we can now see that the error-correction mechanism contains a wealth of information. The ECM separates the short-run dynamics (which are necessary to estimate the model but which may not be of direct interest) from estimates of the long-run properties. It provides three separate types of information: the long-run parameters (A and B); estimates of the short-run dynamics, the Δ terms; and estimates of the speed of adjustment to the long-run.

Finally, we have focused on linear specifications, but the ECM is occasionally treated as a non-linear relationship. In particular, positive equilibrium errors may cause different dynamics from negative errors. For examples of this, and useful discussion, see Burgess (1988, 1992), Granger and Lee (1989), and Granger and Terasvirta (1993).

Cointegration and the ECM

This brings us back to cointegration. It should now be obvious that the notions of cointegration and the ECM are closely linked. In fact, Engle and Granger (1987) showed that if a cointegrating relationship exists, there must be an error-correction specification that can be applied to the data. This result is known as the Granger Representation Theorem. Indeed, if we estimate an ECM for a set of $I(1)$ variables, then they must be cointegrated for this to be a valid regression, for the simple reason that if the variables are not cointegrated, then the levels' terms introduce non-stationarity. On the other hand, if they are cointegrated, then $(y_{t-1} - A - Bx_{t-1})$, the lagged equilibrium error (ε_{t-1}) is stationary and the regression is valid. As a result, the estimate of λ presents a test for cointegration, as discussed above: H_0: $\lambda = 0$.[19]

Multi-stage estimation procedures

Engle and Granger (1987) suggested a two-stage procedure in the estimation of, and testing for, cointegrating relationships. The first step is to run an ordinary least squares regression on the levels of the variables in question, exploiting the superconsistency result. After testing for the existence of cointegration using the ADF test, they advocated imposing the first-stage estimates in a second-stage ECM; that is, to use the fitted values of the equilibrium error $\hat{\varepsilon}_t$ in a standard ECM regression.

This procedure, however, while consistent, is not fully efficient. Moreover, we have no means of performing inference on the long-run parameters; we have no long-run standard errors. The problem really stems from the fact that the first stage produces estimates of the long-run parameters using only the long-run information. This works well for reasons explained above, but we can do better if we use all the information available, and employ the short-run dynamics when we estimate the long-run parameters. Engle and Yoo (1991) propose a three-stage maximum likelihood procedure which does precisely that, using the results from the second-stage ECM to modify the first-stage results.[20] Thus the inference problem turns out to be tractable.

Multiple Cointegrating Vectors

The discussion hitherto has assumed a unique cointegrating vector. This need not be the case. Indeed, multiple cointegrating vectors should be the rule, not the exception. We consider such cases in this section.

The issues

With a set of p variables, the number of cointegrating relationships r may lie between zero and $p - 1$.[21] To see this, take the economic model of supply and demand, illustrated in Fig. 8.9, for some commodity, say mango juice. The demand for mango juice is affected by the price of mangoes, p_m, and the weather, w (the hotter the weather, the higher w, and the higher demand). The supply is also determined by the price, and by the number of mango-picking small boys, b. We assume that supply equals demand and that all the variables are $I(1)$.[22] So we have two long-run relationships, and an equilibrium condition:

$$q^d = \gamma_{10} - \gamma_{11}p_m + \gamma_{12}w \tag{23}$$

$$q^s = \gamma_{20} - \gamma_{21}p_m + \gamma_{22}b \tag{24}$$

$$q^d = q^s \tag{25}$$

All the parameters are positive. The point is that these equations define two long-run relationships that exist in the data: one supply, one demand. We can list the cointegrating variables as $\{q, p_m, w, b\}$. The associated cointegrating vectors are $\{-1, -\gamma_{11}, \gamma_{12}, 0\}$ (demand) and $\{-1, \gamma_{21}, 0, -\gamma_{22}\}$ (supply). Likewise, there are two equilibrium errors:

$$\varepsilon_{1t} = q_t - \gamma_{10} + \gamma_{11}p_{mt} - \gamma_{12}w \tag{26}$$

$$\varepsilon_{2t} = q_t - \gamma_{20} + \gamma_{21}p_{mt} - \gamma_{22}b \tag{27}$$

How are these errors to be embedded in an error-correction mechanism? The simple answer is that there is one ECM for each endogenous variable

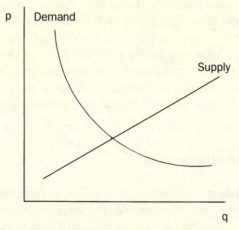

FIG. 8.9 Demand and supply for mangoes

(q, p_m), and that each of the errors may or may not enter either equation. However, both equations must include at least one of the equilibrium error terms. In fact, this is what gives us a notion of endogeneity in this long-run context; endogeneity means that the long-run errors feed back onto a variable in the short run. Similarly, we know, for example, that the weather is exogenous if disequilibrium in supply or demand has no effect on changes in the weather. Thus we might estimate two ECMs for price and quantity as follows, where ε_1 is from the demand equation and ε_2 is from supply:

$$\Delta p_{mt} = dynamics - \lambda_{11}\varepsilon_{1t-1} - \lambda_{12}\varepsilon_{2t-1} \tag{28}$$

$$\Delta q_t = dynamics - \lambda_{21}\varepsilon_{1t-1} - \lambda_{22}\varepsilon_{2t-1} \tag{29}$$

This collection of ECM equations is known as a Vector Error-Correction Mechanism, or VECM. Unpacking the equilibrium errors, it contains a mix of differenced and level terms. Just as a single ECM is a reparameterization of some ARDL, so the VECM is a reparameterization of some vector autoregressive process (VAR).[23] At least one of each of the λ_{ij} must be significant in each equation. We may also be able to make sense of the results. For example, suppose λ_{12} and λ_{21} were insignificant. This would mean that prices respond to disequilibrium in demand and quantities respond to disequilibrium in supply.

In practice, we attempt to identify the number of cointegrating vectors, r, using a suitable systems method, such as the Johansen estimator, described in a subsequent section. If $r = 0$ we stop, as the set of variables does not comprise a cointegrating set. If $r = 1$, then we may proceed by employing the methods discussed in the previous section (although they may not be fully efficient, being single-equation estimators). But if $r > 1$, we generate esti-mates using the same—systems—method. Once we have those uncon-strained estimates, we try to identify the model, using theory.[24]

This is not the place for an extended discussion of the identification prob-lem,[25] but the basic ideas are pretty simple. Suppose we have two cointe-grating relationships with associated errors ε_1 and ε_2. By definition, both of these are $I(0)$. But any arbitrary combination of two $I(0)$ variables is also $I(0)$. If $r = 2$, as we are assuming, then the statistical techniques we use pick two vectors out of a hat.[26] What theory does is to enable us to make a sensible choice of model so that the results can be interpreted. If we are lucky, theory will allow us to test hypotheses, that is, if it is rich enough to suggest 'over-identifying' restrictions. Very often, as in our example, the restrictions are of the exclusion type. That is, we are able to tell demand from supply because weather affects demand but not supply; and the number of small boys affects supply, but not demand. In short, there is one exogenous variable in each equation which is excluded from the other.

The first empirical step in any analysis of non-stationary data, then, is to establish the number of cointegrating relationships, r. Recall $0 < r < (p - 1)$ where p is the number of non-stationary variables. If $r = 0$, then analysis should cease, as there are no equilibrium relationships. If $r = 1$, it is fine (but possibly inefficient) to use single-equation estimators. If $r > 1$, some form of system estimator is required. Finally, if $r = p$, so that the number of 'cointe-grating vectors' equals the number of variables, think again. This can only hold when all p of the variables are themselves stationary.[27]

Rank and cointegration

The material which follows requires some understanding of matrices, otherwise it may be rather difficult to understand the relevant empirical work, or how to implement the method in the regression packages that include the Johansen technique. What we have here is a system of four vari-ables, $z = \{q, p_m, w, b\}$. Using a notation consistent with that employed by Johansen (1990) and his collaborators, we write the p-dimensional VAR as:

$$z_t = A_1 z_{t-1} + \ldots + A_k z_{t-k} + \mu + \delta_t \tag{30}$$

where p is 4, and δ is the residual term. We assume z_t is $I(1)$, although it need not be: z may include $I(0)$ variables. We may transform the model into a Vector Error-Correction Mechanism (VECM):

$$\Delta z_t = \Gamma_1 \Delta z_{t-1} + \ldots + \Gamma_{k-1} \Delta z_{t-k+1} + \Pi z_{t-1} + \mu + \delta_t \tag{31}$$

The existence of r cointegrating relationships amounts to the following hypothesis:

$$H_1(r): \Pi = \alpha\beta' \tag{32}$$

where α and β are $p \times r$ matrices of full rank. The α coefficients are basically the error-correction adjustment terms, which we called λ earlier. The β are the long-run coefficients. The *rank* of a matrix is simply the number of linearly independent rows (or columns). Put simply, the rank tells us how many distinctly different relationships exist. For example, suppose Π were:

$$\begin{bmatrix} 1 & 2 & 3 & 4 \\ 2 & 4 & 6 & 8 \\ 5 & 4 & 6 & 4 \\ -3 & 0 & 0 & 4 \end{bmatrix} \tag{33}$$

This matrix seems to have four different rows, but there is only one independent relationship. The first and second are proportional; the third and fourth add up to the second. So, the rank of the matrix is 1. Thus $H_1(r)$ is the hypothesis of reduced rank of Π. This sounds somewhat daunting, but there is a straightforward way to express it. We know that the number of cointegrating vectors is equal to the rank of the Π matrix. So if we can come up with a test for the rank of Π, we automatically have a test for cointegration. If $r = 1$, then there is just one cointegrating vector. If $r = 0$, there are none. If $r > 1$, then issues of identification arise.[28] In our example, we expect $r = 2$. In this set-up, the error-correction coefficients are known as *loadings*.

In the absence of an a priori theory, there is a problem identifying the structural relationships from the long-run part of the system. The statistical point is simply that not only is ε_i stationary, but so are any linear combinations. Thus an infinite number of vectors satisfy the cointegrating (reduced rank) restriction. Fortunately, as discussed above, our theory offers identifying restrictions. Moreover, some of the loadings may be zero. α_{ij} is the coefficient on the jth-equilibrium error in the ith equation. If $\alpha_{i1} = \alpha_{i2} = 0$, then the ith variable is weakly exogenous with respect to the long-run parameters.

It is important to understand the sense in which exogeneity is being used here. Exogeneity is defined by Engle *et al.* (1983) as the condition where information about the process generating an explanatory variable carries no information about the parameters of interest. Thus the fact that we find a variable to be weakly exogenous does not necessarily imply that the variable is exogenous in the traditional sense, that is, being either strictly exogenous or predetermined. The latter definitions refer to the covariance between an explanatory variable and the error term relating to the dependent variable.[29]

The Johansen method

We discovered earlier that cointegration implies that the rank r of the long-run matrix must lie between 1 and $p-1$. So, if we can develop a test of, say, $H_0: r = p$ against $H_a: r \leq p$, then we have a test for cointegration. This is what the Johansen method does. The method often seems mysterious to those unfamiliar with the notions of canonical regressions and eigenvectors, but it is possible to see the method as a generalization of the simple Dickey–Fuller test. Recall that, the DF test is the test for a unit root in a single variable. We are looking for a unit value of A in the regression:

$$y_t = A_1 y_{t-1} + v_t \tag{34}$$

or

$$\Delta y_t = (A_1 - I) y_{t-1} + v_t \tag{35}$$

or

$$\Delta y_t = \Pi y_{t-1} + v_t \tag{36}$$

Now Π is a (1×1) matrix, and the only way it can have zero rank is if $A_1 = 1$. Extending this to more than one variable so that z is a pth-order vector, then we know that the VECM specification is:

$$\Delta z_t = (A_1 - I) z_{t-1} + v_t \tag{37}$$

or

$$\Delta z_t = \Pi z_{t-1} + v_t \tag{38}$$

where A_1 and Π are now $(p \times p)$ matrices and I is the (pth-order) identity matrix. The number of distinct cointegrating relationships is given by the rank of Π. Writing Π in the form of $(A_1 - I)$, the rank is given by the number of non-zero *characteristic roots*, also known as *eigenvalues*. There can be, at most, p of these, and they can be ordered by size, so that $\lambda_1 > \lambda_2 > \ldots > \lambda_p$. In the univariate case, as we have seen, the rank can only be zero if $A_1 = 1$, when the characteristic root is zero. But in the multivariate case, we know that linear combinations of the elements of Π will produce zero characteristic roots. So if we could develop a test of whether $\lambda_r = 0$, against $\lambda_r > 0$, then we would have a test that the number of cointegrating vectors equals r. This is what the Johansen procedure offers.

The procedure starts from the VECM. The idea is to take out the effect of short-run dynamics by running initial regressions of Δz_t and z_{t-k} on the right-hand side. The residuals from these two regressions are then used to form residual 'product moment' matrices. The maximum likelihood estimate of the long-run coefficients, β, is then obtained as the eigenvectors corresponding to the r largest eigenvalues (of which there are p in total) resulting from the solution to an equation involving these matrices. Johansen then constructs tests that allow us to determine how many relationships exist, based on the eigenvalues; the associated eigenvectors are the corresponding estimates of cointegrating vectors.

Note that if there are multiple vectors ($r > 1$), the particular vectors generated by the procedure are essentially arbitrary, being selected on statistical criteria. There are two main tests of the number of vectors, r, known as the Trace and Maximum Likelihood tests. Once r is established, restrictions on the α_{ij} and β_{ij} may be imposed and tested. It is possible to include $I(0)$ variables in the underlying VECM, as well as intervention (dummy) variables. It is also possible to specify some $I(0)$ variables as exogenous, although it would be natural to assume that all variables are endogenous at the outset, and test this restriction in estimation. The only problem with this approach is that it is sensitive to the specification. The lag length has to be right (longer is preferable to shorter), and the method is unreliable for small samples.

Illustrating Cointegration Analysis

Economic models tend to be fairly specific, certainly compared to social or political models, thus the theory can offer more restrictions to exploit. So, in this section, we look first at a well-defined, albeit simple, economic problem as an example of how to proceed in empirical analysis. As it would be wrong, however, to give the impression that the paraphernalia of first-order conditions and specific functional forms are needed in order to use cointegration analysis, we go on to consider an example from political science. The basic steps we follow are to think about the theory; examine the data; test for the number of cointegrating vectors; estimate those vectors; impose and test identifying restrictions on the vectors; and test for exogeneity. The first example examines a model of employment, hours, and wages in UK manufacturing (Price 1995).

Employment, hours, and wages in the UK

The theoretical starting point in this instance is a simple, static, profit-maximization model. Perfectly competitive firms facing parametric real wages aim to maximize profits given a standard Cobb–Douglas production function.[30] The firm chooses both employment and hours. We assume that marginal labour costs are increasing so more hours raise labour costs. Thus production is given by (output) $Q = A L^{\alpha} H^{\gamma}$, and the cost function $F(H)$ has the quadratic form $\frac{\delta H^2}{2}$, where L is employment and H is hours. Thus profits are given by:

$$\Pi = AL^{\alpha}H^{\gamma} - WL - \frac{\delta H^2}{2}W$$

In log-linear form, the first-order conditions are:

$$l = q - w + a \tag{39}$$

$$h = 0.5q - 0.5w + 0.5(c{-}d) \tag{40}$$

where lower case letters indicate logs (so that q is the log of Q) and Q is output. There are clear theoretical restrictions to test; in particular, the unit coefficients on output and wages in equation (39). More importantly, we have a set of identifying restrictions on the long-run structure, excluding h from the first equation and l from the second. Note that these restrictions are just identifying, and cannot, therefore, be tested. However, if we take the theoretical restrictions seriously, then we do have a set of testable restrictions with the other, specific, parameters in (39) and (40).

Next we examine the data, which, note, come after the theory! Figs. 8.10–8.13 illustrate the logarithms of hours worked, employment, output, and real wages in the UK manufacturing sector. The series have differing characteristics: employment and wages are dominated by strong trends; hours worked show a secular decline; and output falls sharply after 1979 but rises over the whole sample period. Our initial, informal, assessment is that all these variables may reasonably be considered to be $I(1)$.

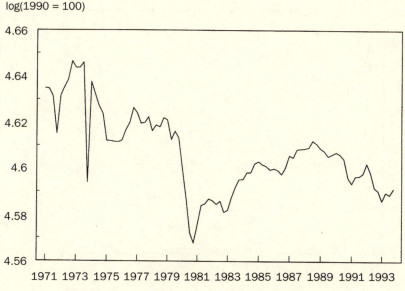

FIG. 8.10 Hours worked in UK manufacturing (log scale)

log(1990 = 100)

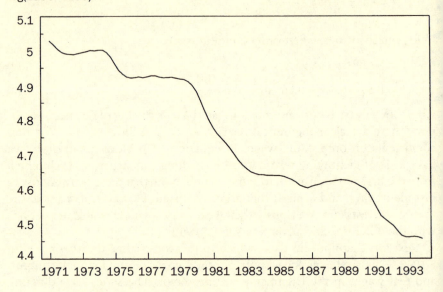

FIG. 8.11 Employment in UK manufacturing (log scale)

log(1990 = 100)

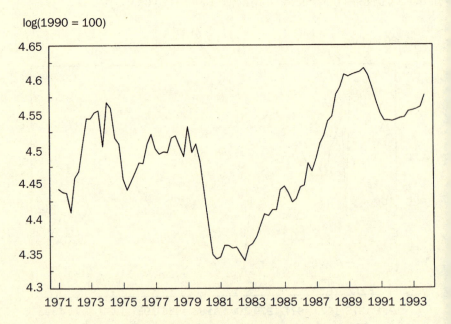

FIG. 8.12 Output in UK manufacturing (log scale)

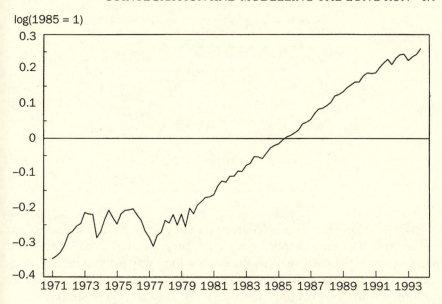

log(1985 = 1)

Fig. 8.13 Real wages in UK manufacturing (log scale)

Some ADF test statistics, which reveal that all the variables are indeed unambiguously $I(1)$, are reported in Table 8.1. The lag length was chosen to ensure the residuals in the underlying equations were white noise.

Although not really in the spirit of the exercise, a useful next step is to look at single-equation estimates, using Engle–Granger first-step level equations and unrestricted ECM relationships. However, any such results are necessarily preliminary and are really data-explorations, as we need to establish the number of cointegrating relationships. In this case, partly as a salutary example of how single equations can mislead, we estimate an ARDL parameterized as an error-correction mechanism, with the change in log(employment)(Δl) as the dependent variable. Testing down[31] from a fifth-order ARDL, including the lagged levels of log(employment), log(output), and log(real wages) as dependent variables, and concentrating on the parameters of interest, we find:

$$\Delta l_t = \ldots - 0.0218 l_{t-1} + 0.0170 q_{t-1} - 0.0236 w_{t-1} \ldots$$
$$ (1.55) (1.19) (1.51)$$

where absolute t-statistics are given in parentheses. Clearly, there is no evidence of the posited cointegrating relationship. The long-run solution is:

$$l = \ldots + 0.779 q - 1.085 w$$
$$ (2.44) (10.4)$$

Table 8.1 Tests for order of integration: ADF(4)

Variable	ADF(4)
l	−0.40
Δl	−3.32
h	−2.23
Δh	−5.15
q	−1.55
Δq	−4.14
w	0.02
Δw	−4.09

Critical value = −2.89

While these long-run t-statistics are apparently large, under the null of no cointegration (which cannot be rejected) they are subject to severe bias. Furthermore, the coefficient on output is a long way from unity. The conclusion may be drawn that, on the face of it, $\{l, q, w\}$ do *not* form a cointegrating relationship, contrary to (39). As we shall see, there are reasons to believe that this conclusion is profoundly mistaken.

The Johansen method assumes Gaussian residuals—that is, normally distributed white noise—and it is important that the general VAR is not misspecified. The way to do this is simply to ensure that the lag lengths are sufficiently long, and that we have included the right selection of $I(1)$ and $I(0)$ variables. It is quite legitimate also to include intervention or dummy variables to capture unusual episodes. In Table 8.2, we report some summary and diagnostic statistics from the fifth-order VAR.

Table 8.2 Diagnostics for unrestricted VAR

Std. dev.	R^2	Ljung–Box $Q(23)$	ARCH(5)
0.0031	0.855	22.274	5.615
0.0062	0.487	14.349	0.535
0.0152	0.465	21.766	5.928
0.0134	0.409	14.551	5.355

Evidently the general VAR is a satisfactory representation of the data, and we proceed to the tests for cointegration. The results of these, presented in Table 8.3, indicate that we cannot reject the hypothesis that there is at least one cointegrating vector, but we can formally reject the hypothesis that $r = 2$. However, the test statistics for $r = 2$ are sufficiently close to the critical values for us to tentatively assume the existence of two vectors. Proceeding on this assumption, the β matrix implied by the reduced rank Π matrix is given in Table 8.4, where we have arbitrarily normalized on employment and hours. Imposing the identifying restrictions, we obtain the results given in Table 8.5.

Looking at β, the point estimates on q and w are close to -1 and 1 respectively in the second (employment) vector, as the Cobb–Douglas technology implies. However, the standard errors show that this hypothesis can be rejected for the real wage. Using likelihood ratio tests, the test statistics are $\chi_1^2 = 0.01$ and 8.09 respectively. So the unit restriction on output is easily accepted, but we reject the unit restriction on real wages.

Turning to the loadings, the α_{ij}, Table 8.6 shows that we have the intriguing result that hours and employment are weakly exogenous: the relevant loadings are insignificantly different from zero. An explicit test of this is that $\alpha_{11} = \alpha_{12} = \alpha_{21} = \alpha_{22} = 0$. This is comfortably accepted: $\chi_4^2 = 3.89$.

This now explains why the OLS results failed to reveal a cointegrating regression. Although at first counter-intuitive, there is a sensible explanation for the pattern of loadings. Well-defined demand functions for employment

Table 8.3 Tests for number of cointegrating vectors

Eigenv.	L-max	Trace	H_0: r	$p-r$	L-max$_{90}$	Trace$_{90}$
0.2312	24.18	46.53	0	4	24.73	43.95
0.1531	15.28	22.34	1	3	18.60	26.79
0.0732	6.99	7.06	2	2	12.07	13.33
0.0007	0.06	0.06	3	1	2.69	2.69

Trace$_{90}$ = 90% confidence for Trace test; L-max$_{90}$ = 90% confidence for L-max test

Table 8.4 Normalized β matrix for $r = 2$

l	h	q	w
0.091	1.000	−0.324	0.206
1.000	−1.389	−0.667	1.000

Table 8.5 β matrix for $r = 2$; identifying restrictions imposed

l	h	q	w
Parameters			
0.000	1.000	−0.234	0.102
1.000	0.000	−0.992	1.142
Standard errors			
0.000	0.000	0.028	0.010
0.000	0.000	0.085	0.029

Table 8.6 α matrix for $r = 2$; identifying restrictions imposed

Vector 1	Vector 2	t-ratio 1	t-ratio 2
0.064	−0.020	1.326	−1.031
−0.126	0.014	−1.247	0.354
0.615	0.083	2.533	0.857
0.376	−0.202	1.757	−2.362

and hours may be identified. However, the structure of the model is that changes in output and wages equilibrate the system, rather than employment or hours. When hours exceed their equilibrium levels, there are two responses: real wages respond to the pressure of demand, $\alpha_{41} > 0$, and firms respond to higher utilization by increasing output ($\alpha_{31} > 0$). These effects are large and significant. By contrast, when employment exceeds the equilibrium value, real wages respond by falling ($\alpha_{42} < 0$); firms require less labour.

Thus, we have a real wage equation that responds to demand pressure in precisely the way anticipated. It may need to be stressed that, despite finding hours and employment weakly exogenous, this does not mean that these two variables are outside a firm's control. This is obviously not the case. In fact, standard Granger causality tests on a fourth-order VAR on the differenced variables clearly show that output causes employment and hours worked.[32]

Government popularity and economic competence

Our second example, taken from political science, examines the relationship between government popularity and economic competence (Sanders and Price 1996). The background here is that it is widely believed that support for the government is largely determined by the public's view of its economic competence. However, this begs the questions of whether competence causes popularity, or popularity causes competence, or whether the two variables are measuring the same thing. We investigate this by looking at the relationship between three variables: government popularity, 'competence', and the tax 'wedge'. All the data are monthly for the period January 1991–August 1995. The percentage intending to vote Conservative 'if there were a general election tomorrow' is denoted as g; the difference between the percentages reporting that the Conservatives or Labour were the more competent economic managers as c; and τ is the difference between the Retail Price Index (RPI) and the Tax and Price Index (TPI).

We do not plot the data, but visual inspection suggests that popularity and competence are linked. A sharp fall in competence (with subsequent recovery) is associated with Britain's exit from the Exchange Rate Mechanism in September 1992. The tax wedge shows a step change in early 1993, associated with the rise in taxes implemented at around this time. This step change suggests that τ might best be modelled as a variable which is stationary around a break, although it is clear from the figure that the series is trended both before and after the break. The appropriate test is by Perron (1989).[33]

Table 8.7 reports some ADF test statistics, which reveal that g and c are unambiguously $I(1)$.[34] The same cannot be said for τ. The Perron test is just below (more negative than) the critical value for stationarity, so it seems likely that this variable is stationary around a break.[35]

Table 8.7 Tests for order of integration: ADF(4)

Variable	ADF(4)
g	−0.74
Δg	−5.22
c	−1.20
Δc	−6.44
τ	0.33
$\Delta \tau$	−6.60
τ^*	−3.95
$\Delta \tau^*$	−4.25

Notes: Sample Jan. 1991–Aug. 1995. N=56. Dummies for Apr. 1992, Oct. 1992, and Apr. 1993 included in regressions. τ^* and $\Delta \tau^*$ allow for a Perron intercept shift after Apr. 1992. Critical value = −4.2. ADF critical value = −2.9.

We test for the existence of a cointegrating vector with the Johansen method. The results are based on a fourth-order VAR, and the diagnostics confirm that the errors are all Gaussian. Table 8.8 reveals that there is evidently a cointegrating vector as the test statistic is well above the 95 per cent level. The estimated relationship is $g = \alpha + 0.22429c$ with a t-ratio of 8.42. Table 8.9 gives the resulting vector error-correction results for the VAR. The loadings on c are insignificant.

Having established the weak exogeneity of c and the existence of a unique cointegrating relationship, we may validly condition g on c and τ using single-equation methods. This is a fully efficient method which may give more precise estimates of the long-run parameters (Kremers $et\ al.$ 1992). It is not hard to see why this may follow, as the VAR is obviously overparameterized (many of the parameters reported in Table 8.9 are insignificant). The single equation results, where $d\tau$ is the shift intercept dummy, are:

Table 8.8 Tests for number of cointegrating vectors; $p = 2$

Eigenv.	L-max	Trace	H_0: r	$p - r$	L-max$_{95}$	Trace$_{95}$
0.38179	25.01	25.87	0	2	14.07	15.41
0.016561	0.86	0.86	1	1	3.76	3.76

Notes: Sample May 1991–Aug. 1995. $N = 52$. Trace$_{95}$ = 95% confidence for Trace test. L-max$_{95}$ = 95% confidence for L-max test.

Table 8.9*a* Regression for Δg: Johansen results

Variable	Coefficient	t-ratio
Δg_{t-1}	0.35	2.00
Δg_{t-2}	0.29	1.93
Δg_{t-3}	0.20	1.33
Δc_{t-1}	−0.05	−0.84
Δc_{t-2}	−0.12	−2.23
Δc_{t-3}	−0.07	−1.20
τ_t	1.91	1.00
τ_{t-1}	−3.99	−2.09
ecm$_{t-1}$	−0.77	−4.32

Notes: Constant and dummies (including step intercept shift) not reported. Sample May 1991–Aug. 1995. $N = 52$. $R^2 =$ 0.58. Serial correlation: $F(12, 26) = 0.96$. Normality: $\chi^2_2 =$ 4.83. Heteroscedasticity: $F(1, 50) = 0.75$.

Table 8.9*b* Regression for Δc: Johansen results

Variable	Coefficient	t-ratio
Δg_{t-1}	1.06	2.86
Δg_{t-2}	0.70	2.18
Δg_{t-3}	−0.39	−1.18
Δc_{t-1}	−0.23	−1.82
Δc_{t-2}	−0.47	−4.09
Δc_{t-3}	−0.14	−1.21
τ_t	0.35	0.09
τ_{t-1}	−1.77	−0.51
ecm$_{t-1}$	−0.29	−0.76

Notes: Constant and dummies not reported. Sample May 1991–Aug. 1995. $N = 52$. $R^2 = 0.76$ Serial correlation: $F(12, 26) = 1.51$. Normality: $\chi^2_2 = 0.62$. Heteroscedasticity: $F(1, 50) = 0.63$.

$$\Delta g_t = 24.8 + 0.27\Delta g_{t-1} + 0.22\Delta g_{t-2} - 0.09\Delta c_{t-2} - 2.15\tau_{t-1} - 2.74\,d\tau +$$
$$(2.47) \qquad (1.68) \qquad (-1.81) \qquad (-3.05) \quad (-3.19)$$

$$5.03d92m4 - 3.74d92m10 - 0.72\,(g_{t-1} - 0.21c_{t-1}\,)$$
$$(3.97) \qquad\quad (-2.93) \qquad\quad (-4.83) \qquad (-7.13)$$

Evidently, there is a well defined long-run relationship here as well, which is close to the Johansen result. Furthermore, the coefficient on the long-run error term (distributed asymptotic standard normal under the null of either stationarity or non-stationarity) is of sensible magnitude and highly significant. Our prior expectation is that adjustment to the long-run should be relatively rapid, and this is the case. The ECM term is large and significant; no less than 72 per cent of the adjustment takes place within one month. This strongly suggests that the correct statistical treatment has been followed. The election and ERM exit dummies are highly significant, but there is no independent effect for the 1993 budget (reflected in the data for τ). The effects of these two dummies can easily be seen from their coefficients: the election campaign added 5 percentage points to the government's popularity; the ERM debacle cost it 3 percentage points, over and above any indirect effects from perceptions of competence, which fell precipitately at the time.[36] As with the Johansen results, the diagnostics are satisfactory: $R^2 = 0.553$; serial correlation, $F(12, 31) = 1.69$; normality, $\chi^2_2 = 2.23$; heteroscedasticity, $F(1, 51) = 1.03$; test of general to specific restrictions, $F(4, 38) = 0.56$.

What we find, then, is that competence and taxes are weakly exogenous to the relevant long-run parameters. That is, neither competence nor taxes are affected by deviations from the long-run relationship between popularity, competence, and taxation. Nevertheless, there are short-run feedbacks from popularity to competence. The clear message is that competence feeds into popularity: governments are not judged competent because they are popular, but are popular because they are judged to be competent. Competence and popularity do not measure the same thing.

What We've Learnt

This has been a long haul, but there are potentially great rewards. The issues involved in analysing the long run have been fairly exhaustively flagged in this chapter, and there are innumerable examples of time-series in the social sciences which are non-stationary, and often trended. This matters a great deal, as the standard statistical techniques are usually invalid when data are non-stationary. It becomes very easy to make misleading inferences, which is the problem of spurious regression. So it is vital to test for the order of integration of data prior to analysis, and if they turn out to be non-stationary, to use appropriate techniques. These techniques have a great deal of leverage. Special attention has to be paid to the identification problem, but we should be doing this anyway. The notion of cointegration may actually help us in this search, because it is legitimate to concentrate our attention on the long run. Tests for cointegration can also be seen as a powerful diagnostic tool. If we have non-stationary data, then there is no point in analysing them unless we can demonstrate the existence of one or more cointegrating vectors. Far from being a problem, this helps us in our search for the 'true' underlying model.

Software

Some of the techniques discussed here, such as the ADF tests, and the Engle–Granger or ECM procedures, need no special software, only ordinary least squares analysis. The Johansen procedure, however, does need a specialist package. Fortunately, many packages now implement these procedures. These include *CATS FOR RATS* (Hansen and Juselius 1994), which has the advantage of being written by Johansen's collaborators, but the disadvantage of being less than user-friendly. But the techniques are also available in popular packages such as *EVIEWS*, *PCGive*, and *MICROFIT*. Each package has different features so it is impossible to make a specific recommendation. Even if one were to do so, the recommendation would be quickly out of date, given the fast development of this rapidly evolving approach. Nevertheless, each of the packages noted here enables estimation of the number of cointegrating vectors and offers tests for restrictions and exogeneity, among other features. Unlike some other areas in econometrics, there is no package with a cointegration procedure which is suitable for the completely inexperienced user. It is necessary to understand the issues, especially regarding integration, before proceeding. But this should be seen as a bonus, not a problem.

Notes

1. Despite the impression given in some texts, not all non-stationary processes have a unit root; e.g. if y_t is generated by the unstable process $y_t = \alpha + 1.2y_{t-1} + \delta_t$, y_t, will grow without limit, does not have a unit root, and cannot be rendered stationary by differencing.
2. δ_t, the error term, is assumed to be a 'white noise' residual here and elswhere, unless otherwise stated. We use ε_t to indicate an *equilibrium error*, a term defined below. ε_t will not, in general, be white noise. Errors denoted v_t should also not be assumed to be white noise.

3. The condition that $y_t = y_{t-i}$ is actually rather restrictive, as the variables we are interested in will often be growing. More generally, in the steady state $y_t^\star = y_{t-1}^\star + g_y$ where g_y is the steady growth in y_t. This can make a difference to the solution of long-run models (Pagan 1985), but the key insight—that in the long run the variance of a trended variable is dominated by the trend—is unchanged.

4. The error is autocorrelated to make the dynamics more realistic.

5. Given by $(1 - \beta)$, 0.05 in this case.

6. The first difference of the log of a variable is the growth rate, so Fig. 8.6 shows the growth of GDP.

7. This should perhaps be amended to stress the importance of a high (close to unity) R^2, which is the key indicator of non-stationary, trended data.

8. The DW statistic lies between 0 and 4, where a value of 2 indicates no auto-correlation. So 0.039 is pretty bad.

9. Phillips (1986) put this on a firmer statistical basis, showing that the t-ratios have no limiting distributions, actually diverging as the time-period increases, leading to ever-greater spurious precision, while the DW statistic tends to zero.

10. There may be more than one such trend, which we shall discuss in the next section.

11. The standard errors have non-standard distributions, however, and should be ignored.

12. The expression is given by: $y^* = \dfrac{\alpha}{(1-\sum_{i=1}^{n}\beta_i)} + \dfrac{\sum_{i=1}^{m}\gamma_i x^*}{(1-\sum_{i=1}^{n}\beta_i)}$.

13. Note that for $\theta \equiv (1 - \sum_{i=1}^{n}\beta_i)$, a necessary (but not sufficient) condition for stability here is that $(-2 < \theta < 0)$, or that $(-1 < \sum_{i=1}^{n}\beta_i < 1)$.

14. Modern computing technology has simplified the task; econometric packages now routinely offer facilities to estimate standard errors of non-linear functions. See Wickens and Breusch (1988) for discussion of the econometric issues.

15. The λ parameter is closely related to the coefficients on the lagged dependent variable terms in the ARDL. In fact $\lambda \equiv -d \equiv (1 - \sum_{i=1}^{n}\beta_i)$, or one minus the sum of the coefficients—the term we use to calculate the long-run effects and check for stability.

16. Remember that λ enters (21) or (22) with a negative sign.

17. The ECM is intimately associated with cointegration and is particularly useful in the analysis of non-stationary variables. But the ECM specification may also be applied to $I(0)$ variables.

18. Strictly, λ may lie between 1 and 2. This is rare in practice. If it does occur, it implies that the process overshoots while still converging asymptotically.

19. Under the null, the regression is invalid as stationarity is violated. Kremers et al. (1992) show that despite this the distribution of λ is asymptotic standard normal

under both the null and the alternative, but in small samples, and especially where the contribution to the variance from the short-run dynamics is relatively small, we should be cautious in applying conventional t-critical values. The ADF critical values are a safe upper bound.

20. The method is clearly explained in Hall, Cuthbertson, and Taylor (1992). Another efficient method enabling inference is due to Saikkonen (1991).

21. A simple proof of this is given in Hall, Cuthbertson, and Taylor (1992).

22. This may not be the best example, as it seems unlikely that either the weather or small boys are $I(1)$, although many parents would agree that small boys are rarely stationary, and, with global warming, perhaps w is trended too. Nevertheless, it serves as a readily understood example of the issues underlying identification.

23. A vector autogressive process (VAR) is simply a collection of ARDL equations with a common lag structure. Each equation contains precisely the same explanatory variables, namely, a distributed lag of all variables in the system.

24. If we cannot do so, perhaps because our model is not strong enough to generate identifying restrictions, then we must include all the estimated vectors in any ECM specification. This is fine statistically but interpretation may be tricky.

25. This is covered in any standard econometrics text; for example, Stewart (1992, ch. 8).

26. This is putting it a little strongly; the Johansen method chooses two vectors that are as orthogonal to each other as possible. This possesses a kind of statistical logic—it is akin to principal component analysis—but, except by accident, they will not coincide with the 'true' relationships.

27. In fact, a test that $r = p$ is a test for the stationarity of a set of variables.

28. See Wickens (1996), Johansen and Juselius (1990, 1992), and Pesaran and Shin (1994, 1995).

29. For more discussion see Hendry (1995) or Banerjee *et al.* (1993).

30. Economists will be familiar with the Cobb–Douglas function, but others may not. The Cobb–Douglas function for two inputs X and Z takes the form $Y = A X^\alpha Z^\beta$. If α and β both lie in the interval $(0, 1)$, then an increase in inputs of X or Z will increase Y, but by less than a proportionate amount so factors exhibit diminishing returns. The function is homogeneous of degree $(\alpha + \beta)$. This means that the sum of the exponents gives the returns to scale. An important case is when $(\alpha + \beta) = 1$; here we have constant returns to scale, which means that if we increase both factors by the same proportion γ, then Y will also rise by γ. In general, the effect on Y will be $(\alpha + \beta)\gamma$. The function is non-linear, but it can easily be linearized; $ln(Y) = ln(A) + \alpha ln(X) + \beta ln(Z)$. Finally, the derivatives with respect to the factors (the marginal products) have a very nice form: $\frac{\delta Y}{\delta X} = \alpha \frac{Y}{X}$, for example.

31. The phrase 'testing down' conceals a multitude of issues. The final equation here is the result of a series of restrictions on a general ARDL specification,

employing the Hendry methodology to ensure the resulting equation is congruent with the data. See Hendry (1995) for the definitive exposition of the method.

32. Pesaran and Shin (1995) advocate the use of traditional autoregressive distributed lag models for the analysis of long-run relations. They suggest that once the order of the ARDL model has been determined, estimation and identification can proceed by OLS or the Bewley (1979) method. The advantage of the Bewley transform is that long-run estimates of parameters and standard errors can be generated in one step; see Wickens and Breusch (1988). Pesaran and Shin (1995) consider only single-equation estimation, but in Pesaran and Shin (1994) they propose a methodology for system estimation. The properties of traditional systems methods have not been explored in the same detail, but it seems likely the superconsistency results on the long-run parameters will be preserved. In Price (1995) the system for output and wages is estimated conditioning on the lagged dependent variables and the two weakly exogenous variables. The results revealed that both specifications produce estimates extremely close to the Johansen results.

33. Perron (1989) employs a semi-parametric Phillips–Perron type approach but we report the ADF version. In this case we know the timing of the exogenous break in taxation, the 1992 budget.

34. As we have added dummies (discussed below) to the test regressions the critical values are approximate and likely to be too low. However, the test statistics for $I(1)$ status are comfortably negative, so it is probably safe to ignore this detail.

35. However, these tests have notoriously low power, so in the paper from which these results are taken we also report results on the assumption that the variable is non-stationary.

36. At first sight the coefficient for the change of competence (Δc_{t-2}) appears to have the 'wrong' sign. In fact, the dynamics have a completely sensible interpretation, entirely in line with our expectations: a rise in competence leads to higher popularity in both the short- and the long-run. To understand this, note that if we expand the relevant part of the regression, the terms in lagged c may be written as:

$$\theta_1 c_{t-1} + \theta_2 c_{t-2} + \theta_3 c_{t-3} + \ldots \tag{41}$$

where in the current specification $\theta_2 c_{t-2} = -\theta_3 c_{t-3}$. Inspection of the estimates suggests that the equation might be reparameterized as:

$$\theta_1 \Delta c_{t-1} + \theta_1 c_{t-3} + \ldots \tag{42}$$

so that competence enters with a rate of change and level effect with equal, positive coefficients. This restriction is pretty clearly indicated by the estimated parameters, at least for those accustomed to looking for similar patterns in estimated coefficients! Formally, the restriction is comfortably accepted; the test statistic is $\chi^2 = 0.36$, which is well below any critical value we might choose. So the dynamics on competence accord with our expectations; it is simply that the effect of the short-run rate of change kicks in straight away, while the long-run level effect comes in with a slightly longer lag.

9

MODELLING SPACE AND TIME: THE EVENT HISTORY APPROACH

NATHANIEL BECK

The analysis of event history, or duration, data is usually treated as a specialized topic, of interest to sociologists, historians, economists, or political scientists who observe event histories, but of little interest to others.[1] Event history, or duration data, are not a special type of data, somehow different from other types of data used by social scientists, however. Duration data, event count data, and binary time-series–cross-section data are all examples of what Flemming and Harrington (1991) call a 'counting process'. Such processes are relevant for data obtained from a number of units over time. Event counts data count the number of events for each unit; duration data measure the time until the first event; event history data mark the transition between various types of events; and binary time-series–cross-section data mark whether a single event has occurred in a series of short intervals.

Examples of the use of these kinds of data abound in the social sciences. In international relations, for example, we can count the number of wars each country engages in, the length of time between wars, and whether a country is at war in a given year. In social policy, we can count how often someone has been on welfare, the length of welfare spells, and whether someone is on welfare in any given month. From an event history perspective, we can examine what happens to nations when war ends, or what individuals do when they are no longer on welfare.[2] All processes which study the behaviour of discrete dependent variables over time and space have a commonality. Investigators may choose different methods to analyse such data, but these are choices made by the investigator; they are not choices based on the inherent properties of the data.[3] While duration analysis appears formidable because it has its own special set of techniques, distributions, and jargon, it loses much of its mystery when it is seen simply as another way to analyse common types of data.

This chapter, first, lays out the basic terminology of duration analysis and discusses the common methods for analysing such data. While it is most common to analyse duration data in a continuous time framework, we shall see that the discrete time framework may be more congenial. As space is limited, only the rudiments of duration analysis are considered here. Fortunately, there are now a number of excellent social science duration texts, including Allison (1984), Blossfeld *et al.* (1989), Peterson (1995), and Yamaguchi (1991) to which readers can refer. The only advanced topic considered in this chapter is the estimation and interpretation of duration-dependence, a topic that often seems a bit obscure. I also show how event history insights can help us to estimate models for binary dependent-variable time-series–cross-section data, a point which seem to have gone largely unnoticed.

Throughout this chapter, a simple substantive example is used, based on a study of the duration of 314 West European governments by King *et al.* (1990). This study examines the relationship between the length of time a cabinet[4] holds power and various features of the parliamentary context: the degree of party polarization ('polar'); whether the cabinet has majority status ('majority'); whether an initial confirmatory, or investiture, vote is required ('invest'); the number of prior attempts to form a cabinet ('format'); whether a cabinet was formed immediately after an election ('eltime'); and whether a cabinet is a caretaker government ('caretaker').[5] Thus, for example, we can ask whether cabinets with a parliamentary majority endure longer than other types of cabinets, and, if so, on average how much longer.

Duration models are standardly applied to the length of marriages, spells of unemployment, lengths of time on welfare, and durations of peace. From an event history perspective, we can examine individual sexual or employment histories. The theoretical and policy implications of such studies are obvious. While these applications are not explicitly discussed, readers can substitute any favourite duration data for my examples. Finally, it should be noted that duration analysis was invented to examine when industrial components would fail and how long patients would survive following some medical treatment. While these are not social science examples, the jargon of duration analysis ('hazard rate', 'failure time', 'survivor function') is heavily influenced by this heritage.

Continuous Time Parametric Duration Models

The most common duration studies analyse the relationship between the length of a series of independent 'spells' and a series of fixed covariates.[6] These fixed covariates are measured at the beginning of each spell, hence they are not caused by the length of that spell. The durations of the various spells are measured continuously. These durations must be positive, since spells of zero or negative length make no sense.

It is possible to analyse such duration data by ordinary least squares, but such analysis can return negative predicted durations. Thus the standard regression set-up, which assumes that the dependent variable is the sum of the effects of the covariates and a normal random variable, is not appropriate. Duration analysts, therefore, turn to more complicated maximum likelihood methods. While these methods are not simple, the ideas which underlie them can be easily understood. Here I focus on the ideas, leaving the mathematics to the footnotes and the various texts already cited.

Maximum likelihood requires specification of the distribution of the dependent variable (given the covariates), and the expected value and variance of the dependent variable (again given the covariates). Maximum likelihood analysis of standard regression models, for example, assumes that the dependent variable is normal, with the mean given by the usual sum of the independent variables and constant variance; logit analysis assumes that the dependent variable is Bernoulli (with parameter P) with its mean (P) given by the usual logit expression. Some distributions, such as the Bernoulli, are completely determined by their mean; others, like the normal distribution, require an additional parameter. The normal distribution is unusual in that the second parameter is the variance; more typically the mean and the second parameter combine to determine the variance. Since likelihood analysis requires the specification of a distribution, these duration methods are all fully parametric.

Exponential models

The simplest duration distribution is the *exponential*. This distribution assumes that durations are 'duration-independent' or 'memoryless'. A duration process is memoryless if its future depends only on the present but not the past. Cabinet duration is memoryless if the probability of a cabinet surviving an additional number of years is the same, regardless of how long the cabinet has already endured. It is duration-independent in that the probability of a cabinet falling in any given period does not depend on how long the cabinet has been in office. This is a very strong assumption. To take a more commonplace example, would we expect that the probability of someone who has just become unemployed being unemployed for a year or longer to be the same as the probability of someone who has been unemployed already for five years being unemployed for six years or longer? Probably not. The assumption of 'duration independence' can be relaxed, but let us maintain it for a moment.

The exponential distribution, like the Bernoulli, is completely determined by its mean. This mean, the expected duration of a given cabinet, is a function of the cabinet's characteristics, the covariates. How can we model the expected length of a cabinet as a function of these covariates? It cannot be as in a linear regression, since then we could have negative expected durations, which are impossible. While this argument only rules out functions that may return negative durations, event history analysts invariably make stronger assumptions about the nature of this function. In particular, they assume that the effect of a covariate on expected duration increases with that duration. It is 'easier' to move an expected cabinet length from four to five years than it is to move it from four to five months. In particular, analysts assume that expected duration is an exponential function of the covariates.[7]

Duration data present an additional complication: the data may be *censored*. Data are censored if for some units we know only that they lasted at least so long. In studies of welfare spells, for example, some people may still be on welfare at the end of our study, so all we know is that they were on welfare for at least the observed duration.[8] We do not know if such people left welfare the day after our study ended or would stay on welfare until death (which is simply another form of censoring). Censoring causes serious problems for any data analysis. For example, consider a simple computation of the mean length of welfare spells with censored observations. If we throw out the censored observations, we are throwing away those who have been on welfare the longest. If we set the value of the censored observations to the length of spell observed, we are again underestimating the mean length of welfare spells. The one thing we are sure of about a censored observation is that its duration would have been at least as long as the observed spell.

Maximum likelihood methods make it easy to handle censoring, although, of course, at the cost of making some assumptions. For a censored observation, we know that, had we been able to observe the exact duration, it would have been at least as long as that observed. Given that durations are exponentially distributed, we can compute the probability of observing a duration as long as, or longer than, the censored duration, and enter that probability in the likelihood function. If our distributional assumptions are wrong, then this probability will be wrong. It must be the case, however, that this approach is better than discarding censored observations, or assuming that the censored observation is the actual duration. But we clearly must be careful in analysing datasets with a large proportion of censored observations.

The cabinet duration data help us to understand the censoring issue. The democracies studied by King *et al.* (1990) all require elections within a maximum of between three and five years. Thus, while we can record the exact duration of each cabinet government, we do not know how long the cabinet would have endured in the absence of a constitutionally mandated election.

King *et al.* treat any cabinet that falls within one year of its constitutionally maximum duration as censored.[9]

Computer programs can then easily estimate the parameters that determine duration (a, b, and d in n. 7) and their standard errors using general maximum likelihood routines. Since maximum likelihood estimates have a normal distribution (for large samples), we can test null hypotheses about these parameters or groups of them. But we can do more than assess statistical significance. We can compute hypothetical expected durations for different combinations of the covariates to assess the substantive effect of the various covariates. To do this we simply exponentiate the weighted sum of the covariate values with the weights being the estimated coefficients.

We can also assess the impact of individual variables. Holding all other covariates equal, the relative expected duration of a cabinet with $X = x_1$ versus another cabinet with $X = x_2$ is just $e^{b(x_1 - x_2)}$. This is even simpler for a dummy variable like 'majority'. The relative expected duration of majority and minority cabinets, all other covariates being equal, is just e^b. For continuous variables, the analogue of a regression coefficient is the derivative of expected duration with respect to a covariate. This is simply the coefficient of that covariate multiplied by the expected duration of a cabinet. As in any non-linear model, the impact of any covariate changes with the values of other covariates.[10]

Table 9.1 reports the results of estimating cabinet durations using the exponential distribution. We see that each of the coefficients is statistically significant. The expected duration of the 'mean cabinet' (that is, a cabinet with all covariates set to their mean values, which may or may not be sensible) is just under nineteen months. To compute this, we first multiply each coefficient by the mean of its covariate, sum these up, and then exponentiate the sum.

Table 9.1 Parametric estimation of cabinet durations

Variable	Exponential		Weibull	
	b	s.e.	b	s.e.
Constant	2.96	0.22	3.00	0.15
Investiture	−0.34	0.16	−0.30	0.11
Polarization	−0.02	0.01	−0.02	0.01
Majority	0.53	0.16	0.48	0.11
Formation	−0.12	0.05	−0.11	0.04
Post-election	0.78	0.17	0.72	0.12
Caretaker	−1.32	0.34	−1.33	0.21
σ			0.78	0.04
Log like	−424.71		−414.09	

For the mean cabinet, a unit change in polarization (which runs from zero to 43 with a mean of about 15) is associated with a decrease (because of the negative sign) in expected cabinet duration of about two weeks (-0.02×18.9 months). For two cabinets that are otherwise identical, a change from a minority to a majority governing coalition increases its expected durability by about 70 per cent ($e^{0.53}$); caretaker cabinets endure only a quarter ($e^{-1.32}$) as long as normal ones; and cabinets formed immediately after an election endure something over twice as long ($e^{0.78}$) as other cabinets. All the coefficients of a duration model are readily interpretable, even if their interpretation is not quite so simple as for the usual linear regression coefficients.

Hazard rates

So far we have dealt with duration models in the same way that we deal with other types of data such as event counts or limited dependent variables, by specifying the probability distribution of the data and then performing maximum likelihood estimation (King 1988). But duration analysis has its own jargon, some of which can actually be helpful. The key notion for duration analysts is the *hazard rate*. This notion, while not difficult in itself, is a bit difficult to define precisely in continuous time. However, it is very easy to define in discrete time. Assume that cabinet durations are only measured to the nearest month (which is actually how King *et al.* measure them). The hazard rate in a given month is the probability of a cabinet falling in that month, given that it survived to the beginning of the month. In continuous time, the hazard rate similarly reflects the propensity of a government to fall at any given time given that it has survived up to that time.[11] The probability of a spell ending at some time-point, given that the spell has lasted to that time-point, is the critical feature of a hazard rate. In survival jargon, the cabinets that have endured through, say, one year are said to still be 'at risk'. It is good to be at risk! From the duration analyst's perspective, governments either have already fallen or are at risk of falling in the future.

Duration analysts use the hazard rate because it is often easier to think about hazard rates than survival rates. Duration analysts define the survivor function, $S(t)$, as the proportion of the population that is still at risk at time t.[12] It is hard to think about the survivor function for cabinet governments, but it is relatively easy to think about their hazard function. When a government is newly formed it is likely to be quite fragile, that is, to have a relatively high hazard rate. If a government survives the first few months, its chance of failing—the hazard rate—probably declines. Then perhaps, over time, crises build up, so the chance of a government falling after being in power for several years increases. While we could come up with other ideas about the hazard rates for cabinets, it does seem as though we can meaningfully think about the hazard function in a way that it is difficult to do for the survivor function.[13]

The assumption of duration independence in an exponential duration model is equivalent to the assumption that the hazard rate is constant over time. This makes sense. If the hazard rate is constant, then the probability of a failure in any short time-interval is the same, and hence does not depend on how long a cabinet has been in power. There is also a simple relationship between the constant hazard rate and the expected duration time for any government (remember, the hazard rate does not vary with time, but it does vary from cabinet to cabinet as a function of their covariates). The hazard rate is simply the inverse of expected duration, So, recalling that we computed the expected survival of the mean coalition as 18.9 months, then, for the mean cabinet, the time invariant hazard is 1/18.9 or 0.053. The units of this hazard are per month, so, loosely speaking, a cabinet has a probability of falling of about one in twenty each month.

Weibull models

The assumption of duration independence is both strong and usually implausible.[14] There are many other failure-time distributions that allow for duration dependence, with the simplest being the Weibull. It allows for hazard rates to be either rising or falling, but whether rising or falling, the Weibull requires them to be monotonic. That is, Weibull hazard rates may be either always rising ($\sigma < 1$), always falling ($\sigma > 1$) or flat ($\sigma = 1$), in which case the Weibull is the same as the exponential.[15]

The Weibull is estimated similarly to the exponential, except that it has one additional shape parameter, σ. If $\sigma = 1$, the Weibull reduces to the exponential, that is, the exponential is a special case of the Weibull. Since maximum likelihood estimates are normal (for large samples), we can test if the exponential is adequate by comparing $\frac{\sigma - 1}{se(\sigma)}$ to a standard normal.

Table 9.1 shows the results of estimating the cabinet duration data with a Weibull failure time distribution. The estimate of σ is less than one, which means that hazard rates are increasing over time. A test of the null hypothesis that the true model is exponential (that is, H_0: $\sigma = 1$) yields a z statistic of over 5. The probability of getting such a z by chance is zero to as many decimal places as one likes. Thus we can easily reject the null hypothesis of duration independence. We return to the interpretation of this rejection of the null hypothesis in the next subsection. But whatever the interpretation, the statistical meaning of this rejection is that parameters estimated using the exponential distribution are not optimal, and the estimated exponential standard errors are not correct.[16]

Turning to the estimated coefficients, we note that all remain statistically significant and are close to their exponential counterparts. The Weibull standard errors are about a third smaller than their exponential counterparts. Since the Weibull standard errors are more accurate, tests and confidence intervals computed with the Weibull coefficients and standard errors are superior to their counterparts computed with exponential coefficients and standard errors.

One advantage of the exponential is that it is easy to compute the expected durations of cabinets with various configurations of the covariates, and it is easy to compute the effect of any covariate on durations. This is also possible for the Weibull model (and any other mathematical model), but the computations are more complex. But complex computations are little bother for modern computers, which can easily produce graphs of the hazard rate, expected duration rates, and the effects of the various covariates.[17]

A graph of the hazard rate, as a function of time, for the mean cabinet is shown in Fig. 9.1. This graph shows clearly the pattern of rising hazards. In interpreting this graph it is important to remember that the Weibull distribution imposes the assumption of monotonically rising (or falling) hazards, and the general shape of the hazard plot; the only thing that the data speak to is the rate at which hazards are rising. As we can see in Fig. 9.1, the initial hazard rate, for the mean cabinet, is under 0.03; this doubles over the next three years. The exponential model asserted that the probability of a cabinet falling was about 5 per cent per month, regardless of duration. The Weibull model has a lower figure for this failure rate early in the life of a cabinet, but a failure rate half as large again for cabinets that have endured as long as legally possible. The hazard plot in Fig. 9.1 shows that the estimated Weibull hazard exceeds the exponential hazard for any cabinet that lasts longer than eight months.

This higher general hazard should be reflected in a lower mean survival rate for cabinets when we use the superior Weibull model. Under the exponential model the expected duration for the mean cabinet is just under 19 months; the Weibull model suggests that a more correct estimate is about 16.5 months. Since the estimated Weibull coefficients are similar to their exponential counterparts, the Weibull effects of the covariates on relative expected durations is similar to that which we found for the exponential effects. Thus, for example, the effect of moving from minority to majority coalition status increases expected duration by 60 per cent under the Weibull model, compared to 70 per cent under the exponential model. Other relative effects decrease similarly.

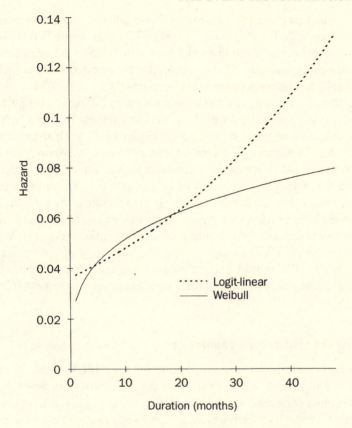

Fɪɢ. 9.1 Hazard function for mean cabinet

Interpretation of duration dependence

The Weibull model of cabinet durations is clearly statistically superior to the exponential model. Because the exponential is a special case of the Weibull, we can do classical hypotheses tests which clearly reject the exponential in favour of the Weibull. But, in doing so, we must keep in mind what it means for an estimation to reveal duration dependence.

The recent literature on cabinet stability has featured a controversy between Warwick (1992) and Alt and King (1994) over whether cabinet durations show rising hazards. While there is little doubt that the rising hazard Weibull model is statistically superior to the constant hazards exponential model, this does not mean that, over time, there is an inherent tendency for cabinets to be likely to fall. What it does mean is that, given the variables used by King et al., we can improve estimation by allowing hazards to rise over time. But this is simply because we have left out some variables that should explain why hazards rise. One possibility, as argued by Warwick (1995: ch. 5), is that the Weibull model omits the state of the economy, and this explains rising hazards. That is, when the state of economy is included in the model, the resulting hazard rate becomes flat.

So whether the hazard rate is constant, rising, or falling is a property of a particular model, not the real world. To explain cabinet durations by saying that hazards are rising is clearly not a good explanation. Such an explanation would be akin to allowing for a time trend or correlated errors. Omitting such items may lead to statistically incorrect estimations; these corrections hardly provide satisfying explanations of the phenomena under study. A model with non-constant hazard rates begs for amplification; we can regard non-constant hazard rates as a signal of an inadequately specified model. This does not mean that we should prefer exponential models to Weibull models when the Weibull model is superior, as is the case for our cabinet duration model. We should, rather, continue to investigate this model, as Warwick did, until we can explain duration dependence by observable variables.

Extending the model: split populations

Once we have written down the likelihood for the basic Weibull (or exponential) duration model, it is easy to extend it in a variety of ways. For example, suppose observations are truncated, so that only unemployment durations of more than four weeks are observed (individuals may not be eligible to receive unemployment compensation until they have been unemployed for a minimum period). To handle such data, all we need to do is to realize that the observed data are distributed so that the probability of observing a duration of four weeks or less is zero, and the density of longer observations is the Weibull (or exponential), inflated[18] so as to make the densities integrate to one.

This idea has been extended in an interesting manner in what criminologists call the 'split population' model. Criminologists have long used duration models to study recidivism, or at least the length of time until a released prisoner returns to jail. Those who never return are considered to be censored, that is, they would return to jail if we waited long enough. Schmidt and Witte (1989) make this model more realistic by assuming there are two types of former prisoners: recidivists (either observed or potential) and non-recidivists. With a probit model to estimate whether an individual is recidivist, it is easy to write down the likelihood for, and then estimate, a split-population duration model. All we need to do is to write down the density of the observed times of return to prison and the probability of a former prisoner never returning. The former is just the product of the probability that the individual is a potential recidivist multiplied by the density of returning at any particular time (using, say, the Weibull). The latter is just the sum of the probabilities that the individual is not a potential recidivist and the probability that he is but his return time is censored (again using the Weibull). While the reader interested in details of this model should consult Schmidt and Witte, the basic idea of the model should be clear. The ability to extend maximum likelihood models to take into account particular features of some data is a great strength of parametric duration models.

Semi-parametric Duration Models

Even though the Weibull is more flexible than the exponential duration model, it still makes strong assumptions about durations. Other continuous time models, such as gamma or the Gompertz, make other, but equally strong assumptions. Many survival analysts use a more flexible, semi-parametric, technique devised by Cox (1975). We look at Cox's technique first, and then discuss another duration method based on semi-parametric discrete time methods.

Cox's technique

Cox's insight was that most of the information in survival data comes when one of the units exits. The hazard for the unit exiting should be the greatest among all the units still at risk. Thus, suppose we have three cabinets still at risk at, say, forty months, and one falls at that time. The relative chance of this cabinet (say cabinet 1) falling is $\dfrac{h_1(40)}{h_1(40)+h_2(40)+h_3(40)}$. Cox called this fraction the *partial likelihood*. It contains most of the information that is available in the full likelihood (ignoring information based on the exact timing of exits).

Using this partial likelihood, Cox noted that he could use weaker assumptions than those underlying the fully parametric models. He assumed only that the hazard rates are 'proportional'. Proportional hazards are the product of two components: an unspecified 'baseline' hazard which varies with time in an unspecified manner, but does not vary across units; and a unit-specific but time-invariant component. Duration analysts typically assume that the unit-specific hazard is exponential in the covariates, as in the fully parametric models.[19] While the assumption of proportional hazards is strong, it is weaker than the assumption that the duration distribution is Weibull (or exponential) since Weibull (and exponential) hazards are themselves proportional.

The proportional hazard assumption is useful because the unspecified 'baseline' hazard drops out of the partial likelihood. Thus the partial likelihood can be maximized using standard methods. While the partial likelihoods are not likelihoods, the parameter estimates from a Cox analysis have the same large sample properties as maximum likelihood estimates. Researchers have also shown that there is little efficiency loss in using Cox's method.

Estimates of the cabinet duration model using Cox's method are in the left columns of Table 9.2.[20] The Cox estimates, with signs reversed, are interpreted in the same manner as for the exponential duration model. The Cox estimates are very close to those of the exponential and Weibull models, with any differences between the sets of estimates varying by less than one standard error. The exponential and Weibull models differed in their standard errors. While it is difficult to compare the Cox and Weibull estimates and standard errors, it is the case that the t-ratios of the Cox estimates are very close to the Weibull t-ratios; both of these differ from the (incorrect) exponential t-ratios.

Discrete hazard models

The exponential and Weibull models assume that duration data are continuous, that is, any positive duration length is possible. While the Cox procedure also works with continuous time, only the discrete set of exit times affects the estimation. Social science duration data, however, are never actually continuously measured. Rather, they are measured at some set of discrete intervals. Thus the King *et al.* (1990) cabinet durations are measured to the nearest month (although they could have been dated more finely). Durations of unemployment spells are similarly measured monthly. Even if we could get finer measurements, would it matter? Do we care if a government falls after thirty-six days rather than forty-two days?

Table 9.2 Semi-parametric estimation of cabinet durations

Variable	Cox		Logit	
	b	s.e.	b	s.e.
Constant			−3.27	0.20
Investiture	0.38	0.14	0.41	0.14
Polarization	0.02	0.01	0.02	0.01
Majority	−0.58	0.13	−0.63	0.14
Formation	0.13	0.04	0.14	0.05
Post-election	−0.85	0.14	−0.91	0.15
Caretaker	1.54	0.28	1.84	0.32
Month			0.03	0.01

Discrete duration data can be easily analysed with continuous methods. But they can also be analysed using discrete time methods. These methods are easier to comprehend, since they are simple extensions of the well-known logit or probit model. We can also use discrete time methods to analyse data, such as time-series–cross-section data with a binary dependent variable, that are usually not thought of as duration data.

Duration models are all driven by an underlying model of the probability of a unit surviving beyond a given time. The laws of probability tell us that the probability of a government surviving beyond a certain month is the probability of it surviving beyond the previous month multiplied by the probability of it surviving the final month, given that it reached that month. The latter conditional probability is exactly the discrete time hazard function. One advantage of discrete time models is that the hazard function is very intuitive.[21]

The discrete hazard—that is, the conditional probability of surviving through a given month, given that a cabinet survived to a given month—can be estimated by standard binary dependent-variable procedures such as probit or, more commonly, logit.[22] Thus, we could do a logit analysis on the cabinet duration data, where each observation represents one month of a cabinet's life. This logit would use the same independent variables that we have been using with the dependent variable being whether or not the cabinet fell in that month. The logit coefficients yield estimates of the discrete hazard function.

Each of the units that is uncensored (that is, observed until exit) contributes a series of observations with a dependent variable of zero for all but the last observation. Censored units simply contribute a series of observations, each having a dependent variable of zero. If we were to do a simple logit analysis on such data, we would be assuming duration independence. This is because the discrete hazard would be a function of the covariates, but not of time. Thus, the simple logit set-up is the discrete time analogue of the exponential model.

What if we are unwilling to make the very strong assumption of duration independence? We could proceed very generally, and allow the discrete hazard at month m to be a different function of the covariates for each m. But this is too general, and would not allow for accurate estimation of parameters. The same logic that leads to a proportional hazards model leads to a much simpler, and estimable model, which at the same time allows for duration dependence.

We can add to the independent logit model a term which marks how long a cabinet has been in power. If this term has no effect, then the hazard rate is independent of time, that is, we would have duration independence. If, however, duration belongs in the logit, then we have duration dependence. The simplest way to enter duration into the logit analysis is to add a dummy variable for each month. Thus, in the cabinet duration study, we would have just under forty-eight-monthly variables added to the substantive covariates in a logit analysis.[23] This approach allows for a reasonable estimation of the effects of the covariates. But it uses up many degrees of freedom, and makes it difficult to estimate the form of duration dependence, since each of the coefficients of the dummy variables will have large standard errors.

We could attempt to parameterize the dummy variables as, say, lying on a low-order polynomial in time. This would be the exact analogue of modelling distributed lags in time-series analysis via Almon polynomials. (The unrestricted dummy variable approach corresponds to estimating an unrestricted distributed lag model.) But such an approach is inflexible, and may not pick up the correct pattern of duration dependence. Therefore, I prefer to model the monthly dummy variables by a *cubic spline*. Cubic splines join together a series of cubic polynomials as 'knots', with the cubic term and the number of knots being chosen such that the resulting function appears to be fairly smooth.[24]

After estimating the logit model with a cubic spline in duration, it appeared that duration should enter the logit in a simpler, linear form. A χ^2 test failed to reject the null hypothesis that the cubic spline was no better than a simpler, linear term (with a p-value of about 0.50).[25] Although I simply use a linear term 'month' in the logit analysis, it should be stressed that researchers cannot assume that a linear form, or even a monotonic form, will always be correct. The logit model with smoothed duration allows us to test various hypotheses about the form of duration dependence. At that point, as here, we might choose to model duration dependence by a simple parametric term, or terms.

The estimates from the logit analysis with duration dependence are shown in the right-hand columns of Table 9.2. We see that the logit estimates (with duration dependence) are similar to the Cox estimates. Since the Cox results are similar to the Weibull results, this means that including 'month' in the logit does a good job of picking up duration dependence.[26]

The logit duration-dependent model also shows that the hazard of a cabinet falling increases monotonically over time. Thus, the monotonic hazard rate assumed by the Weibull is correct. To use the Weibull, we had to assume that duration dependence is monotonic; the logit analysis can demonstrate that it is so. The shape of the discrete hazard function (with all covariates set to their mean) is shown in Fig. 9.1. The shape is similar to that of the Weibull hazard for the first two years. At that point, the discrete hazard continues to rise at an increasing rate while the Weibull hazard rises at a falling rate.[27]

Thus, whether we use a Weibull or discrete approach, it appears that the King *et al.* model shows duration dependence, with an unexplained tendency for cabinets to face an increasing risk of falling as they age. We can gauge the substantive impact of this increasing hazard by comparing its effect in the underlying linear latent model with that of other variables. A change from being a majority to a minority government, for example, has the same effect on cabinet fragility as does an increased cabinet age of about two and a half years. These increasing hazards cause problems for estimation techniques which ignore it. But they are also substantively non-trivial.

Binary time-series–cross-section models

Using logit analysis to analyse discrete duration data is not new (*cf.* Allison 1982), but it seems less well known that we can use event history ideas to improve on some logit analyses. The analysis of time-series–cross-section data with binary dependent variables (BTSCS) is becoming more common, especially in international relations research.[28] Analysts interested in the causes of war (Maoz and Russett 1993, for example) commonly take as their unit of analysis the dyad-year, with the dependent variables being whether or not the dyad was at war, and independent variables measuring whether the dyad was democratic, economically interdependent, and the like. Such studies are invariably estimated via independent logits.

These logit analyses assume that the observations are temporally independent. This is an untenable assumption and may lead to severe estimation problems. There is no simple correction for interdependent observations with time-series–cross-section data with binary dependent variables, as there would be with continuous time-series–cross-section data. But just as we analyse duration data using discrete methods, we can think of time-series–cross-section data with binary dependent variables as event histories. Consider the example of whether a dyad is at war or peace in any given year. The dependent variable can be thought of as an event history. That is, we observe an initial spell of peace, followed by a spell of war, followed perhaps by another spell of peace, and so forth. The binary yearly dependent variable simply tells us how long these spells are. Dyads ending with a spell of peace are simply treated as censored.

We can, then, analyse time-series–cross-section data with binary dependent variables in the same manner as we analyse discrete duration data: we simply add a smooth term in duration to the logit model. We can then test for whether this smooth term is required. If not, the data are duration independent and the simple, independent, logit is appropriate. This method works best if the time-series–cross-section data with binary dependent variables look like duration data; that is, long spells with the dependent variable being zero followed by a very short spurt where it is one. Thus the method is best for rare events, such as militarized disputes.[29] Standard logit and probit methods work least well for dependent variables which are almost always zero. But event history methods are exactly right for such data. In the cabinet's data, over 95 per cent of the cabinet-months revealed no cabinet fall. We would hope that students of divorce or death would be studying similarly rare events. The discrete time event history approach is the only simple way to estimate models using time-series–cross-section data with binary dependent variables.

Time-varying covariates and multiple destinations

The discrete duration approach also simplifies two issues which often prove difficult: time-varying covariates and multiple destinations. Until now I have assumed that the covariates are constant over the life of a government. But covariates may change over time, as in Warwick's use of the economy to explain the fall of cabinets. While it is possible to use time-varying covariates in either the Cox model or the fully parametric models, the data set-up for these analyses is not simple.[30] Time-varying covariates, are, however, not only not difficult for discrete duration models, they are the natural way to proceed. Some of these covariates may remain constant over the life of a cabinet, others may vary from month to month. But time-varying covariates are completely straightforward and natural in the discrete duration context.

Having said this, one must take care to ensure that the covariates are exogenous; that is, that there are no simultaneities between the covariates and the duration being explained. Thus, for example, in a study of marriage durations, we might allow for the health status of the spouses as a time-varying covariate (unless one believed that impending divorce were a serious cause of illness). The birth of children would not, however, be a legitimate covariate, since we might hope that people take marriage durability into account in their family-planning decisions. Simultaneities are on the frontier of duration analysis; readers interested in such issues should consult Peterson (1995).

A second issue on the frontiers is known as *multiple destinations*. So far we have assumed that a cabinet either survives or falls. However, we might be interested in different types of failure, perhaps differentiating between cabinet reshuffling and major changes. For unemployment spells, we might want to know not only how long someone is unemployed, but whether they leave unemployment for a job, illness, or perhaps a welfare programme. Such issues are difficult in the parametric or Cox approaches. But in the discrete approach, we merely replace the simple logit with a multinomial logit. We probably should not be too optimistic about getting good estimates for the probability of exit in a given manner. After all, most of the discrete observations will be in months when a government has not exited, so we would have very few observations to provide information on the direction of exit.

But if multiple destinations are important, the discrete duration approach, with multinomial logits, seems the simplest way to proceed.[31]

Conclusion

The analysis of duration data and event histories is becoming more common in the social sciences. The nature of the dependent variable for such data, and the presence of censored data, require the use of maximum likelihood techniques. While these techniques are computationally complex, we have seen that the estimates produced by these techniques have clear substantive interpretations. Event history analysts should always report their conclusions in terms of the durations or event histories of interest, rather than just providing a list of coefficients, standard errors, and t-ratios.

Event history data often show duration dependence, that is, the model operates differently as the process ages. There was only a moderate amount of duration dependence in our running example, so taking duration dependence into account did not have huge effects on the estimated coefficients. Ignoring duration dependence leads to incorrect standard errors; taking duration dependence into account reduces those errors by about a third. In any event, it is easy enough to estimate models, such as the Weibull, that take duration dependence into account. Once such a model is estimated, it is possible to test for whether the data actually show duration dependence. If not, a simpler model can be re-estimated.

Duration-independent models, such as the exponential, make it easier to interpret results. Thus, we might want to stick with a simpler model even if a test indicates a small amount of duration dependence. This situation is similar to that in time-series analysis, where it is often worth while ignoring a small amount of serial correlation in the errors in order to make it easier to communicate results.

The analogy with serially correlated errors also helps us to understand the meaning of duration dependence. Like serially correlated errors, ignoring duration dependence leads to inefficient estimation and incorrectly estimated standard errors. But, as with serially correlated errors, duration dependence cannot be considered a satisfactory explanation of an event history. Simply to say that hazards rise over time is no more an explanation of a phenomenon than saying that large errors follow large errors. Thus, if we find duration dependence we must seek models which provide a substantive explanation of this dependence. But until we find such a model we must allow for duration dependence in estimation.

The parametric Weibull model makes very strong assumptions about the form of duration dependence. Both the Cox model and the discrete logit model make it possible to account for duration dependence without making such strong assumptions. The Cox model is the most widely used duration model in applied work. The discrete logit model is easy to use and to implement; it ties in very nicely with data that do not look like standard duration data, such as binary time-series–cross-section data; and it is easy to extend to time-varying covariates and multiple destinations. But while the semi-parametric methods have strong advantages, the fully parametric methods also have advantages. In particular, they can be more easily extended in interesting ways, such as the split-population models. Given the ease of modern computation, there is no reason for researchers to limit themselves only to either fully parametric or semi-parametric techniques. Thus, for example, the discrete logit approach was once shunned because it involved estimation with enormous data sets. Today, estimating such models on a common desktop computer is trivial. To convince readers that this is so, the chapter is rounded off with a note about software for duration analysis.

Software

A decade ago most duration analysts used specialized software. Today, many of the most common general purpose packages, such as *SAS*, contain a reasonable set of duration routines. There are several statistical packages which have special strengths for analysing duration data. *SPLUS* has a wonderful set of Cox routines, and seems to be the package of choice among bio-statisticians. It is not a particularly easy package to work with, however, and is not widely used among social scientists. Most of the analyses in this chapter were performed using *LIMDEP*. This package has an excellent set of parametric routines, and allows the user to undertake many specialized analyses, such as the split-population models, the generalized gamma, or the use of continuous time-varying covariate data.

The latest version of *STATA* (*STATA 5*), released at the end of 1996, has tremendous capabilities for analysing complex duration data in either the Cox or Weibull frameworks. This package makes it relatively painless to analyse repeated events, delayed entry, time-varying covariates, and other features that complicate the life of event history analysts. *STATA* also produces excellent graphical output, and provides a wide range of diagnostic statistics. Since *STATA* is commonly used as a general purpose package, the routines available in *STATA 5* almost certainly make it the package of choice for event history analysts who do not need the full range of parametric routines available in *LIMDEP*. *STATA*, or *SPLUS*, can also be used to produce the smooth duration terms for the analysis of binary time-series–cross-sectional data. A combination of *LIMDEP* and *STATA* should meet the needs of almost anyone engaged in event history analysis. The more econometrically oriented analyst will probably want to start with *LIMDEP*, while the more sociologically oriented will probably look first at *STATA*.

It is easy to undertake technical analyses of duration and event history data with any of this software. The difficult part, of course, is coming up with good theoretical specifications to analyse. Event history analysts also spend much time collecting interesting data; event history data seldom come on convenient CD-ROMS! But once the data are collected and the models formulated, modern computers and software make the analysis of these data and models relatively painless. Understanding the models makes interpretation similarly painless.

Obviously, only the surface of event history analysis has been scratched here. In particular, questions of specification testing have been completely ignored. In addition, I have only touched on analytic issues on the frontier of event history analysis: simultaneities, multiple destinations, and repeated spells. Research on these topics is in its infancy. But this infant is growing fast! It is an exciting time to study event histories.

Notes

1. This chapter draws on several collaborations with Simon Jackman, Jonathan Katz, and Richard Tucker. Thanks also to Jim Alt, Rob Engle, Gary King, and Glenn Sueyoshi for numerous discussions about duration models, and to Gary King for supplying the data. Special thanks to all my Summer School students who allowed me to hone my ideas while claiming to be teaching them, and to the *Essex Summer School in Data Analysis and Collection* for creating an environment where this could be done.
2. Duration analysis examines the time until the first event, while event history analysis deals more with transitions between a variety of events. The distinction is not sharp. My interest here is in the simpler duration data. The analysis of simple durations is a critical building block in the analysis of event histories. For ease of exposition, I use the two terms more or less interchangeably throughout.
3. For a recent argument in this vein, see Alt *et al.* (1996).
4. Cabinet and government are used as synonyms.
5. The data were originally collected by Strom (1988). I trust readers have an intuitive understanding of these variables since they are simply referred to in the chapter by the short names in parentheses with little discussion of their substantive meaning. Measurement details may be found in Strom (1988) and King *et al.* (1990). Warwick (1995) provides an excellent recent book on these issues.
6. Fixed covariates remain constant over an entire spell; they are distinguished from time-varying covariates which vary over the course of a spell. This distinction will be made clearer below.

7. Mathematically, if the covariates for a cabinet are X and Z, the expected duration of that cabinet is $e^{a+bX+dZ}$. It should be stressed that the exponential form for the mean has nothing to do with the distribution being exponential. We are stuck with this unfortunate coincidence of nomenclature. Even when we abandon the exponential distribution, event history analysts still assume that the relationship between the covariates and durations has an exponential component.

8. This is what is known as 'right censoring' since we know when spells began but do not know when some end. Data are 'left censored' if we do not know when spells began, as would be the case if we asked people in a monthly panel if they were on welfare and observed some people on welfare at the beginning of the panel. I treat only simple right censoring here, assuming that the censoring mechanism is unrelated to the process under study.

9. Warwick (1995) has argued that censoring should never be imposed by the analyst but only by the data collection process. Hence, from his perspective a British cabinet that endures for 53 months is a duration of exactly 53 months. But we do not know how long such a cabinet would have endured in the absence of constitutionally set maximum durations. Thus it seems that the King et al.'s (1990) censoring argument is reasonable. King et al. censor the data a year before a mandated election since they do not consider the exact timing of when an election is called to be relevant to their theory of the parliamentary determinants of cabinet durations. In any event, here I use the coding on censoring employed by King et al.

10. $\frac{\partial E(t)}{\partial X} = bE(t)$ for the duration model in n. 7.

11. More formally, let $h(t)$ be the hazard rate as a function of time; $h(t)$ is not a probability, and can exceed one. (It is mathematically like a density.) The probability of a cabinet failing in the interval from time t to $t + \Delta t$ given that it survived up to time t is $h(t)\Delta t$ for very small values of Δt.

12. $F(t)$ is the distribution of failure times, so $S(t) = 1 - F(t). h(t) = \frac{f(t)}{S(t)}$ where $f(t)$ is the density of failure times. When we use an exponential duration model, we are assuming the F follows an exponential distribution.

13. To give another example, what does the original survivor function, that for human lifetimes, look like? It is hard to answer this. But we do have the intuition that the human hazard rate is fairly high at birth, declines after that, stays low for a while, perhaps increases again for teenage males, then perhaps declines, and then inexorably rises. It is easier to think about the conditional probability of a 60-year-old dying in his 61st year than it is to think about the probability of any random person dying in their 61st year. While the hazard function seems mathematically more complex than the survivor function, it is actually more intuitive. Of course the two functions are mathematically related.

14. This assumption is exactly the same as the assumption of independence in event counts, which leads to the use of a Poisson distribution. If event counts are Poisson distributed, then the time until the first event is exponentially

distributed. Since event count analysts seldom find the Poisson to be acceptable, we would not expect the exponential to be the duration distribution of choice.

15. Other common distributions, such as the gamma or the Gompertz, do not require monotonic hazards. But these other distributions, containing the same number of shape parameters as the Weibull, cannot be more flexible than the Weibull. They simply impose different shape requirements, which may, in some cases, fit the data better. There is one more general distribution, the 'generalized gamma' (Lancaster 1990: 38–40) which has two shape parameters. In theory this more general distribution could be used to sort out whether the gamma or Weibull is correct, since it contains both as special cases. In practice, this distribution appears to be too flexible in that it seems hard to estimate the two shape parameters with any degree of accuracy.

16. To be more precise, even if the exponential is rejected, its estimates of the coefficients are still consistent, albeit inefficient. Its estimated standard errors are not consistent, and so may not even be correct for large samples. The degree of inefficiency, and inaccuracy of the standard errors, depends on how far σ is from 1. In large samples we may reject the null hypothesis that $\sigma = 1$ even when it is close to 1. In such cases the exponential estimates may still be adequate.

17. For those who like to know what their computers are doing, the various formulae are given. Using the example of two covariates, X and Z, as before, and standard duration notation, we write $\lambda = e^{-(a + bX + dZ)}$ for interesting values of the covariates. These are most commonly the means of X and Z but could easily be other interesting combinations, especially with dummy variables. For simplicity, we use the notation $p = 1/\sigma$ and let Γ be the Gamma function. (Note that some computer programs report p, others report σ, and they all use differing notation. It is very important that users of a computer program are sure about what is reported.) The Weibull hazard as a function of time for that cabinet is $h(t) = \lambda p (\lambda t)^{p-1}$. The expected duration for any cabinet is given by $\frac{\Gamma(1+\sigma)}{\lambda}$. Note that if $\sigma = p = 1$ the hazard function reduces to λ and the expected duration is just $1/\lambda$ which is exactly what we have for the exponential. Since σ (and p) does not vary from cabinet to cabinet, the effect on expected duration of any continuous covariate is calculated similarly to the exponential effect, but multiplied by $\Gamma(1 + \sigma)$. If $\sigma < 1$ this multiplicative factor is between 0.9 and 1.0. Only in the rarely seen case of large σ's is this multiplicative factor very different from 1. In our cabinet example, $\sigma = 0.78$. Since $\Gamma(1.78) = 0.92$, the Weibull coefficient overstates impacts by about 8 per cent. Since σ does not vary from cabinet to cabinet, we can easily compare relative expected durations of two cabinets. For example, for two cabinets which are identical except for one having $X = 1$ while the other has $X = 0$, the relative expected duration remains e^b.

18. By $\frac{1}{1 - P(Y < 4)}$ where Y has a Weibull distribution.

19. In symbols, let $h_0(t)$ be the baseline hazard, which is some unknown function of time but does not vary by unit. If we let $h_i(t)$ be the hazard function for unit i,

Cox assumed that $h_i(t) = h_0(t)e^{-(a+bX_i+dZ_i)}$. The hazards are proportional in that $\frac{h_i(t)}{h_j(t)} = \frac{e^{-(a+bX_i+dZ_i)}}{e^{-(a+bX_j+dZ_j)}}$ which varies with the individual covariates but not with time. If unit 1 exits at time t, with units $2, \ldots, n$ still at risk at time t, the partial likelihood for this observed exit is $\frac{e^{-(bX_1+dZ_1)}}{\sum_{i=1}^{n} e^{-(bX_i+dZ_i)}}$. Tied exit times cause problems for Cox's method. There are now several standard ways of handling ties, which vary in computational complexity. Users of data with many tied exit times should be aware of this issue.

20. The Cox method does not estimate a constant term, since the constant term drops out of the partial likelihood.

21. The probability of surviving beyond month m is just $P(t > m) = P(t > m - 1)P(t > m \mid t > m - 1)$. We can iterate this backwards to get $P(t > m) = P(t > m \mid t > m - 1)P(t > m - 1 \mid t > m - 2) \ldots P(t > 1)$ so the unconditional probability of a cabinet surviving beyond m months is the product of the series of discrete hazards at months $1, 2, \ldots, m$.

22. The situation is a bit more complicated than this, since the logit or probit models are not what would emerge if we started with a standard continuous time duration model and then converted it to a discrete time model. Thus the logit and probit models do not have the proportional hazards property. To my mind this is a theological issue, since we choose specific continuous time distributions for reasons of mathematical convenience, not for their social science implications. Thus we could equally criticize the continuous models for not being the limit of a logit or probit. The relationship between continuous and discrete time models is laid out very clearly in Sueyoshi (1995). Alt *et al.* (1996) assert the reasonable point that models should be invariant to arbitrary measurement decisions.

23. Just under 48 because months in which no cabinet fell do not contribute anything to the likelihood and must be dropped. This only happens in a few months right before the maximum censoring point. Note how similar this is to the Cox analysis, which also analyses only months where at least one cabinet fell.

24. In other work, I have used cubic 'smoothing splines' (Hastie and Tibshirani 1990) for the smooth duration term. For our purposes, the difference between the two types of spline is not great, and either could be used as the smoothed duration term.

25. The spline is shown in Beck and Jackman (1998). The only departure from linearity is that it appears to be flat after about 30 months.

26. I estimated a simple logit model without a month term; that is, assuming duration independence. Coefficient estimates for this model are similar to our other estimates, but its t-ratios are closer to the exponential model t-ratios. Since both the simple logit and the exponential assume duration independence, we should expect estimates and standard errors using these models to be similar.

27. Again, it should be noted that the hazard rate estimated with a cubic spline levels off after about 30 months. Thus the late period discrepancy between the

Weibull and the discrete hazard in Fig. 9.1 is largely an artefact of having entered time linearly in the discrete hazard model. It should also be remembered that most cabinets have either failed or are marked as censored by 36 months, so there is not a lot of information available for precise estimation of hazard rates at long durations.

28. It is important to distinguish time-series–cross-section data with binary dependent variables (BTSCS) from panel data. Panel data have many units observed for short periods of time, while BTSCS have a number of fixed units observed for many time periods. This section does not treat issues involved with binary panel data, which, of course, have a long literature of their own, most of which is not particularly relevant to BTSCS data.

29. Applications of this idea to international relations BTSCS data may be found in Beck and Tucker (1996).

30. It is also the case that many duration programs do not allow for time-varying covariates for all the different approaches they support.

31. Duration dependence would still be modelled via a smooth function of time. All of the assumptions required for cross-sectional multinomial logit would obviously have to be met for a discrete multiple destinations analysis.

PART III
NEW PERSPECTIVES

10

THE GLASS BEAD GAME: TESTING GAME-THEORETIC MODELS OF POLITICS

HUGH WARD

Rational choice theory is based on a straightforward claim: 'When faced with several courses of action, people usually do what they believe is likely to have the best overall outcome' (Elster 1989: 22). Since first developed in the 1950s, rational choice theory has had an enormous impact on most major sub-fields of political science, if only negatively, by provoking strong critical reactions.[1] Orthodox rational choice theory [2] has a number of other core commitments. First, that individuals are self-interested; but exactly what this highly elastic term means is open to dispute. Second, that explanations of social phenomena should build upwards from the beliefs and goals of individuals, although this principle of methodological individualism often has little impact on the actual practice of rational choice analysis in which structural factors are introduced without attempts to explain them away. Third, that individuals have the rational capacity, time, and emotional detachment necessary to choose a best course of action, no matter how complex the choice; or, if they do not, that some process of social selection will eliminate them from 'the game', so long-run survivors act 'as if' they had these capacities.

In recent years, the trickle of critical commentary on rational choice theory has grown into a spate as the approach has become more central to, in particular, American political science.[3] Elsewhere (Ward 1996a), I have provided a route map for this body of critical literature by dividing it into four broad categories: (i) the internal critique of rational choice 'heretics', who wish to emphasize 'bounded rationality' and technical problems in game theory; (ii) the sociological critique, which centres on the way rational choice theory appears to downplay social structure and holistic modes of explanation; (iii) the arguments by psychologists that individuals often do not act rationally in the standard sense, but are motivationally and psychologically complex; and (iv) the critique from mainstream political science, based on the implausibility of the assumptions made and the predictive failures of the model. In this chapter, I focus specifically on this last line of criticism.

The most important version of the critique coming from mainstream political science is Green and Shapiro's book, *Pathologies of Rational Choice Theory* (1994). Their arguments are extensive but the essentials can be summarized in six points (see, particularly, pp. 34–46):

1. Many rational choice models are slippery, as they contain crucial unobservable variables that are impossible to operationalize and measure. As a consequence, theorists can always generate some combination of unobservables fitting any empirical observation, so that the model cannot be falsified.
2. When empirical tests are carried out, they often amount to *post hoc* explanations of known facts, which is all too easy given the slippery nature of the models.
3. The models seldom generate novel predictions which are open to clear falsification.
4. When testable hypotheses are generated, alternative theories are often ignored when testing is carried out, so there is a failure to control for potentially important variables and to construct null hypotheses that provide a realistic test for the model.
5. When evidence does falsify the models, it is selectively ignored, whereas evidence that confirms the model is accumulated.
6. Attention is steered away from applications in which the model does not seem to work, leading to an imbalance in evaluating the paradigm.

All these deficiencies are seen to derive from the desire to construct a universalist theory of human behaviour, and, consequently, an unwillingness to acknowledge exceptions. In their turn, however, Green and Shapiro's arguments have been subject to a considerable barrage of criticism from those sympathetic to rational choice theory.[4]

This chapter sets out to illustrate the power of rational choice theory, or game theory, to produce novel, empirically testable, and confirmed propositions in an area of interest to political scientists: local campaigning strategy by political parties. The chapter also has two subsidiary purposes. First, to show something of how game theory works in a relatively simple context. Then, secondly, to draw attention to some problems of empirically testing game-theoretic models to which Green and Shapiro give inadequate attention. These are, in particular, the problems associated with an approach that generally does not make point predictions, and the problems of operationalizing basic concepts when the theory tells us that the information we have is liable to be false, as there are incentives for rational actors to mislead us.

start by introducing some ideas from game theory, after which I examine the literature on local party campaigning.

A Rough Guide to Game Theory

There are several excellent introductions to game theory,[5] and what follows is no more than the briefest sketch. The simplest decision problem arises when each action has a single, known outcome; there is no risk or uncertainty, and no other agent's actions affect the consequences of the choice made. In such instances, in order to make a decision, all that is needed is a rank ordering of the outcomes. Thus, for any pair of alternatives a and b, the decision-maker can say whether a is better than b, b is better than a, or the two outcomes are indifferent; and the transitivity property is satisfied, so that if a is better than b and b is better than c, then a is better than c.

The first complication is that decision-makers may not know for sure what the consequences of their actions will be. It has been shown that, granted certain assumptions, individuals choose as if they were maximizing expected utility. This can be thought of as the 'long-term average' pay-off if the same decision were to be made repeatedly, taking account of the various possible outcomes the action could lead to and the probabilities of their occurrence.[6] The so-called *cardinal utilities* needed to represent decision-making here can be derived, at least in principle, from experiments in which individuals rank order lotteries over the outcomes. Cardinal utilities can be interpreted as containing information about preference intensity, which is inessential to predicting choice under certainty.

The second complication, and one central to game theory, is that the outcome may be the consequence of the actions of two or more players, say A and B. So A cannot predict the consequences of her actions from knowledge of her own action alone. Moreover, A may anticipate the decisions being made by B in reaction to her choice and realize that her best choice of action depends on what B does. Game theory deals with rational choice where there is this sort of strategic interdependence.

The most important idea in game theory is that of a *strategy equilibrium*. A strategy is a complete plan for playing the game which tells the player exactly what action to choose at all points in the game when the player has to make a choice. In non-cooperative games, in which binding agreements between players are impossible, an equilibrium is a set of strategies, one for each player, such that no player can increase their pay-off by changing strategy given that no other player changes strategy. In games, there is a possible infinite regress of the form: 'If he thinks I will choose a then he will choose b; but if he chooses b, I will choose c; but if I choose c, he will choose d, . . .'

When strategies are in equilibrium, this does not occur. Suppose that the strategies S and T are in equilibrium, and that it is common knowledge that both players are rational and have the pay-offs they do. If A expects B to choose T, he cannot improve his pay-off by changing from S; and if A believes that B thinks he will choose S, then B will choose T, justifying A's assumption about B's choice being T. The same argument applies to B. So, in equilibrium, players' choices of strategy and expectations are consistent. Moreover, equilibria are self-enforcing: consistent with the assumption that binding agreements cannot be made, the actors' pay-offs must provide the reasons for sticking with an equilibrium; and this is certainly the case since none can gain from a unilateral change of strategy. Game-theoretic models predict that rational players will choose strategies that are in equilibrium.

Rational Resource Distribution in Party Campaigning

It is part of political folk wisdom that parties should focus their campaign efforts and resources on swing voters and marginal constituencies. For example, in 1996 the Conservative Party in Britain decided to produce a free newspaper containing 'good news' as part of its general election campaign but distributed it only in marginal constituencies. Denver and Hands (1992: 33–41) examined several aspects of campaigning activity and found positive correlations with a measure of marginality, although the Conservative Party appeared to campaign as hard in safe seats as in marginal seats. Many political scientists, at least as far back as Downs (1957: ch. 4), have claimed that it is important to allocate scarce political resources efficiently across groups. This has often been taken to mean a spatial distribution of benefits favouring constituencies that are marginal.[7] The problem with this literature is that it relies on informal or 'soft' rational choice arguments to justify the claim that the party will, thus, do better in marginal seats or among swing voters (Ward and John 1996).

   In relation to marginal seats, it is taken as obvious by local party activists and academic commentators alike (Denver and Hands 1992: 528; Pattie *et al.* 1995: 976–7) that resources should be steered in their direction, because there is more chance that this will affect the outcome. Actually it is not at all obvious! Is it rational to distribute resources to marginal seats when, by the same argument, the opposition should be doing exactly the same thing? At least to some degree, these efforts will cancel out one another. Moreover, if it is rational to direct resources into marginals, how marginal has a constituency to be before it gets additional resources? And how much will seats with different degrees of marginality get relative to one another? The 'soft' rational choice arguments cannot answer these questions. Rather, they can be answered only within a game-theoretic model that takes into account the strategic interdependence of the parties' decisions. As I shall show, it is generally not rational to behave in the way assumed in the literature.

Interest in this topic has been reactivated by evidence that what happens at constituency level can have an impact on constituency results, and, hence, on national outcomes. The conventional wisdom in Britain, exemplified by the Nuffield election studies, has been that local campaigning makes little or no difference to the outcome in a constituency; swings are largely uniform across constituencies and are determined by national campaigning, not by the quality of the local campaign or the candidate.[8] Recent empirical work, however, suggests that constituency campaigning can make a difference to outcomes (Denver and Hands 1992: 542–4; Whiteley *et al.* 1994: ch. 8), at least for the challengers in a seat if not for the incumbent party (Pattie *et al.* 1995: 979–81). This may be because it is easier to gain support from a lower base. As I shall show, the evidence is that politically significant extra resources are allocated to some constituencies.

A game-theoretic model of constituency campaigning

The assumptions of the model are that:

1. there are two parties competing in a national-level election;
2. the parties are unitary actors;
3. by distributing campaigning effort across the constituencies, parties aim to maximize the expected number of seats they win;
4. there is an upper limit on the quantity of mobile resources that parties can allocate in a discretionary way to campaigning at constituency level;
5. other things being equal, increased local campaigning effort increases the chances of a party winning a particular seat.

The argument here concerns mobile resources that can be moved between constituencies by the central party organization, not those resources which are under the control of the local constituency associations. The idea is to model the way in which the central party machine steers resources towards target constituencies (Denver and Hands 1992: 41). Some resources, such as advertising expenditure, clearly can be targeted in this way.

The number of constituencies is N and each constituency has n voters who turn out. Let p_i be the probability that a randomly chosen voter in constituency i votes for the opposition; $(1 - p_i)$ is the probability that she votes for the government; and that $0 < p_i < 1$. The maximum resources that the parties can allocate to all constituency campaigning are C_{Opp} and C_{Gov} for the opposition and government, respectively. The resources employed in the i-th constituency are $c_{Opp,i}$ and $c_{Gov,i}$ respectively. For each constituency i, $p_i = p_{i,0} + k\,(c_{Opp,i} - c_{Gov,i})$ where: $p_{i,0}$ is the posterior probability that a voter in constituency i votes for the opposition if neither party campaigns in the constituency; $k > 0$, so that the probability of an elector voting for the opposition in constituency i is a linearly increasing function of opposition campaigning effort in that constituency and a linearly decreasing function of government campaigning effort in that constituency. It is assumed that the effects of local campaigning are sufficiently small to ensure that $p_{i,0} - k{\star}C_{Gov} > 0$ and $p_{i,0} + k{\star}C_{Opp} < 1$, so that even the maximum possible effects of constituency campaigning are not great enough to eliminate the uncertainty in both parties about voter behaviour and outcomes.

For an even value of n, under a plurality voting system, the government wins constituency i if the number of votes for the opposition is less than w, where w is the integer $n/2$.[9] The probability that the government wins the i-th constituency is the probability that the number voting for the opposition is less than or equal to w. Assuming that the voting behaviour of electors is statistically independent, this is given by the cumulative distribution function for the binomial distribution:

$$\sum_{r=0}^{w} \binom{n}{r} p_i^r (1-p_i)^{n-r} \tag{1}$$

where the terms being summed are the probability that r out of the n electors vote for the opposition. The expected number of constituencies that the government wins—its expected utility given that utility is a linearly increasing function of seats won[10]—is:

$$\sum_{i=0}^{N} \sum_{r=0}^{w} \binom{n}{r} p_i^r (1-p_i)^{n-r}$$

The constraints facing the government are: $C_{Gov} - \sum_{i=0}^{N} c_{Gov,i} \geq 0$. That is, the government cannot spend more resources than it has, and: $C_{Gov,i} \geq 0$ for all i. That is, no constituency can be allocated a negative quantity of resources. Similarly, the opposition wishes to maximize its number of seats and faces constraints like those on the government.

In Fig. 10.1 the probability that the government wins constituency i, given by expression (1), is sketched as a function of p_i, assuming that n is very large. This is the case for constituencies in Britain which average about 65,000 voters. As suggested by this sketch, the function will closely approximate a discontinuous function taking on the value 1 for $p_i < \frac{1}{2}$, and the value zero for $p_i > \frac{1}{2}$. The behaviour of the voters in the constituency constitutes a large number of independent 'trials' of the same 'experiment', where the outcome is either a vote for the government or a vote for the opposition with fixed probability across the trials. By the Strong Law of Large Numbers, as the number of trials increases to infinity, the proportion of trials in which 'vote opposition' occurs will approach p_i. So, with a 'large' number of voters, the proportion voting for the opposition will 'almost certainly' be a majority if $p_i > \frac{1}{2}$ and will 'almost certainly' be less than a majority if $p_i < \frac{1}{2}$. The discontinuous function shown in Fig. 10.1 is an approximation; the actual function falls from left to right, but very slowly except in the neighbourhood of $p_i = \frac{1}{2}$, as shown in a deliberately exaggerated way by the elongated z-shaped dotted function.

In effect, the discontinuous approximation ignores the fact that there is some real uncertainty about which way constituencies with p_i close to $\frac{1}{2}$ will go. In the model here, so long as the government can get a constituency 'onside' by ensuring that $p_i < \frac{1}{2}$, it believes it will win. A further simplification assumes that if $p_i = \frac{1}{2}$, the probability that the opposition wins the constituency is seen as 1 by each side, although strictly speaking it is ill-defined. This eliminates the need to consider messy problems about limits and vanishingly small changes.

With the approximation made in the previous paragraph, the game between the government and opposition is easy to visualize. The constituencies are initially positioned as points on the interval of the real line (0, 1), the position of constituency i being $p_{i,0}$. Constituencies 'just' to the left of

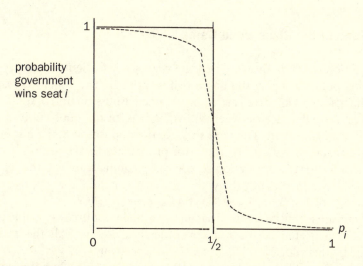

FIG. 10.1 The probability of winning a seat as a function of the probability of a randomly chosen voter voting for the opposition

½ are government marginals and constituencies 'just' to the right of ½ are opposition marginals. The governing party has campaigning resources which enable it to move constituencies to the left. But the total leftward movement it can bring about, summing across the movements made in each constituency, is limited by the government's constraint to C_{Gov}/k, that is, its total campaigning resources divided by the unit cost of reducing the probability of electors voting for the opposition in any constituency. Similarly, the opposition can move constituencies to the right, but there is a limit on the sum of rightward movements it can bring about. The government's expected pay-off is the number of constituencies with p values strictly less than ½ *after* each side has distributed its resources according to its campaign strategy; and the opposition's pay-off is the number of constituencies with p values which end up as greater than, or equal to, ½. The game is fixed-sum, so there is complete conflict of interest. In other words, the constituencies are like glass beads that can be moved around in a series of grooves, one for each constituency, on a board. The aim is to get as many as possible on your side of the half-way mark in each groove, but you are limited to a certain total 'yardage' of movement and can only move the beads in your own direction.[11]

In general, the equilibria of a game can be different, depending on the order in which players choose their strategies and whether any player knows the choice of the others. It will make for a simpler, more graphic presentation if we assume that the government chooses its strategy first, then the opposition chooses in full knowledge of how the government has moved.[12]

Equilibria in the Glass Bead Game

This section starts by showing that the way political scientists have typically assumed politicians play the game is not rational. The usual suggestion is that the resources allocated are a linearly decreasing function of the absolute value of the difference between the vote share of the opposition in a constituency and one-half. The vote share of the opposition at the last election is a reasonable proxy for $p_{i,0}$, the prior probability that a randomly chosen elector votes for the opposition before campaigning starts. So the resources allocated to constituency i by the government and the opposition are assumed to be $f_{Gov}(1-2|p_{i,0}-0.5|)$ and $f_{Opp}(1-2|p_{i,0}-0.5|)$, with f_{Gov} and f_{Opp} strictly positive constants such that all the mobile resources available to each party are allocated across the constituencies. Let us call the strategies implied by this allocation M_{Gov} and M_{Opp} respectively.

The effects of these strategies are shown in Fig. 10.2. Here it is assumed that the government has more resources to allocate than the opposition, but

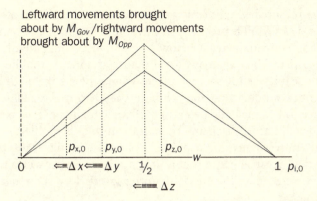

Fig. 10.2 The strategy combination (M_{Opp}, M_{Gov}) is not likely to be an equilibrium

similar arguments arise if the opposition has more resources. The position of constituency i before the campaigns start is $p_{i,0}$. The effect of the government's strategy on constituency x, for example, is to move it $k f_{Gov}(1-2\,|\,p_{x,0} - 0.5\,|)$ to the left; while the effect of the opposition's strategy is to move it $k f_{Opp}(1-2\,|\,p_{x,0}-0.5\,|)$ to the right. The net effect on x is Δx, a leftward movement equivalent to the difference between the height of the government and opposition movement functions at $p_{x,0}$.

The strategy pair (M_{Gov}, M_{Opp}) will typically not be an equilibrium. For example, given the government's strategy, the opposition can increase its pay-off by reallocating resources away from seats it will lose anyway to a seat it could have won if it had focused its resources on it. (Often numerous other reallocations also exist that it would be rational to make given that the other side's strategy is fixed.) This is illustrated in Fig. 10.2. The opposition would lose seats x and y whether or not it put resources into them, because $p_{x,0}$ and $p_{y,0}$ are less than one-half and because the government allocates more resources than the opposition. On the other hand, the opposition could prevent constituency z from moving on to the government's side by reallocating to z all the resources given to x and y. Leaving all the rest of the opposition's resource allocation unchanged, this pushes up the opposition's expected pay-off by 1. More generally, if there is a seat such as z, which the opposition can keep on its side by reallocating resources to it from any number of other seats that it will lose or win whether or not it allocates resources to them, then (M_{Gov}, M_{Opp}) is not an equilibrium. So it is a necessary condition for an equilibrium that no such seat as z exists.

It is possible, but extremely unlikely, that this, and similar, necessary conditions will be satisfied, given that there are a large number of constituencies and they are reasonably uniformly spread on both sides of ½. In other words, (M_{Gov}, M_{Opp}) is an equilibrium only in extreme cases, such as when the prior position of all constituencies is below ½.[13] The intuition is that it is usually irrational to play M_{Opp} against M_{Gov} because it spreads mobile resources 'thinly' over seats, wasting them in places where they make no difference to the outcome. By refocusing them where they can make a difference, an increased pay-off can usually be earned. If we actually observe parties playing strategies like this, the game-theoretical model is falsified—unless the prior distribution of constituencies is exceptional. This illustrates the important point that because game-theoretical models rule out certain forms of behaviour as irrational, the models can be falsified by showing that such behaviour occurs.

Now we turn to the question of what strategies are in equilibrium in this game. In order to define the government's strategy focused on here, we need to order the constituencies to the left of ½ sequentially according to their prior marginality, $p_{i,0}$. Any constituencies with the same prior marginality can be numbered in some arbitrary way without the argument being affected. So constituency 1 is to the left of, and nearest to, ½ and so on, as illustrated in Fig. 10.3a. Then we can define the government's strategy S as follows: (i) start with constituency 1, and allocate resources to it until they run out, in which case stop, or its marginality is the same as that of constituency 2; (ii) allocate equal resources to constituencies 1 and 2 until resources run out, in which case stop, or their marginality is the same as that of constituency 3; (iii) repeat stage (ii) until resources run out. The effects of S are illustrated in Fig. 10.3b. The position of constituency i in this figure is $p_{i,Gov}$, that is, the probability that a randomly chosen elector in that constituency would vote for the opposition given the government's resource allocation and if the opposition allocated no resources to campaigning in it.

To define the opposition's strategy, we need another numbering of the constituencies. This time we order constituencies to the left of ½ sequentially according to the value of $p_{i,Gov}$. Constituencies with the same marginality after the government's move can be numbered in any way without affecting the argument. The opposition's strategy T is defined as follows: (i) start with constituency 1, and, if it is feasible to do so, allocate enough campaigning resources to move it to ½; if it is not, stop without allocating any resources; (ii) if the algorithm has not stopped, go to constituency 2, and, if it is feasible, allocate enough campaigning resources to move it to ½; if it is not, stop; (iii) repeat step (ii) until the algorithm terminates. In short, whatever the government's first move, T 'captures' constituencies sequentially, starting with those nearest to ½ and moving on to constituencies that are harder to capture, until no more constituencies can be captured. The effects of employing T on the distribution in Fig. 10.3b are illustrated in Fig. 10.3c.

(a) Prior marginalities before the government's move

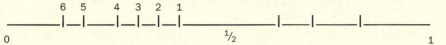

(b) Marginalities after the government's move

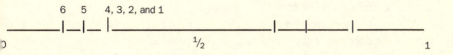

⇐⇐⇐⇐⇐⇐   4, 3, 2, and 1 moved to the same
position; 5 and 6 not moved

(c) Posterior marginalities after both the opposition's and the government's moves

⇒⇒⇒⇒⇒⇒⇒⇒⇒   1 and 2 moved to 1/2;
no others moved

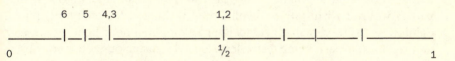

Fɪɢ. 10.3 A visualization of the strategies *S* and *T*

To show that *S* is a best reply to *T* requires some care but no deep mathematics. The proof goes as follows: start with any reply that the first player could adopt to *T*, say *S*(1); show that *S*(1) can be transformed on a step-by-step basis to *S* through a finite sequence of intermediate strategies *S*(2), *S*(3), . . . , *S*(I), . . . , *S*(N − 1), to *S*(N) = *S*, each step involving a reallocation of resources across constituencies; show that at each step the government's pay-off never decreases; and conclude that *S* is at least as good against *T* as *S*(1). The trick lies in proving that the intermediate steps never make things worse for the government. The proof of this is set out in the Appendix to this chapter; those who wish to get a feel for how proofs in rational choice theory operate are advised to try to follow it! Why *T* is the best reply to *S* is also discussed in the Appendix.

Testable and Untestable Implications of the Equilibrium (*S*, *T*)

If the strategies chosen by the two sides are *S* and *T*, a number of predictions can be made. First, if we know the campaign resources of the two parties and the prior marginalities of constituencies, we can work out how many, and which, constituencies will be won. However, it is far from clear how this could be empirically tested. As the result is essentially probabilistic, it can only be tested over a large number of elections; resources change over time whereas testing the predictions demands that they remain constant. Moreover, we are unlikely to be able to obtain believable estimates of the parties' campaign resources.

As Green and Shapiro suggest, some predictions made by using rational choice models are difficult, if not impossible, to test because we cannot directly observe a key parameter of the model. In this case, resources cannot be observed; other problems are players' preferences, beliefs, or the true 'rules of the game'. The unobservability of some theoretical entities is, of course, an endemic problem in the social sciences (and the natural sciences), necessitating the use of proxies and indirect empirical tests. Yet rational choice and game theory, *by their very nature*, would seem to have special problems. The assumption is that players are rational. If this is true, it will often pay them not to divulge information—even to give misleading information—for this may aid them strategically. In the case at hand, it is likely that parties will not wish fully to divulge their resources; for one thing, public opinion seems to view high campaign spending in a poor light. By its very nature, the approach being tested leads us to be suspicious about any observation of, or proxy for, a theoretical term where there is likely to be a premium on keeping the information private.

A model can generate insights without having testable predictions, but any model claiming to contribute to political science ought to have testable implications. Fortunately, the model here has such implications. This illustrates the way that Green and Shapiro underestimate rational choice and game theory: to say that *some* of the predictions of a model are inherently untestable does not mean that *all* of them typically are.

In Fig. 10.4*a*, the distribution of campaign resources by the government is sketched as a function of the prior marginality of constituencies. Recall that the prediction is that all constituencies getting any resources end up with the same marginality after the government's first move. The nearer that any constituency getting resources is to ½ initially, the further it is moved; and as the costs of moving a constituency are linear in distance, the total resources it receives will be linearly increasing with its prior marginality, as shown in Fig. 10.4*a*. Constituencies with values of $p_{i,0}$ greater than ½ get nothing; and constituencies with values of $p_{i,0}$ lower than some critical value get nothing. So the relationship predicted is 'triangular' and discontinuous. This is very different from the continuous relationship between marginality and campaign resources which, as we shall see, is typically assumed in 'soft' rational

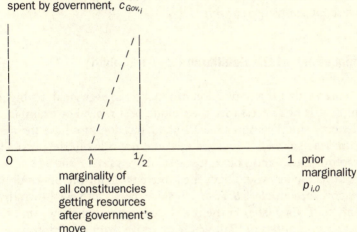

(a) The government's distribution of campaigning resources

Campaign resources
spent by government, $c_{Gov,i}$

0   ↑̂ $^{1}/_{2}$ 1   prior

marginality of   marginality
all constituencies $p_{i,0}$
getting resources
after government's
move

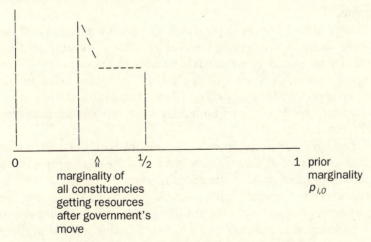

(b) The opposition's distribution of campaign resources under T

Campaign resources
spent by opposition, $c_{Opp,i}$

0   ↑̂ $^{1}/_{2}$ 1   prior

marginality of   marginality
all constituencies $p_{i,0}$
getting resources
after government's
move

FIG. 10.4 The distribution of campaigning resources under strategies S and T

choice discussions of this topic. Moreover, it is a somewhat counter-intuitive prediction from the model. Of course, to test the qualitative prediction of a 'triangular', discontinuous relationship, we still need a proxy measure of resources.[14] As we shall see, there are good reasons to believe that a good correlate of campaign resources is the declared campaign expenses of the candidates. However, because this is a correlate, it cannot be used to test point predictions about which constituencies will get what, or who will win which seats. But it can be used to test the qualitative prediction of a 'triangular', discontinuous relationship.

Non-uniqueness of the Equilibrium and Testability

While no reply that the opposition can make can ever yield it a higher pay-off than T, it is not necessarily the unique best reply. For example, in Fig. 10.3c the opposition captures seats 1 and 2 but does not have the resources to capture seat 3 as well. However, this does not rule out the possibility that it can capture seats 1 and 3 but not seat 2, or even seats 2 and 3 but not seat 1. Each of these replies would have the same pay-off for the opposition, given that the government plays S. Also, consider the way it was shown that S is a best reply to T. Each step in the proof (see Appendix) shows that the government's pay-off does not fall when we move from any arbitrary strategy 'in the direction of' S. It is not shown that the government's pay-off increases; and for any particular prior distribution of constituencies and resources, there will be very many strategies as good (though no better) than S against T. This suggests that (S, T) is unlikely to be the only equilibrium of this game.

Although this outcome depends on the precise positions of the constituencies before campaigning and the government's strategy, there will typically be an infinity of equilibria. One way to see this is to observe that strategy T can end up not utilizing all the available resources. Because mobile resources are infinitely divisible and transferable, if there is a surplus it can typically be divided up in infinitely many ways without affecting the equilibrium.

Here we have a major problem with game theory that Green and Shapiro do not seem to have noticed. Except in a few of the most simple two-player, two-strategy games, such as one-shot Prisoners' Dilemma, it is seldom the case that there is a unique equilibrium. Recently, much attention has been given to finding further assumptions which allow the implausible equilibria that arise in some games to be eliminated (Morrow 1994), but there is no consensus about how this should be done (see Hargreaves-Heap et al.: ch. 7), and the suggested methods of refinement are of no help here. It might seem that the situation is empirically hopeless: with an infinity of equilibria, any observed pattern of resource distribution will be compatible with one of them, so the model cannot be falsified. There are reasons to suggest that this is not the case, however.

First, the game being analysed here is a zero-sum game. The Minimax Theorem, first proved by von Neumann and Morgenstern, the founding fathers of game theory (Luce and Raiffa 1989: ch. 4), implies, among other things, that if there is more than one equilibrium for a zero-sum game, the pay-offs for the players in each of these equilibria will be exactly the same. Now, if we know the prior positions of the constituencies and the parties' resources, we can easily calculate their pay-offs in the equilibrium (S, T); that is, how many constituencies they expect to win and to lose. No matter what the equilibrium, this will still be the prediction. In principle, this is a point prediction that is open to falsification. However, I have already noted that getting direct measures of parties' campaign resources to test this is difficult.

The Minimax Theorem guarantees that if the government adopts any strategy associated with an equilibrium of the game, T will always be in equilibrium with this strategy, too; and if the opposition adopts any strategy associated with an equilibrium of the game, S will always be in equilibrium with this strategy, too. The algorithms for implementing S and T are straightforward to write down and the implied allocations of resources are easy to calculate. T is always a best reply, no matter what strategy the government adopts, although it is easy to find opposition strategies to which S is not a best reply. For these reasons, the equilibrium (S, T) might have the property of 'obviousness' or 'prominence'; it might stand out from potential alternatives. When faced with numerous equilibria, game theorists often invoke Schelling's (1960) argument that players will coordinate on a prominent equilibrium. The trouble with this application, as with all applications, of Schelling's idea is that there is no general theory of prominence, and the factors that are said to make equilibria prominent typically derive from cognitive psychology or normative social theory, not rational choice theory.

To summarize, because (S, T) is very unlikely to be the only equilibrium of the game, we are forced to resort to arguments from outside game theory and rational choice, such as strategic simplicity, to justify using (S, T) to make predictions. If the predictions based on (S, T) are false, it may be possible to find another equilibrium that does fit the observed facts. However, this is the sort of *post hoc* theorizing about which Green and Shapiro rightly complain.

Actually, it is possible to characterize the whole class of equilibria of this game by showing that 'best-response' strategies have to meet certain necessary conditions. Observing the distribution of resources in a way that does not meet these conditions would falsify the model. Such a complex analysis is not pursued here. There are also other implications of the model that are testable in principle, such as those about pay-offs in equilibrium mentioned above and that the behaviour implied by the strategies M_{Gov} and M_{Opp} should not be observed because they are not in equilibrium when played against each other. However, the problem identified here is not easy to eradicate from empirical applications of game theory.

Assumptional Realism and Falsification

In Britain today, there are almost always more than three candidates in any constituency at a general election. However, to avoid the additional difficulties with analysing a multinomial probability model and an n-person game, the model proceeds under the assumption that there are only two candidates. Indeed, if the campaigning of the two main parties in the constituency does not affect the vote of the third (and smaller) parties, it could be argued that things may operate as if the contest is a two-horse race. Then competition is about which party gets a majority from a fixed number of electors who vote for one or other of the major parties. It still needs to be recognized, of course, that the two main contenders are not always Labour and Conservative.

These are not the only problems: the size of constituencies differ, and so does turnout. Marginality is likely to be correlated with turnout (Denver and Hands 1985), and campaigning may mobilize electors to turn out (Denver and Hands 1992: 31, 43). The problem here is that the cost of shifting the probabilities of an opposition vote might be different in constituencies of different size; poster campaigns, for example, have enormous economies of scale so that the cost of reaching a given voter will hardly differ with the number of voters. This is not true of door-to-door campaigning, where more would have to be spent to get a higher number of votes.

No doubt many other problems can be identified. To many of these, the game theorist will reply that the model is a useful 'first approximation'; that any model has to simplify reality to be tractable; and, by definition, it is a model, not reality. Models are to be used, not believed! However, there is an issue here about the logic of model testing. Any empirical test is about the logical conjunction of all the assumptions that feed into the prediction, not any single assumption. So, if the prediction of the model does not hold, a game theorist could say that this is because the model is, after all, only a 'first approximation'; that the core of the model is correct; and that only some of the auxiliary assumptions needed to apply it to the British case are false. The game theorist might also quote the logical truth that, from a set of assumptions containing at least one that is false, it must always be possible to derive at least one false conclusion—the point being, again, to say that failure to fit the British or some other case can leave the core of the model intact.

Green and Shapiro (1994), and other critics of rational choice, see these sorts of arguments as evasions, and their deployment as a damning criticism of rational choice and game-theoretical work. However, as I have argued elsewhere (1996b), this is because they are näive about the logic of theory testing and because they make a fetish of model falsification. Arguments derived from Kuhn (1970) and Lakatos (1974) suggest that problems of this kind are endemic to the social and the natural sciences. An apparent falsification of a model can always be evaded by fiddling around with the 'protective belt' of auxiliary assumptions and/or the assumptions which always have to be made when actually confronting the data. The key point here is that we should abandon our original approach if the predictions derived from it are repeatedly shown to be empirically questionable; if the approach spends more time explaining known anomalies in *ad hoc* ways rather than in predicting novel and interesting phenomena; and if there is some alternative approach that is not as bad a 'fix'. This perspective points to the centrality of empirical testing in the possibility of scientific progress without fetishizing falsification in the way that Green and Shapiro do. We now move on to test some of the predictions of the model.

Testing the Model

Direct measures of campaigning effort at constituency level are not available for most constituencies, although Seyd and Whiteley (1992) provide various measures of campaigning effort by local Labour activists for a sample of constituencies, and Denver and Hands (1992) have collected detailed data from a sample of Conservative local agents. Recently, several studies have used the campaign expenses of candidates as a proxy measure for overall campaigning effort.[15] These data are readily available since, by law, candidates are required to declare their campaign expenses (Blackburn 1995: 281–6). There are some doubts about whether the published figures fully reflect candidates' expenditure and whether campaign expenses correlate positively with other dimensions of campaign effort (Gordon and Whiteley 1980). Even so, there is now evidence that this proxy is probably quite a good guide to relative campaigning effort.[16] The dependent variable here, then, is Conservative candidates' campaign expenses in the 1992 general election ('expenses'), measured in pounds.[17]

According to Pattie *et al.* (1995: 969), the campaign expenses of Conservative candidates are mostly funded by local constituency parties. It is difficult to be sure that this is the case; there is no legal requirement for political parties to produce full accounts and the accounts of the Conservative Party are notoriously sketchy (Blackburn 1995: 314–15). The hypothesis about the distribution of resources across constituencies concerns those resources which the central party machine can control. It is unlikely, given the degree of autonomy enjoyed by Conservative constituency associations, that effective control of all relevant resources lies in the hands of the party's Central Office. It is equally unlikely that full control is exerted locally. This suggests that, in seeking to explain a candidates' expenses, we need to allow for the resources controlled at constituency level. Again, it is notoriously difficult to do this directly: even obtaining accurate membership totals is extremely difficult (Whiteley *et al.* 1994).

In searching for proxy measures of the likely financial resources of Conservative constituency associations, census data were examined first. I assumed that more resources are likely to be available to the local party the higher the socio-economic profile of the constituency and the better the local economic circumstances. Exploratory analysis suggested that two variables obtainable at constituency level from the 1991 census are powerful proxies: the proportion of the population belonging to the Registrar-General's social class 2 ('sclass2') for the class profile; and the percentage younger than 18 who were unemployed ('youthun') for economic conditions. These variables were included in an attempt to control for local contributions to expenses that were outside the power of Central Office. The cases were the 631 English, Welsh, and Scottish constituencies.[18]

We know that many people join Conservative constituency associations as a way of progressing in local (and sometimes then national) politics, and also, perhaps, in local business circles (Whiteley *et al.* 1994: ch. 4). It makes sense that in historically rock-solid Labour seats, or seats which have been continuously held by a third party, the local Conservative association will tend to be less well resourced, other things being equal. Local politics tends to follow national politics, so it is unlikely that the party will control the political preferment (and economic contacts) at the local level to attract the ambitious. The converse is true in solid Conservative seats. This suggests that, in controlling for locally directed resources, we need to control in some way for the past success of the Conservative Party in a constituency. Excluding the Conservative Party, the party obtaining the highest vote total in each constituency ('chall') was identified and the number of votes it obtained. In most seats, that party was Labour, although in a few it was either the Liberal Democrats or one of the nationalist parties. As 'chall' emerged as strongly negatively correlated with 'expenses', I interpreted it as picking up the effect of past Conservative success. Other interpretations are possible, including the idea that Conservative Central Office does not try hard in seats it looks unlikely to win.

There are legal limits on how much candidates can spend on campaigning, and on what they can spend the money.[19] The formula is linear, an addition being allowed for each registered elector in addition to a lump sum, but the restrictions are more lax in rural seats. These limits might seem to suggest that the dependent variable should be expenses as a proportion of the legal maximum, as in some recent studies (Pattie *et al.* 1995: 978–9). However, this was not the variable about which the model makes a prediction. Moreover, examination of the published returns suggests that actual expenditure never hits the upper bound. Thus, instead, the upper bound on expenditure was controlled for, on the assumption that it exerted *downwards pressure* as opposed to *truncating* observations on the independent variable. Indeed, the number of registered electors in 1987 ('elect') was a strong correlate of 'expenses', as this argument suggests.

The theoretical prediction from the equilibrium is that the resources controlled by Conservative Central Office will be distributed in the general way shown in Fig. 10.4*a;* that is, that there is a 'triangular', discontinuous relationship between the prior probability that a randomly chosen elector in the constituency votes for the governing party and how much discretionary resources a constituency receives. The first problem in operationalizing this relationship was to find a proxy for the prior probability as seen by the (Conservative) government. Although it might be argued that the local party would use by-election results and electoral trend data from constituency-level polls, it was assumed that the government's probability calculation was based on the result of the 1987 election. So I calculated [Pprob = chall/(chall + Con87)], which varies between zero and one. This was taken as a proxy for the perceived prior probability in 1992.[20] The most marginal constituencies from the Tories' viewpoint, then, are those for which [chall = Con87].[21]

There is yet another difficulty. As already noted, we have no way of knowing the total resources that Conservative Central Office has to allocate. Without this information, looking again at the 'triangular', discontinuous relationship in Fig. 10.4*a*, we have no way of directly operationalizing the cut-off point to the left of the prior probability of ½ beyond which constituencies are allocated no resources centrally. In face of this difficulty, a series of variables of the general form shown in Fig. 10.5 were created.

For values of Pprob between $X/100$ and 0.5, DX50 takes on the value Pprob $- X/100$. Everywhere else it takes on the value 0. So, for example, D3050 takes on the value Pprob $- 0.3$ for values of Pprob in the semi-open interval (0.3, 0.5) and zero elsewhere. Controlling for 'sclass2', 'youthun', 'chall', and 'elect', a series of models was run including the variable DX50 for values of X from 0.0 to 0.45 in steps of 0.05. The hypothesized relationship between DX50 and 'expenses' was, of course, positive. Conditional upon the relationship actually being positive (which it was in all cases), the value of X chosen by this search procedure was the one that maximized the corrected R^2, given the other variables included. It turned out that D3050 was the best

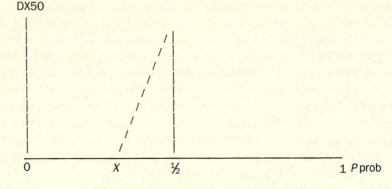

FIG. 10.5 The form of the variable DX50

version of the DX50 variable on this criterion. The results are shown in the first column of Table 10.1 (regression model 1).

The signs of the regression coefficients are all as expected on theoretical grounds and all are easily significant at the 95 per cent level. The coefficient of 8263.7 on D3050 indicates that in a constituency with a score of 0.5 on Pprob (the most marginal constituency on our proxy), 'expenses' would be

Table 10.1 Results of three regression models

	Regression Model 1	Regression Model 2	Regression Model 3
Constant	2005.5	1512.1	2449.7
	(4.101)	(3.211)	(4.847)
Sclass2	49.10	53.03	53.11
	(6.152)	(6.903)	(7.026)
Chall	−0.100	−0.108	−0.104
	(−9.021)	(−9.974)	(−9.747)
Elect	0.0692	0.0742	0.0697
	(12.515)	(13.989)	(13.124)
Youthun	−37.91	−32.517	−34.15
	(−3.992)	(−3.536)	(−3.771)
D3050	8263.7	—	—
	(10.886)		
D3055	—	7613.8	4557.4
		(13.070)	(5.220)
Marg	—	—	−3557.5
			(−4.642)
Adjusted R^2	0.64053	0.66413	0.67481

Notes: Entries are regression coefficients; *t*-values are shown in parenthesis.

[8263.7*(0.5 − 0.3)] £1,652.7 higher, other things equal, than a constituency scoring zero on D3050, that is, in a constituency with a value for Pprob outside the interval (30, 50). The mean value of 'expenses' over all cases was £5,781; with the range running from £22 to £8,617. Recalling that 'expenses' is a proxy for overall campaigning effort, the results suggest that very substantial extra effort was directed into the most marginal constituencies.

Around 64 per cent of the variance is explained by regression model 1. This compares reasonably with the fit obtained by others (*cf.* Pattie *et al.* 1995: 978–9). Besides the factors already alluded to, it is plausible that the characteristics of candidates might affect campaign expenses. Candidates or their agents ultimately have to sanction all campaign expenditure, and candidates will differ in their energy, readiness to speak publicly, and the personal financial assets they can put into campaigning. We could expect the proportion of the variance explained to increase if the personal characteristics of candidates were controlled for in theoretically relevant ways. To investigate this possibility, however, would be to go beyond the scope of this chapter.[22]

As suggested above, the equilibrium in which the government gives no discretionary resources to constituencies with prior probability values greater than ½ is typically not the only one. There may well be equilibria in which marginals with prior probability values greater than ½ get something, too. Actually, the prediction that constituencies with prior probabilities greater than ½ get no discretionary resources is a consequence of the dichotomous approximation to the relationship between the prior probability and the probability that the seat will be won. Starting with the normal approximation to the cumulative binomial, the predicted relationship is still 'triangular' and discontinuous, but some constituencies with prior probabilities greater than ½ get discretionary resources (Ward and John 1996). For these reasons, I carried out a grid search for the values of X and Y that maximized the adjusted R^2 when D3050 was replaced in regression model 1 by DXY, where DXY = Pprob − X/100 if X/100 ≤ Pprob < Y/100; and Pprob is 0 otherwise. Under the constraints that $X < Y$, $X > 0.0$, and $Y < 0.65$, the search suggested that the best fit was obtained with the variable D3055. As shown in the second column of Table 10.1 (regression model 2), the coefficient on this is positive and significant, as expected on theoretical grounds. This time the constituencies getting most as a consequence of the marginality effect are predicted to be the ones with Pprob = 0.55. Expenses are predicted to be [7613.8 * (0.55 − 0.3)] £1,903.45 higher than in a constituency similar in all other respects but scoring 0 on D3055.

A tough-minded critic might argue that regression model 2 falsifies the prediction, from the model, that constituencies with prior probabilities greater than ½ should get no discretionary resources. But the fact that D3055 is significant, and that the fit is a slight improvement over regression model 1, indicates that some constituencies with higher prior probability values probably do get such resources. Notoriously, it is never that simple to falsify a model in the social sciences. It has already been noted that some equilibria in the model would probably fit this finding; besides, an enormous number of auxiliary hypotheses are assumed to be true when we accept the findings of regression model 2. Any one of them could be false. For example, the auxiliary assumption that Conservative Central Office sees marginality in the way suggested by Pprob might be unreasonable given that the very big shifts in opinion polls since 1987 could have made many relatively safe seats look marginal in 1992.

Leaving these points aside, another peculiar problem with testing rational choice theory is illustrated here. Game-theoretic models are *models*; they are known, and intended, to be highly stripped down representations of reality. Given this, we might be inclined to charity: if the model is 'approximately true' in that it predicts the general form of the relationships found in the data, this is all we can expect; and we live in hopes (drawn from experience in the natural sciences) that a slightly more 'realistic' model (using the normal approximation instead of the dichotomous, say) would be a better approximation, so we could get as close to explaining the observed 'facts' as is consistent with parsimony. But what are the bounds of charity? That there are no widely agreed hard and fast rules is an endemic problem, and this leads to very different evaluations of rational choice theory.

Game theory tells us what we should not observe as well as what we should observe. As noted at the start, 'soft' rational choice arguments suggest concentrating electoral campaigns in seats that could go either way and with less emphasis on safe seats, as under strategies M_{Gov} and M_{Opp}. This idea is usually operationalized by using a variable such as marg $= |P\text{prob} - 0.5|$, that is, the absolute value of the difference between the share of the vote obtained by the government's nearest challenger and ½. The hypothesis is that this should show a negative relationship with 'expenses'. Evidence for such an effect has frequently been found.[23] Going back to Table 10.1, the results shown for regression model 3 come from rerunning regression model 2 with 'marg' inserted; 'marg' is significant and has the theoretically expected sign. The estimate is that in the most marginal constituencies with a value of $P\text{prob} = $ ½, an extra $[0.5* 3557.5]$ £1,778.75 is spent compared with seats where Pprob is zero or one, according to the effect picked up by 'marg'.

That 'marg' has a significant negative relationship with 'expenses' might, on the face of it, seem to falsify the game-theoretic approach; it is very unlikely that (M_{Gov}, M_{Opp}) is an equilibrium, as argued above. An alternative interpretation is that the effect being picked up by 'marg' is due to constituency associations in marginal seats trying harder to mobilize resources that they control. If a constituency association wants a Conservative win because of the advantages it brings in local elections or local patronage, it might well be rational for the local party to put more non-mobile resources into close fights. Local associations do not have to consider the inter-constituency trade-offs that Central Office has to make in allocating resources.

In regression model 3, D3055 is still significant after controlling for 'marg' and it still has the expected sign. The coefficient now indicates that [(0.55 − 0.3)* 4557.4] £1,139.4 extra is spent in the most favoured marginals compared to a constituency scoring zero on D3055—a non-negligible sum. Clearly, in regression model 2, D3055 was picking up some of the explanatory effect of 'marg' in the interval (0.3, 0.5). Nevertheless, there continues to be evidence for the kind of discontinuous 'triangluar' relationship predicted for the equilibrium (S, T). This could be the empirical trace of the steering of mobile resources by Conservative Central Office. Empirical studies that have ignored this effect are mis-specified and risk biased estimates of the effect picked up by 'marg'.[24] Rather than falsifying the game-theoretic approach, the empirical results point up the importance of distinguishing between the centrally directed and the locally directed components of campaigning. Only if variables like D3055, capturing the predicted discontinuous 'triangular' relationship, had proven insignificant when controlling for 'marg' would there have been a fairly clear falsification of the approach.

Conclusion

The purpose of this chapter was to illustrate that game theory is capable of making predictions which are surprising, testable, and substantively important. This is directly counter to Green and Shapiro's argument, which is where we started. If this was an isolated counter-example, there would still be a great deal to be said for Green and Shapiro's position. However, it is easy to cite numerous other areas where game theory has important testable implications (see Ward 1996b). One virtue of the example used here is that it brings into sharp focus two characteristic problems of testing game theory: finding proxies for variables about which players have strategic reasons for giving false or inadequate information; and the problem of multiple equilibria. These seem to be much the more significant problems about rational choice theory.

APPENDIX
Proofs that (S, T) is an equilibrium

Lemma 1
Suppose the government adopts a strategy $S(I)$ under which it does not allocate all the campaign resources available to it. If the opposition uses the strategy T, there is a strategy $S(I+1)$ under which the government allocates all its resources which is at least as good against T as $S(I)$

Suppose that, under its strategy T, the opposition can capture at least one constituency after the government has allocated its resources according to $S(I)$. Let m be the most marginal constituencies that the opposition captures, so that $(m + 1)$, $(m + 2)$, *etc.* are not captured. Denote the set of constituencies other than m that are captured by the opposition as X. Denote the opposition's cost of capturing a constituency by $\kappa_i = \frac{1}{2} - p_{i,Gov}$ for $p_{i,Gov} < \frac{1}{2}$. Suppose that the opposition cannot capture all the government's constituencies when the government's allocation is that in $S(I)$. Then:

$$K = \kappa_{m+1} + \kappa_m + \sum_{\chi \in X} \kappa_\chi > C_{Opp} > \kappa_m + \sum_{\chi \in X} \kappa_\chi$$

that is, given its total resources, the opposition can bear the total cost of capturing m and all seats in X, but it cannot also capture even a most low-cost additional marginal seat like $(m + 1)$.

Let all the resources not allocated under $S(I)$ be allocated to m under $S(I + 1)$ with the allocations to all other seats the same. In order to capture more seats given this new allocation, the opposition must first capture all the seats in X, and then capture the two most marginal seats to the left, as T captures seats sequentially from the right. The additional two seats are either m and $(m + 1)$, or, if m is now at or to the left of $(m + 2)$, under the new allocation $S(I + 1)$, $(m + 1)$ and $(m + 2)$. The total cost of either option is greater than K and is, therefore, infeasible: the cost of capturing m goes up while the cost of capturing $(m + 1)$ stays the same under the new allocation. So the first option is infeasible. As $\kappa_{m + 2} \geq \kappa_{m + -1} \geq \kappa_m$, the second option is infeasible.

If T captures all the seats under the allocation in $S(I)$, it cannot do better under $S(I+1)$, as the cost of capturing m has increased and all other things are equal.

Finally, suppose the opposition can capture no seats when the government uses $S(I)$. Then allocating the extra resources to m under $S(I + 1)$ still leaves it unable to capture any seats.

Lemma 2
Suppose the government adopts a strategy $S(I)$ under which it allocates resources to some constituency i such that $p_{i,0} > \frac{1}{2}$. Then if the opposition uses the strategy T, there is a strategy $S(I + 1)$ under which the government allocates no resources to i which is at least as good against T as $S(I)$.

Suppose, first, that $p_{i,Gov} \geq \frac{1}{2}$. If the government allocates no resources to i and keeps the rest of its allocation the same, its pay-off will be the same, as i is won by the opposition in both cases, given $p_{i,0} \geq \frac{1}{2}$. So the resources allocated to i under $S(I)$ are wasted. Reallocate these resources to m as in lemma 1. The rest of the proof is exactly the same as for lemma 1.

Secondly, suppose that $p_{m,Gov} \leq p_{i,Gov} < \frac{1}{2}$, so that i is captured by T. Then, under the strategy $S(I + 1)$, reallocate all the resources i receives to m, keeping the allocation to all other constituencies the same, as illustrated in Fig. 10.6. As m is among the most marginal constituencies captured given the distribution under $S(I)$,

$$K = \kappa_{m+1} + \kappa_m + \sum_{\chi \in X} \kappa_\chi + \kappa_i > C_{Opp} \geq \kappa_m + \sum_{\chi \in X} \kappa_\chi + \kappa_I$$

where X is the set of constituencies captured in the distribution shown in Fig. 10.6a excluding i and m. Given the reallocation under $S(I + 1)$, m moves $x = (p_{i,0} - p_{i,Gov})$ to the left. As T captures constituencies sequentially from the right, in order to capture more constituencies in the distribution shown in Fig. 10.6b, all constituencies in X and the three next most marginal constituencies must be captured out of m, $(m + 1)$, $(m + 2)$, $(m + 3)$; that is, either m, $(m + 1)$ and $(m + 2)$ must be captured or $(m + 1)$, $(m + 2)$, and $(m + 3)$ must be captured. Neither of these possibilities is feasible:

$$\kappa_{m+1} + \kappa_{m+2} + \kappa_m + x + \sum_{\chi \in X} \kappa_\chi \geq K$$

as $x > 0$ and $\kappa_{m+2} \geq \kappa_i$;

$$\kappa_{m+1} + \kappa_{m+2} + \kappa_{m+3} + \sum_{\chi \in X} \kappa_\chi \geq K$$

as $\kappa_{m+2} \geq \kappa_m$ and $\kappa_{m+3} \geq \kappa_i$.

Now suppose that i is not captured under $S(I)$. This time:

$$K = \kappa_{m+1} + \kappa_m + \sum_{\chi \in X} \kappa_\chi > C_{Opp} \geq \kappa_m + \sum_{\chi \in X} \kappa_\chi$$

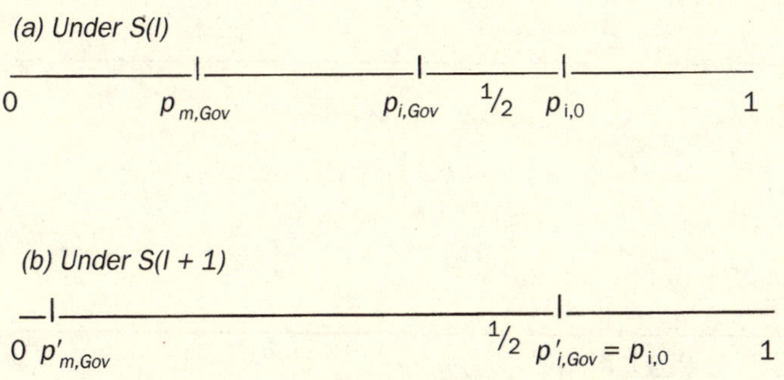

(a) Under S(I)

```
_____|_____|_____|_____
0      p_m,Gov          p_i,Gov  1/2  p_i,0      1
```

(b) Under S(I + 1)

```
—|_____|_____
0 p'_m,Gov                       1/2 p'_i,Gov = p_i,0      1
```

FIG. 10.6 The redistribution in lemma 2

which means that to capture more constituencies when all resources are reallocated from i to m, all constituencies in X and the next two most marginal constituencies must be captured. These are either $(m + 1)$ and $(m + 2)$ or m and $(m + 1)$. Neither option is feasible:

$$\kappa_{m+1} + \kappa_{m+2} + \sum_{\chi \in X} \kappa_\chi \geq K$$

since $\kappa_m \leq \kappa_{m+2}$;

$$\kappa_{m+1} + \kappa_m + x + \sum_{\chi \in X} \kappa_\chi \geq K$$

as $x > 0$.

Lemma 3

Let a and b be two feasible allocations of the government's resources which only differ with respect to the allocations to two constituencies, i and j, such that: $p'_{j,Gov} = p_{j,Gov} + x$; $p'_{i,Gov} = p_{i,Gov} - x$; $p'_{j,Gov} \leq p'_{i,Gov}$; $p_{j,Gov} < p_{i,Gov} < \frac{1}{2}$, where the primes denote probability values in distribution b. Then the government's pay-off is never lower if its first move brings about distribution a than if it brings about distribution b, if the opposition uses strategy T.

The situation is pictured in Fig. 10.7. Let the set of constituencies excluding m and (if it is captured) i that the opposition captures in distribution a be denoted by X.

Case (i): $\frac{1}{2} > p_{m,Gov} > p_{i,Gov}$
As the opposition cannot capture i or any constituency to the left of it in the distribution shown in Fig. 10.7a, it captures all members of X and m for both distributions, and the government's pay-off is the same for both distributions.

Case (ii): $p_{i,Gov} \geq p_{m,Gov} > p'_{i,Gov}$
As m is the most marginal constituency that the opposition can capture in the distribution shown in Fig. 10.7a,

distribution (a)

distribution (b)

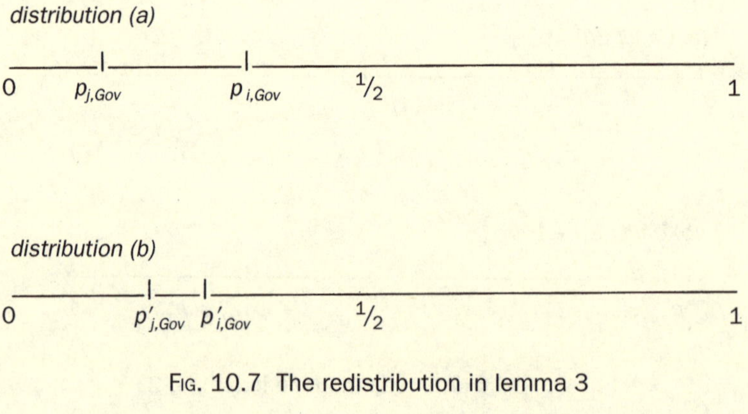

FIG. 10.7 The redistribution in lemma 3

$$K = \kappa_{m+1} + \kappa_m + \kappa_i + \sum_{\chi \epsilon X} \kappa_\chi > C_{Opp} \geq \kappa_m + \kappa_i + \sum_{\chi \epsilon X} \kappa_\chi$$

In order to capture a greater number of constituencies in the distribution shown in Fig. 10.7b using T, the opposition must, first, be able to capture all constituencies in X and m. Then it must capture the two next most marginal constituencies to m in distribution (b). These are either $(m + 1)$ and $(m + 2)$, $(m + 1)$ and i, or i and j.[25] None of these options is feasible:

$$\kappa_{m+2} + \kappa_{m+1} + \kappa_m + \sum_{\chi \epsilon X} \kappa_\chi \geq K$$

as $\kappa_{m+2} \geq \kappa_i$;

$$\kappa_{m+1} + \kappa_m + \kappa_i + x + \sum_{\chi \epsilon X} \kappa_\chi \geq K$$

as $x > 0$;

$$\kappa_i + x + \kappa_j - x + \kappa_m + \sum_{\chi \epsilon X} \kappa_\chi \geq K$$

because $\kappa_j \geq \kappa_{m+1}$ as j is either the most marginal seat the opposition does not capture in distribution a or is to the left of it.

Case (iii): $p'_{i,Gov} \geq p_{m,Gov} > p'_{j,Gov}$
In order to capture a greater number of constituencies in the distribution shown in Fig. 10.7b under T, the opposition must, first, be able to capture all constituencies in X, m, and i. Then it must capture either $(m + 1)$ or j, whichever is cheaper to capture. Neither of these options is feasible:

$$\kappa_{m+1} + \kappa_m + \kappa_i + x + \sum_{\chi \epsilon X} \kappa_\chi > K$$

as $x > 0$;

$$\kappa_j - x + \kappa_m + \kappa_i + x + \sum_{\chi \epsilon X} \kappa_i \geq K$$

because $\kappa_j \geq \kappa_{m+1}$ as j is either the most marginal seat the opposition does not capture in the distribution shown in 10.7a or is to the left of it.

Case (iv): $p'_{j,Gov} \geq p_{m,Gov} > p_{j,Gov}$
In order to capture a greater number of constituencies in the distribution shown in Fig. 10.7b under T, the opposition must, first, be able to capture all constituencies in X and m. Then it must capture the two most marginal constituencies out of $(m + 1)$, i, and j, that is, $(m + 1)$ and i, or i and j. Neither of these options is feasible, as shown in case (iii) above.

Case (v): $p_{j,Gov} \geq p_{m,Gov} > 0$

The total cost of capturing both i and j is the same in both distributions since resources are redistributed between them. As m is not to the right of j in the distribution shown in Fig. 10.7a, both i and j will be captured in both cases, and the set of other constituencies captured will be the same, too.

Lemma 4

Suppose that under the allocation of resources in strategy $S(I)$ there are two constituencies i and j such that $\frac{1}{2} > p_{i,0} > p_{j,0}$ and $p_{i,Gov} < p_{j,Gov} \leq p_{j,0}$. Then there is another strategy $S(I + 1)$ which is at least as good as $S(I)$ against T such that the allocations to all constituencies apart from i and j are the same but:

$$p'_{i,Gov} = p'_{j,Gov} = (p_{j,Gov} + p_{i,Gov})/2 < p_{j,Gov}$$

This is a direct consequence of lemma 3 taking x as $(p_{i,Gov} - p_{j,Gov})/2$.

Lemma 5

Suppose that under the allocation of resources in strategy $S(I)$ there are two constituencies i and j such that $p_{j,0} < p_{i,0}$, $p_{i,0} \geq p_{i,Gov}$, and $p_{j,Gov} < p_{j,0}$. Then there is another strategy $S(I + 1)$ which is at least as good as $S(I)$ against T such that the allocations to all constituencies apart from i and j are the same but either:

$$p'_{j,Gov} = p_{j,0} \leq p'_{i,Gov} < p_{i,Gov} \text{ or } p'_{j,Gov} = p'_{i,Gov} < p_{j,0}.$$

In the first case $(p_{i,Gov} + p_{j,Gov})/2 \geq p_{j,0}$. In lemma 3, take $x = (p_{j,0} - p_{j,Gov})$, so that j now gets no resources and all the resources are reallocated to i. The redistribution between cases i and j is illustrated in Fig. 10.8. As $p'_{i,Gov} \geq p'_{j,Gov}$ the conditions for lemma 3 to apply hold, and the result follows directly from it.

In the second case $(p_{i,Gov} + p_{j,Gov})/2 < p_{j,0}$. In lemma 3, take $x = (p_{i,Gov} - p_{j,Gov})/2$, so that the resources are reallocated in a way that leave i and j in the same position.

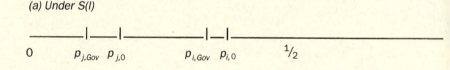

(a) Under S(I)

$$0 \qquad p_{j,Gov} \quad p_{j,0} \qquad\qquad p_{i,Gov} \quad p_{i,0} \qquad \tfrac{1}{2}$$

(b) Under S(I + 1)

$$0 \qquad\qquad p'_{j,Gov} = p_{j,0} \qquad p'_{i,Gov} \qquad \tfrac{1}{2}$$

Fig. 10.8 The first redistribution in lemma 5

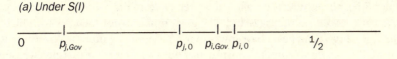

(a) Under S(I)

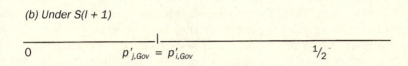

(b) Under S(I + 1)

FIG. 10.9 The second redistribution in lemma 5

The situation is illustrated in Fig. 10.9. As $p'_{i,Gov} = p'_{j,Gov}$ the conditions for lemma 3 to apply hold, and the result follows directly from it.

Theorem 1
S is at least as good a reply to T as any other strategy.
   Let $S(1)$ be any strategy that does not imply the same allocation as S.

   1. If some resources are unallocated under $S(1)$, allocate them to m in the way suggested in the proof of lemma 1 to get a strategy $S(2)$ which is at least as good as $S(1)$ against T.
   2. If, under $S(2)$, the government allocates resources to some constituency, i, such that $p_{i,0} > \frac{1}{2}$, then reallocate the resources to m in the way suggested in the proof of lemma 2 to get a strategy $S(3)$ which is at least as good against T as $S(2)$.
   3. Repeat the reallocation just discussed until no constituencies remain which have been allocated resources and which were originally to the right of $\frac{1}{2}$ that now obtain a positive resource allocation to get a strategy $S(I)$ at least as good as $S(1)$ against T, by repeated application of lemma 2.
   4. Suppose that under the allocation of resources in strategy $S(I)$ there are two constituencies i and j such that $p_{j,0} < p_{i,0} < \frac{1}{2}$; and $p_{i,Gov} < p_{j,Gov} \leq p_{j,0}$. Then reallocate resources only between i and j to give $p'_{i,Gov} = p'_{j,Gov} = (p_{j,Gov} + p_{i,Gov})/2$ under a strategy $S(I + 1)$ at least as good as $S(1)$ against T, according to lemma 4.
   5. Suppose that under the allocation of resources in strategy $S(I+1)$ there are two constituencies i and j such that $p_{j,0} < p_{i,0} < \frac{1}{2}$, $p_{i,Gov} \leq p_{i,0}$, and $p_{j,Gov} < p_{j,0}$. Then reallocate resources only between i and j to give $p'_{j,Gov} = p_{j,0} \leq p'_{i,Gov} < p_{i,Gov}$ or else $p'_{j,Gov} = p'_{i,Gov} < p_{j,0}$ under a strategy $S(I + 2)$ that is at least as good as $S(I + 1)$ against T, according to lemma 5.
   6. Repeat the sort of reallocations discussed under (4) and (5) until there are no more pairs i, j to which the conditions apply, to get a strategy $S(N)$ at least as good against T as $S(1)$ by repeated application of lemmas 4 and 5.

Under $S(N)$, all resources are allocated (step (1)); no opposition constituency is allocated any resources (steps (2) and (3)); government constituencies with higher prior marginality values never have lower marginality values after the government's first move than any government constituency with a lower prior marginality value (steps (4) and (6)); no government constituency with a lower prior marginality value ends up with a lower marginality value after the government's first move than any government constituency with a higher prior marginality value (steps (5) and (6)). So all the resources are used on government seats; the initial order of the seats from left to right according to prior marginality is preserved for government seats after the government's first move; and all seats allocated any resources have the same marginality after the government's first move, or else steps (5) and (6) would have to come into play. But this means $S(N)$ gives the same allocation as S. So S is at least as good against T as $S(1)$ for any $S(1)$.

In order to prove that (S, T) is an equilibrium, we have now to show that T is a best reply to S. In informal terms, the reason that T allocates resources in a way that cannot be bettered when played against S is that it wastes no campaign resources on constituencies the opposition will win anyway; it only allocates enough campaign resources to any given constituency to ensure that it will be won; it never wastes campaign resources by pushing up the probability that voters will vote for the opposition, but not to the point where the constituency will be won; and it starts with the most easily winnable constituency and carries on allocating to the most winnable constituency at each stage. So no resources are wasted on paying a higher than necessary price for the next winnable constituency. Clearly a formal proof that T is a best reply to S would be similar to the proof of Theorem 1. Space constraints mean that the formal proof is not given here. It is also obvious that T is a best reply to any strategy the government could adopt since the informal argument for its efficiency applies whatever is the government's first move.

Theorem 2
(S, T) is an equilibrium of the game.

By theorem 1, S is a best reply to T and by the informal argument T is a best reply to S.

Notes

1. For wide-ranging overviews, see McLean (1987), Mueller (1989), and Ordeshook (1986) in increasing order of technical complexity.
2. See e.g. Ward (1996a,b), in which heterodox forms of rational choice theory are also discussed.
3. See e.g. Barry (1970); Cook and Levi (1990); Hargreaves-Heap *et al.* (1992); Hindess (1988); Hollis and Nell (1975); Lewin (1991); Mansbridge (1990); Moe (1979); Monroe (1991); Self (1993); Zey (1992).
4. See esp. the contributions to *Critical Review* (1985: 9, nn. 1–2); Ward (1996b).

5. See e.g. Brams (1975); Luce and Raiffa (1985); Morrow (1994); Ordeshook (1986).

6. See e.g. Elster (1989: 13–30); Hargreaves-Heap *et al.* (1992: 3–26, 93–130); Harsanyi (1986: 82–108).

7. See e.g. Johnston (1978, 1979); Pattie *et al.* (1995); Raimond (1983); Reid (1980); Whiteley *et al.* (1994: 206).

8. See e.g. Kavanagh (1970); Pattie *et al.* (1995: 970); cf. Denver and Hands (1992: 528).

9. For an odd value of n the government wins if the number of votes for the opposition is less than or equal to w, where w is the next integer below $n/2$.

10. So long as the parties' utility functions are strictly increasing in the number of seats they win, the argument is unaffected. So if there is a sharp drop in the utility of extra seats once the party expects to win a majority of seats, as might be plausible empirically, the same arguments hold.

11. In Herman Hesse's novel *The Glass Bead Game* an intellectual élite plays an elaborate game of analogy construction, rich in cultural resonance but with no real pay-off for society as a whole. This is the picture of rational choice that its critics like to paint.

12. There is some justification for this assumption in the British context. Constitutionally the government has the right to choose the date of general elections, up to a maximum five-year term. Although surprise is an important weapon for the government, it is likely to plan the disposition of its electoral forces across constituencies before the election is announced; and it is likely that the opposition plans its campaign with some (no doubt imperfect) knowledge of the government's plan. Notice that the assumption is that the planning of campaign moves is sequential, but not the carrying out of the plan.

13. Seeing what happens 'in the limit' as more and more constituencies are introduced gives an insight into why this is the case. In Fig. 10.2, the effect of government campaigning in a constituency initially located at w would be to move it to position 0.5. Now, suppose that at least one constituency is located in any neighbourhood, however small, of a sub-interval of $(0, 1)$, say (p, q). Suppose that $p < \frac{1}{2}$ and $q > w$. Because there are constituencies initially located as close as you like to get and below w, we can pick a constituency, say z, such that its position after allowing for the effects of government campaigning is arbitrarily close to, and below, $\frac{1}{2}$. Denote as y the constituency with an initial location as close as we can get to, and below, the position of z after allowing for the effects of government campaigning. We can always find such a y because of the way the interval (p, q) is defined and because there is a constituency in every neighbourhood. Consider a strategy just the same as M_{Opp} except that it allocates no resources to y and reallocates all resources to z. If the reallocation does not ensure that the prior position of z is now greater than 0.5, choose another constituency $z1$ that is below but even closer to 0.5 after the effects of government campaigning. Repeat the argument as many times as necessary. Eventually, the opposition will increase its pay-off, because it relocates a quantity of resources greater than a lower bound higher than 0; but the distance these resources have to move

the constituency to the right to get it on the opposition's own side can be made arbitrarily small. So (M_{Gov}, M_{Opp}) cannot be an equilibrium.

14. The functional form of the opposition's distribution of resources depends on the size of its resources relative to the government's. The prediction is that the opposition will, first, move as many as possible of the seats to which the government has allocated resources onto its own side; then, if it can, it will sequentially move other government seats onto its own side until this is no longer feasible. This implies the functional form shown in Fig. 10.3*b* when the opposition has enough resources to capture all the seats to which the government has allocated resources. Again this is a discontinuous relationship. Testing this prediction is not attempted here.

15. See Pattie *et al.* (1995); Whiteley *et al.* (1994: ch. 8).

16. See Pattie *et al.* (1995: 970); Whiteley *et al.* (1994: 193).

17. Ideally, we should also statistically model the expenses of opposition candidates but this is precluded by space constraints.

18. Northern Ireland is excluded because no Conservative Party candidates are fielded in Ulster. For the English and Welsh constituencies, 1991 data were used; problems of data availability meant using 1981 data for the Scottish constituencies.

19. But notoriously there are no constraints on what the parties can spend on the national campaign so long as particular candidates are not mentioned; see Blackburn (1995: ch. 6).

20. There is a case for calculating this probability as the Tory vote in 1987 divided by the total number of votes cast. It makes very little difference if this alternative method is adopted.

21. Of course a seat may also be marginal because two other parties ran neck-and-neck.

22. This could affect the findings as the type of candidate may be correlated with the type of constituency; perhaps 'good' candidates are those who will campaign hard even in solid Tory seats. But none of the regressions reported in Table 10.1 suffers from any obvious estimation problems.

23. See e.g. Denver and Hands (1992: 32); Pattie *et al.* (1995: 978–9); Whiteley *et al.* (1994: 207).

24. See Ward and John (1996) for similar problems in models that attempt to explain the geographical distribution of government spending by reference to 'soft' rational choice arguments about marginality. Denver and Hands' (1992) argument that the Conservative Party campaigned as hard in safe seats as in marginal seats, concerns total campaigning effort and the sort of relationship captured by 'marg'. My hypothesis, however, is that marginals will be favoured with extra resources steered from Central Office and a 'triangular', discontinuous relationship.

25. The third possibility can only occur when $p'_{i,Gov} = p'_{j,Gov}$.

11

POLITICAL ANALYSIS IN A WORLD WITHOUT FOUNDATIONS

BOBBY SAYYID AND LILIAN ZAC

In the short story *Death and the Compass* by Jorge Luis Borges, the 'daring perspicacity' of detective Erik Lonnrot is challenged by the murder of Marcell Yarmolinsky, a famed Talmudic scholar. A paper is discovered at the scene of the crime on which is written, 'The first letter of the name has been spoken'. To solve the mystery and apprehend the killer, Lonnrot begins an intensive study of Yarmolinsky's work in an endeavour to uncover the reason for the rabbi's murder. Lonnrot thinks that by understanding the logic of Yarmolinsky's world, he will also come to understand the world of the murderer, and thus discover the identity of the murderer.

Lonnrot's approach has much in common with discourse analysis. We explain why in four steps. First, we examine the background to a discourse-theoretical approach to analysing political phenomena, referring to a number of trends and developments in contemporary scholarship, such as continental philosophy, structural linguistics, and psychoanalysis, and illustrate how these developments have contributed to the formulation of discourse theory. In the second step, we outline some of the main tools and categories of such an approach. Thirdly, we say a brief word about the charge of relativism laid against discourse theory by its critics. In the fourth step, we come back to Lonnrot to reveal what happens in his quest for truth, pointing out what the detective's work tells us about discourse theory, and, so, reveal the limits of discourse theory.

As discourse theory presents a major challenge to the assumptions and conventions of empirical social science, the first question is: why adopt a discourse-theoretical approach? What can discourse theory achieve that other, more established political science methodologies cannot? The quick and conciliatory answer is 'nothing'. But an answer more in keeping with the spirit of discourse theory is to argue that the question itself is wrong. The decision to adopt such an approach is not made by comparing and contrasting accounts based on discourse theory against accounts based on empiricist approaches. It is not that discourse theory can provide better answers, or more statistically significant results, than quantitative methods. In a strict sense, discourse theory is not comparable with quantitative social science analysis. On questions of prediction, reliability, falsification, replication, and similar ways of assessing the validity of research methodologies, discourse theory is silent—or should be. What discourse theory can do is offer a different way of thinking about the world, and thus address the concerns of politics from a different perspective. Let us start by identifying a number of conceptual themes that are central to discourse theory.

Conceptual Themes

The world according to discourse theory is without foundations. In this sense, discourse theory can be described as a sustained meditation on the consequences of anti-foundationalism for the social sciences. In this section, we review the major concepts, or conceptual themes, of discourse theory arising from anti-foundationalism and touch upon some of the most frequently voiced critiques of the approach.

Anti-foundationalism

An anti-foundationalist perspective aims at understanding political phenomena without relying on given foundations such as the will of God, human nature, or social cycles as the ultimate grounding of history. The main proposition is that truth is not discovered, but fabricated. Anti-foundationalism questions the possibility of building knowledge on, or around, apparently permanent categories or essences. That is, there are no a priori categories to explain political processes, nor are there elements in the world which remain 'untouched' by the ever-changing processes by which meaning and identities are produced. Once the notion of essence is destabilized, meaning itself becomes unstable ground. Political analysis becomes a question of examining the unevenness, and the relative permanence, of certain ensembles of meaning.

According to an anti-foundationalism perspective, there are no foundations to rely upon for an understanding of the world. Thus socio-political phenomena have to be understood by looking at the way in which actors, objects, and politics are constructed within a discourse. In other words, instead of explaining, for example, Latin American populism as stemming from class divisions, class consciousness, the cultural attributes of the Latin American people, or the charismatic character of populist leaders, discourse analysts focus on the way in which, within a populist discourse, the identity

of both the populist leader and the people are constituted in a unique relationship. The analytic objective is to know how the identity of the nation
within the populist discourse produces a common ground, and how the
unity of the discourse is achieved by establishing a frontier and an enemy—
the oligarchy, say—against which the identity of the leader and the people
can be defined.

As there are no a priori foundations, and as identities are constructed,
these identities do not pre-exist in a (relatively) unified form before undergoing their construction. Rather, their unity is defined in that construction.
The complete and unified object does not exist prior to its construction. This
is why founding moments, such as the establishment of a new political order
(for example, the constitution of the USA), involve the production of new
identities (for example, American citizens and the Founding Fathers).

In this important sense, then, discourse theory is a working through of
the implications of anti-foundationalism for the social sciences. Indeed, the
usefulness of discourse theory depends in large part on the extent to which
one takes anti-foundationalism to heart. So, next, we consider some of
the specific themes, central to discourse theory, which arise from anti-
foundationalism.

Anti-essentialism

Diana Fuss (1989: ix) defines essentialism as 'a belief in the real, true essence
of things, the invariable and fixed properties which define the "whatness" of
a given entity'. Anti-essentialism rejects this view and proposes, instead, that
the 'whatness' of any given entity is socially constructed. In adopting an anti-
essentialist perspective, discourse theory is concerned with the construction
of meaning and identities, and rejects claims about the 'necessary' character
of historical and political phenomena. According to discourse theorists,
there are no categories which, in themselves, can explain political processes
a priori. That is, there are no variables, or concepts, which can, a priori, serve
to understand political processes in all possible situations, and which might
become 'ultimate' explanations, be they class, gender, race, or the collective
unconscious. Therefore, the analysis of political processes cannot rely on categories which are prior to or 'outside' the process itself. If, for example, race,
gender, or colour are significant factors in understanding specific phenomena, it is only because they have been constructed as such in that specific context. In other words, discourse theorists see political processes in terms of
the social construction of both the *elements* of a process and the concepts
deployed to *analyse* that process.

Identity and difference

The conceptualization of *identity* in discourse theory is based on Saussure's (1983: 118) dictum that all identities are negative and relational. The meaning of a sign arises out of its difference from other signs. For example, the identity of pieces in a chess set is determined by the role they play in a game of chess. The identity of any piece is negative in that it does not rely on some substantive quality (a pawn can be made of wood or ivory, can have this or that shape), and is relational in that it is established by its relation to, and difference from, other pieces. That is, a pawn moves in ways different from the other pieces, and has a different function from the other pieces. In the same way, the construction of categories involves their insertion into a system of differences, and the identity of any specific element is given by its relation to other elements in the same system.

Post-structuralism

The idea that we can understand the world by discovering the system of rules, or structure, which defines how that world operates, presumes that the structure is determinative and ultimately closed. All that happens, happens because of, and according to, the structure, and there can be nothing outside the rules of this structure, as, for example, in a game of chess. Politics, however, is not like a game of chess. In politics, it is possible to break the rules of the game, by, for instance, kicking over the political equivalent of the chess board. Kicking over the chessboard is not internal to the game of chess; it is not incorporated in the rules of chess. Politics, by contrast, is precisely a game which is ultimately open ended, and is geared towards making the rules and drawing the boundaries of those rules.

Events in Algeria in the early 1990s provide an example of the point we are making here. In the first round of the 1992 elections, the Islamic Salvation Front (FIS) won 188 of the 231 seats in the National People's Assembly, leaving it to win only another twenty seats to secure a majority. Thus, according to the rules of the electoral game, the FIS looked poised to form the next government. Days before the second round, however, the constitution was suspended and the President resigned. The High Security Council announced a 'state of exception', declared martial law, and cancelled the second round of the elections to prevent the FIS coming to power. The Francophone élite argued that this was necessary in order to safeguard democracy. This development entailed the formulation of new rules which redefined the boundaries of the Algerian political game.[1]

According to discourse theory, structures cannot determine action. If that were the case, there would be no possibility of action outside the limits of

that structure. Equally, discourse theory does not take the opposite view—
held by many methodological individualists and American behaviouralists—
which asserts the autonomy and sovereignty of the subject. The core of the
argument is that social behaviour is ultimately the aggregation of individual
subjects exercising their will through various mechanisms (the market, community, kinship, class, and the like), and that these subjects and their wills are
not conditioned or modified by their association with other subjects. In
other words, social links do not affect subjective phenomena. If that were so,
the structural aspects of social relations would dominate.

Between the devil of the subject and the deep blue sea of structure, falls a
shadow. This shadow reflects, on the one hand, the inability of structures to
achieve final closure or provide ineluctable and complete rules, and, on the
other hand, the inability of the subject to be sovereign and complete with a
closed identity, unmodified by its own decisions. This shadow is a 'never-
closed-gap' which disrupts and prevents the structure from closing, so pre-
cluding the subject from being whole, full, and enclosed in a definitive
identity. This 'never-closed-gap' is precisely the condition of the possibility of
political life. It is here that we find the tension between agency and structure.
And it is this which is the domain of the political.

That the political is primary is central to discourse theory. It is the practice
of politics that constructs our world. Accordingly, discourse theory widens
and radicalizes the problem set out by Machiavelli: how does a prince maintain his position? The problem for a contemporary prince, or princess, is
more difficult, since many of the props upon which Machiavelli's Prince
could rely are not available. Post-modern princes cannot take comfort in the
permanence of their instruments of rule. Moreover, the foundations of their
principality are the remains of the work of former princes, and, as such, they
are temporary constructs. Their temporary nature, however, does not mean
that every principality is a *tabula rasa*. Even in the wake of revolutionary
upheavals, the rules of principalities are already inscribed. However, some of
the writing is in stone and some in chalk, and the successful prince knows
how to reinterpret the former and rewrite the latter. What is important here
for discourse theory is that structures do not have necessary and permanent
elements and rules. Rather, they are contingent, and their permanence
depends on their degree of politicization.

In approaching questions of this kind, discourse theory distinguishes
between categories not in terms of their division into permanent and temporary (that is, as necessary or contingent), but, rather, according to their
degree of politicization. For example, in modern democratic states, women's
suffrage is no longer a political issue; it is now part of the 'common sense'
that women should have the right to vote. Women's right to abortion on
demand, by contrast, is a politically charged issue. There is no consensus

around the abortion versus pro-life conflict; no 'common sense' has yet formed. And, according to the anti-foundationalist stance of discourse theorists, there are no rules by which the matter might be determined: the world is without a solid foundation. It is only the will of the prince, the locus of power, that gives the illusion of cohesion.

Of course, the idea that our world is held together by the contingencies or vagaries of the political is an uncomfortable one. Thus, it is only too easy to be lured away from confronting the insecurities of a world without foundations, especially by the temptations of materialist arguments, on the one hand, and, on the other, by focusing on the apparently paradoxical character of discourse theory.

The materialist temptation

A common caricature of discourse theory is that it is idealist (see, for example, Geras 1987; Meiksins-Wood 1986) and that, within the terms of the theory, 'anything goes' (some versions do, indeed, degenerate into that). In response to the challenges of discourse theory, these critics constantly attempt to find foundations, and thus reduce the role of the political. The first temptation is the appeal to materiality, or facticity. Such temptations range from asserting the facticity of material objects (rock is rock, an earthquake is an earthquake, and the like) to asserting that the intrinsic properties of objects provide true foundations (sand cannot be eaten, water cannot be used in place of firewood). The temptation here is to uncover the 'reality' beneath the cover of the language games, which, according to critics, discourse theorists play. That is, 'materialist' arguments endeavour to find in the hardness of rocks or the movement of an earthquake, for example, something which is immune to discursive articulation. Such appeals to materiality as a way of locating foundations, however, are based on a number of misunderstandings about the discourse-theoretical approach.

Discourse theorists do not claim that things are created simply by uttering words; language does not create entities. But discourse theorists do maintain that reality is only accessible through the descriptions made in language; and descriptions have to be located in some signifying practice. Moreover, changing descriptions has an important effect on how we understand reality. Richard Rorty (1989: 5) puts it this way:

Truth cannot be out there—cannot exist independently of the human mind—because sentences cannot so exist, or be out there. The world is out there, but the descriptions of the world are not. Only descriptions of the world can be true or false. The world on its own—unaided by the describing activities of human beings—cannot. . . . When the notion of 'descriptions of the world' is moved from the level of criterion-governed sentences within language games to language games as wholes, games which we do not choose between by reference to criteria, the idea that the world decides which descriptions are true can no longer be given a clear sense.

In other words, discourse theorists maintain that descriptions of the world are the means by which we socially construct reality. Descriptions of the world are our handles upon it. This, however, does not mean that descriptions cannot change. The labels that we use to understand reality are not the labels of reality itself. For example, until fifty years ago we thought that the universe was made of atoms and that there was nothing smaller than atoms. Nowadays, we understand that the universe is constructed from subatomic particles. The universe has not changed; only our metaphors for describing it. Moreover, there is no guarantee that, in the future, our descriptions will not change again. The ways in which descriptions change (or how social relations are (re-)constructed) are not a matter of individual wills. The articulation of discourse is a social and political process. It is also a process which involves both linguistic and extra-linguistic elements. We do not enter the world by labelling and relabelling all the things around us. We are rarely at the moment of initial baptism; and, in any case, such a moment is always a collective one.

Materialist arguments (*cf.* Meiksins-Wood 1986) assume that the 'best' discourse is one that corresponds to the 'nature of things'. But the materialist tempters conflate two separate arguments: one concerning how things are inserted within discourses; the other concerning the nature of things themselves. The first argument assumes that the nature of things is not the product of discourse, so it defines away the claims at issue. The second argument claims that the way in which science, or contemporary knowledge, describes things is the way that things really are. This, it is argued, can be confirmed by the way in which a correct understanding of the nature of things makes it possible to manipulate them. Both of these claims are rejected by discourse theorists who see in them a return to foundationalism.

The paradoxical temptation

The second temptation that might lure us away from the discomforts of a world without foundations is based on trying to demonstrate the paradoxical character of discourse theory. This is done by claiming that discourse theory is inherently incoherent. If truth is constructed, as discourse theorists accept, then, according to critics (see Geras 1987) the statement 'truth is constructed' is also a construction. If that is the case, discourse theory is inherently self-referential; it is unable to validate itself by appealing to canons of evidence which are external to its discourse. As such, analyses based on discourse theory can only be justified in terms of discourse theory. In other words, if the terms of discourse theory reject appeals to empiricism, and emphasize the constructed character of social categories, they provide no grounds for accepting the conclusions derived from applying discourse theory. By abandoning notions of 'objectivity' and 'scientific method', discourse theory is unable to distinguish between the social sciences and literature (Rorty 1982: 201).

The paradoxical character of discourse theory is only apparent, however, if one continues to hold on to foundationalism. That discourse theory appears to be paradoxical is a product, not of the incoherence of discourse theory, but, rather, of the incommensurability of the criteria culled from, on the one hand, the tradition of foundationalism, and, on the other hand, the terms of discourse theory. Discourse theory is not (and should not) be read as another royal road to wisdom. Its usefulness can be judged only as one would judge a piece of literature or cinema. Namely, is the story that it tells compelling? There may be many strategies for telling a compelling story, but these are strategies, not algorithmic solutions, about how to tell compelling stories. These strategies may include following generic rules, such as the rules of academic discourse; they may also include appeals to greater explanatory power. But there are no guarantees that the application of generic rules will always produce a compelling narrative.

According to discourse theory, both the materialist and the paradoxical temptations are based on perpetuating what Nietzsche (1994: 24, 119) called the 'longest lie': that there is something outside our human practices that we can appeal to by following the correct procedures. For discourse theorists, there is no way that we can step outside ourselves to see the world from a non-human point view. As a consequence, all that our knowledge industries can do is to tell us human tales about human actors. Discourse theory cannot ground itself in anything other than its own concepts and its own narration.

Tools of the Trade

Having rejected the siren calls of materialism and the theoretical paradox, we go on to examine the three main conceptual tools on which the discourse-theoretical approach relies to yield some sense of the world. These tools are used to understand a world without foundations, enabling us to make the leap from an analysis of the representation of political phenomena to an explanation of the construction of the political through signifying practices.

Discourse

The term 'discourse' has become very fashionable in recent years. In many instances it is loosely used as a synonym for text, or merely for speech. As used to refer to speech, it has become widely used by analysts who rely on the distinction between what people say and what they do (for example, in electoral campaigns). However, discourse theorists regard discourse as more than verbal or written speech. It includes actions, thoughts, and beliefs. According to discourse theory, discursive configurations include both linguistic and non-linguistic elements.

This approach owes a great deal to the linguistic school initiated by Saussure (1983) whose pioneering work on the sign lies at the heart of the notion of discourse. Saussure defines the sign as the closed relationship between a *signifier* and a *signified*. The signifier is an acoustic image, the signified is a concept, and the relationship between them is uniquely based on convention (that is, it is arbitrary). So, for instance, the word 'tree' is the sign which identifies the outcome of the relationship between the acoustic image 'tree' and the concept of tree. The arbitrary nature of this relationship, according to Saussure (1983: 100), lies in the fact that the same concept can have different names. That a tree has different nominations in different languages is proof of this. A crucial point in Saussurean linguistics is that language is a system of signs, each of which acquires its identity in relation to the identity of other signs. For instance, the sign 'day' only has meaning in its relationship to other signs such as 'night'. The same goes for the sign 'tree'; it only acquires meaning from its relation to other signs like seed, plant, leaf, soil, or even in relation to that which it is not (for example, human or manufactured).

Although Benveniste (1971) queried Saussure's notion of the arbitrariness of the sign, other theorists, coming from very diverse disciplines, developed further the notions of signifier and signified and the link between them. Taking his lead from Saussure, the French theorist Roland Barthes sought to found a new discipline, semiology, as a science of signs. He applied the linguistic model and the notion of the sign to different systems (the fashion system, the highway code, films, the food system, for example) in order to uncover the structure of the signs in these systems. According to Barthes (1973), the closed structure of signs could explain all possible variations within each of these systems. He thought that by finding the fundamental rules which define and exhaust, for example, the food system, he could account for all possible occurrences of eating; that is, the way people eat in Japan, Europe, or Uzbekistan. Semiological analysis would involve finding this structure and working through the different levels of meaning to find the last layer—or 'the first order language'—on which all the other layers lean.

In his later work, however, Barthes gave up what he called the 'dream of semiology', turning, instead, to questioning the very notion of the sign as a transparent medium of signification. He argued that there is not simply a real and unmediated concept, the signified, to which we have access through an acoustic image, the signifier. In this later post-structuralist period of his work, Barthes (1990: 8–11) claimed that meaning is constructed via the very production of the link between a signifier, or a chain of signifiers, and a signified; it is in this process that the signified is produced. Thus, according to Barthes, there is no pre-existing signified prior to its relationship to a signifier or a chain of signifiers. Therefore, there is no transparent language through which we have direct access to reality. There is no 'first-order language'. Rather, Barthes claims, the notion of a first-order language is an illusion. Meaning is produced, rather than reflected, in language.

If meaning is a construction and there is no pre-existing signified (objective reality) before signification, then there are no pre-given identities—objects as such—before meaning. All of them are constructions. In other words, if all signification is constructed, then so are identities and the relations between them. As signification involves the construction of identity, there is no identity before meaning. Not only does identity come into existence through signification, but its construction involves the construction of its link to other identities. Thus, for example, the construction of the identity 'woman' before the construction of feminist discourse involved its inscription as subordinate within a certain hierarchy (for example, in its relation to 'man'), in a specific place within a certain form of family structure (for example, in its association with 'mother'), and/or in a marginal location in the labour force (for example, in relation to male workers). But now, following the dissemination of feminist discourse, we see how the construction of 'woman' has changed; the subordinate position of women has been questioned and new forms of identity are being asserted. Moreover, transformation of the identity of woman also involves changes in the identities of man, father, or workers.

In Saussurean linguistics, discourse refers to any individual utterance longer than a sentence. However, as Saussure was wedded to the Cartesian notion of the subject, he was unable to conceive a general theory of discourse. Since whatever is uttered by an individual constitutes discourse yet individuals are unique, it becomes impossible—within Saussure's approach—to develop a general theory of what would constitute the speech of individuals. Thus, following Barthes' expansion of Saussure's linguistics, how to identify the elements of a general system of signification became an important question. In his early work, Barthes used common sense notions (such as the food system, the fashion system) to describe the limits of his semiological studies. But once he made the move to post-structuralism and abandoned the closure of structures, this was clearly an inadequate way of defining objects of study. As post-structuralism entails the claim that no system can be fully closed, the notion that systems have a priori boundaries is crucially weakened. Thus, a problem arises: how do we identify any system if the boundary of what constitutes a system cannot be closed? For instance, how can we distinguish between what elements are part of the fashion system and what elements are part of the food system if we cannot establish the boundaries of either system?

Although coming from very a different intellectual tradition, Michel Foucault encountered similar problems. His attempt to study systems of thought over time was fraught with the difficulties of identifying the unity and limits of these various systems of thought. Foucault focused on the statements proper to each system, which led him to reject four methods for identifying the unity of a group of statements. First, since objects are the products of statements, a network of statements cannot be identified on the grounds that the statements all refer to a common object. Foucault did not assert that there are no entities prior to statements, but, rather, that the identity of objects—in Rorty's terms, the way we label them—is given by the statements made about them. Secondly, since the signifying practice can include a variety of statements from different *genres*, the unity of a signifying practice cannot be given by a common style. For example, in clinical discourse, Foucault (1973: 33) found statements about 'ethical choices, therapeutic decisions, institutional regulations, teaching models'. Nor, thirdly, can a signifying practice be unified in terms of persistent concepts, since these concepts are also subject to transformations over time. An obvious example is the concept of madness which has been transformed from a purely neurological concept to a psychoanalytic concept. And, fourthly, unity is not possible by identifying underlying themes because the same theme can generate more than one signifying practice. The theme of pathology, for instance, can be found in the discourses of medicine, law, and criminology.

Foucault's solution for these difficulties is to theorize unity as 'regularity in dispersion'. A discourse is a signifying practice in which statements have a regular and dispersed relationship. What is missing from Foucault's account, however, is the notion of boundary or frontier. 'Regularity in dispersion' cannot tell us where one signifying practice ends and another begins, since there is no apodeictic means of deriving regularity. The limits of a discourse must be found within the discourse itself; that is, by uncovering how, in a particular discourse, the boundaries are drawn. For otherwise we would need to devise another discourse which would establish 'from the outside', as it were, the limits of the first discourse, which would require a third discourse on the limits of the second discourse, and so on. The discourse of astronomy, for example, marks itself off from astrology, but discourse defined as 'regularity in dispersion' would not be adequate for distinguishing between these two practices.

Having said that the never-entirely-closed boundaries of any system are constituted within the discourse itself, we can go on to say that discourse is a means of resolving the destabilization produced by the post-structuralist move. Bearing in mind the discussion in the previous section about the lack of ultimate foundations (anti-foundationalism) and the never-entirely-closed system, or structure, of meaning (post-structuralism), we can define discourse as that never-entirely-closed organization of meaning and identities. That is, discourse is the relatively unified and coherent organization of meaning which is historically constructed but which always entails a gap. It is this gap which precludes a full, final closure of the discourse.

There are two sides to discourse, then. On the one hand, there is a relatively stable unity of meaning and identities; on the other, there is that gap which prevents full closure. It is the latter—the gap—which marks precisely the domain of the political: that arena in which contestation takes place with the aim of suturing, or closing, the gap. In all discursive formations, there will be various projects trying to close the gap, to master the political arena, to found a unified discourse by means of complex operations. The organization of unity requires at least two things. First, the construction of the limits of an ensemble of meaning; signifying practices cannot have any form of unity or stability without boundaries which mark them off as distinct from other signifying practices. Second, a unified ensemble of meaning is constituted by means of a set of narratives, logics, or rules, whose articulations constitute the structure. It is these features of discourse, primarily, which are the concern of discourse theory.

In short, discourse theorists study political phenomena by looking at the limits of discursive formations, tracing and unweaving the logics that structure a discourse. Their tools, or concepts, are borrowed from a wide variety of disciplines: linguistics (sign, signifier, signified), psychoanalysis (subjectivity, identification, repression), philosophy (deconstruction of binary oppositions, pragmatism), political science and political theory (concepts such as hegemony and power). Analysts using the discourse-theoretical approach are concerned with how, in given historical circumstances, different elements of a discourse are put together and unified. This involves a pragmatic reading of the constructed coherence of social practices (rather than a quest for hidden underlying unities or an external essence). Coherence and the limits of the discourse (what keeps the ensemble a cohesive, meaningful whole) could be explained as an effect of the production of meaning. This coherence, however, is never totally realized, due to the existence of conflict, counter-practices, and other forms of disruption.

Discourse theory enables analysts to study political phenomena by tracing and disentangling these operations. A discursive approach to political analysis does not entail, as sometimes claimed by practitioners or critics, the end of 'traditional' political concerns and their replacement by the analysis of text, whether verbal or written. Such misconceptions are grounded in the politics of representation, which maintains a distinction between meaning and politics, between saying and doing. The discursive approach, by contrast, focuses on the way in which communities construct their limits; their relationship to that which they are not or that which threatens them; and the narratives which produce the founding past of a community, its identity, and its projections of the future.

Hegemony

The notion of discourse is the first step in an anti-foundationalist approach to political analysis. However, there is still the question of how signification, or a system of significations, acquires a certain stability. In other words, it is necessary to look not only at the construction of a discourse—its unity and its limits—but also to look at what gives that ensemble a certain permanence. It is at this point that the concept of hegemony becomes central. This is where the significance of the link between meaning and politics becomes more visible.

The advent of so-called 'new right' political thought prompted many political thinkers on the left to re-consider the work of Antonio Gramsci. These thinkers focused, in particular, on Gramsci's attempt to examine the possibility of radical change in advanced capitalist societies (see, for example, Hall 1988). This interest led to a reworking of Gramsci's notion of hegemony, a category previously used mainly by Marxist thinkers. Coming from a Marxist tradition, Gramsci still thought of the economy as the domain where identities and interests are ultimately grounded. At the same time, however, by putting ideology at the forefront of change, he broke with the Marxists' two-tier view of the world in which structure fully determines superstructure. Gramsci's insistence on the 'materiality of ideology' and the need for 'intellectual and moral leadership' as a means of gaining and holding power, opens up the possibility of studying the construction of political projects. It also invests the cultural domain with political importance. For Gramsci, an 'organic leader' would focus on the transformation of culture as a means of acquiring power. What this entails, of course, is a shift of focus from the economy to culture as a structural phenomenon.

A post-structuralist notion of hegemony disposes of the commonly voiced criticism that the loss of a fixed ground necessarily involves the end of politics and the 'empire of gaming'.[2] The success of any political project is measured by its ability to fix meaning, at least relatively, within a specific context. This is what discourse theorists call hegemony. The apparent closure of a discursive field is the outcome of strategies designed to achieve hegemony. As we noted earlier, however, the hegemonic project which aims to 'close the gap', to master the political arena by means of complex manœuvres, can never be entirely successful. But, at the same time, a hegemonic discourse involves the creation of a certain stability of meaning. Traditional politics relies on this stability, insofar as political actors require a certain space, albeit limited, where uncertainty can be circumscribed, as in the case, for instance, of elections, parliamentary politics, or voting systems in international bodies. The construction of domains where uncertainty can be controlled, where there are established rules by which subjects are expected to behave, are the products of the historical operation of hegemony.

A hegemonic project can be judged successful when it achieves two things. First, when it succeeds in making its proposed logics and rules the 'natural' rules of the community, and its proposed limits define the 'natural' limits of the community. Secondly, it is successful insofar as it contributes to the deactivation, or 'forgetting', of the other projects against which it was struggling. But these other, contending, projects do not dissolve. Here, the post-structuralist notion of hegemony, especially in regard to the theorization and analysis of resistance, and the limits of hegemony, are crucial points to note. By the way in which its limits are constructed, a successful hegemonic project creates rules for dealing with resistance. Discourses of resistance to the hegemonic project attempt to subvert those rules and those limits, and since a hegemonic discourse can never enjoy full-fledged stability, resistance always has a chance. Resisting discourses will struggle to make their own space, endeavouring to subvert the rules of the hegemonic discourse and its limits. Thus, the study of a hegemonic discourse cannot account for all discourses within that field, since that would be to reduce all other projects to the hegemonic discourse. Hegemony is always possible but it can never be total.

Subject/identity

Although generally neglected in political theory, issues of identity have been extensively discussed recently within cultural theory, philosophy, and feminist studies.[3] The debates involve reviewing the links between representation, subjectivity, and politics, and a critique of the subject as an explanatory category. The critical question here is: what is the status of the subject in the analysis of political action if the subject is neither the unique sovereign, nor the origin of meaning, nor is determined by structure? This question raises further questions: how is the unity of a political formation constituted?; and how do we explain and analyse the construction of political identities?

Within discourse analysis, identity is used in two senses. In one sense, we talk about identity in relation to the way social agents can be identified and identify themselves within a certain discourse (as workers, women, atheists, British, for example). In the other sense, the notion of identity is related to the unity of any object or subject. In fact, both ways of talking about identity are intimately connected, since the category of identity in both senses involves the constitution of a relatively fixed unity.

Recall the earlier discussion emphasizing that the identity of any element within a discourse is not given a priori but is constituted within a discourse by its relation to other elements. The identity of any subject involves the same principle; that is, the identity of a subject will be given by its insertion within a discourse. Moreover, the subject occupies a certain position within the discourse: powerful, subordinated, marginalized, central, or whatever. However, since no discourse is ever entirely closed, the identity of the subject can always change. In which case, the obvious questions are: how is an identity 'acquired', and how can an identity change?

Foucault's (1977) answer relies on the notion of a strategy without a strategist and the subject as constituted *within* discourse as an effect of that strategy. Psychoanalysis and the theory of deconstruction provide further clues to Foucault's insights. The notion of the undecidability of the frontiers of any unity, drawn from deconstruction theory, has important implications for the notion of subject and identity. Undecidability entails that no identity within a system can be fully constituted but is always precarious and contingent. Thus, to Foucault's notion that the identity of the subject is constituted within discourse, Derrida's contribution is to add that identity is always precarious and contingent.

The psychoanalytic notion of identification sheds light on the construction of identity in that it focuses on the process by which a subject's identity is constituted and how it can change. Identification involves a process of exchange between an 'inside' and an 'outside' (the object of identification) to produce identities within a certain context. Yet the distance between the result of the identification process (the acquired identity) and what it identifies (the subject) shows the impossibility of constituting a full and complete identity (see Laclau and Zac 1994). The subject is never identical to its acquired identity; the result of the process of identification—the acquired identity—is not identical to the 'model' or object of that identification. In short, the subject is always something more than its identity. Thus, the dialectics of the split subject are established, insofar as instability is a constitutive element of any identity. The identity of the subject is modified by a new act of identification and by its adherence to a new project. In other words, the identity of a subject is constituted in a unifying process but the process is never entirely closed. This impossibility of closing and exhausting the subject with an act of identification is mirrored in the impossibility of the closure of the discourse within which that subject operates.

To clarify this point, we have to distinguish between the subject, and subjectivity or identity. Subjectivity or identity defines the multiple ways by which the subject identifies itself, but which never exhausts the subject. As we noted, a subject can play a part in the many logics and narratives at play in a discourse. Hence, a subject can have various subjectivities: as a student at university, as an employee or employer in the workplace, a husband or wife at home, a mother or child in a family, a Conservative or Labour supporter at election times. Moreover, in any of these narratives, a particular subject would occupy a place in a hierarchy of some kind.

Subjects within a discourse acquire, through the process of identification, an identity, or identities, defining their positioning relative to others, the nature of their relationship to others, and the scope of their behaviour. As discourse theory is concerned with studying the logics at play in a discourse, unravelling the narratives that endow the discourse with a past and a sense of the future, and examining the way its limits are constructed, so examining the way subjectivities are constituted, is crucial to the enterprise. Thus, we have to consider how agents become 'sutured' into a discourse, defining their place in that ensemble and their links to other subjectivities.

We have to bear in mind, however, that given the inherent instability of any discourse, the identity of a subject can always change. The scope of that change will be dictated by the relative success of hegemony. The more stable the hegemonic hold of a discourse, the less scope there is for a change in subjectivities; and, for the subject, the more restricted the space available for identification outside the hegemonic patterns of identification and subjectivities. Nazi discourse, for example, inscribed a certain scope for identification: as a member of the Aryan nation, a soldier of the Reich, a worker labouring for the common good, as a true believer in national socialism. In these logics, the identity of the subject would be inscribed within a certain hierarchical order: as a man or woman in the Ayran community, as a general or a private in the German army, as a worker or manager in industrial relations. There was even scope for indifference. Certain forms of identification, however, as Jews, Gypsies, communists, or disabled, were strictly excluded from the community. According to Nazi discourse, such groups threatened the purity of the Aryan nation, so they fell outside the limits of the community as defined by the discourse. Moreover, the tight hold of Nazi discourse meant that anybody who challenged that exclusion, defying the Nazi *diktat* against identification with the victims of Nazism, would also be excluded by marginalization or death.

Particularities of Discourse Theory

The anti-foundationalist rejection of essentialism involves a critique of universalism, that is, the endeavour to apply one standard or criterion across cultures, histories, or societies. For example, classical economics engages the notion of *homo economicus*—the rational, utility-maximizing individual—who acts according to a cost-benefit calculus regardless of the particularities of his, or her, subjectivity. Relativism arises, it is argued, as a consequence of abandoning universalism. If there is no longer one template by which we can order the world, we will be faced with a Hobbesian war of all against all, in which there is no way to adjudicate between different claims. Thus, the charge—or fear—of relativism is used to ward off anti-foundationalist arguments. Insofar as discourse theory reflects the consequences of anti-foundationalism for political theory, it is compelled to confront questions arising out of debates between universalists and their critics. In other words, anti-foundationalism is not simply a critique of foundations as such, but is also critical of the notion that foundations can be located within one cultural formation. It is the very idea of foundations, and the identity of those foundations, which are the focus of an anti-foundationalist critique (see Sayyid 1997).

Analysts employing discourse theory are sometimes prey to the illusion that their reading of a discourse somehow captures the world of the subjects of that discourse. That is to claim too much. All that discourse theory can enable us to do is to advance an interpretation of the way a specific discourse is constructed: how identities are constituted, how narratives are articulated, and how the ensemble of narratives is rendered coherent. To make larger claims about discourse analysts unveiling the minds of subjects and having access to their thoughts is simply a phenomenological illusion. Discourse analysis cannot give us access to the mind and inner thoughts of an other; it cannot overcome the inevitable distance that exists between the analyst and the object of study, between any object of identification and the result of that identification.

Lonnrot's Quest for Truth

The impossibility of having access to the minds of others, to fully identify with them, is also shown by the failure of the detective Lonnrot in Borges' short story. Lonnrot did not discover the identity of Yarmolinsky's murderer, and his efforts to do so led to three further deaths, including, finally, his own. It was rumoured that he had uncovered the pattern underlying the vicious crimes, but Lonnrot's discovery was the result of the cunning machinations of his sworn enemy Scharlach (the Dandy), who conspired to lead Lonnrot on a merry chase through the city 'amid the boundless odour of the eucalypti'.

In the end, Lonnrot met his death because he persisted in trying to establish a priori the limits of a discourse. Lonnrot's certainty that the crime involving a rabbi must be a crime with Talmudic connotations reveals that a discourse constructs its own limits; the task of the analyst is to reveal those limits, not to establish them before investigation. In this sense, Lonnrot's failure illustrates one of the limitations of discourse theory. Analysts using discourse theory cannot dismiss that which disrupts the coherence of a discursive universe; rather, the analyst should always look for both the limits and coherence of a discourse and at the nuances, disruptions, or conflicts contained within the discourse. To emphasize again: no hegemonic discourse can fully account for what goes on within that universe. There are always going to be moments when the coherence of that discourse is challenged or encounters insurmountable obstacles. The construction of 'the other' in an hegemonic discourse cannot fully account for the identity of that other. In this instance, Lonnrot's mistake was to assume that Yarmolinsky's murder was a crime belonging to the 'history of Jewish superstition'. He could only think of Yarmolinsky as a Jew and a rabbi. He could not think that Yarmolinsky's Jewishness or rabbinical status was simply incidental to his death.

Lonnrot's essentialism (Yarmolinsky was essentially a rabbi) led him to assume, a priori, the limits of the discourse of the murderer. He privileged the rabbinical belonging of the victim and projected that privileging on to the murderer. The motive for the killing had to be linked with Yarmolinsky's status as a rabbi. Lonnrot established the 'history of Jewish superstition' as the limits of that discourse. From there onwards, and within these limits, Lonnrot attempted to reconstruct the crime and its motive by divining the rules and logics of rabbinical discourse; by reading the narratives that sutured the rabbi and his killer to the discourse. The cunning of Scharlach was precisely to play a deadly game with Lonnrot's vision of the crime; he played on Lonnrot's attempt to reconstruct the rules of the killer's game. He became an accomplished 'organic intellectual', articulating the rules which would lead the detective to his death. In this sense, Scharlach acted as an anti-foundationalist; he put into question all the certainties and regularities on which Lonnrot depended. Sharlach did not read Lonnrot's mind. Rather, he ensnared Lonnrot by weaving into the dectective's logic further articulations linked to rabbinical texts, so bracketing, and thus preventing, the possibility that the accidental death of the rabbi would disrupt the coherence of Lonnrot's logic. The detective was outplayed by Scharlach's 'perspicacity' in understanding that diverse narratives are possible. Thus, he could draw Lonnrot to his death.

Notes

1. It might be argued that suspending the elections and declaring martial law was merely the addition of a new rule. The point here is that this 'addition' (establishing that an election could be suspended if a certain result was likely) transformed the game so radically that it could no longer be thought of as the same game. In this sense, the major players would have acted in a different way and would have had different strategies for the game. Indeed, they would, themselves, have been modified by the new rule.
2. Many figures associated with anti-foundationalism are also associated with particular visions of a political order; Rorty (1989) and 'post-modern bourgeois liberalism' is a case in point. Thus, it is often assumed that discourse theory underwrites a particular vision of politics. This slippage between discourse theory as way of analysing political events to discourse theory as a way of advocating certain political arrangements represents, in effect, a bid for hegemony. There is nothing in discourse theory that makes it more or less susceptible to any type of political regime. Discourse theory can do nothing to prevent, for example, the rise of authoritarian or fascist regimes, nor does it endorse any particular political tendency.
3. See e.g. Butler (1987); Dallmayr (1981); Derrida (1978, 1981); Hall (1983); Irigaray (1985); Levinas (1981).

12

DISCOURSE THEORY AND POLITICAL ANALYSIS
DAVID HOWARTH

A proliferation of theories and methodologies challenging positivist approaches to the social sciences have emerged in recent years. Researchers have drawn upon a range of interpretative and critical traditions, such as Marxism, hermeneutics, psychoanalysis, deconstruction, literary theory, structural linguistics, and cultural anthropology to account for social and political phenomena (see, for example, Dallmayr and McCarthy 1977; Gibbons 1987; Shapiro 1981). One consequence has been a blurring of the once important division between, on the one hand, an objective, value-neutral, empirical social science, and, on the other, those approaches stressing interpretative and essentially evaluative methods of inquiry. Another consequence has been a questioning of the very foundations of the human and social sciences, evident in the development of anti-foundationalist and post-modernist standpoints (for example, Bernstein 1983; Rorty 1980, 1989).

The epistemological commitments and methodological implications of these new approaches, however, remain largely underdeveloped, which has led, *inter alia*, to charges of irrationalism, methodological anarchism, relativism, and idealism (*cf.* Bhaskar 1989; Geras 1990; Habermas 1990). An exception is the work of Ernesto Laclau and Chantal Mouffe, who have articulated a rigorous discursive approach to empirical research based on an explicitly post-foundational stance. The aim of this chapter is to present the main contours of Laclau and Mouffe's approach, and to explore its implications for social science research, particularly the analysis of politics.

The first section of the chapter sets Laclau and Mouffe's conception of discourse in the context of contemporary debates about ideology and discourse. In the second section, I examine the main political concepts and logics in Laclau and Mouffe's theory of discourse. Some of the epistemological issues pertinent to a critical assessment of discourse theory are raised in the third section, and in the fourth section the research strategies and techniques of discourse analysis are outlined. Finally, in the fifth section, some criticisms of the discursive approach to social and political analysis are considered.

From a Critique of Ideology to a Theory of Discourse

The development of Laclau and Mouffe's theory of discourse can be traced back to Althusser's (1971, 1977) account of ideology, which emerged out of an epistemological and sociological confrontation with certain accounts of Marxist theory. The epistemological issue centred on Althusser's defence of Marxist science (manifest in Marx's later writings) against theoretical humanism (symptomatic of the 'Young Marx'), and was predicated on the idea that every science is constituted by breaking with a prescientific ideological past. This 'epistemological break', as Althusser called it, drawing on Barchelard's philosophy of science, involved a science producing its own irreducible and authentic object of investigation, around which theoretical labour could be organized.[1] The sociological issue concerned the role of ideology in the production and reproduction of social relations, in which ideology is a 'lived', albeit 'imaginary', relation that a subject has to the real conditions of existence. In so doing, Althusser challenges the view that ideology is a mere reflection of an already existing social reality, substituting instead the idea that ideology is integral to the structure of social relations, carrying with it real material effects.

These two sites of theoretical struggle are not, however, completely separated in Althusser's writings. Ideology as a lived relation is also connected to questions of truth and falsity, and, by extension, to problems of epistemology. The obviousness of the world in which the subject 'sees' and 'lives' is a function of ideology; the apparent truthfulness of the world for the subject is marked by a 'misrecognition' of its real conditions. Thus, the misrecognition of exploitation in capitalist society by workers, who are constituted as free and equal citizens, represents one of the crucial means by which capitalist relations of production are reproduced. In short, Althusser links his critique of empiricism and idealism on a philosophical plane to the modes by which subjects seemingly experience a world of objects without mediation or misrecognition.

Ideology is not, however, to be equated with a form of 'false consciousness', as this would imply that ideology is simply to do with the mental representations, or ideas, which subjects experience, albeit in a false form.[2] Such a view of ideology presupposes an empiricist epistemology in which subjects represent the way the world is, whether correctly or incorrectly. By contrast, Althusser views ideology as a 'practice' of constituting individuals as subjects with particular attributes and 'class outlooks'. Moreover, these 'class outlooks' are embodied in social institutions and rituals, materializations which underwrite beliefs and forms of consciousness.

As numerous commentators have suggested, Althusser's theorization of ideology rejuvenated a moribund aspect of Marxist theory and contributed to the reworking of Marxist political and cultural theory (cf. Hirst 1979; Laclau 1977). However, Althusser's theorization is not without its difficulties, even for those who share some of his objectives. In the first place, although Althusser's attack on theoretical humanism sought to 'de-centre' the subject by drawing attention to its production in and through ideology, the mechanism by which ideology functions—interpellation—supposes an already constituted subject which subsequently 'recognizes/misrecognizes' itself. As Althusser (1971: 174) puts it:

[I]deology 'acts' or 'functions' in such a way that it 'recruits' among the individuals (it recruits them all) by that very precise operation which I have called *interpellation* or hailing, and which can be imagined along the lines of the most commonplace everyday police (or other) hailing: 'Hey, you there!'

Assuming that the theoretical scene I have imagined takes place in the street, the hailed individual will turn around. By this one-hundred-and-eighty-degree physical conversion, he becomes a *subject*. Why? Because he has recognized that the hail was 'really' addressed to him (and not someone else).

This view emphasizes the way in which the social structure determines the positioning of subjects in a social formation *before* they are interpellated (Hirst 1979: 64–8). It also assumes a unified subject which is centred by the imaginary relation conferred in the 'hailing' process.

Althusser's social ontology presents a further problem. In his conception, social formations are composed of three systems of practice (economic, political, and ideological), as well as theoretical (scientific) practice, each with their own relative autonomy and efficacy in reproducing what Althusser calls the 'complex structure-in-dominance' which makes up society. However, which system is to be the most important is determined by the economy, albeit 'in the last instance' (Althusser 1977: 163–218). This conception, however, fails to deconstruct fully the determinism and functionalism of the Marxist social totality, so that the relative autonomy of the ideological and political superstructures is confined to maintaining the reproduction of capitalist relations of production. Moreover, the grounds for separating the different systems are not spelled out (Cutler *et al.* 1977: 207–21; Laclau and Mouffe 1985: 97–105). The consequence of these difficulties is to militate against a relational conception of different systems of social practice, an idea presaged in Althusser's borrowing of Freud's concept of overdetermination to account for the mutual imbrication of social relations.[3] Finally, Althusser's representation of social relations as pre-existing the interpellation of individuals as social subjects provides little theoretical space for conflicting forms of identification, which may challenge the prevailing 'structure-in-dominance', so confirming the functionalist tones of the theoretical schema.

One path out of Althusser's cul-de-sac is provided by Foucault's work. Foucault replicates Althusser's concerns with the analysis of bodies of knowledge, which he names 'discursive formations' (or simply discourses), and the historical examination of systems of knowledge/power and their effects on social practices, but he changes the terrain of investigation. In what has been dubbed his 'archaeological phase' (Dreyfuss and Rabinow 1982: 104), Foucault (1970) introduces the concept of a 'discursive formation' to account for the production of forms of knowledge—understood as the enunciation of scientific statements—in specific historical periods. Reflecting on his empirical investigations, Foucault (1972: 31–9) argues that discursive formations are not individuated by reference to a common object of investigation, or a shared style in producing statements, nor by a constancy of concepts, or reference to a common theme. Rather, it is the *regularity* of dispersed statements, governed by, and produced within, a historically specific set of rules of formation, which provides the principles of unity for discourses.

In this respect, Foucault shares Althusser's 'decentring' of theoretical humanism—the notion that knowledge is a product of sovereign subjects—and accepts that knowledge is itself a discursive practice. However, he does not draw a sharp distinction between science and ideology. Rather, Foucault argues that the distinction—at least in Althusser's terms—retains an untheorized commitment to objectivity. That is, for Althusser, a science is constituted by creating a theoretical object of investigation to provide knowledge of 'real objects', and is thus an unwarranted support for epistemological discourse. In Foucault's archaeological description of knowledge, by contrast, theoretical objects are constructed within discursive formations, which are, in themselves, neither true nor false (see Brown and Cousins 1980; Foucault 1972; Hindess and Hirst 1977; Lecourt 1970).

In his later 'genealogical' studies, Foucault (1977, 1979) shifts attention to the social practices and power relations that give rise to the different institutional regimes, complexes of power/knowledge, and logics of subjectification which, in his view, form the modern world. In moving away from a quasi-phenomenological description of discursive practices and formations to a critique of 'non-discursive practices', as he calls them, Foucault displaces the symbolic and linguistic emphases of his earlier writings, leading him to consider the way in which forms of knowledge (or discourses) intersect with, and bolster, systems of domination. This break reinforces Foucault's (1980: 118–19) suspicion of the concept of ideology as a form of false consciousness, to be deciphered and demystified in the name of truth and science.

Laclau and Mouffe's (1985) theory of discourse emerges from engaging with these theoretical developments. While acknowledging Althusser's stress on the material character of ideology, they abandon the split between science and ideology, arguing that this simply confirms the appearance/ reality or false consciousness/true consciousness distinctions in classical Marxism. Further, they question the social ontology of practices underpinning Althusser's account of ideology, arguing that there are no abstract and transhistorical reasons for separating systems of practices and relations. Thus, they query the idea that ideology (which, following Foucault, they redefine as discourse) provides the subject with an imaginary—that is, distorted and illusory—relation to its real conditions of existence. Similarly, while they affirm the practical character of discourse, as produced in determinate historical conditions, Laclau and Mouffe reject an a priori separation of different types of practice in which the economic is determining. Rather, they argue that all practices have an articulatory character, that no system of practices is completely immune from the effects of others, and, thus, ultimate determinacy is impossible. Finally, although they accept Foucault's endeavour to displace an epistemological critique of discursive configurations, particularly his view that theoretical objects are wholly internal to discourses, they question his division of practices into the 'discursive' and the 'non-discursive'. In Laclau and Mouffe's (1985: 146) view, all objects are discursively constituted by articulatory practices such that the determinants and limits of discursive formations are not an extra-discursive 'reality' but other discourses.

In developing their alternative conception, Laclau and Mouffe extend to all social relations Lacan's (1977a: 147) dictum that 'the unconscious is structured like a language': the social itself is articulated and structured like a language. Drawing from Levi-Strauss (1967) and Saussure (1983), they argue that all social phenomena can be redescribed as an ensemble of linguistic differences in which the identity of any element depends on its relation to other elements in the system. Central here is Laclau and Mouffe's (1985: 113) concept of an *articulatory practice*:

The practice of articulation . . . consists in the construction of nodal points which partially fix meaning; and the partial character of this fixation proceeds from the openness of the social, a result, in its turn, of the constant overflowing of every discourse by the infinitude of the field of discursivity.

Three further theoretical specifications are required to make this concept intelligible: the characteristic unity of discourses; the openness or contingency of discourses; and the various dimensions of the discursive. I examine each in turn.

First, Laclau and Mouffe (1985: 106) argue that discourses consist of a system of dispersed elements which can 'in certain contexts of exteriority . . . be *signified* as a totality' (emphasis added). Here they are borrowing directly from Saussure (1983) and Benveniste (1971: 19) for whom language is char- acterized as a formal system of differences such that all identity is relational, and all relations have a necessary character. For Laclau and Mouffe, however, this perspective would reduce all linguistic differences to the internal *moments* of a system, in which case there would be no possibility of an articu- latory practice. Every practice would simply repeat the existing system of differences, and there would be no possibility of constructing new 'nodal points which partially fix meaning'.

Articulatory practices are, thus, only possible given the 'openness' or con- tingency of discourses. Here, Laclau and Mouffe distinguish between the infinitude (or contingency) of a 'field of discursivity'—what they call 'a sur- plus of meaning'—with the finitude (or necessity) of concrete discourses. Instead of prioritizing one pole of this opposition, Laclau and Mouffe elab- orate a more complex dialectic between the contingent and the necessary. They argue that any social formation, consisting of moments of a system, fails to exhaust the field of possible meaning, such that there are always ele- ments which are not integrated.[4]

To theorize this view, Laclau and Mouffe draw upon those currents of thought—post-structuralism, post-modernism, and post-analytical philo- sophy—which have questioned the assumption that meanings can be foun- dationally fixed. Derrida's (1974: 27–65) deconstructive reading of the linguistic sign, for instance, questions a homologous relation between signi- fier (sound-image) and signified (concept).[5] He claims that the essence of a sign is that its meanings can never be determined once and for all by a given linguistic system, but always has the capacity to break with a context and take on different connotations. The sign is thus overflowed by a plurality of signification, which cannot be finally stabilized. As Derrida (1982: 320–1, last two emphases added) puts it:

Every sign, linguistic or nonlinguistic, spoken and written (in the usual sense of this opposition), as a small or large unity, can be *cited*, put between quotation marks; thereby it can break with every given context, and engender infinitely new contexts in an absolutely nonsaturable fashion. This does not suppose that the mark is valid outside its context, but on the contrary that *there are only contexts without any center of absolute anchoring*. This citationality, duplication, or duplicity, this *iterability* of the mark is not an accident or anomaly; but is that (normal/ abnormal) without which a mark could no longer even have a so-called 'normal' functioning. What would a mark be that one could not cite? And whose origin could not be lost on the way?

For Laclau and Mouffe's conception, the impossibility of a final closure of signification is analogous with their view that the structuring of 'elements' into 'moments' is never complete. This means that social formations are 'impossible' objects of construction in that they can never totally hegemonize the social meanings of a given discursive field. This means that every 'necessity' or 'social objectivity' is surrounded (and, as we shall see, 'penetrated') by a discursive exterior which renders all social identity contingent. It is this dialectical play between relations of necessity and contingency which makes articulatory practices possible. In other words, the impossibility of a final closure of meaning opens the space for all social practices to be articulatory, that is, to constitute new meanings and identities by being both partially internal and external to the discourses which define them (Laclau and Mouffe 1985: 111–14).

The third aspect of Laclau and Mouffe's theorization endeavours to deconstruct the distinction between discursive and non-discursive practices. This has proved to be one of the most controversial elements in their theory. Criticizing Foucault's retention of a dichotomy between discursive and non-discursive practices, Laclau and Mouffe (1985: 107) argue that all objects are constituted as objects of discourse and that there is no ontological difference between 'the linguistic and behavioural aspects of a social practice'. Two important qualifications are added here. First, the discursive characterization of objects does not deny their 'real existence' outside of discursive configurations, but, rather, denies their constitution as meaningful objects outside of discourse. Second, discourse has a material, rather than mental, character. Drawing on the writings of the later Wittgenstein (1958), and others, they problematize a sharp separation between an objective world, on the one hand, and language or thought on the other, in which the latter is simply a representation or expression of the former.[6] Discourses are not confined to an inner realm of mental phenomena, but are those frameworks of meaning which constitute the intersubjective rules of social life.

The Primacy of Politics

We have seen that Laclau and Mouffe's social ontology is predicated on the radically open texturedness of any discourse and, therefore, the contingent character of social identity. However, they are faced with an immediate paradox. On the one hand, borrowing from Saussure and structuralist thought more generally, they claim that all identity is relational, depending on a system of differences for its existence. However, drawing on Derrida's poststructuralist critique, they also assert that this system of differences can never, in principle, be closed, as every sign is overflowed with a plurality of meanings not reducible to any one signified. How, then, is any identity possible? Are we condemned to a total dissemination of meaning in which identities are dissolved into a 'play of differences', as some visions of (post-) modernity suggest?[7]

It is here that Laclau and Mouffe affirm the primacy of politics in their social ontology. Systems of social relations—or discourses—are always political constructions, and, as such, involve the exercise of power in their formation. It is political practices which serve to constitute (and undermine) discourses and the identities they form. Moreover, because social systems have a fundamentally political character, they are rendered vulnerable to those forces which are excluded in the process of political constitution. It is around these processes that Laclau and Mouffe seek to erect a political theory of discourse. In doing so, they introduce three central concepts: social antagonism, political subjectivity, and hegemony. Each needs examining in greater detail.

Antagonisms

The construction and experience of social antagonisms are central for Laclau and Mouffe's theory of discourse. First, antagonisms are not subsumable under a greater rationality, such as universal laws of history or the preconstituted interests of social agents, but are *constitutive* of identity and social objectivity. Further, in introducing an element of radical negativity into the social, antagonisms also show the *contingency* of all identity and social objectivity. This dual constituting and destabilizing means that the concept of antagonism has strong resonances with Derrida's notion of a 'constitutive outside' (Staten 1984: 23–4). In his deconstructive readings of metaphysical texts, Derrida shows how the privileging of certain poles of key binary oppositions—essence/accident, mind/body, speech/writing—are predicated on a simultaneous relation of exclusion and dependence. That is to say, efforts in the Western tradition to prioritize one pole of the dialectic are shown to fail in that the dominant term requires for its identity that which is excluded, thus problematizing a clear hierarchical relation between the two.

What are social antagonisms in Laclau and Mouffe's perspective? In opposition to traditional conceptions of social conflict in which antagonisms are represented as the clash between social agents with fully constituted identities, Laclau and Mouffe insist that social antagonisms occur because of the failure of social agents to attain their identity. Thus, antagonism occurs when 'the presence of [an] "Other" prevents me from being totally myself. The relation arises not from full totalities, but from the impossibility of their constitution.' This 'blockage' of identity is a mutual experience for both the antagonizing force and the force being antagonized:

Insofar as there is antagonism, I cannot be a full presence for myself. But nor is the force that antagonizes me such a presence: its objective being is a symbol of my non-being and, in this way, it is overflowed by a plurality of meanings which prevent it being fixed as full positivity. (Laclau and Mouffe 1985: 125)

The task of the discourse analyst, therefore, is to explore the different forms of this impossibility, and the mechanisms by which the blockage of identity is constructed in antagonistic terms by social agents.

To illustrate this conception, let us consider a clash between miners and management over laying off workers in a drive by the mineowners to cut costs and increase efficiency. The miners, represented by their union, oppose the measure and call for strike action. The obdurate management, backed by the government of the day, refuses to change its decision, and a period of struggle ensues. Typically, we have here an antagonism between management (and the government), who construct the union and militant mineworkers as a threat to the long-term prospects of the mining industry, and workers who see their identity as workers threatened by the closure of the mine and the long-term destruction of the mining industry. In this instance, we see that social antagonism arises because of the mutual impossibility of differently located social agents achieving their identities—as 'workers' or 'managers'—rather than a clash between pre-existing forms of identity. Strike action, and its possible extension into other spheres of society, establishes a political frontier separating the two sides, while simultaneously constituting different identities.

In short, antagonisms do not just reveal a fundamental 'negativity' or 'lack' in social relations, in that they show the impossibility of agents achieving their identity, but are also formative of social objectivity itself. A social formation is thus constituted by the construction of antagonistic relations and the institution of political frontiers between agents. In this way, antagonisms are evidence of the boundaries of a social formation, showing the points where identity is no longer stabilized in a differential system but is contested by forces which stand outside, or at the limit, of that order. In so doing, the experience of antagonism bolsters Laclau and Mouffe's thesis that social formations (and identities) are not reducible to the underlying laws of history or the self-interested actions of rational agents, but are political and historical phenomena undergoing constant deformation and redefinition, according to the ways in which social divisions are instituted.

How, then, are antagonisms discursively constructed? How are these subversive forms possible? Here, Laclau and Mouffe must provide an understanding of the way in which a discursive system is threatened by the construction of an antagonism. To show this, a place must be found for a purely negative identity, an identity which is not recuperable into an existing system of differences. To do so, Laclau and Mouffe introduce the concept of the *logic of equivalence*. This logic operates through creating equivalent identities, which express the negation of a discursive order.

The discourse of the Black Consciousness Movement in South Africa during the late 1960s and 1970s provides an example of this logic. This resistance discourse endeavoured to link together a diverse set of ethnic, racial, class, gender, and political differences against the prevailing apartheid order. To establish this linkage, these different positions were rendered equivalent by reference to a common 'white racism', which was the 'constitutive outside' of the movement. A political frontier in South Africa was achieved by drawing a clear division between whites (the enemy) and blacks (friends), and by internally policing the frontier between 'non-whites' and 'blacks' within the oppressed camp; between those who 'collaborated' with apartheid and those who were prepared to challenge it (Howarth 1995a, 1997). For example, a pamphlet distributed by the Black People's Convention in 1973, in the immediate aftermath of the 'Durban strikes', attacked the idea that there are major ethnic differences ('African', 'Indian', 'Coloured') amongst the black population, and called for black solidarity in the face of a common white oppression:

African workers have put out their hands for support from the rest of the black community. But the rest of the black community has not responded positively. *We must remember that we are not different from each other*—it is only the white man who makes us feel this way by separating us and paying us different wages. None of us can afford to sit on our backs and say: 'I don't want to be involved!'. Whether we like it or not we are involved, and we are involved together. And it is time that we got together as OPPRESSED people—Africans, Coloureds and Indians—who are affected by APARTHEID, GROUP AREAS, JOB RESERVATION . . . the injustices are endless. Our suffering is the same. WE ARE ALL BLACK PEOPLE. (Black People's Convention 1973; italicized emphasis added)

The production of signifiers such as 'white oppression' and 'the black people' in Black Consciousness discourse were critical to the emergence of antagonisms in South Africa during the period of 'total apartheid'. They served to dissolve differences being institutionalized in apartheid discourse, and provided the discursive resources to enable black political activists to construct a political identity in opposition to the prevailing system of domination.

In addition to the logic of equivalence, Laclau and Mouffe also introduce a *logic of difference* in the construction of antagonisms and the structuring of social spaces. Whereas the logic of equivalence splits a system of differences, the logic of difference consists in expanding a system of differences by disarticulating existing chains of equivalence and incorporating the elements into an expanding order. Thus a project employing a logic of difference attempts to weaken and displace an antagonistic polarity, while endeavouring to relegate that division to the margins of society (Laclau and Mouffe 1985: 127–34). For example, as Torfing (1991: 86–7) argues, welfare states in post-war Europe were able 'to articulate a social imaginary making possible an almost infinite integration of identities as legitimate differences'. This logic of difference went hand-in-hand with a particular logic of equivalence: 'The constitutive outside of the modern welfare state is established by a chain of equivalence collapsing the differences between the political left and the political right into a sameness of "extremity".'

Political subjectivity and agency

Questions about political subjectivity and agency—the way agents acquire and 'live out' their identities—are paramount for Laclau and Mouffe's theory of discourse. To explicate their conceptualization, I begin by citing their views in relation to Althusser's theorization, touched upon earlier. In opposing perspectives such as phenomenology, empiricism, or rational choice theory, which view subjects as originators of their own ideas, values, or economic interests, Althusser insists that subjects are constructed—'interpellated' or 'hailed'—by ideological practices. For Laclau and Mouffe, however, Althusser's analysis is problematic in at least two respects. First, ideological practices are regarded as a 'relatively autonomous' region of a social formation, a proposition which, as we saw earlier, runs counter to the idea of discourses including all types of social practice. Second, subjects are constituted by ideological practices, which are, in turn, determined by underlying social structures. This reduces the autonomy of social agents to the mere effects of pre-existing social structures.

Thus, while Laclau and Mouffe accept Althusser's critique of a unified and self-transparent subject, and so accept that the identities of subjects are discursively constructed, they do not affirm its deterministic connotations. Rather, they distinguish between *subject positions* and *political subjectivity*.[8] The concept of subject positions refers to the positioning of subjects within a discursive structure (Laclau and Mouffe 1985: 115). Rather than a homogeneous subject with particular interests, this means that any 'concrete individual' can have a number of different subject positions. An empirical agent, at any point in time, might identify herself, or be positioned, as 'black', 'working class', 'Christian', and a 'woman'.[9]

The concept of political subjectivity, by contrast, concerns the way in which social agents act. To go beyond Althusser's privileging of structure over agency, without recourse to a dualistic conception of structure and agency, such as proposed by Giddens (1984: 1–40), Laclau argues that the actions of subjects emerge because of the contingency of those discursive structures through which subjects obtain their identity. This presupposes the concept of *dislocation*, which refers to the process by which the contingency of discursive structures is made visible (Laclau 1990: 39–41). This 'decentring' of the structure through social processes, such as the extension of capitalist relations to new spheres of social life, shatters already existing identities and literally induces an identity crisis for the subject. It is this 'failure' of the structure, and of those subjectivities which are part of such a structure, which 'compels' the subject to act. In this sense, the subject is not simply determined by the structure. Nor, however, does the subject constitute the structure. The subject is forced to take decisions—to identify with certain political projects and the discourses they articulate—when social identities are in crisis and structures need to be recreated. It is in the process of this identification that political subjectivities are formed. Once formed, and stabilized, they become those subject positions which 'produce' individuals with certain characteristics and attributes.

Hegemony

The concept of hegemony is central to Laclau and Mouffe's political theory of discourse: hegemonic practices are an exemplary form of political articulation which involves linking together different identities into a common project, and the creation of new forms of social order from a variety of dispersed elements. This conception emerges out of a detailed critique of Gramsci's concept of hegemony and the Marxist theory of politics and society from which it was derived. For Lenin, hegemony was conceived as a political strategy involving an alliance of class forces under working-class leadership in which the interests of the working class were guaranteed by the vanguard political party. The alliance of class forces was a strategic and conjunctural necessity in that its sole objective was the 'smashing' of existing state institutions, and their replacement with the 'dictatorship of the proleteriat'. Laclau and Mouffe argue that although Lenin's conceptualization of hegemony expanded the role of intellectuals and activists in the vanguard party, this did not undermine the underlying Marxist conception of history in which the working class has the necessary task of bringing about socialist transformation. In other words, the necessary relationship between social classes and their historically allocated tasks (determined by the laws of historical materialism) was not questioned.

Gramsci's conception of hegemony, by contrast, was not just concerned with securing a temporary alliance between distinct class forces and interests. Rather, it involved the articulation of different forces by the working class such that it could transcend its narrow corporate interests to become a more universal representative of 'the people' or the 'nation' as a whole. Thus, hegemony was not simply a political strategy, but a general political logic involving the construction of a new 'common sense'—what Gramsci calls 'intellectual, cultural, and moral leadership'—which could structure an emergent 'historical bloc' (Gramsci 1971: 181–2).

Laclau and Mouffe's radicalization of Gramsci's concept of hegemony involves deconstructing two assumptions which reinforce the logic of necessity in Gramsci's thinking. First, his insistence on the role of a 'fundamental social class'—in capitalist societies, the working class—in bringing about social change; and, secondly, his commitment to 'a decisive nucleus of economic activity' around which societies are structured (Gramsci 1971: 161). Ultimately, according to Laclau and Mouffe, these assumptions mean that society is still portrayed as a self-enclosed and rational totality, whose character is determined and comprehended by objectively given laws of history.

For discourse theorists there is no underlying logic of history which secures, a priori, the unity of social formations; nor is there a privileged social agent which can effect historical change (see Sayyid and Zac, this volume). On the contrary, Laclau and Mouffe's theory of discourse is predicated on the ultimate impossibility of societal closure, an impossibility which makes articulatory practices and political agency possible. According to Laclau and Mouffe (1985: 136), hegemonic practices entail two further conditions of possibility: the existence of antagonistic forces, and the instability of the political frontiers which divide them. Thus, hegemonic practices presuppose a social field criss-crossed by antagonistic relations, and the presence of elements which can be articulated by opposed political projects striving to hegemonize them. The major aim of hegemonic projects is to construct and stabilize what Laclau and Mouffe call *nodal points*, which form the basis of concrete social orders.[10] From this perspective, Hall (1983), for example, examines the various hegemonic strategies employed by Mrs Thatcher and her colleagues during the crisis-ridden 1970s in transforming the Conservative Party in Britain from a party of 'one nation Toryism' and qualified supporter of the welfare state into an advocate of free market economics and radical critic of the post-war consensus. Hall, and others, show how this new hegemonic project, structured around the nodal points of a 'free economy' and a 'strong state', instituted a new discursive configuration for reorganizing state and society in Britain.[11]

Understanding, Explanation, and Truth

Having outlined the development of discourse theory, let us turn to some associated epistemological questions. I begin with the general philosophical orientation of discourse theory, concentrating on the relationship between understanding and explanation. I then move on to consider the particular theory of knowledge accompanying discourse theory.

Discourse and hermeneutics

Discourse theory is placed within the hermeneutical, rather than naturalistic, tradition of inquiry. This means that discursive accounts are concerned with understanding and interpreting socially produced meanings, rather than explanations of observed behaviour based on universal laws of cause and effect.[12] Discourse theorists share Winch's distrust of philosophers of science such as J. S. Mill who attempted to base the analysis of society on the methods of natural science, with its endeavour to formulate causal laws and establish objective statistical correlations. Instead, Winch takes the object of social sciences to be meaningful social behaviour. Borrowing from the later Wittgenstein, he describes such behaviour as 'rule governed', and stresses the 'central role which the concept of understanding plays in the activities . . . characteristic of human societies' (Winch 1990: 22). Contrasting a hermeneutical perspective with the objective and predictive requirements of the natural sciences, Winch (ibid. 115, emphases original) argues:

The difference is precisely analogous to that between being able to formulate statistical laws about the likely occurrences of words in a language and being able to understand what was being *said* by someone who spoke the language. The latter can never be reduced to the former; a man who understands Chinese is not a man who has a firm grasp of the statistical probabilities for the occurrence of the various words in the Chinese language . . . 'Understanding', in situations like this, is grasping the *point* or *meaning* of what is being said or done. This is a notion far removed from the world of statistics and causal laws: it is closer to the realm of discourse and to the internal relations that link the parts of a realm of discourse.

In the language of discourse theory, this implies that the work of discursive analysis is to discover those rules and conventions which structure the production of meaning in particular contexts; investigating why and how these systems of meaning change; and how social agents come to identify themselves in discursive terms.

This way of putting things, however, begs the question of the relationship between understanding and explanation. Naturalistic approaches to social science give priority to explanation, but what of the hermeneutical tradition? Following Winch, a more complex relationship between interpretation and explanation in social analysis can be elaborated from within a hermeneutic approach. As Winch (1990: x) puts it:

Understanding is the goal of explanation and the end-product of successful explanation. But of course it does not follow that there is understanding only where there has been explanation; neither is this in fact true . . .

Unless there is a form of understanding that is not the result of explanation, no such thing as explanation would be possible. An explanation is called for only where there is, or at least thought to be, a deficiency in understanding. But there has to be some standard against which such deficiency is to be measured: and that standard can only be an understanding that we already have.

In this reformulation, explanation in the social sciences comes after, and depends upon, understanding. Thus, the task of explanation, couched in terms of a particular conceptual language—'antagonism', 'equivalence', 'the other', 'lack', 'hegemony'—is to supplement a less than complete understanding of a discursive context, and to provide a new perspective on familiar phenomena.

This position, however, begs a further question: does it result in a circularity which an objective causal account might overcome? That is, should the explanations providing further understanding be causal, as in the natural sciences? The answer depends, naturally enough, on the form of causal explanation employed. From a discursive perspective, certain forms of causality are ruled out, such as those which depend on assumptions about the essential nature of things, or which are deduced from (putative) universal laws of human behaviour. But other, looser forms of 'causal explanation' are compatible with a hermeneutical perspective. In other words, questions about why and how certain discourses emerged and flourished while others did not, or why certain forms of identity were constructed, and how they came to prevail over others in certain historical contexts, are central to discursive accounts of politics.

Put more concretely, discourse theorists reject the essentialist, reductionist, totalizing, and deterministic explanations offered by many research programmes, whether of a Marxist, rational choice, or structural functionalist persuasion. They oppose, for instance, explanations of political identity which hearken back to some pristine historical origin, or assume them to be eternal forms exhibiting an unproblematic unity. These essentialist 'explanations', although common in studies of nationalism, racism, and ethnicity foreclose investigating the complex production of identity in specific historical situations. For instance, Said (1978) shows how the constitution of 'the West' or 'the Occident' was predicated on the negation of 'the East' or 'the Orient'. This was made possible, he argues, by imposing an essentialist conception of 'the Orient' as unchanging, static, passive, non-autonomous traditional, and 'non-Occidental'. This presumption of fixed characteristics about 'the Orient' prevented the investigation of important historical, cultural, and political facts about 'the Orient', and precluded the exploration of exchanges between 'the Occident' and 'the Orient'.

Discourse theorists, then, begin from the premiss that political identities are always relational and historical entities, politically fabricated out of diverse elements. Their 'explanations' do not seek an essence of identity, or reduce them to other more determinate logics of society, such as economic variables. Rather, discourse theorists set out to demystify essentialist forms of identification and thinking by showing identities to be contingent and inherently unstable constructions. In this way, discourse theorists engage in critique in their analyses of empirical phenomena. For example, returning to the Black Consciousness Movement in South Africa, the construction of black identity in the context of apartheid was far from natural or inevitable, but a deliberate and contingent product of political struggle in a determinate historical conjuncture. Until the intervention of the Black Consciousness Movement, black identity did not register in the South African field of discursivity.

Epistemological questions

Just as Laclau and Mouffe's social ontology stresses contingency, so their epistemological position is set against an essentialist theory of knowledge and all forms of empiricism, idealism, and realism. As Althusser puts it, in all these conceptions, 'to know is to abstract from the real object its essence, the possession of which by the subject is called knowledge' (Althusser and Balibar 1970: 36–7). By contrast, discourse theorists adopt a more complicated stance towards the production of truth and the 'verification' of knowledge, which originates in a different conception of the subject and object, and which accepts an irreducible gap between objectivity and its representation.

First, following developments in the French epistemological tradition (by, for example, Canguilhem, Bachelard, and Foucault), theoretical objects are not 'given' by the world of experience and facts, but are constructed in historically specific systems of knowledge. In *Madness and Civilization*, for instance, Foucault shows that the object of mental illness is produced by the intersecting 'rules of formation' of psychiatric discourse, and 'does not pre-exist itself'. As he puts it in *The Archaeology of Knowledge* (1972: 44–5), 'the object does not await in limbo the order that will free it and enable it to become embodied in a visible and prolix objectivity'; rather, 'psychiatric discourse is characterized not by privileged objects, but by the way in which it forms objects that are highly dispersed'.

Secondly, questions of truth and falsity are not determined by a theory-free world of objects, but are relative to the standards set by systems of knowledge. In this respect, discourse theory draws upon a long tradition, stretching back to Heidegger, Wittgenstein, Kuhn, and Foucault, which questions the privileging of validity and 'objectivity' over meaning. For instance, Heidegger (1962: 261) argues:

To say that an assertion 'is true' signifies that it uncovers the entity as it is in itself. Such an assertion asserts, points out, 'lets' the entity 'be seen' in its uncoveredness. The *Being true* of the assertion must be understood as *Being-uncovering*. Thus truth has by no means the structure of an agreement between knowing and the object in the sense of a likening of one entity (the subject) to another (the Object).

Being-true as Being-uncovering is in turn ontologically possible only on the basis of Being-in-the-World. This latter phenomenon . . . is the *foundation* for the primordial phenomenon of truth.

As Heidegger suggests, the question of validity, in the usual sense of propositional truth, presupposes a world of meaningful discourse through which we identify and encounter objects (*cf.* Foucault 1981: 60–1). Therefore, while the truth-value of a statement might well be decided by its 'correspondence' or 'lack of correspondence' with an 'external reality', this already assumes that there are certain linguistic rules and conventions which define what that external reality is, as well as how propositions about it are to be articulated. This does not mean that there are never disputes about the validity of statements, nor that they are in principle unresolvable. It does mean, however, that the truth or falsity of statements is settled within orders of discourse using criteria established by those same orders.

Research Strategies and Techniques

Three methodological questions are addressed in this section. First, how are viable research problems defined from within discourse theory? Second, what techniques are used in investigating empirical phenomena? Third, what is the relationship between the concepts and logics of discourse theory and empirical cases?

Defining objects of research

For Laclau and Mouffe, theoretical objects of investigation are not given in experience, but constructed within particular discourses. But how are objects of investigation defined? What problematizations are closed off or opened up by the ontological assumptions of the research programme? Clearly, from what has been said so far, two areas of investigation stand out: the formation and dissolution of political identities, and the logic of hegemonic articulation (both the forms of domination and resistances to those forms). Both of these objects of investigation are premissed on the centrality of social antagonisms in constituting identity and social objectivity by drawing political frontiers between social agents.

To demonstrate the process of defining and addressing problems within discourse theory, let us consider Norval's (1990, 1995) work on apartheid. Norval is critical of accounts which reduce the apartheid system to the racial prejudices of embattled Afrikaner nationalists or the economic interests of an emergent Afrikaner petty bourgeoisie. She also rejects studies which have accorded a determining role to the logics of capitalist development, or which attempt a synthesis of racial and class variables (cf. Wolpe 1988: 1–20). Instead, she treats apartheid as a politically constructed and complex discursive formation: 'Rather than trying to penetrate below the surface of apartheid, this study takes as its object of investigation the discourse of apartheid: the multifarious practices and rituals, verbal and non-verbal, through which a certain sense of reality and understanding of society were constituted and maintained' (Norval 1995: 2).

Viewing apartheid as a discourse enables Norval to avoid reducing it to a spurious 'objectivity' even while analysing its changing 'horizon of meanings, conventions and practices, and the . . . modes of subjectivization instituted by it' (Norval 1995: 7). Instead, Norval traces the interacting logics of equivalence and difference by which the political frontiers of apartheid were drawn and redrawn. She shows how, in the 1940s, apartheid discourse established a distinctive Afrikaner identity in which the unity of the fragmented Afrikaner 'volk' was forged by reference to a series of 'others' (the 'swart gevaar', or black peril, British imperialists, English-speaking capitalists) who were represented as impeding the creation of an Afrikaner identity. During the 1960s and 1970s, this discursive logic was extended to all ethnic and national groups in South Africa, such that all 'volke' (peoples) were differentially located in the apartheid system. This period of 'Grand Apartheid' witnessed the predominance of a logic of difference, as the various groups were allocated separate identities and concomitant political forms of identification. It was not until the rebirth of political resistance to the apartheid system in the 1970s and 1980s that new political frontiers were instituted around different logics of equivalence: white versus black, apartheid versus the people.

Two techniques of discourse analysis

Here we touch on two research techniques stemming from the writings of Foucault and Derrida.[13] Towards the end of his life, Foucault's endeavours to clarify his methodological presuppositions led him to the strategy of problematization. In Foucault's (1987: 11) words, this was 'a matter of analysing, not behaviour or ideas, nor societies and their "ideologies", but the *problematizations* through which being offers itself to be, necessarily, thought— and the *practices* on the basis of which these problematizations are formed.'

Problematizing phenomena engages what Foucault calls the archaeological and the genealogical dimensions: 'The archaeological dimension of the analysis made it possible to examine the forms themselves; its genealogical dimension enabled me to analyse their formation out of the practices and the modifications undergone by the latter' (ibid. 11–12).

In his earlier writings on madness, medicine, and the human sciences, Foucault employed the archaeological method. It consisted in isolating the 'rules of formation' of discursive practices, that is, delimiting the discursive conditions of existence for the production of statements, objects, enunciative modalities (or 'subject positions'), theoretical themes, and strategies in different historical epochs. Thus, the archaeological method entailed a 'quasi-transcendental' approach which bracketed questions of truth and serious meaning in favour of a *description* of discursive orders, and the conditions which made them possible, without recourse to a constitutive subjectivity or animating consciousness.

Difficulties arose in the archaeological method, however, particularly in the idea of pure description without interpretation, the detached role of the archaeologist in the production of knowledge, and the ambiguous status of the rules 'underlying' discursive formations (see Dreyfus and Rainbow 1982; Visker 1995: 41–6). These led Foucault, inspired by Nietzsche, to the genealogical approach, in which the investigative strategy is not to isolate the rules of discursive practices, but to give an account of the historical emergence and political constitution of the rules themselves. According to Foucault (1984: 76, 77, 83):

[G]enealogy . . . record[s] the singularity of events outside of any monotonous finality . . . [It] does not oppose itself to history as the lofty and profound gaze of the philosopher might compare to the molelike perspective of the scholar; on the contrary, it rejects the metahistorical deployment of ideal significations and indefinite teleologies. It opposes itself to the search for 'origins' . . . Genealogy . . . seeks to establish the various systems of subjection: not the anticipatory power of meaning, but the hazardous play of dominations.

In short, the genealogist examines the political and historical construction of objectivity, aiming not to record and confirm the identity and meaning of an unchanging reality, but to show its contingency, and, at times, to seek its dissolution. In this way, genealogy is explicitly critical and overtly engaged. The genealogist is always 'inside' the practices investigated, and can never assume the neutral, 'outsider', viewpoint of the archaeologist. Thus, the genealogist is preoccupied with the practices being accounted for and engages to dissolve imposed forms of identity. This means that the epistemological stance of the genealogist is interpretative rather than representational; the task is not to record a (false) objectivity, but 'to follow the complex course of descent' and 'to maintain passing events in their proper dispersion' (Foucault 1984: 83). Thus, although these two strategies are quite different in their objects of investigation, Foucault suggests that they are complementary techniques of investigation, and both are required in empirical investigation. Archaeology delimits a field of practices for investigation whereas genealogy endeavours to account for their emergence and installation.

Whereas Foucault was concerned with the rules and conditions for discursive practices, Derrida's technique of deconstruction is a practice of reading which takes the written metaphysical text (broadly construed) as its object. What Derrida sometimes calls a 'double reading' aims at rigorously reconstructing a text while showing its 'limits'; identifying those impossible 'points of closure' in a text, which both allow the text to function but, simultaneously, undermine it. As Derrida (1981a: 6) puts it:

To 'deconstruct' philosophy . . . would be to think—in the most faithful, interior way—the structured genealogy of philosophy's concepts, but at the same time to determine—from a certain exterior that is unqualifiable or unnameable by philosophy—what this history has been able to dissimulate or forbid, making itself into a history by means of this somewhere motivated repression.

A deconstructive stance, however, is not just a neutral methodological device. It includes a substantive and critical outlook informed by the view that metaphysical texts are constituted around the privileging of certain conceptual oppositions and logics—what Derrida calls 'the metaphysics of presence'—and the repression of others. Derrida's double reading aims to pinpoint these oppositions, while endeavouring to reverse and reinscribe their effects by articulating new conceptual 'infrastructures' which contain and redistribute the oppositions in different ways (see Gasché 1986).

The 'method' of deconstruction is useful for discourse theorists in several ways. Theoretically, deconstructive practice opens up possibilities closed off by dominant interpretations. The rethinking of the structure–agency dichotomy in social and political theory discussed earlier is predicated on a deconstructive reading of those positions which attempt to privilege and essentialize one pole of the structure–agent distinction in such a way that the minor pole is reduced to a mere supplement of the dominant pole. The deconstructive infrastructure offered by Laclau and Mouffe seeks to show the mutual imbrication of structure and agency, showing that political agency is only possible given the 'failure' or 'dislocation' of a structure.

Deconstructive methods have informed a number of studies employing a discursive perspective. Norval's deconstructive account of apartheid discourse locates a crucial 'undecidability' in the political frontiers—the logics of simultaneously excluding and including that which was 'other' in the discourse—by which apartheid functioned. My own reading (1995, 1997) of black consciousness discourse in South Africa contests the dominant interpretation by showing how the Black Consciousness Movement overturned the white–black division in South African society. I also show how the movement endeavoured to reinscribe a different, more complex, relationship between white and black, predicated on the idea of a 'universal humanity'. This attempt at 'infrastructural' reinscription was based on a complex interplay between the universal and the particular, rather than a simple prioritization of one over the other. Further, drawing on Derrida's concept of the essential *iterability* of the sign, I have shown how Black Consciousness activists were able to reanimate the discursive resources upon which they drew while, at the same time, giving them a different meaning. Their articulation of 'black communalism' as a distinctive economic programme, for example, referred back to a pristine and egalitarian African 'state of nature' pre-existing the ravages of Western imperialism, but was also used to enunciate an essentially modern, social democratic strategy for economic growth and redistribution.

The application problem

Efforts by discourse theorists to circumvent the difficulties of theoreticism and empiricism result in the 'application problem'. Put briefly, although discourse theorists acknowledge the centrality of theoretical frameworks in determining their objects and methods of research, they are concerned to avoid theoretical concepts subsuming the empirical cases they are investigating. Thus, instead of applying pre-existing theory to empirical objects of study, Laclau (1990: 208–9) argues for the *articulation* of concepts in each particular instance of empirical research. In this respect, discourse theorists meet up with other methods of reading and research. Derrida, for instance, speaks of the 'singularity' of each deconstructive reading, which cannot be reduced to any general theory and 'method' of deconstruction. The enactment of each deconstructive reading is also evident in Foucault's 'genealogies' of punishment, subjectivity, and sexuality. Each genealogy is seen as a specific 'history of the present', designed and executed around concerns which provoke inquiry into how they became an issue, and how particular forms can be transfigured.

The condition for this perspective on research is that the concepts and logics of the theoretical framework must be sufficiently 'open' and flexible to be adapted, deformed, and transformed in the process of application. This conception excludes essentialist and reductionist theories of society, but, rather, endeavours to arrive at novel accounts of phenomena while also contributing to theoretical development.

Some Remaining Questions

Laclau and Mouffe's elaboration of discourse theory has attracted considerable critical commentary, much of it directed at their underlying assumptions. In large part, this is because their approach constitutes an epistemological and methodological challenge to mainstream social and political science. One of the main charges is the supposed idealism of their approach, or, more narrowly, its purported textualism, a position which more or less entails a relativist conception of knowledge. For example, Woodiwiss (1990: 68–9) argues:

Ontologically, Laclau and Mouffe are anti-realist, but they seem to be unaware that they must be idealist . . . [They] are mistaken if they think they can hold that discourse has a material character and that 'literality is, in actual fact, the first of metaphors.' The latter statement repeats their idealist theory of reference, whilst the former seeks to deny that it is idealist. Thus they may best be characterized as 'irrealists' or as unwilling 'objective idealists', since while their anti-realism leads them to deny that objects outside of discourse may be known, their materialism leads them to claim that the objects that exist in discourse are real. There is, therefore, an incoherence here, which may only be corrected by either retaining the theory of reference and acknowledging its idealism or abandoning it altogether on the grounds that its claimed materialist character does not prevent it from being axiomatically idealist on the grounds of its anti-realism.

Here, Woodiwiss is trying to drive a wedge between Laclau and Mouffe's denial of an extra-discursive realm of objects, on the one hand, and their affirmation that all objects are precarious and unstable objects of discourse on the other, as if this corresponds to a realist–idealist divide. However, as we have seen, Laclau and Mouffe do not deny the existence of a reality external to thought. What they do deny, however, is that real objects have a meaning independently of the discourses in which they are constituted as objects. Thus, Laclau and Mouffe (1985: 136) write:

An earthquake or the falling of a brick is an event that certainly exists, in the sense that it occurs here and now, independently of my will. But whether their specificity as objects is constructed in terms of 'natural phenomena' or 'expressions of the wrath of God', depends upon the structuring of a discursive field. What is denied is not that such objects exist externally to thought, but the rather different assertion that they could constitute themselves as objects outside any discursive condition of emergence.

In short, whereas Woodiwiss argues that there are only two ontological options from which to choose—idealism or realism—Laclau and Mouffe propose radical materialism as a *tertium quid* between idealism and realism.

The charge of relativism is the main thrust of the critique launched by Geras (1987: 67):

However frequently these may be denied . . . a pre-discursive reality and an extra-theoretical objectivity form the irreplaceable basis of all rational enquiry, as well as the condition of meaningful communication across and between differing viewpoints. This foundation once removed, one simply slides into a bottomless, relativist gloom, in which opposed discourses or paradigms are left with no common reference point, uselessly trading blows.

This critique raises several issues; in particular, the problem of truth and falsity. If the meaning of objects, and the facts about those objects, are conditioned by a discourse, how is it possible to judge within and between discourses? Are all judgements equally valid? Underlying this line of questioning is the classical discourse of epistemology—particularly the correspondence theory of truth—and the assumption that all discourses are hermetically sealed, and thus necessarily incommensurable.

Both suppositions are questioned in Laclau and Mouffe's approach. In the first place, they do not do away with the truth and falsity of statements within discourses. Rather, they claim that we have to share some criteria as to what the world is like before we can make claims about that world. If not, we would not know what we were talking about. This does not mean that we cannot judge whether some beliefs are true or false, but, simply, that such judgements depend on the standards agreed upon by the form of life in which we are situated. Secondly, precisely because discourses are not hermetically sealed, there is always the possibility of exchange and communication between different, perhaps even competing, discourses. Moreover, accounts originating in discourse theory may be better than others. Demonstrating this would entail attacking the theoretical assumptions of competing approaches, and would involve producing accounts which are more persuasive.

So far, we have considered how Laclau and Mouffe's theory of discourse displaces a series of epistemological concerns by concentrating on the ontological suppositions of the concept of discourse. However, while their dismissal of classical epistemological postulates, such as the correspondence theory of truth and the independence of theory from observation, is convincing (and in line with much contemporary philosophical thought), other issues remain. For one, Laclau and Mouffe have to provide criteria by which to judge the persuasiveness of accounts derived from applying discourse theory. Following Kuhn, these might be adduced from studies which serve as exemplars for practitioners in the field, showing how problems are constituted and investigated. So far, however, there are few empirical studies which might serve this purpose (cf. Smith 1994; Norval 1995).

In addition, Laclau and Mouffe need to lay down, however minimally, a set of methodological guidelines for practitioners, as well as a set of questions and hypotheses (à la Lakatos) for clarification and development. Thus far, the only clear methodological rule consists in a 'non-rule': rules can never be simply applied to cases, but have to be articulated in the research process. This radical rereading of Wittgenstein not only subverts the idea of methodological procedures but also blurs the line between the rule and its application. Thus, the specificity of rules is lost, and we are unable to determine what rule is being applied in different contexts. Again, we would be left with no criteria to guide us in the proper application of discourse theoretical concepts.

The lack of adequate responses to these epistemological and methodological questions pose significant problems for researchers working within discourse theory. Most important, in this regard, is the difficulty of individuating discourses. Ironically, this is precisely the question which animates Laclau and Mouffe's (1985: 145–6) critique of Foucault's conception of discourse:

The problem can be formulated . . . as follows: if what characterises a formation is regularity in dispersion, how then is it possible to determine the limits of the formation? Let us suppose that there is a discursive entity or difference which is exterior to the formation, but which is absolutely regular in this exteriority. If the sole criterion at stake is dispersion, how is it possible to establish the 'exteriority' of that difference?

Although this is an entirely legitimate criticism of Foucault,[14] the problem for Laclau and Mouffe centres on which boundaries are central for individuating discourses. For instance, how are discourses different from practices such as playing chess or voting in an election, or Wittgenstein's 'primitive language game' in which A and B are building a wall? How do discourses differ from the collective social imaginaries, such as Christianity, the Enlightenment project, or communism, which Laclau (1990: 64) has introduced in his more recent writings?

We might presume that part of Laclau and Mouffe's response would depend on their definition of politics: for discourses to be valid objects of investigation for political theorists, they must be assumed to have political import. The difficulty with this solution lies in defining the political. Mouffe (1993: 2), for instance, defines the political in terms of the 'friend–foe' opposition: the political centres on the 'existence of an element of hostility among human beings'. Again, this leaves us without a clear criterion for distinguishing between important political divisions and relatively minor disagreements. In practice, Laclau and Mouffe have circumvented the problem by focusing, empirically, on Italian Fascism, Thatcherism, Peronism in

Argentina, and Chartism in England—all discourses associated with political projects operating within clearly defined state boundaries. What still remains to be defined are the criteria by which such discourses can be regarded as discourses in the first place. Establishing such criteria, in both theoretical and empirical terms, has to be the work of practitioners currently working in the field of discourse analysis.

Notes

1. For the relation between Bachelard and Althusser, see Young (1990).
2. In this respect, Althusser is targeting 'historicist' Marxists such as Lukacs; see Lukacs (1971).
3. This conception was taken up in later writings by Poulantzas (1978), and, as we shall see, by Laclau and Mouffe.
4. Laclau and Mouffe (1985) distinguish between the moments and the elements of discourses: moments are those objects which are internal and partially fixed by a discursive practice whilst elements, sometimes referred to as 'floating signifiers', are not. This position is radicalized in Laclau (1990) by the argument that all discursive structures are, by definition, 'undecidable', that is, their constitution is necessarily marked by an exteriority which functions both as its condition of possibility and impossibility.
5. Or, as it is theorized in the Anglo-American tradition, between a word and its referent. Note, however, that signifer and signified do not correspond to a word and its object, as the former relationship takes place entirely within a linguistic system.
6. This line of thinking is also evident in the theorization of ideology by Gramsci (1971) and Althusser.
7. For apocalyptic and/or celebratory visions of post-modernity, see Baudrillard (1988) and Kroker (1988).
8. Cf. Laclau (1990), Laclau and Mouffe (1985), and Laclau and Zac (1984).
9. This notion of a dispersion of subject positions does not mean a complete separation of positions in that various subjectivities can, and are, articulated into discourses which hold together different positions in a contingent unity. A socialist, populist, or nationalist discourse may try, for example, to weld various subjectivities into an overdetermined subject position, thus modifying the meaning of its component parts.
10. According to Laclau and Mouffe (1985: 136), 'a social and political space relatively unified by the institution of nodal points and the constitution of tendentially relational identities' is called a 'hegemonic formation', a concept which has strong affinities with Gramsci's (1971) idea of a historical bloc. See also, Sassoon (1987: 119–25).
11. See Gamble (1990); Hall (1983, 1988).

12. Although situated in the hermeneutic tradition, Laclau and Mouffe's approach by no means exhausts the possibilities opened up by such a philosophical horizon. As indicated in the previous two sections, their theory of discourse articulates an ontology in which social relations are marked by the primacy of politics, the interweaving of necessity and contingency, and the historicity of social relations. This ontology differs from other hermeneutic approaches, such as Habermas's theory of communicative action, or Giddens's structuration theory, and serves two functions: to criticize approaches to social analysis which provide distorted accounts; and as the basis for a new mode of empirical research. These functions close off avenues which are considered incompatible with its core ontological assumptions, while opening up new areas of empirical and theoretical research.

13. Two important qualifications are in order here. First, 'techniques', does not refer to the various methods—qualitative and quantitative—that may or may not be compatible with a discourse theory perspective, such as data generated by interviews or large-scale surveys. Rather, 'techniques' refers to the different styles of research, investigation, and analysis which are 'internal' to the philosophical and substantive commitments of discourse theory. Lacan's introduction of the 'variable session' represented an important innovation in the practice and method of psychoanalysis, but it was internally connected to Lacan's 'return to Freud' and the development of his substantive psychoanalytic theory. Second, as Wittgenstein (1953: n. 133) suggested, there is not *a* method of discourse analysis, but a number of different techniques of research which are compatible with its assumptions, each of which has to be developed in any particular research project.

14. The only question about their characterization is the claim that Foucault is not concerned with boundaries and frontiers, which is an odd claim given its centrality in Foucault's writings. This is apparent in his concern with the demarcation of orders and practices from their 'others'.

REFERENCES

Aitkin, M., Anderson, D., and Hinde, J. (1981). 'Statistical modelling of data on teaching styles', *Journal of the Royal Statistical Society*, Series A 144: 148–61.

—— and Longford, N. (1986). 'Statistical modelling in school effectiveness studies', *Journal of the Royal Statistical Society*, Series A 149: 1–43.

Aldrich, J. H. (1993). 'Rational choice and turnout', *American Journal of Political Science* 37: 246–78.

—— and Nelson, F. D. (1984). *Linear Probability, Logit Series, and Probit Models*, Sage University Papers 45 (London: Sage).

Alker, H. S. (1969). 'A typology of ecological fallacies', in M. Dogan and S. Rokkan (eds.), *Quantitative Ecological Analysis* (Cambridge, Mass.: MIT Press).

Allerbeck, K. (1977). 'Analysis and inference', in A. Szallai and R. Petrella (eds.), *Cross-national Comparative Survey Research: Theory and Practice* (London: Pergamon).

Allison, P. D. (1982). 'Discrete-time methods for the analysis of event histories', in S. Leinhardt (ed.), *Sociological Methodology* (San Francisco: Jossey-Bass).

—— (1984). *Event History Analysis: Regression for Longitudinal Data* (Newbury Park, Calif.: Sage).

Alogoskoufis, G., and Smith, R. (1991). 'On error correction models: specification, interpretation, estimation', *Journal of Economic Surveys* 5: 97–128.

Alt, E. J., and King, G. M. (1994). 'Transfers of government power: The meaning of time dependence', *Comparative Political Studies* 27: 190–210.

—— —— and Signorino, C. (1996). 'Estimating the same quantities from different levels of data: Time dependence and aggregation in event count models.' Paper presented at the Annual Meeting of the Midwest Political Science Association, Chicago.

Althusser, L. (1971). 'Ideology and ideological state apparatuses', In L. Althusser (ed.), *Lenin, Philosophy, and Other Essays* (London: New Left Books).

—— (1977). *For Marx* (London: New Left Books).

—— and Balibar, E. (1970), *Reading Capital* (London: New Left Books).

Banerjee, A., Dolado, J., Galbraith, J. W., and Hendry, D. F. (1993). *Co-Integration, Error-Correction, and the Econometric Analysis of Non-Stationary Data* (Oxford: Oxford University Press).

—— —— Hendry, D. F., and Smith, G. W. (1986). 'Explaining equilibrium relationships in econometrics through static models: Some Monte Carlo evidence', *Oxford Bulletin of Economics and Statistics* 48: 253–77.

Barry, B. (1970). *Sociologists, Economists, and Democracy* (London: Collier-Macmillan).

Barthes, R. (1973). *Mythologies* (London: Paladin).

—— (1990). *S/Z* (Oxford: Blackwell).

Baudrillard, J. (1988). *America* (London: Verso).

Beck, M. L. (1980). *Applied Regression* (Beverly Hills, Calif.: Sage).

Beck, N. (1992). 'Comparing dynamic specifications: The case of presidential approval', in J. A. Stimson (ed.), *Political Analysis*, iii (Ann Arbor, Mich.: University of Michigan Press).

—— and Jackman, S. (1998). 'Beyond linearity by default: Generalized additive models', *American Journal of Political Science* 42: 596–627.

—— and Katz. J. (1995). 'What to do (and not to do) with time-series cross-section data', *American Political Science Review* 89: 634–47.

—— and Tucker, R. (1996). 'Conflict in space and time: Time-series–cross-section analysis with a binary dependent variable.' Paper presented at the Annual Meeting of the American Political Science Association, San Francisco.

Belsey, D. A., Kuh, E., and Welsch, R. E. (1980). *Regression Diagnostics* (New York: Wiley).

Beneviste, E. (1971). *Problems in General Linguistics* (Coral Gables, Miami, Fla.: University of Miami Press).

Bentler, P. M. (1995). *EQS Structural Equation Program Manual* (Encino, Calif.: Multivariate Software Inc.).

Bernstein, R. (1983). *Beyond Objectivism and Relativism* (Oxford: Blackwell).

Berry, M., and Feldman, S. (1985). *Multiple Regression in Practice* (Beverly Hills, Calif.: Sage).

Best, N. G., Spiegelhaltyer, D. J., Thomas, A., and Bryne, E. G. (1996). 'Bayesian analysis of realistically complex models', *Journal of the Royal Statistical Society, Series A* 159: 323–42.

Bewley, R. (1979). 'The direct estimation of the equilibrium response in a linear dynamic model', *Economic Letters* 3: 357–61.

Bhaskar, R. (1989). *Reclaiming Reality* (London: Verso).

Black People's Convention (1973). 'The "Great Zulu Strike" ', William Curren Library Collection: University of Witwatersrand, mimeo.

Blackburn, R. (1995). *The Electoral System in Britain* (London: St Martin's Press).

Blossfeld, H. P., Hamerele, A., and Mayer, K. U. (1989). *Event History Analysis* (Hillsdale, NJ: Lawrence Erlbaum).

Bollen. K. A. (1989). *Structural Equations with Latent Variables* (New York: Wiley).

Borges, J. L. (1985). *Fictions* (London: John Calder).

Boswell, T., and Sweat, M. (1991). 'Hegemony, long waves and major wars: A time series analysis of systemic dynamics, 1496–1967', *International Studies Quarterly* 35: 123–49.

Box, G. E. P., and Jenkins, G. M. (1976). *Time Series Analysis: Forecasting and Control* (San Francisco: Holden-Day).

—— and Tiao, G. C. (1975). 'Intervention analysis with applications to economic and environmental problems', *Journal of the American Statistical Association* 70: 70–92.

Brams, S. J. (1975). *Game Theory and Politics* (New York: Free Press).

Brennan, G., and Lomasky, L. (1993). *Democracy and Decision: The Pure Theory of Electoral Preference* (Cambridge: Cambridge University Press).

Breusch, T. S., and Pagan, A. R. (1979). 'A simple test for heteroscedasticity and random coefficient variation', *Econometrica* 47: 1287–94

Brook, L., Prior, G., and Taylor, B. (1992). *British Social Attitudes Survey 1991: Technical Report* (London: Social and Community Planning Research).

Brown, B., and Cousins, M. (1980). 'The linguistic fault: The case of Foucault's archaeology', *Economy and Society* 9: 251–78.

Bryk, A. S., and Raudenbush, S. W. (1992). *Hierarchical Linear Models: Applications And Data Analysis Methods* (Newbury Park, Calif.: Sage).

—— —— Seltzer, M., and Congdon, R. (1988). *An Introduction to HLM: Computer Program and User's Guide*, 2nd edn. (Chicago: University of Chicago, Dept. of Education).

Bullen, N. I., Jones, K., and Duncan, C. (1997). 'Modelling complexity: Analysing between-individual and between-place variation a multilevel tutorial', *Environment and Planning,* Series A 29: 585–609.

Burgess, S. (1988). 'Employment adjustment in UK manufacturing', *Economic Journal* 98: 81–103.

—— (1992). 'Nonlinear dynamics in a structural model of employment', *Journal of Applied Econometrics* 7: S101–18.

Butler, D., and Stokes, D. (1969). *Political Change in Britain* (London: Macmillan).

Butler, L. (1987). *Subjects of Desire: Hegelian Reflections in Twentieth-Century France* (New York: Colombia University Press).

Casella, G., and Berger, R. L. (1990). *Statistical Inference* (Belmont, Calif.: Duxbury Press).

Castles, F. G. (1982). *The Impact of Parties* (Beverly Hills, Calif.: Sage).

Cattell, R. B. (1966). 'Patterns of change: Measurement in relation to state dimension, trait, change, lability, and process concepts' in R. B. Cattell (ed.), *Handbook of Multivariate Experimental Psychology* (Chicago: Rand McNally).

Charemza, W. W., and Deadman, D. F. (1992). *New Directions in Econometric Practice* (Aldershot, Hants.: Edward Elgar).

Clarke, H. D., Mishler, W., and Whiteley, P. F. (1990). 'Recapturing the Falklands: Models of Conservative Party support, 1979–83', *British Journal of Political Science* 20: 63–81.

—— and Stewart, M. C. (1994). 'Prospections, retrospections and rationality: The "bankers" model of presidential approval reconsidered', *American Journal of Political Science* 38: 1104–23.

—— —— and Whiteley, P. F. (1997). 'Tory trends: Party identification and the dynamics of Conservative support since 1992', *British Journal of Political Science* 27: 299–331.

Clegg, A. (1993). *Childhood Immunization Uptake: Geographical Perspectives.* Unpublished PhD thesis Dept. of Geography, University of Portsmouth.

Coleman, J. S. (1990). *Foundations of Social Theory* (Cambridge, Mass.: Harvard University Press).

Connolly, W. E. (1991). *Identity and Difference* (Ithaca, NY: Cornell University Press).

Cook, K. S., and Levi, M. (eds.) (1990). *The Limits of Rationality* (Chicago: Chicago University Press).

Cox, D. R. (1975). 'Partial likelihood', *Biometrika* 62: 269–76.

Cutler, A., Hindess, B., Hirst, P., and Hussain, A. (1977). *Marx's Capital and Capitalism Today* (London: Routledge & Kegan Paul).

Dallmayr, F., and McCarthy, T. (eds.) (1977). *Understanding and Social Inquiry* (Paris: University of Notre Dame Press).

Davidson, J. E., Hendry, D. F., Srba, F., and Yeo, S. (1978). 'Econometric modelling of the aggregate time-series relationship between consumer expenditure and income in the United Kingdom', *Economic Journal* 88: 661–92.

De Leeuw, J., and Kreft, I. (1995*a*). 'Not much disagreement it seems', *Journal of Educational and Behavioural Statistics* 20: 239–40.

—— —— (1995*b*). 'Questioning multilevel models', *Journal of Educational and Behavioural Statistics* 20: 171–89.

Dempster, A. P., Laird, N. M., and Rubin, D. B. (1977). 'Maximum likelihood from incomplete data via the EM algorithm', *Journal of the Royal Statistical Society, Series B* 39: 1–38.

Denver, D., and Hands, G. (1985).'Marginality and turnout in general elections in the 1970s', *British Journal of Political Science* 15: 381–8.

—— —— (1992). 'Constituency campaigning', *Parliamentary Affairs* 45: 528–44.

Derrida, J. (1973). *Speech and Phenomena* (Evanston, Ill.: Northwestern University Press).

—— (1974). *Of Grammatology* (Baltimore: Johns Hopkins University Press).

—— (1978). *Writing and Difference* (London: Routledge & Kegan Paul).

—— (1981*a*). *Dissemination* (Chicago: University of Chicago).

—— (1981*b*). *Positions* (Chicago: Chicago University Press).

—— (1982). *Margins of Philosophy* (Brighton: Harvester Press).

Dickey, D. A., and Fuller, W. A. (1981). 'Likelihood ratio statistics for autoregressive time series with a unit root', *Econometrica* 49: 193–220.

—— Bell, W., and Miller, R. (1986). 'Unit roots in time series models: tests and implications', *American Statistician* 40: 12–26.

DiPrete, T., and Forristal, J. (1994). 'Multilevel models: methods and substance', *Annual Review of Sociology* 20: 331–57.

Downs, A. (1957). *An Economic Theory of Democracy* (New York: Harper & Row).

Draper, D. (1995). 'Inference and hierarchical modelling in the social sciences', *Journal of Educational and Behavioural Statistics* 20: 115–47.

Dreyfus, H., and Rabinow, P. (1982). *Michel Foucault: Beyond Structuralism and Hermeneutics* (Brighton: Harvester).

Duncan, C., Jones, K., and Moon, G. (1993). 'Do places matter? A multilevel analysis of regional variations in health-related behaviour in Britain', *Social Science and Medicine* 37: 725–33.

—— —— —— (1995). 'Multivariate multilevel models for blood pressure, age, and gender', in G. Woodhouse (ed.), *A Guide to Multileveln for New Users* (London: Institute of Education University of London).

Duncan, C., Jones, K., and Moon, G. (1996). 'Health-related behaviour in context: A multilevel modelling approach', *Social Science and Medicine* 42: 817–30.

Duncan, O. D. (1979). 'Indicators of sex typing: Traditional and egalitarian, situational, and ideological response', *American Journal of Sociology*, 85: 251–60

—— Sloane, D. M., and Brody, C. (1982). 'Latent classes inferred from response consistency effects' in K. G. Jöreskog and H. Wold (eds.), *Systems Under Indirect Observation* (Amsterdam: North Holland).

Elster, J. (1989). *Nuts and Bolts for the Social Sciences* (Cambridge: Cambridge University Press).

Enders, W. (1995). *Applied Econometric Time Series* (New York: Wiley).

Engle, R. F., and Granger, C. W. (1987). 'Cointegration and error-correction: Representation, estimation, and testing', *Econometrica* 55: 251–76.

—— —— (eds.) (1991). *Long-Run Economic Relationships* (Oxford: Oxford University Press).

—— Hendry, D., and Richard, J. F. (1983). 'Exogeneity', *Econometrica* 51, 277–304.

—— and Yoo, B. S. (1991). 'Cointegrated economic time series: An overview with new results', in R. F. Engle and C. W. Granger (eds.), *Long-Run Economic Relationships* (Oxford: Oxford University Press).

Finkel, S. E. (1995). *Causal Analysis with Panel Data* (Thousand Oaks, Calif.: Sage).

Flemming, T. R., and Harrington, D. P. (1991). *Counting Process and Survival Analysis* (New York: Wiley).

Foucault, M. (1970). *The Order of Things* (London: Tavistock).

—— (1972). *The Archaeology of Knowledge* (London: Tavistock).

—— (1977). *Discipline and Punish*, 2nd edn., 1978 (Harmondsworth: Penguin).

—— (1979). *The History of Sexuality* i (Harmondsworth: Penguin).

—— (1980). *Power/Knowledge* (New York: Pantheon Books).

—— (1981). 'The order of discourse', in R. Young (ed.), *Untying the Text: The Post-Structuralist Reader* (London: Routledge).

—— (1984). 'Nietzsche, genealogy, history', in P. Rabinow (ed.), *The Foucault Reader* (Harmondsworth: Penguin).

—— (1984). 'What is an author?', in P. Rabinow (ed.), *The Foucault Reader* (Harmondsworth: Penguin).

—— (1987). *The Uses of Pleasure* (Harmondsworth: Penguin).

Fuss, D. (1989). *Essentially Speaking: Feminism, Nature, and Difference* (London: Routledge).

Gamble, A. (1990). *The Free Economy and the Strong State* (London: Macmillan).

Gasché, R. (1986). *The Tain of the Mirror: Derrida and the Philosophy of Reflection* (Cambridge, Mass.: Harvard University Press).

Geras, N. (1987). 'Post-Marxism?', *New Left Review*, 163: 3–27.

—— (1990). *Discourses of Extremism* (London: Verso).

Gibbons, M. (ed.) (1987). *Interpreting Politics* (New York: New York University Press)

Giddens, A. (1984). *The Constitution of Society* (Cambridge: Polity Press).

Gilbert, C. L. (1986). 'Professor Hendry's econometric methodology', *Oxford Bulletin of Economics and Statistics* 48: 283–307.

—— (1990). 'Professor Hendry's econometric methodology', in C. Granger (ed.), *Modelling Economic Series* (Oxford: Oxford University Press).

Gilks, R., Clayton, G., Spiegelhalter, D., Best, N., McNeil, A., Sharples, L., and Kirby, A. J. (1993). 'Modelling complexity: Applications of Gibbs Sampling in medicine', *Journal of the Royal Statistical Society*, Series B 55: 39–102.

Goldstein, H. (1984). 'The methodology of school comparisons', *Oxford Review of Education* 10: 69–74.

—— (1986). 'Multilevel mixed linear model analysis using iterative generalised least squares', *Biometrika* 73: 43–56.

—— (1987). *Multilevel Models in Educational and Social Research* (Charles Griffin: London).

—— (1991). 'Nonlinear multilevel models with an application to discrete response data', *Biometrika* 78: 45–51.

—— (1994). 'Multilevel cross-classified models', *Sociological Methods and Research* 22: 364–75.

—— (1995). *Multilevel Statistical Models* (Edward Arnold: London).

—— Healy, M. J. R., and Rasbash, J. (1994). 'Multilevel time series models with applications to repeated measures data', *Statistics in Medicine* 13: 1643–55.

—— and Spiegelhalter, D. (1996). 'League tables and their limitations: Statistical issues in comparisons of institutional performance', *Journal of the Royal Statistical Society*, Series A 159 (3): 385–443.

—— and Thomas, S. (1993). *Guardian A-Level analysis 1993: Technical Report* (University of London, Institute of Education).

Goodman, L. A. (1974). 'The analysis of systems of qualitative variables when some of the variables are unobservable, Part I: A modified latent structure approach', *American Journal of Sociology*, 79: 1179–259.

—— (1978). *Analyzing Qualitative/Categorical Data* (Cambridge, Mass.: Abt Books).

Gordon, I., and Whiteley, P. (1980). 'Comment: Johnston on campaign expenditure and the efficacy of advertising', *Political Studies* 27: 291.

Gramsci, A. (1971). *Selections from the Prison Notebooks of Antonio Gramsci* (London: Lawrence & Wishart).

Granger, C. W. J., and Lee, T. H. (1989). 'Investigation of production, sales, and inventory relationships using multicointegration and non-symmetric error correction models', *Journal of Applied Econometrics* 4: S145–59.

—— and Newbold, P. (1974). 'Spurious regression in econometrics', *Journal of Econometrics* 2: 111–20.

—— —— (1986). *Forecasting Economic Time Series* (New York: Academic Press).

—— and Terasvirta, T. (1993). *Modelling Nonlinear Economic Relationships* (Oxford: Oxford University Press).

Green, D. P., and Shapiro, I. (1994). *Pathologies of Rational Choice Theory: A Critique of Applications in Political Science* (Cambridge, Mass.: Yale University Press).

Gujarati, D. (1995). *Basic Econometrics* 3rd edn. (London: McGraw-Hill).

Haberman S. J. (1978). *Analysis of Qualitative Data* i (New York: Academic Press).

—— (1979). *Analysis Of Qualitative Data* ii (New York: Academic Press).

Habermas, J. (1990). *The Philosophical Discourse of Modernity* (Cambridge: Polity Press).

Hagenaars, J. A. (1990). *Categorical Longitudinal Data: Log-Linear Analysis of Panel, Trend, and Cohort Data* (Newbury Park, Calif.: Sage).

—— (1994). *Loglinear Models with Latent Variables* (Newbury Park, Calif.: Sage).

—— and Luijkx, R. (1987). 'LCAG: Latent class models and other loglinear models with latent variables', Tilburg University: Dept. of Sociology, Working Paper 17.

Hall, S. (1983). 'The great moving right show', in S. Hall and M. Jacques (eds.), *The Politics of Thatcherism* (London: Lawrence & Wishart).

—— (1988). *The Hard Road to Renewal* (London: Verso).

—— and Martin J. (1983). *The Politics of Thatcherism* (London: Lawrence & Wishart).

Hall, S. G., Cuthbertson, J. M., and Taylor, M. P. (1992). *Applied Econometric Techniques* (London: Philip Allan).

Hansen, H., and Johansen, S.(1993). 'Recursive estimation in cointegrated var-models' (University of Copenhagen: Institute of Mathematical Statistics 1).

—— and Juselius, K. (1994). 'Manual to cointegration analysis of time series: CATS in RATS' (University of Copenhagen, mimeo).

Hargreaves-Heap, S., Hollis, M., Lyons, B., Sugden, R., and Weale, A. (1992). *The Theory of Choice: A Critical Guide* (Oxford: Blackwell).

Harris, R. (1995). *Cointegration Analysis in Econometric Modelling* (London: Harvester Wheatsheaf).

Harsanyi, J. C. (1986). 'Advances in understanding rational behaviour' in J. Elster (ed.), *Rational Choice* (Oxford: Blackwell).

Hastie, T. J., and Tibshirani, R. J. (1990). *Generalised Additive Models* (London: Chapman & Hall).

Hauser, R. M. (1970). 'Context and consex: A cautionary tale', *American Journal of Sociology* 75: 645–64.

Heath, A., Jowell, R., and Curtice, J. (1985). *How Britain Votes* (London: Pergamon).

—— —— —— (1991). *Understanding Political Change* (London: Pergamon).

—— —— —— (eds.) (1994). *Labour's Last Chance: The 1992 Election and Beyond* (Aldershot: Dartmouth).

Heidegger, M. (1962). *Being and Time* (Oxford: Blackwell).

Hendry, D. F. (1980). 'Econometrics: Alchemy of science?', *Economica* 47: 387–406.

—— (1995). *Dynamic Econometrics* (Oxford: Oxford University Press).

Hibbs, D. A. (1987). *The Political Economy of Industrial Democracies* (Cambridge, Mass.: Harvard University Press).

Hindess, B. (1988). *Choice, Rationality, and Social Theory* (London: Unwin-Hyman).

—— and Hirst, P. (1977). *Mode of Production and Social Formation* (London: Macmillan).

Hirst, P. (1979). *On Law and Ideology* (London: Macmillan).

Hollis, M., and Nell, E. (1975). *Rational Economic Man: A Philosophical Critique of Neo-Classical Economics* (Cambridge: Cambridge University Press).

Howarth, D. (1995a). *Black Consciousness in South Africa: Resistance and Identity Formation under Apartheid Domination* (Unpublished PhD thesis, University of Essex).

—— (1995b). 'Discourse theory', in D. Marsh and G. Stoker (eds.), *Theories and Methods in Political Science* (London: Macmillan).

—— (1997). 'Complexities of identity/difference: Black consciousness ideology in South Africa', *Journal of Political Ideologies* 2: 51–78.

Hox, J. J., and Kreft, I. G. (1994). 'Multilevel analysis methods', *Sociological Methods and Research* 22: 283–99.

Irigaray, L. (1985). *This Sex Which Is Not One* (Ithaca, NY: Cornell University Press).

Jagodzinski, W., and Kühnel, S. M. (1987). 'Estimation of reliability and stability in single-indicator multiple-wave models', *Sociological Methods and Research* 15: 219–58.

Jenkins, G. M. (1979). *Practical Experience with Modelling and Forecasting Time Series* (St Helier, Jersey: Jenkins & Partners).

Jessop, B. (1982). *The Capitalist State* (Oxford: Robertson).

Johansen, S. (1988). 'Statistical analysis of cointegration vectors', *Journal of Economic Dynamics and Control* 12: 231–54.

—— and Juselius, K. (1990). 'The full information maximum likelihood procedure for inference on cointegration with applications to the demand for money', *Oxford Bulletin of Economics and Statistics* 52: 168–210.

—— —— (1992). 'Testing structural hypotheses in a multivariate cointegrating analysis of the PPP and the UIP for UK', *Journal of Econometrics* 53: 211–44.

Johnston, R. J. (1978). 'The aggregation of federal money in the United States: Aggregate analysis by correlation', *Policy and Politics.* 6: 279–97.

—— (1979). *Political, Electoral, and Spatial Systems: An Essay in Political Geography* (Oxford: Oxford University Press).

Jones, K. (1996). 'Multilevel approaches to modelling contextuality: From nuisance to substance in the analysis of voting behaviour' in G. Westert and R. Verhoeff (eds.), *Places and People: Interactions between Macro and Micro Level* (Royal Dutch Geographical Society: Netherlands Geographical Studies).

—— and Bullen, N. J. (1993). 'A multilevel analysis of the variations in domestic property prices: Southern England, 1980–87', *Urban Studies* 30: 1409–26.

—— —— (1994). 'Contextual models of urban house prices: A comparison of fixed- and random-coefficient models developed by expansion', *Economic Geography* 70: 252–72.

—— and Duncan, C. (1995). 'Individuals and their ecologies: Analysing the geography of chronic illness within a multilevel modelling framework', *Health and Place* 1: 27–40.

—— —— (1996). 'People and places: The multilevel model as a general framework for the quantitative analysis of geographical data', in P. Longley and M. Batty (eds.), *Spatial Analysis: Modelling in a GIS Environment* (London: Longman).

—— Gould, M. I., and Watt, R. (1996). 'Multiple contexts as cross-classified models:

The Labour vote in the British general election of 1992' (University of Portsmouth: Dept. of Geography, University of Portsmouth, mimeo).

Jones, K., Gould, M. I., and Watt, R. (1998). 'Multiple contexts as cross-classified models: The Labour vote in the British general election of 1992', *Geographical Analysis* 30: 65–93.

—— Johnston, R. J., and Pattie, C. J. (1992). 'People, places and regions: Exploring the use of multilevel modelling in the analysis of electoral data', *British Journal of Political Science* 22: 343–80.

—— and Moon, G. (1991). 'Re-assessing immunisation uptake as a performance measure in general practice', *British Medical Journal* 303: 28–31.

—— —— and Clegg, A. (1991). 'Ecological and individual effects in childhood immunisation uptake: A multilevel approach', *Social Science and Medicine.* 33: 501–8.

—— Tonkin, P., and Wrigley, P. (1996). 'Individual and constituency characteristics: Analysing the geography of voting behaviour within a multilevel modelling framework', University of Portsmouth: Dept. of Geography, Working Paper No. 12.

Jöreskog, K. G. (1994). 'On the estimation of polychoric correlations and their asymptotic covariance matrix', *Psychometrika* 59: 381–9.

—— and Sörbom, D. (1989). *LISREL 7. A Guide to the Program and Applications*, 2nd edn. (Chicago: SPSS Inc.).

—— —— (1993*a*). *LISREL 8 User's Reference Guide* (Chicago: Scientific Software Inc.).

—— —— (1993*b*). *PRELIS 2 User's Reference Guide* (Chicago: Scientific Software Inc.).

Kavanagh, D. (1970). *Constituency Electioneering in Britain* (London: Longman).

Kendall, M. (1973). *Time Series*, 2nd edn. (New York: Macmillan).

Keynes, J. M. (1939). 'Professor Tinbergen's method', *Economic Journal.* 49: 558–68.

Kim, K., and Schmidt, P. (1990). 'Some evidence on the accuracy of Phillips–Perron tests using alternative estimates of nuisance parameters', *Economic Letters* 34: 345–50.

King, G. (1988). *Unifying Political Methodology: The Likelihood Theory of Inference* (New York: Cambridge University Press).

—— Alt, J., Laver, M., and Burns, N. (1990). 'A unified model of cabinet dissolution in parliamentary democracies', *American Journal of Political Science* 34: 846–71.

Kleinherz, T. (1995). *Die Nichtwähler. Ursachen der sinkenden Wahlbeteiligung in Deutschland* (Opladen: Westdeutscher Verlag).

Kreft, I. G., de Leeuw, J., and Van der Leeden, R. (1994). 'Comparing five different statistical packages for hierarchical linear regression: BMDP-5V, GENMOD, HLM, Multilevel 3, and VARCL', *American Statistician* 48: 324–35.

Kremers, J. J. M., Ericsson, N. R., and Dolado, J. J. (1992). 'The power of cointegration tests', *Oxford Bulletin of Economics and Statistics* 54: 325–46.

Kroker, A. (1988). *The Postmodern Scene: Excremental Culture and Hyper-Aesthetics* (Montreal: New World Perspectives).

Kuhn, T. (1970). *The Structure of Scientific Revolutions* (Chicago: Chicago University Press).

Kwiatowski, D., Phillips, P., Schmidt, P., and Yongcheol, S. (1992). 'Testing the null hypothesis of stationarity against the alternative of a unit root', *Journal of Econometrics* 54: 159–78.

Lacan, J. (1977*a*). *Four Fundamentals of Pyschoanalysis* (Harmondsworth: Penguin).

—— (1977*b*). *Ecrits: A Selection* (London: Tavistock Publications).

Laclau, E. (1977). *Politics and Ideology in Marxist Theory* (London: New Left Books).

—— (1990). *New Reflections on the Revolution of Our Time* (London: Verso).

—— and Mouffe, C. (1985). *Hegemony and Socialist Strategy* (London: Verso

—— —— (1987). 'Post-marxism without apologies', *New Left Review*, 166: 79–106.

—— and Zac, L. (1994). 'Minding the gap: The subject of politics', in E. Laclau (ed.), *The Making of Political Identities* (London: Verso).

Laird, N. M., and Louis, T. A. (1987). 'Empirical Bayes confidence intervals based on bootstrap samples', *Journal of the American Statistical Association* 82: 739–57

—— —— (1989). 'Empirical Bayes confidence intervals for a series of related experiments', *Biometrics* 45: 481–95.

Lakatos, I. (1974). 'Falsification and the methodology of scientific research programmes', in I. Lakatos and A. Musgrave (eds.), *Criticism and the Growth of Knowledge* (Cambridge: Cambridge University Press).

Lancaster, T. (1990). *The Econometric Analysis of Transition Data* (New York: Cambridge University Press).

Langford, I., Leyland A., Rasbash, J., and Goldstein, H. (1996). 'Multilevel modelling of the geographical distributions of rare diseases', *Proceedings: Varying Parameter Models Conference* (Odense University).

Lazarsfeld P. (1950*a*). 'The logical and mathematical foundation of latent structure analysis', in S. Stouffer (ed.), *Measurement and Prediction* (Princeton, NJ: Princeton University Press).

—— (1950*b*). 'The interpretation and mathematical foundation of latent structure analysis', in S. Stouffer (ed.), *Measurement and Prediction* (Princeton, NJ: Princeton University Press).

Lazowska, E. (1997). 'The real impact of computing is yet to come' (http://www.cs.washington.edu/homes/lazowska/cra/future.html).

Leamer, E. E., (1983). 'Let's take the con out of econometrics', *American Economic Review* 73: 31–44; repr. in C. W. J. Granger (ed.), *Modelling Economic Series* (1991) (Oxford: Oxford University Press).

Lecourt, D. (1970). *Marxism and Epistemology: Bachelard, Canguilhem, Foucault* (London: New Left Books).

Levi-Strauss, C. (1967). *Structural Anthropology* (New York: Doubleday).

Levinas, E. (1989). *The Levinas Reader*, ed. S. Hand (Oxford: Blackwell).

Lewin, L. (1991). *Self-Interest and Public Interest in Western Politics* (Oxford: Oxford University Press).

Leyland, A., and Rice, N. (1996). 'Multilevel models: Applications to health data', *Journal of Health Services Research and Policy* 1: 154–64.

Longford, N. T. (1987). 'A fast-scoring algorithm for maximum likelihood estimation in unbalanced mixed models with nested random effects', *Biometrika* 74: 817–27.

Longford, N. T. (1993). *Random Coefficient Models* (Oxford: Clarendon Press).

—— and Muthen, B. O. (1992). 'Factor analysis for clustered populations', *Psychometrika* 57: 581–97.

Luce, R. D., and Raiffa, H. (1985). *Games and Decisions: Introduction and Critical Survey* (New York: Dover).

Lukacs, G. (1971). *History and Class Consciousness* (London: Merlin).

McCleary, R., and Hay, R. A. (1980). *Applied Time Series Analysis for the Social Sciences* (Beverly Hills, Calif.: Sage Publications).

Machiavelli, N. (1979). *The Prince* (Harmonsworth: Penguin).

McCutcheon, A. L. (1987). *Latent Class Analysis* (Beverly Hills, Calif.: Sage).

—— and Hagenaars, J. A. (1997). 'Comparative social research with multi-sample latent class models', in R. Langeheine and J. Rost (eds.), *Applications of Latent Trait and Latent Class Models in the Social Sciences* (New York: Waxman).

McDonald, R. P. (1994). 'The bilevel reticular action model for path analysis with latent variables', *Sociological Methods and Research* 22: 399–413.

MacKinnon, J. G. (1991). 'Critical values for co-integration tests', in R. F. Engle and C. W. J. Granger (eds.), *Long Run Economic Relationships* (Oxford: Oxford University Press).

MacKuen, M. B., Erikson, R., and Stimson, J. (1992). 'Peasants or bankers? The American electorate and the U.S. economy', *American Political Science Review* 86: 597–611.

McLean, I. (1987). *Public Choice* (Oxford: Blackwell).

Malkiel, B. G. (1973). *A Random Walk Down Wall Street* (New York: Norton).

Mansbridge, J. J. (ed.) (1990). *Beyond Self-Interest* (Chicago: University of Chicago Press).

Maoz, Z., and Russett, B. B. (1993). 'Normative and structural causes of democratic peace, 1946–1986', *American Political Science Review* 87: 639–56.

Mason, W. M. (1995). 'Comment', *Journal of Educational and Behavioural Statistics* 20: 221–7.

—— Wong, G. Y., and Entwistle, B. (1984). 'The multilevel model: A better way to do contextual analysis', in S. Leinhardt (ed.), *Sociological Methodology* (San Francisco: Jossey-Bass).

Meiksins-Wood, E. (1986). *The Retreat from Class: A New True Socialism* (London: Verso).

Moe, T. M. (1979). 'On the scientific status of rational models', *American Journal of Political Science* 23: 215–43.

Monroe, K. R. (ed.) (1991). *The Economic Approach to Politics: A Critical Reassessment of the Theory of Rational Action* (New York: HarperCollins).

Morgan, M. (1990). *The History of Econometric Ideas* (Cambridge: Cambridge University Press).

Morrow, J. D. (1994). *Game Theory for Political Scientists* (Princeton, NJ: Princeton University Press).

Mouffe, C. (1993). *The Return of the Political* (London: Verso).

Mueller, D. C. (1989). *Public Choice II* (Cambridge: Cambridge University Press).

Mulhall, S. (1996). *Heidegger and Being and Time* (London: Routledge).

Nickell, S. J. (1985). 'Error correction, partial adjustment and all that: An expository note', *Oxford Bulletin of Economics and Statistics* 47:119–29.

Niemi, R. G., and Weisberg, H. F. (1993). 'Why don't more people vote?' in R. G. Niemi and H. F. Weisberg (eds.), *Controversies in Voting Behaviour*, 3rd edn. (Washington DC: Congressional Quarterly).

Nietszche, F. (1994). *On the Genealogy of Morality* (Cambridge: Cambridge University Press).

Norpoth, H. (1986). 'Transfer function analysis', in W. D. Berry and M. S. Lewis-Beck (eds.), *New Tools for Social Scientists* (Beverly Hills, Calif.: Sage).

—— (1987). 'Guns and butter and government popularity in Britain', *American Political Science Review* 81: 949–59.

—— (1992). *Confidence Regained: Economics, Mrs Thatcher, and the British Voter* (Ann Arbor, Mich.: University of Michigan Press).

—— (1995). 'Is Clinton doomed? An early forecast for 1996' *Political Science and Politics* 28: 201–7.

—— (1996). 'Presidents and the prospective voter', *Journal of Politics* 58: 776–92.

Norval, A. (1990). 'Letter to Ernesto', in E. Laclau (ed.), *New Reflections on the Revolution of Our Time* (London: Verso).

—— (1995). *Deconstructing Apartheid Discourse* (London: Verso).

Nuttall, D. L., Goldstein, H., Prosser, R., and Rasbash, J. (1990). 'Differential school effectiveness', *International Journal of Educational Research* 13: 769–76.

Olson, M. (1965). *The Logic of Collective Action: Public Goods and the Theory of Groups* (Cambridge, Mass.: Harvard University Press).

Oppenshaw, S. (1987). 'Spatial units and locational referencing', in *Handling Geographic Information: Report of the Committee of Enquiry chaired by Lord Chorley* (London: HMSO).

Ordeshook, P. C. (1986). *Game Theory and Political Theory* (Cambridge: Cambridge University Press).

Pagan, A. R. (1985). 'Time series behaviour and dynamic specification', *Oxford Bulletin of Economics and Statistics* 47: 125–39.

Page, B. I., and Shapiro, R. Y. (1983). 'Effects of public opinion on policy', *American Political Science Review* 76: 175–90.

Paterson, L., and Goldstein, H. (1992). 'New statistical methods for analysing social structures: An introduction to multilevel models', *British Educational Research Journal* 17: 387–93.

Pattie, C. J., Johnston, R. J., and Fieldhouse, E. A. (1995). 'Winning the local vote: The effectiveness of constituency campaign spending in Great Britain, 1983–1992', *American Political Science Review* 89: 969–83.

Perron, P. (1989). 'The great crash, the oil shock, and the unit root hypothesis'. *Econometrica* 57: 1361–402.

Pesaran, M. H., and Shin, Y. (1994). 'Long-run structural modelling' (Cambridge: University of Cambridge, mimeo).

—— —— (1995). 'An autoregressive distributed lag modelling approach to cointegration analysis', Cambridge: University of Cambridge, mimeo).

Peterson, T. (1995). 'Analysis of event histories', in G. Arminger, C. Clogg, and M. Sobel (eds.), *Handbook of Statistical Modelling for the Social and Behavioural Sciences* (New York: Plenum).

Phillips, A. W. (1954). 'Stabilisation policy in a closed economy', *Economic Journal* 64: 290–333.

—— (1957). 'Stabilisation policy and the time form of lagged response', *Economic Journal* 67: 265–77.

Phillips, P. C. (1986). 'Understanding spurious regressions in econometrics', *Journal of Econometrics* 33: 311–40.

—— and Perron, P. (1988). 'Testing for a unit root in time series regression', *Biometrika* 75: 335–46.

Pollins, B. (1996). 'Global political order, economic change, and armed conflict: Co-evolving systems and the use of force', *American Political Science Review* 90: 103–17.

Poulantzas, N. (1978). *State, Power, Socialism* (London: New Left Books).

Price, S. (1995). 'Employment, hours, wage adjustment, and supply in UK manufacturing: Identifying a long-run structure' (London: Economics Dept., City University, Discussion Paper).

Raftery, A. (1985a). 'Choosing models for cross-classifications', *American Sociological Review* 51: 145–6.

—— (1985b). 'A note on Bayes factor for log-linear contingency table models with vague prior information', *Journal of the Royal Statistical Society*, Series B 48: 249–50.

—— (1995). 'Baysian model selection in social research', *Sociological Methodology* 25: 111–63.

Raimond, H. (1983). 'The political economy of state intergovernmental grants', *Growth and Change* 14: 7–23.

Rao, B. B. (1994). *Cointegration for the Applied Economist* (London: Macmillan).

Rasbash, J., and Goldstein, H. (1994). 'Efficient analysis of mixed hierarchical and cross-classified random structures', *Journal of Educational and Behavioural Statistics* 19: 337–50.

Raudenbush, S. W. (1988). 'Educational applications of hierarchical linear models: A review', *Journal of Educational Statistics* 13: 85–116.

—— (1993). 'A crossed random effects model for unbalanced data with applications in cross-sectional and longitudinal research', *Journal of Educational Statistics* 18: 321–49.

—— and Bryk, A. S. (1986). 'A hierarchical model for studying school effects', *Sociology of Education* 59: 1–17.

Reid, J. N (1980). 'Politics, program administration, and the distribution of grants-in-aid: A theory and a test', in B. S. Runquist (ed.), *Political Benefits* (Lexington, Ky.: Lexington University Press).

Riker, W. H., and Ordeshook, P. C. (1968). 'A theory of the calculus of voting', *American Political Science Review* 62: 25–43.

Robinson, W. S. (1950). 'Ecological correlations and the behaviour of individuals', *American Sociological Review* 15: 351–7.

Rorty, R. (1980). *Philosophy and the Mirror of Nature* (Oxford: Blackwell).

—— (1982). *The Consequences of Pragmatism* (Hemel Hempstead: Harvester Wheatsheaf).

—— (1989). *Contingency, Solidarity, and Irony* (Cambridge: Cambridge University Press).

Rubin, D. B. (1980). 'Using empirical Bayes techniques in the law school validity studies', *Journal of the American Statistical Association* 75: 801–16.

Said, E. (1978). *Orientalism* (Harmondsworth: Penguin Books).

Saikkonen, P. (1991). 'Asymptotically efficient estimation of co-integrating regressions', *Econometric Theory* 7: 1–21.

Salmon, M. (1982). 'Error correction mechanisms', *Economic Journal* 92: 615–29.

Sanders, D. (1993). 'Why the Conservatives won—again', in Anthony King *et al.*, *Britain at the Polls 1992* (Chatham, NJ: Chatham House).

—— and Price, S. (1996). 'Disentangling the relationship between party support and perceived economic competence: Some evidence from the UK, 1991 to 1995' (London: Economics Dept., City University, Discussion Paper).

—— Ward, H., and Marsh, D. (1987). 'Governmental popularity and the Falklands war: A reassessment', *British Journal of Political Science* 17: 281–313.

Sargan, J. D. (1984). 'Wages and prices in the United Kingdom: A study in econometric methodology', in P. E. Hart, G. Mills, and J. K. Whitaker (eds.), *Econometric Analysis for Economic Planning* (London: Butterworth).

—— (1988). 'Wages and prices in the United Kingdom: A study in econometric methodology', in *Contributions to Econometrics* i (Oxford: Blackwell).

Särlvik, B., and Crewe, I. (1983). *Decade of Dealignment* (Cambridge: Cambridge University Press).

Sassoon, A. S. (1987). *Gramsci's Politics* (London: Hutchinson).

Saussure, F. de (1983). *Course in General Linguistics* (London: Duckworth).

Sayer, A. (1984). *Method in Social Science: A Realist Approach* (London: Hutchinson).

Sayyid, B. S. (1997). *A Fundamental Fear: Eurocentrism and the Emergence of Islamism* (London: Verso).

Schelling, T. C. (1960). *The Strategy of Conflict* (Cambridge, Mass.: Harvard University Press).

Schmidt, P., and Witte, A. (1989). 'Predicting criminal recidivism using split population survival time models', *Journal of Econometrics* 40: 141–59.

Self, P. (1993). *Government by the Market? The Politics of Public Choice* (Basingstoke: Macmillan).

Seyd, P., and Whiteley, P. (1992). *Labour's Grass Roots: The Politics of Party Membership* (Oxford: Clarendon Press).

Shapiro, M. (1981). *Language and Political Understanding* (New Haven, Conn.: Yale University Press).

Skinner, C. J., Holt, D., and Smith, T. F. (eds.) (1989). *Analysis of Data from Complex Surveys* (Chichester: Wiley).

Smith, A. M. (1994). *New Right Discourse* (Cambridge: Cambridge University Press).

Sowell, F. (1992*a*). 'Maximum likelihood estimation of stationary fractionally integrated time series models', *Journal of Econometrics* 50: 165–88.

—— (1992*b*). 'Modelling long-run behaviour with the fractional ARIMA Model', *Journal of Monetary Economics* 29: 277–302.

Staten, H. (1984). *Wittgenstein and Derrida* (Lincoln, Nebr.: University of Nebraska Press).

Stewart, J. (1992). *Econometrics* (London: Philip Allan).

Stewart, M. C., and Clarke, H. D. (1992). 'The (un)importance of party leaders: Leader images and party choice in the 1987 British Election', *Journal of Politics* 54: 447–70.

Stimson, J. A., MacKuen, M. B., and Erikson, R. S. (1995). 'Dynamic representation', *American Political Science Review* 89: 543–65.

Strom, K. (1988). 'Contending models of cabinet stability', *American Political Science Review* 82: 922–30.

Sueyoshi, G. T. (1995). 'A class of binary response models for grouped duration data', *Journal of Applied Econometrics* 10: 411–31.

Swank, D. (1992). 'Politics and the structural dependence of the state in democratic capitalist nations', *American Political Science Review* 86: 38–54.

Taylor, C., and Jodice, D. (1983). *World Handbook of Political and Social Indicators* (New Haven, Conn.: Yale University Press).

Thorndike, E. L. (1939). 'On the fallacy of imputing the correlations found for groups to the individuals or smaller groups composing them', *American Journal of Psychology* 52: 122–4.

Torfing, J. (1991). 'A hegemony approach to capitalist regulation', in R. Bertramsen, J. Frolund, and J. Torfing (eds.), *State, Economy, and Society* (London: Unwin-Hyman).

Tukey, J. W. (1977). *Exploratory Data Analysis* (Reading, Mass.: Addison-Wesley).

Vermunt, J. K. (1993). 'Lem: Log-linear and event history analysis with missing data using the EM algorithm', Tilburg University, WORC Paper 93.09.015/7.

Visker, R. (1995). *Michel Foucault: Genealogy as Critique* (London: Verso).

Ward, H. (1996*a*). 'Rational choice theory', in D. Marsh and G. Stoker (eds.), *Theory and Methods in Political Science* (Basingstoke: Macmillan).

—— (1996*b*). 'The fetishisation of falsification: The debate on rational choice', *New Political Economy* 1: 283–96.

—— and John, P. (1996). 'Targeting benefits for electoral gain: Constituency marginality and the distribution of grants to English local authorities', University of Essex: Unpublished working paper).

Ware, J. H. (1985). 'Linear models for the analysis of longitudinal studies', *American Statistician* 39: 95–101.

Warwick, P. V. (1992). 'Rising hazards: An underlying dynamic of parliamentary government', *American Journal of Political Science* 36: 857–76.

—— (1995). *Government Survival in Parliamentary Democracies* (New York: Cambridge University Press).

Whitaker, K. (1988). 'Econometric analysis for economic planning', in J. D. Sargan (ed.), *Contributions to Econometrics* i (Cambridge: Cambridge University Press).

White, H. (1980). 'A heteroskedasticity-consistent estimator and a direct test for heteroskedasticity', *Econometrica* 48: 817–38.

Whiteley, P. F. (1979). 'Electoral forecasting from poll data: The British case', *British Journal of Political Science* 9: 219–36.

—— and Seyd, P. (1998). 'The dynamics of party activism in Britain: A spiral of demobilisation?' *British Journal of Political Science* 28: 113–17.

—— —— and Richardson, J., and Bissell, P. (1993). 'Explaining party activism: The case of the British Conservative Party', *British Journal of Political Science* 24: 79–94.

—— —— —— (1994). *True Blues: The Politics of Conservative Party Membership* (Oxford: Oxford University Press).

Wickens, M. R. (1996). 'Interpreting cointegrating vectors and common trends', *Journal of Econometrics* 74: 255–67.

—— and Breusch, T. S. (1988). 'Dynamic specification, the long-run, and the estimation of transformed regression models', *Economic Journal* 98: S189–205.

Williams, L. J., Bodzdogan, H., and Aiman-Smith, L. (1996). 'Inference problems with equivalent models', in G. A. Marcoulides and R. E. Schumacker (eds.), *Advanced Structural Equation Modelling: Issues and Techniques* (Mahwah, NJ: Lawrence Erlbaum Associates).

Winch, P. (1990). *The Idea of a Social Science and Its Relation to Philosophy* (London: Routledge).

Winship, C., and Mare, R. (1989). 'Loglinear models with missing data: A latent class approach', *Sociological Methodology* 19: 331–67.

Wittgenstein, L. (1953). *Philosophical Investigations* (Oxford: Blackwell).

Wlezien, C. (1996). 'Dynamics of representation: The case of US spending on defence', *British Journal of Political Science* 26: 81–103.

Wolpe, H. (1988). *Race, Class, and the Apartheid State* (London: James Curry).

Woodhouse, G. (1995). *A Guide to MLn for New Users* (London: Institute of Education, University of London).

—— Yang, M., Goldstein, H., and Rasbash, J. (1996). 'Adjusting for measurement error in multilevel analysis', *Journal of the Royal Statistical Society*, Series A 159: 201–12.

Woodiwiss, A. (1990). *Social Theory after Postmodernism* (London: Pluto).

Yamaguchi, K. (1991). *Event History Analysis* (Newbury Park, Calif.: Sage).

Yang, M., Goldstein, H., and Rasbash, J. (1996). *MLn Macros for Advanced Mutilevel Modelling* (University of London: Institute of Education).

Young, R. (1990). *White Mythologies* (London: Routledge).

Yule, G. U. (1926). 'Why do we sometimes get nonsense correlations between time series?', *Journal of the Royal Statistical Society* 89: 1–64.

Zey, M. (ed.) (1992). *Decision Making: Alternatives to Rational Choice Models* (Newbury Park, Calif.: Sage).

Zivot, E., and Andrews, D. W. K. (1992). 'Further evidence on the Great Crash, the oil-price shock, and the unit-root hypothesis', *Journal of Business and Economic Statistics* 10: 251–70.

Zizek, S. (1989). *The Sublime Object of Ideology* (London: Verso).

—— (1990). 'Eastern Europe's Republics of Gilead', *New Left Review* 183: 50–62.

—— (1992). *Enjoy Your Symptom! Jacques Lacan in Hollywood and Out* (London: Routledge).

NAME INDEX

Aitkin, M. 95, 115, 120
Aldrich, J. H. 52, 58
Alker, H. S. 100
Allerbeck, K. 21
Allison, P. D. 128, 192, 205
Alogoskoufis, G. 168
Alt, E. J. 192, 199, 209, 212
Althusser, L. 269, 270–1, 278, 283
Anderson, D. 115
Andrews, D. W. K. 164

Balibar, E. 283
Banerjee, A. 161, 188
Barry, B. 248
Barthes, R. 257, 258
Baudrillard, J. 292
Beck, M. L. 50
Beck, N. 7, 127–8, 143, 212–13
Bell, W. 144
Belsey, D. A. 113
Bentler, P. M. 55, 69
Berger, R. L. 55
Bernstein, R. 268
Berry, M. 50
Best, N. G. 99
Bewley, R. 189
Bhaskar, R. 268
Blackburn, R. 233, 248
Blossfeld, H. P. 192
Bollen. K. A. 55, 56, 70
Borges, J. L. 9, 249, 265
Boswell, T. 154
Box, G. E. P. 128–30, 137–9, 140–1, 143
Brams, S. J. 246
Brennan, G. 59
Breusch, T. S. 155, 167, 187, 189
Brook, L. 71
Brown, B. 271
Bryk, A. S. 100, 114, 115, 121, 123
Bullen, N. I. 107, 121
Bullen, N. J. 111, 119
Burgess, S. 170
Burns, N. 192
Butler, D. 52
Butler, L. 267

Casella, G. 55
Castles, F. G. 154
Cattell, R. B. 18
Charemza, W. W. 145, 151

Clarke, H. D. 7, 138, 144, 146, 151–2, 154–5, 167
Clegg, A. 120
Coleman, J. S. 59
Cook, K. S. 246
Cousins, M. 271
Cox, D. R. 201, 202, 204, 206, 207, 208, 212
Crewe, I. 52
Curtice, J. 52
Cuthbertson, J. M. 188
Cutler, A. 270

Dallmayr, F. 267, 268
Davidson, J. E. 167
de Leeuw, J. 97, 122
Deadman, D. F. 145, 151
Dempster, A. P. 86
Denver, D. 220–1, 232–3, 247–8
Derrida, J. 263, 267, 273–5, 285, 287–8
Dickey, D. A. 144, 145, 161, 163, 175
DiPrete, T. 121
Dolado, J. J. 183, 187
Downs, A. 59, 220
Draper, D. 120, 122
Dreyfus, H. 271, 286
Duncan, C. 5, 107, 109, 119, 122–3
Duncan, O. D. 87

Elster, J. 217, 247
Enders, W. 144, 145, 155
Engle, R. F. 144–5, 148, 155, 167, 170–1, 174, 179, 186, 209
Entwistle, B. 123
Ericsson, N. R. 183, 187
Erikson, R. S. 154

Feldman, S. 50
Fieldhouse, E. A. 220
Finkel, S. E. 128
Flemming, T. R. 191
Forristal, J. 121
Foucault, M. 259, 263, 271–2, 283–8, 291
Fuller, W. A. 144, 145, 161, 163, 175
Fuss, D. 251

Gamble, A. 292
Gasché, R. 287
Geras, N. 254–5, 268, 290
Gibbons, M. 268
Giddens, A. 278, 293

Gilbert, C. L. 153, 155
Gilks, R. 121
Goldstein, H. 97, 99, 107–9, 113–16, 123
Goodman, L. A. 71, 85
Gordon, I. 233
Gould, M. I. 122
Gramsci, A. 261, 279–80, 292
Granger, C. W. J. 143–5, 148, 156, 165, 167, 170, 179, 182, 186
Green, D. P. 218, 228, 230, 231, 233, 239
Gujarati, D. 154

Haberman, S. J. 71, 85
Habermas, J. 268, 293
Hagenaars, J. A. 71, 85–6, 94
Hall, S. 188, 261, 267, 280, 292
Hamerele, A. 192
Hands, G. 220–1, 232–3, 247–8
Hansen, H. 186
Hargreaves-Heap, S. 230, 246, 247
Harrington, D. P. 191
Harris, R. 145, 151, 155
Harsanyi, J. C. 247
Hastie, T. J. 212
Hauser, R. M. 119
Hay, R. A. 138
Heath, A. 52
Heidegger, M. 283, 284
Hendry, D. F. 143, 151, 153, 155, 165, 167, 174, 188–9
Hibbs, D. A. 154
Hinde, J. 115
Hindess, B. 246, 271
Hirst, P. 270–1
Hollis, M. 246
Holt, D. 96
Howarth, D. 9, 277
Hox, J. J. 121

Irigaray, L. 267

Jackman, S. 209, 212
Jagodzinski, W. 70
Jenkins, G. M. 128–30, 140–1, 143
Jodice, D. 19
Johansen, S. 145, 153, 172–3, 175–6, 180, 183, 185–6, 188–9
John, P. 220, 237, 248
Johnston, R. J. 116, 220, 247
Jones, K. 6, 107, 109, 111, 116, 119, 120, 122–3, 131
Jöreskog, K. G. 56, 57, 69
Jowell, R. 52
Juselius, K. 186, 188

Katz, J. 128, 209
Kavanagh, D. 247
Kendall, M. 127
Keynes, J. M. 4, 143
King, G. 192, 194–6, 199, 202, 204, 209–10

Kleinherz, T. 60
Kreft, I. G. 97, 121–2
Kremers, J. J. M. 183, 187
Kroker, A. 292
Kuh, E. 113
Kuhn, T. 233, 283, 290
Kühnel, S. M. 4, 70

Lacan, J. 272, 293
Laclau, E. 9, 268, 270–80 passim, 283–93 passim
Laird, N. M. 86, 113
Lakatos, I. 233, 291
Lancaster, T. 211
Langford, I. 99
Laver, M. 192
Lazarsfeld P. 85
Leamer, E. E. 20
Lecourt, D. 271
Lee, T. H. 170
Levi, M. 246
Levi-Strauss, C. 272
Levinas, E. 267
Lewin, L. 246
Leyland A. 122
Lomasky, L. 59
Longford, N. 95, 100, 120–1, 123
Louis, T. A. 113
Luce, R. D. 231, 246
Luijkx, R. 86
Lukacs, G. 292

McCleary, R. 138
McCutcheon, A. L. 5, 42, 85, 94
McDonald, R. P. 100, 121–2
Machiavelli, N. 253
MacKuen, M. B. 154
McLean, I. 246
Malkiel, B. G. 131
Maoz, Z. 205
Mare, R. 94
Marsh, D. 138, 154
Mason, W. M. 100, 123
Mayer, K. U. 192
Meiksins-Wood, E. 254–5
Miller, R. 144
Mishler, W. 138, 154
Moe, T. M. 246
Monroe, K. R. 246
Moon, G. 109, 113, 119, 120, 122
Morgan, M. 127
Morrow, J. D. 230, 246
Mouffe, C. 9, 268, 270–80 passim, 283–93 passim
Mueller, D. C. 246
Muthen, B. O. 100

Nell, E. 246
Newbold, P. 143, 156, 165
Nietzsche, F. 256, 286

Norpoth, H. 6, 128, 138, 141, 154
Norval, A. 285, 287, 290
Nuttall, D. L. 117

Olson, M. 59
Oppenshaw, S. 25
Ordeshook, P. C. 70, 246

Pagan, A. R. 155, 187
Page, B. I. 154
Paterson, L. 114
Pattie, C. J. 116, 220, 221, 233, 235, 237, 247, 248
Perron, P. 164, 183, 189
Pesaran, M. H. 188–9
Peterson, T. 192, 206
Phillips, P. C. 164, 167, 187, 189
Pollins, B. 154
Poulantzas, N. 292
Price, S. 7, 134, 143, 145, 176, 182, 189
Prior, G. 71

Rabinow, P. 271
Raftery, A. 89
Raiffa, H. 231, 246
Raimond, H. 247
Rao, B. B. 128
Rasbash, J. 99, 109, 113, 122
Raudenbush, S. W., 100, 114, 115, 121–3
Reid, J. N 247
Rice, N. 122
Richard, J. F. 174, 209, 254
Richardson, J. 221
Riker, W. H. 70
Robinson, W. S. 100
Rorty, R. 254, 256, 259, 267–8
Rubin, D. B. 86, 115–16
Russett, B. B. 205

Said, E. 282
Saikkonen, P. 188
Sanders, D. 4, 138, 140, 144, 147, 154, 182
Sargan, J. D. 167
Särlvik, B. 52
Saussure, F. de 257–8, 272–4
Sayer, A. 120
Schelling, T. C. 231
Schmidt, P. 200, 201
Seyd, P. 128, 221, 233
Shapiro, I. 218, 228, 230–1, 233, 239
Shapiro, M. 268
Shapiro, R. Y. 154
Shin, Y. 188, 189
Showstack, S. A. 292
Signorino, C. 209
Skinner, C. J. 96, 120
Smith, A. M. 290
Smith, R. 168
Smith, T. F. 96, 122

Sörbom, D. 57, 69
Sowell, F. 164
Spiegelhalter, D. J. 122
Srba, F. 167
Staten, H. 275
Stewart, M. C. 146, 151, 154–5, 188
Stimson, J. A. 154
Stokes, D. 52
Strom, K. 209
Sueyoshi, G. T. 209, 212
Swank, D. 154
Sweat, M. 154

Taylor, B. 71
Taylor, C. 19
Taylor, M. P. 188
Terasvirta, T. 170
Thomas, S. 120
Thorndike, E. L. 100
Tiao, G. C. 138, 139
Tonkin, P. 119
Torfing, J. 278
Tucker, R. 209, 213
Tukey, J. W. 2, 14, 16

Vermunt, J. K. 86
Visker, R. 286

Ward, H. 138, 154, 217, 220, 237, 239, 246, 248
Ware, J. H. 97
Warwick, P. V. 199–20, 206, 209–10
Watt, R. 122
Welsch, R. E. 113
White, H. 155
Whiteley. P. F. 6, 70, 128, 138, 154–5, 221, 233–4, 247–8
Wickens, M. R. 167, 187–9
Williams, L. J. 70
Winch, P. 281
Winship, C. 94
Witte, A. 200, 201
Wittgenstein, L. 274, 281, 283, 291, 293
Wlezien, C. 154
Wolpe, H. 285
Woodhouse, G. 113, 121
Woodiwiss, A. 289
Wrigley, P. 119

Yamaguchi, K. 192
Yang, M. 109, 113, 122
Yeo, S. 167
Yoo, B. S. 145, 155, 171
Young, R. 292
Yule, G. U. 165

Zac, L. 8, 9, 263, 280, 292
Zey, M. 246
Zivot, E. 164

SUBJECT INDEX

aggregate analysis 19, 35, 100, 114, 118, 120, 127–8, 152
AIC test statistic 89, 90, 94
AID 25
Almon polynomials 204
ANCOVA 110–11
ANOVA 110–11
anti-essentialism 251
anti-foundationalism 8, 250–1, 254, 260–1, 265–8
ARDL model 167–8, 172, 179, 187–9
ARIMA models 128–9, 131–3, 137–43 *passim*, 152–4
atomistic fallacy 100
augmented Dickey–Fuller (ADF) test 161, 163, 167, 170, 179, 183, 186, 188
autocorrelation 96–7, 99, 115, 133–4, 137, 154, 156, 163–5, 187

baseline hazards 201–2
Bayesian estimators 17, 111, 121
Bentler–Weeks model 55, 69
Bewley transform 189
BIC test statistic 89, 90, 94
binary time-series–cross-section models 191, 205–6, 208
BIRAM 121
Black Consciousness Movement 277, 283, 288
BLUE 33, 34
bootstrapping 113
Box–Jenkins 128–30, 140, 143
Britsh Household Panel Study (BHPS) 35

campaign strategy 218, 220–2, 224–6, 228, 230–3, 237–9
canned solutions 12, 14, 15, 23, 145, 152–3
cardinal utilities 219
categorical data analysis 5, 29, 42, 56, 71, 83, 93, 108–9, 116, 121
censored data 7, 99, 194–5, 200–7, 210, 213
characteristic roots 175
chi-square difference test 45, 58, 61–2, 64–5
Cobb-Douglas function 176, 181, 188
cointegrated variables 6, 148, 157
    cointegrating set 166–7
    cointegrating vector 146, 166, 171–4, 176, 183
cointegration 7, 128, 153, 166, 186
    analysis 176
    and ECM 167, 170
    modelling 6, 156
    relationships 146, 149–51, 157, 167, 170–1, 173, 175, 178, 180
    stationary series 144–5

techniques 164, 180
testing 157, 174–5
vectors 166, 171–6, 183
compositional effects 117–19
    see also contextual effects
computer-aided analysis 12–13
computing power 12, 16, 21–2, 24
confidence intervals 15, 16, 52, 113–15, 198
contextual effects 5, 17, 114, 118–19
    see also compositional effects
Cox models 206–8
cross-classified multilevel model 116
cubic spline 204

data archives 18–19, 25
data exploration 14, 179
data structure cross-classified 99
    long-run 177
    multi-level 95–109 *passim*
data visualization 21, 24
data warehouses 22
database management 13, 18, 19, 23
decision rules 15–17, 33
deconstruction 263, 268, 287–8
design effects 16, 115, 262
Dickey–Fuller (DF) test 161, 163
discourse analysis 1, 3, 7–9, 249, 263, 285, 292–3
    theory 8, 9, 249–57, 260, 264–8, 280–1, 284–5, 289–91, 293
discrete duration data 205–6
discursive formations 260, 271–2, 286
dummy variables 35, 110, 180, 204
duration data 191–210 *passim*
    dependence 7, 192, 197, 199, 200–8 *passim*
    independence 193, 197, 203
    models 7, 99, 191–210, 203, 206
dynamic equilibrium 144, 146
    specification 139

ecological fallacy 100
econometric models 6, 7, 128
    techniques 6, 7, 145, 187
eigen vectors (and values) 175–6
endogenous variable 54, 171
EQS 69
equilibrium 132, 143–4, 166, 169, 235
    error 166, 168–72, 174, 186
    strategy 70, 219–20, 225–6, 228–32, 235, 237–40, 246, 248
error correction mechanism (ECM) 146, 149, 152, 167–8, 170

essentialism 8, 250–1, 265–6, 273, 283
event duration models 99
event history 7, 128, 191–2, 205–9
exogeneity 174, 176, 183, 186
exploratory data analysis 14, 21, 24, 49
exponential model 198–9, 200, 203
factor analysis 17, 48, 54–5, 84, 121
failure time 192, 197
fixed effects 107, 110
fractional integration 164

game theory 219, 238
Gauss 26, 146
    Gaussian errors 183
    residuals 180
generalized gamma model 208, 211
generalized least squares 56
GENSTAT 26, 120, 122
geographical information systems 18
Gompertz model 201, 211
goodness-of-fit statistics 14, 58, 61, 68, 70
government competence 7, 182, 185
    popularity 6, 7, 130, 134, 138–40, 142, 156, 182,
        185, 189

hazard rate 7, 192, 196–8, 200, 204
hegemony 9, 260–2, 279–80
heterogeneity 6, 95, 107–8, 121
hierarchical data structures 77, 96
hypothesis testing 3, 113

idealist 254, 289
identity 8, 52, 257–9, 262–6, 283–5
    and contingency 275
    and difference 252, 273–8
ideology 9, 36, 45, 48, 261, 268–72, 292
inferential statistics 16, 25
information technology 12, 24
interaction effects 4, 77, 79, 81, 110–11, 115, 118
Internet 3, 19, 23

Johansen procedure 145, 153, 173, 175–6, 180, 183,
    186
Jöreskog–Keesling–Wiley model 69

Koyck lag 154

Lagrangian multiplier test 58, 65
latent variables 54–6, 61, 64, 71, 82–9
levels of analysis 100
likelihood ratio chi-square 77, 181
LIMDEP 208, 209
linear probability 37, 40, 49, 50
    regression 4, 6, 53–4, 194, 196
    relationships 32, 120
    transformation 168
linguistics 9, 249, 257–8, 260, 268
LISREL 57, 59

log likelihood statistic 44–5
log-linear models 42, 71, 82, 85, 93
log odds 43, 45, 49
logic
    of difference 277–8, 285
    of equivalence 277–8
logit analysis 193, 203–5
    model 109, 203–8, 212
    multinomial 206, 213
    transformation 43
longitudinal data 122
long-run relationships 7, 143, 157–8, 166, 171, 185,
    189

manufacturing employment 7, 176–7
    output 7, 177, 182, 189
    wages 7, 176–7, 182, 277
Markov Chain Monte Carlo 121
materialist arguments 254–6, 289
mathematics 2, 13, 57, 198, 210
matrix sample design 98
maximum likelihood estimation 44, 48, 81, 86, 171,
    175, 193–4, 196
measurement error 20, 55–6, 61–2, 82–3, 93, 113
    model 64
memory 131–2, 140, 193
meta analysis 100
methodologic decision rules 12, 15, 17, 25
    pluralism 2–4, 20–2
models 157, 173–4, 186
    identification 56, 157, 173–41, 186, 188–9
    multinomial 109, 232
    over-identified 56
    spatial multilevel 99, 128
    statistical 13–14, 24, 29, 103–4, 128
    structural-equation multilevel 100
modification 62, 286
moving average processes 137, 143
multi-collinearity 52
multi-stage design 96, 114
multiple cointegrating vectors 171
multiple destinations 206–9, 213

natural sciences 13, 228, 233, 281–2
negative binomial distribution 109
non-linear distributions 4, 43, 48, 109, 121–2, 167–8,
    187–8
    models 109
non-stationarity 143–4, 157, 161

objectivity 256, 271, 274–6, 283–6, 290
odds ratios 52, 74–6
order of integration 131, 157, 159
ordinary least squares regression 3–4, 29–31, 34, 37,
    40, 42–4, 48–50, 115–16, 170

panel design 97
partial likelihood 201–2

party identification 35–6, 40, 45, 48, 51, 65–9 *passim*, 109, 144, 146–52 *passim*, 155
path diagram 53–4, 59, 61–2, 64
performance analysis 97, 98, 114–15, 120
Phillips–Perron test 164, 183, 189
Poisson distribution 109, 121
political identity 263, 277, 282, 284
polychoric correlation 56
pooled analysis 110–11, 127–8
post-structuralism 252, 259, 273
posterior residual estimates 111
precision weighted 111, 115–16
PRELIS 57
prime ministerial popularity 129–30, 134, 137, 139, 142
probit models 109, 200, 203, 212
  methods 60, 206
  regression 60
proportional hazards 201, 203
pseudo R^2 45
psychoanalysis 9, 249, 260, 263, 268

Q test statistic 137
qualitative research 120
  indicators 19

random effects 100, 110
random walk 131–3, 143, 165
  randomizing 140
rank of matrix 174–5, 219
rational choice 58–63, 66, 217–20, 227–9, 233, 238–9
reduced rank hypothesis 174
relativism 249, 265, 268, 290
reparametrization 167–8, 172
repeated measures 97, 99, 114–15, 121
research design 15, 17–18, 20, 79
residuals 31, 34, 40, 87, 105, 107, 113, 137, 149, 151, 163, 164, 175

sample design 17, 20, 114
  size 50, 110–11, 114
SAS 26, 52, 120, 123, 153, 208
school performance analysis 97, 120
semi-parametric tests 163, 189, 201, 208
semiology 257–8
shrinkage 111
sign 36, 59, 146, 252, 257–8, 273
  signified 257–8, 273
  signifier 257–8, 273, 277
significance tests 15, 33, 40, 44, 113
smoothing spline 212
social identity 274
  ontology 274–5
soft rational choice 66, 220, 229, 238, 248

software 24, 94, 97, 121–3, 145, 153, 186, 209
split population model 200, 208
SPLUS 208
spurious regression 143–4, 165–6, 185
standardized regression coefficients 62
STATA 208–9
stationarity 133, 146, 154, 157, 159, 183
strategies resource allocation 244–5, 247
  campaign 218, 224
  changing of 219–20
  government and opposition 224–6, 230–1, 240–2, 246
  strategy equilibrium 219, 226, 228–31
structure and agency 278, 287
  and discourse 278–9
  of signs 257
  of social relations 269–70, 279
subjectivity 260, 262, 264, 275, 278, 288
super-consistent 167
support scale 36–7, 48, 95–6, 100, 120
survival models 98–9
survivor function 192, 196–7, 210

test statistics 61, 77, 89, 137, 145, 179, 183
threshold model 56
time-series analysis 6, 7, 127–9, 133, 138, 152–3, 191
  cross-sectional 191–2, 203, 205–6, 208, 213
  data 6, 7, 127, 148, 152
  models 99, 128
time-varying covariates 206, 208, 209
transfer function analysis 140
truncated data 200

unit roots 128, 152, 157–9, 161, 163–4, 175
universalism 265

value-added analysis 120
  performance 119
variables observed 54–6, 61, 69
Vector Error-Correction Mechanism (VECM) 172–3, 175–6
voting behaviour 26, 35, 45, 52, 61, 95–7, 114, 122, 222
  and economy 140, 146, 154
  expressive 66
  and income 100–1, 103
  intention 63–4, 65–6, 109, 144, 151
  and place 114, 116–18
  recall 68
  turnout 5, 58–61, 63, 65–6

weak exogeneity 151, 183
Weibull model 197–202, 207, 211
white noise 130–1, 133, 137, 139, 141–2, 154, 158, 163–4, 179, 186

RESEARCH STRATEGIES IN THE SOCIAL SCIENCES